RELIGIOUS DISSENT AND THE AIKIN–BARBAULD CIRCLE, 1740–1860

Recent criticism is now fully appreciating the nuanced and complex contribution made by Dissenters to the culture and ideas of the eighteenth and nineteenth centuries in Britain. This is the first sustained study of a Dissenting family – the Aikins – from the 1740s to the 1860s. Essays by literary critics, historians of religion and science, and geographers explore and contextualize the achievements of this remarkable family, including John Aikin senior, tutor at the celebrated Warrington Academy, and his children: poet Anna Letitia Barbauld, and John Aikin junior, literary physician and editor. The latter's children in turn were leading professionals and writers in the early Victorian era. This study provides new perspectives on the social and cultural importance of the family and its circle – an untold story of collaboration and exchange, and a narrative which breaks down period boundaries to set Enlightenment and Victorian culture in dialogue.

FELICITY JAMES is Lecturer in Eighteenth- and Nineteenth-century Literature at the University of Leicester.

IAN INKSTER is Research Professor of International History in the Faculty of Humanities, at Nottingham Trent University, UK, and Professor of Global History in the Department of International Studies at Wenzao Ursuline College, Kaohsiung, Taiwan ROC.

RELIGIOUS DISSENT AND THE AIKIN–BARBAULD CIRCLE, 1740–1860

EDITED BY

FELICITY JAMES

AND

IAN INKSTER

CAMBRIDGE
UNIVERSITY PRESS

CAMBRIDGE UNIVERSITY PRESS
Cambridge, New York, Melbourne, Madrid, Cape Town,
Singapore, São Paulo, Delhi, Tokyo, Mexico City

Cambridge University Press
The Edinburgh Building, Cambridge CB2 8RU, UK

Published in the United States of America by Cambridge University Press, New York

www.cambridge.org
Information on this title: www.cambridge.org/9781107008083

First published 2012

Printed in the United Kingdom at the University Press, Cambridge

A catalogue record for this publication is available from the British Library

ISBN 978-1-107-00808-3 Hardback

Contents

Contents

Notes on the editors and contributors

EDITORS

FELICITY JAMES is Lecturer in Eighteenth- and Nineteenth-century Literature at the University of Leicester. Her first book, *Charles Lamb, Coleridge and Wordsworth: Reading Friendship in the 1790s* (2008) rereads Lamb's position as an urban, Dissenting Romantic. She has recently published articles on Coleridge, Mary Hays and Harriet Martineau, and is currently working on a study of life writing and Dissent across the Romantic and Victorian periods, which stems from research undertaken during a British Academy Postdoctoral Fellowship at Christ Church, Oxford (2005–8).

IAN INKSTER was born in Warrington and is Research Professor of International History at Nottingham Trent University (UK) and Professor of Global History at Wenzao Ursuline College, Kaohsiung, Taiwan. Work on British culture and the process of industrialization is illustrated in his collected essays *Scientific Culture and Urbanisation in Industrialising Britain* (1997) and his recent paper, 'Potentially Global: A Story of Useful and Reliable Knowledge and Material Progress in Europe *circa* 1474–1914', *International History Review*, 28 (2006), 237–86. Editor of *History of Technology* (UK) since 2001, Inkster is the author of *The Japanese Industrial Economy: Late Development and Cultural Causation* (2001) and *Science and Technology in History: An Approach to Industrialisation* (1991).

CONTRIBUTORS

STEPHEN DANIELS holds the Chair of Human Geography as Professor of Cultural Geography at the University of Nottingham where he has worked since 1980. Since 2005 he has been Director of the Arts and Humanities Research Council's programme in landscape and environment, and was elected a Fellow of the British Academy in 2009. His works on long eighteenth-century subjects include *Humphry Repton: Landscape Gardening and the Geography of Georgian England* (1999) and *Joseph Wright* (1999), the exhibition catalogue *Paul Sandby 1731–1809: Picturing Britain* (2009) co-edited with John Bonehill, and book contributions on the art and aesthetics of Loutherbourg, Turner and Uvedale Price.

PAUL ELLIOTT is Lecturer in History at the University of Derby and a special lecturer at the University of Nottingham. His research interests include eighteenth- and nineteenth-century urban history, scientific and intellectual history and the history of education, and he has published *The Derby Philosophers: Science and Culture in British Urban Society, 1750–1850* (2009); *Enlightenment, Modernity and Science* (Tauris, 2010); and (co-authored with Charles Watkins and Stephen Daniels) *The British Arboretum* (2011).

ANNE F. JANOWITZ is Professor of Romantic Poetry at Queen Mary, University of London. She is the author of *England's Ruins: Poetic Purpose and the National Landscape* (1990), *Lyric and Labour in the Romantic Tradition* (1998) and *Women Romantic Poets: Anna Barbauld and Mary Robinson* (2005). She is at present writing about the night sky in eighteenth-century poetry.

MICHELLE LEVY is Associate Professor of English at Simon Fraser University, in British Columbia. She is the author of *Family Authorship and Romantic Print Culture* (2008), a study of the conjunction of authorship and family life as a distinctive cultural formation of the Romantic period that examines the literary practices and texts of the Aikins, Wordsworths, Coleridges, Godwins and Shelleys. She has recently completed, with Anne K. Mellor, an edition of Lucy Aikin's *Epistles on Women and Other Works* (2011).

WILLIAM McCARTHY is the author of *Anna Letitia Barbauld, Voice of the Enlightenment* (2008), winner of the ASECS Annibel Jenkins Biography Prize 2011. He is co-editor, with Elizabeth Kraft, of Barbauld's collected poems (1994) and the anthology *Anna Letitia Barbauld: Selected Poetry and Prose* (2002).

KATHRYN READY is Assistant Professor of English at the University of Winnipeg. Her general field is eighteenth- and early nineteenth-century British literature and culture, with particular interests in women writers, religious Dissent, and science and literature. Dr Ready has published articles on various members of the Aikin family in *Eighteenth-century Life*, *Eighteenth-century Women*, *History of European Ideas*, *Symbiosis* and *Women's Writing*. She has received a Social Sciences and Humanities Research Council of Canada Standard Research Grant for a monograph project,' "The Freedom of the Mind": The Aikin Family and the Legacy of Rational Dissenting Sociability', and is planning a second monograph project on the eighteenth-century literary physician.

DAVID L. WYKES is Director of Dr Williams's Trust and Library, and, with Professor Isabel Rivers, Co-Director of the Dr Williams's Centre for Dissenting Studies. He is also an honorary reader at Queen Mary, University of London. He edited *Parliament and Dissent*, with Stephen Taylor (2005), and with Isabel Rivers *Joseph Priestley, Scientist, Philosopher, and Theologian* (2008) and *Dissenting Praise: Religious Dissent and the Hymn in England and Wales* (2011). He has published many essays and articles on Dissenting and Unitarian history. Together with Isabel Rivers he is currently working on a major new study, *A History of the Dissenting Academies in the British Isles, 1660–1860*, in association with Richard Whatmore of Sussex University.

Foreword

This study of the Aikin–Barbauld circle is the fourth volume to result from the work of the Dr Williams's Centre for Dissenting Studies. Established in September 2004, the Centre is a collaboration between the School of English and Drama, Queen Mary, University of London, and Dr Williams's Library, Gordon Square, London. Its objectives are to promote the use of the Library's unique holdings of Puritan, Protestant Nonconformist and Dissenting books and manuscripts; to encourage research into and dissemination of these resources; and to increase knowledge and understanding of the importance of Puritanism and Protestant Dissent to English society and literature from the sixteenth century to the present.

To further these aims the Centre has developed an extensive programme of conferences, seminars, workshops and publications. The annual one-day conferences have led to five volumes of essays: *Joseph Priestley, Scientist, Philosopher, and Theologian* (2008), and *Dissenting Praise: Religious Dissent and the Hymn in England and Wales* (2011), both edited by Isabel Rivers and David L. Wykes; *Women, Dissent, and Anti-Slavery in Britain and America, 1790–1865* (2011), edited by Elizabeth J. Clapp and Julie Roy Jeffrey; and *Dissent and the Bible in Britain, 1650–1950* (forthcoming), edited by Scott Mandelbrote and Michael Ledger-Lomas, all from Oxford University Press; and now *Religious Dissent and the Aikin–Barbauld Circle* from Cambridge University Press. In addition the Centre's postgraduates have published the following electronic editions online: *The Letters of Joseph Priestley to Theophilus Lindsey 1769–1794*, edited by Simon Mills (2007); *A Bibliography of the Writings of William Hazlitt 1737–1820* (2009) and *New College, Hackney (1786–96): A Selection of Printed and Archival Sources* (2010), both edited by Stephen Burley; and *Dissenting Education and the Legacy of John Jennings, c.1720–c.1729*, edited by Tessa Whitehouse.

The Centre's Dissenting Academies Project, in association with the Sussex Centre for Intellectual History, is funded by the Leverhulme Trust and the Arts and Humanities Research Council. It will produce both print and online publications: *A History of the Dissenting Academies in the British Isles, 1660–1860*, edited by Rivers and Wykes, with Richard Whatmore as associate editor, to be published by Cambridge University Press, and two relational databases to be published online on the Centre's website. The Centre is also supporting the publication of a new edition of *Reliquiae Baxterianae* by Neil Keeble, John Coffey and Tim Cooper, to be published by Oxford University Press, as well as a number of other major initiatives such as an edition of Henry Crabb Robinson's diary and correspondence.

ISABEL RIVERS
DAVID L. WYKES
The Dr Williams's Centre for Dissenting Studies
London

Acknowledgements

We would like to thank Professor Isabel Rivers and Dr David Wykes, whose excellent day conference at Dr Williams's Library on 17 May 2008, 'The Dissenting Mind: the Aikin Circle, c.1760s to c.1860s', formed the starting point for this collection, and who have offered encouragement and support throughout. We would especially like to thank Cambridge University Press, and our editor Linda Bree, for the time and care she has taken in guiding the collection to completion, as well as the others involved in producing this book, including Christina Sarigiannidou and Martin Barr. We are enormously grateful for the hard work and patience of our contributors, and the many stimulating exchanges around these essays.

Felicity James would particularly like to thank David Wykes for his generously shared knowledge on the history of Rational Dissent, and his help with the volume. She also owes a special debt to the British Academy, whose postdoctoral funding allowed her to start work on this collection, and to her colleagues at the University of Leicester, whose support enabled her to finish it. Others who helped with conversation and guidance include Stuart Andrews, Jon Mee, Alexandra Harris, Stephen Bernard, David Higgins and the 'Creativity Project' seminar at Leeds, and the 'Restoration to Reform' group at Oxford; she is especially grateful to Peter Collings, and to Margaret and Teddy James for the best sort of family conversations.

Ian Inkster would particularly like to recall the memory of the great, late Sidney Pollard, who in 1970 encouraged his move into history from economics and as a research supervisor was so sympathetically alert to the historical relations between social and economic processes at all times and in all places.

CHAPTER I

Religious Dissent and the Aikin–Barbauld circle, 1740–1860: an introduction

Felicity James

We have no portrait of the Aikin family actually *en famille*, despite their extraordinary achievements and their powerful presentation of themselves as a group. The Edgeworths are famously pictured clustering around a manuscript; Isaac Taylor shows his family joyfully at ease in their garden – but despite the Aikins' similarities to both these writing dynasties, no image remains of them together. The closest we can come to a group portrait of the Aikin–Barbauld circle is an engraving commissioned for Thomas Macklin's *The Poets' Gallery*, by Francesco Bartolozzi from a drawing by Henry William Bunbury. Macklin intended to commission one hundred paintings illustrating the works of the English poets; this 1791 engraving celebrates 'The Mouse's Petition', by Anna Letitia Barbauld (1743–1825) (see Figure 1).[1]

Barbauld – then Anna Letitia Aikin, before her marriage to Rochemont Barbauld in 1774 – was visiting the theologian and experimental scientist Joseph Priestley in Leeds in 1771 when she wrote the poem, one of her most popular and widely reprinted. It intercedes on behalf of a mouse, 'found in the trap where he had been confined all night by Dr. Priestley, for the sake of making experiments with different kinds of air':

> Oh! hear a pensive prisoner's prayer,
> For liberty that sighs;
> And never let thine heart be shut
> Against the wretch's cries.[2]

In the engraving, a woman – dressed in white, and looking the very picture of sensibility – lectures a sage figure, as he studies the imprisoned mouse, watched by another woman and a child, the whole set in a pastoral glade. The image invites obvious comparison with the figures of the Aikin–Barbauld circle: the woman lecturing evokes Barbauld, and the seated sage, Priestley. The other woman in the picture could well be Joseph Priestley's wife, Mary, to whom the subsequent verse, 'To Mrs. P ---- .; With Some

Figure 1 'The Mouse's Petition', Macklin's *British Poets*, print by Francesco Bartolozzi, after Sir Henry Bunbury, pub. Thomas Macklin (London: 1791). © Trustees of the British Museum.

Drawings of Birds and Insects', in *Poems* (1773) is dedicated. The little boy who eagerly looks on surely represents Barbauld's adopted son, Charles Rochemont, the child of her brother John Aikin. Barbauld's celebrated series of *Lessons for Children* (1778–9) were written to teach little Charles to read, tracing his development from 2 to 4 years old; countless eighteenth-century and Victorian readers learned along with Charles.

And yet the image is hardly a faithful portrait of the Aikin–Barbauld circle. It is a representation which in many ways works to downplay some of the potentially disturbing aspects of the circle, and of the poem itself – not least the radical implications of the mouse's plea for liberty. Recent criticism has brought out the political edge of 'The Mouse's Petition', as well as its potential feminist critique of oppression.[3] Furthermore, by 1791, the defence of the 'free-born mouse', with its echo of 'free-born Englishman', had taken on a still more dangerous aspect.[4] The print is dated 20 November 1791; in July of that year, Joseph Priestley had had his house and laboratory burnt down in the Birmingham riots. In the early 1790s, his image was far more frequently to be seen in the caricatures of Gillray and Cruikshank; widely denounced, and even burnt in effigy alongside Tom Paine, he became, as David Wykes has recently put it, 'a national figure of hate'.[5] If the Aikin–Barbauld circle was one of sensibility, polite poetry, familial and friendly conversation, it was also, simultaneously, one which grappled with Revolutionary ideals, with experiments both scientific and social, with moral problems, and with radical politics. This is perhaps why the image evades direct representation of the figures to whom it alludes: Priestley becomes transformed into a figure reminiscent of Rousseau, his Leeds laboratory transfigured into a shadowy glade. Both 'Gunpowder Joe' and the radical aftershocks of Barbauld's poem are defused in this pastoral setting, safely placed in a context of familial and friendly interaction.[6]

The ways in which the poem and its illustration pull away from one another make this image a particularly appropriate starting point for this volume. 'The Mouse's Petition' shows how a domestic moment might open onto wider social and political questions. It encapsulates a moment of Enlightenment exchange, as the literature of sensibility speaks to the language of science, and the drive towards discovery and experiment is tempered by larger ethical considerations. Yet, from its publication, it was read against its author's intentions: Barbauld complained that reviewers accused Priestley of cruelty towards the mouse, and inserted an indignant footnote in the third edition to argue that 'cruelty could never be apprehended from the Gentleman to whom this has been addressed'.[7] Its 1791 illustration, however, perpetuates, in William McCarthy's words, 'Barbauld's public image as a preceptress on the ethics of benevolence to animals'.[8] The difficult political and social questions raised by Barbauld are closed down into a scene of domestic sensibility: indeed, the poem itself is only represented by a few verses. Its evasive representation of Barbauld and Priestley also prompts us to consider changes in attitude between the 1770s and the 1790s: a reflection of the way in which the whole collection attempts to trace the troubled passage of Enlightenment figures and ideals through the shifting perspectives of the later eighteenth and nineteenth centuries. These essays set out to explore the changing stories and histories of the Aikin–Barbauld circle from the 1740s to the 1860s, across a range of disciplines – theology, education, medicine, geography, literature and history. The essays function both as a means of recovering the extraordinary achievements of the individuals within the Aikin family, and also, collectively, as an exploration of a particularly powerful familial ethos and its shifts across the generations. They ask, too, how the Aikin–Barbauld circle has been read, reread and misread through the centuries, and probe their legacies.

As in the engraving, Anna Letitia Barbauld is in some ways at the centre of this group: certainly, she is the member who has prompted most recent critical work. Of late, Barbauld scholarship has emphasized the importance of reading her poetry as part of a larger context of family and friends. Scott Krawczyk, for example, shows how her poems and political pamphlets conduct a responsive conversation with the work of her brother, and Michelle Levy persuasively argues that Anna Barbauld and her brother 'stand as the period's exemplary family authors': indeed, 'collaboration with family lay at the root of their literary practices and ideals'.[9] For Anna Barbauld was surrounded on all sides by talented relations. Her father, John Aikin senior (1713–80), was first a schoolmaster, and then a tutor at the celebrated Warrington Academy; her brother John junior (1747–1822) was a physician, literary critic, geographer and editor. John junior's children were also widely accomplished: Arthur Aikin (1773–1854) was a natural scientist and author; Charles Rochemont (1775–1847), adopted by his aunt, became a surgeon and chemist; Edmund (1780–1820), was an architect, and Lucy Aikin (1781–1864), an author, memoirist and historian. The creativity continued into further generations with Charles Rochemont's daughter, the writer and family memoirist Anna Letitia Le Breton (1808–85). Every member of the family over three generations has an entry in the *New Oxford Dictionary of National Biography*, together with the circle of intellectuals associated with them. As Anne Janowitz explores in our final chapter, the very creation of these entries in both editions of the *ODNB* is bound up with the way in which the family reputation has been created and maintained across the nineteenth and twentieth centuries: they were tenacious chroniclers of their own doings and legacies, and their memoirs were informed by the structuring image of themselves as an ideal family unit. This volume examines these memoirs critically and analyses the enduring power of their reputation, asking how and why the Aikins have been read, and setting their achievements in a broader context of religious belief, family creativity and sociable networks of the eighteenth and nineteenth centuries. We aim to offer a form of group biography, setting family members and disciplines in conversation, and suggesting the subtle patterns of change and continuity across different time periods, and different forms of writing.

The chapters move across the generations, beginning with a close look at Kibworth School in the days of John Aikin (senior). David Wykes shows us how his teaching methods there, and his pupils – who have not previously been traced – afford a valuable insight into the educational structures of

Dissent. Aikin's children inherited his skills as educator and took his legacy forward in different ways: William McCarthy explores Anna Letitia Barbauld's range of writing, from her children's work to her elegant and lively poetry, while Kathryn Ready considers John Aikin (junior) as literary physician, and Stephen Daniels and Paul Elliott demonstrate his importance as a geographer. In the next generation, Ian Inkster outlines the family's contributions to science and industry through the work of Arthur and Charles. Lucy Aikin's innovative historical writing is reread by Michelle Levy, and my own chapter traces some of the tensions in Lucy's family biographies. Our closing chapter, by Anne Janowitz, looks back at these pieces, and at the family's own conception of itself, critically exploring not only the Aikins' individual achievements, intellectual and literary, but also the shaping of their reputation against a changing backdrop of religious and secular preoccupations.

The different chapters of this volume, then, not only try to recover the important contributions of this family but to see them *as* a family, working together, returning to particular issues, furthering ideas from one generation to the next – or, alternatively, differing from one another, diverging from each other and struggling to establish their own perspectives. This sense of a larger network of voices and ideas connects with recent critical preoccupations with sociable groups and modes of collaboration. '[W]e need to recover the significance of sociability', argue Gillian Russell and Clara Tuite, 'as a kind of text in its own right, a form of cultural work', which has been obscured by 'Romanticism's traditional identification with the lone poet'.[10] Instead of the solitary bard, brooding on the mountain, we have the crowded theatre, clusters of voices in the periodical, at the coffee house, in the streets and shops of the metropolis, and in the domestic circle. Work is being done to investigate different forms of sociability and sociable places: the family is one such site, where boundaries of private and public, individual and community, are negotiated. The Aikin–Barbauld circle, with its close ties of affection, intellectual connection and religious belief, allows us to see this culture of sociability at work, and to examine a particular form of collaborative creativity.

'Family connexions', wrote Noel Annan in his 1955 essay, 'The Intellectual Aristocracy', 'are part of the poetry of history'.[11] Annan was thinking of the great webs of kinship and intermarriage represented by the Macaulays, the Gurneys, the Darwin–Wedgwoods, the Stephen and Strachey families, stretching from industrial potteries to the heart of Bloomsbury, from the nineteenth to the twentieth century. Furthermore, these families were rooted in Nonconformity – the Clapham sect, the

Quaker Gurneys and Frys, the Unitarian Wedgwoods – even if their sons
and daughters did sometimes end by turning to the Anglican church.
Annan's is a somewhat impressionistic gallop through Victorian intelligentsia and into the society columns, but his 'sketch' has larger implications.
He closes the essay with the thought that this is 'an aristocracy that shows
no signs of expiring', and although the world he describes has faded, the
interest in family connections as a key to exploring larger cultural questions
in the eighteenth and nineteenth centuries is still growing. Of course
historians have long been interested in defining the nature, and the changing structure, of English family life. We might point to the discussions
of what might constitute a 'household' by Peter Laslett and others, or
Lawrence Stone's influential narrative of the rise of 'affective individualism',
or Leonore Davidoff and Catherine Hall arguing for the close connections
between 'the sexual division of labour within families' and 'the development of capitalist enterprise'.[12] More recently, critics have been particularly
interested in how ideas of family might connect with broader networks of
relationship, as in Naomi Tadmor's study of friendship and kinship ties
through the eighteenth and early nineteenth centuries, or Adam Kuper's
Incest and Influence, which goes back to Annan's sets of families to demonstrate the complex dynasties of cousin-marriage underpinning them.[13] As
Davidoff and Hall comment in their introduction to the 2002 edition of
Family Fortunes, fifteen years after its first publication, 'the family itself may
no longer be considered as a unitary thing but rather a set of practices and
expectations in process'.[14] Looking at the Aikin family across time perhaps
helps to give a sense of how those expectations might develop and shift,
from the 1740s to the 1860s.

The process takes on a further aspect, moreover, in the context of
religious Dissent. The enormous intellectual and cultural contribution
religious Dissenters made to English society in the eighteenth and nineteenth centuries is now beginning to be appreciated in scholarship and
criticism. Recent studies of the experimental scientist and theologian
Joseph Priestley, of the radical rhetoric of Richard Price, of the networks
of publisher and bookseller Joseph Johnson, or, in the nineteenth century,
of figures such as Harriet Martineau and women writers of Dissent, represent a small handful of the ways in which we are recognizing Dissent as
central to our understanding of the culture, literature and politics of the
period. Yet more work still needs to be done on identifying Dissenters, and
on establishing denominational differences, which are so often overlooked.
The Aikins' commitment to Rational Dissent, for example, remains strong
throughout this period, but their precise sectarian denomination is harder

to pin down. John Aikin (senior) may be described as English Presbyterian with Arian views; by the nineteenth century, Unitarianism had become the main form of heterodoxy with respect to the Trinity, and thus Lucy Aikin identifies herself specifically with Unitarianism. We hope this study, with its local focus, helps towards an understanding of the nuances of Dissent, and the involvement of particular Dissenters in social, political and literary life, both nationally and at the local level.

We hope, too, that it gives an insight into the creative power of Dissent. There is a long tradition of denigrating Dissenters' capacity for imaginative response. Burke's description of the '*hortus siccus* of dissent', for instance, suggests that Dissenters are hopelessly entangled in dry – yet potentially dangerous – controversy and dispute. From a different background, William Hazlitt's uncompromising conclusion that 'it would be in vain to strew the flowers of poetry round the borders of the Unitarian controversy' carries the same implication.[15] Indeed, many of the male Romantic poets' comments on Barbauld – despite their debts to her – contribute to this impression of Dissent as disputatious, cold and lacking in imagination. Robert Southey, Samuel Taylor Coleridge and Charles Lamb all joined in general denigration of 'Mrs Bare-bald', and Coleridge not only made snide remarks on her inability to interpret 'The Rime of the Ancient Mariner' correctly, but also cruelly commented on the suicide of her husband. Rochemont Barbauld 'must have had a very warm constitution', Coleridge is reported to have said, 'for he had clasped an icicle in his arms for forty years before he found it was cold'.[16] This denigration may have shaped Matthew Arnold's view of Dissent as narrow and constrained – a 'life of jealousy of the Establishment, disputes, tea-meetings, openings of chapels, sermons' directly opposed to 'sweetness, light, and perfection'.[17] However, the richness and lyric power of Barbauld's work is now once more appreciated by critics, as William McCarthy discusses in Chapter 3, and Anne Janowitz in Chapter 9. After a long period of neglect, she is now fully recognized as a vital voice in the transition between Enlightenment and nineteenth-century poetry, and in the formation of Romantic litera-ture. Her bold, lively voice sets the tone for early Romantic poetry such as Coleridge's conversation poems; lyrics such as 'The First Fire' question and adapt Romantic conventions with, in John Anderson's words, 'subtlety and spirit'.[18] More broadly, studies such as Daniel White's *Early Romanticism and Religious Dissent* uncover the great debt that Romantic culture – from Godwin to Coleridge to Southey – owes to Dissent, not simply in terms of context but on a deeper, formal level. Similarly, Helen Thomas, in *Romanticism and Slave Narratives: Transatlantic Testimonies* has followed

up the traces of Dissenting spiritual narrative in Romanticism, and Richard
E. Brantley and Jasper Cragwall have argued for the intense importance of
Evangelical Nonconformism to Wordsworth's development as a poet, and,
in Brantley's case, to wider Anglo-American Romanticism.[19] The essays
which follow celebrate the creative power of Rational Dissent through the
imaginative, lively, varied work of the Aikin family, from educational
material to polemical articles, from lyric poetry to historical memoir and
biography.

Indeed, part of the aim of this collection is to think about what we might
learn from the different models of creativity put forward by the Aikin
family. They were, for example, innovative biographers; Michelle Levy's
contribution (Chapter 7) explores Lucy Aikin's court histories in light of her
theory that 'it is from intimate views of private life in various ages and
countries that the *moral* of political history is alone to be derived'.[20]
Similarly, several of the chapters in this volume are interested in the ways
in which domestic and private lives might uncover larger stories, how a
family story might open onto wider meanings, and how biography of the
Aikin family – and the Aikin family's biographies themselves – might
inform our understanding of eighteenth- and nineteenth-century life writing. We have also tried to reflect the interdisciplinary interests of the family
and their wider circle: the volume attempts to continue their conversations
between different disciplines and areas of expertise, bringing together
religious history, literary criticism, geography and the history of science.
In so doing, we hope to uncover some of the intricate, multilayered
connections between families and intellectual circles, disciplines and
institutions.

The story of this collection begins in a village south-east of Leicester,
Kibworth Harcourt, in an imposing house on the road to London. The 'Old
House', a fine Restoration brick building, is in a dominant position – 'one
of the best houses in Kibworth', as William McCarthy reminds us, just
across from the village green, with its cross and pump.[21] This is where John
Aikin senior began his school in 1742, and where, in 1743 and 1747, his two
children, Anna Letitia and John junior, would be born. More generally, it
offers a useful insight into the situation of the Aikin family in the eighteenth
century. They were important members of the community, both locally and
nationally: the distinguished appearance of the house is matched by the
reputation of Aikin's establishment there in the 1740s. As David Wykes
traces in Chapter 2, Aikin's was a forward-looking, intellectually adven-
turous provincial school, which serves to remind us of the broad intellectual and scholarly contribution Dissenters made to English society and

to education in particular in the eighteenth century. Although the village might at first glance seem a pastoral retreat, nestled in Leicestershire fields – Barbauld remembered 'Kibworth's tufted shade' fondly in a poem of 1768 – it was one of the hubs of Nonconformist activity in the East Midlands. A short walk from the 'Old House' was the building which had housed John Jennings' Dissenting academy, where Philip Doddridge had been a student. Doddridge would, in turn, become tutor to John Aikin senior, and it was at Doddridge's academy in Northampton that John Aikin would meet his wife, the Jennings' daughter, Jane, whom Doddridge had himself courted at one time. Doddridge would send his own son, Philip junior, to study with his former pupil at Kibworth. It is hard to find definite evidence of other pupils at Kibworth, but those traced, as Wykes shows in the appendix to Chapter 2, represent an important insight into Aikin's school, including divines such as Newcome Cappe and Thomas Belsham, one of the founders of the Royal Humane Society, Thomas Cogan, and businessmen such as John Coltman. The Aikin house at Kibworth was therefore well connected, both geographically and socially, to a wider Dissenting network which stretched across the country, from the Midlands to Glasgow, from Somerset to Sheffield.

Yet in spite of this standing in the community, the Aikins were also, in some senses, outsiders, thanks to their religious views. Dissenters occupied an uneasy place in relation to the establishment, supposedly excluded from public office and from Oxford and Cambridge because of their unwillingness to sign the Thirty Nine Articles. In practice, they could evade the Test and Corporation Acts by the practice of occasional conformity, and could matriculate at Cambridge (but not Oxford) without signing, although they could not receive a degree without doing so. Despite this ambiguity, they were 'often capable of wielding considerable local power', and thus frequently viewed with suspicion.[22] The Aikin family may have felt their marginal position as Dissenters the more keenly since the major landowner in Kibworth was Merton College, Oxford; the impressive 'Old House', after all, was only rented for a relatively short time, from 1742 to 1758. When Aikin first established his school, moreover, it had been less than a decade since Doddridge had been prosecuted for not having a licence to teach at his academy in Northampton, when Aikin himself had been studying there and assisting Doddridge to teach. By the mid-eighteenth century, Dissenters might not have been openly persecuted, but the sense of their difference persisted. 'Not a few amongst us', warned Anglican clergyman-turned-Dissenter Theophilus Lindsey at the opening of the Essex Street Chapel in 1774, 'lye undeservedly under the terror of severe, unjust, penal laws, made in bad and dark times'.[23] Although he went on in optimistic Enlightenment tone to point out that 'these laws sleep', it is clear that the history of the previous century was constantly present for Dissenters. This would come to the fore in the 1790s. As Ian Inkster discusses, Dissent had multiple links to radical activity; in a climate of post-Revolutionary anxiety, and of Dissenters' disappointment at the failure of the proposed Repeal of the Test Acts, this was to prove an explosive combination. As we have heard, Priestley was attacked, and, less violently, both Barbauld and John Aikin (junior) also suffered. Barbauld was critically attacked; for Horace Walpole, previously an admirer, she became a danger-ous 'prophetess', a Crown and Anchor 'poissonnière'. John Aikin, as Kathryn Ready details, lost his Yarmouth practice. For all the solid respect-ability of the Kibworth house, Dissenters occupied an uneasy social position through the eighteenth century.

This possibility of persecution and social exclusion from establishment groups meant that those extended networks of worship, education, busi-ness and family took on special importance. We might see this at work, for example, in Barbauld's obituary poems, 'On the Death of Mrs. Jennings' and 'On the Death of Mrs Martineau', both celebrating family members who were also powerful in the Dissenting community. Anna Letitia Wingate Jennings was Barbauld's grandmother, wife of Dissenting minister John Jennings, who had officiated at the Kibworth Academy; after Jennings' death, his old pupil Doddridge had become her lodger and, as William McCarthy puts it, 'unofficial household chaplain'.[24] The subject of the other poem, Sarah Meadows Martineau, the descendant of a Unitarian minister, was matriarch of the Norwich Martineau clan, who had sent her children (including the future surgeon Philip) to the Barbaulds' school at Palgrave; she was the grandmother of Harriet Martineau and related through marriage to the Taylors of Norwich. 'An Israelite indeed', exclaims Barbauld about her grandmother, turning her own family of Dissenters into a chosen race; the Martineaus, similarly, are seen as children of Israel, in verse which celebrates Sarah Meadows Martineau and echoes Psalm 78:

> –Long may that worth, fair Virtue's heritage,
> From race to race descend, from age to age!
> Still purer with transmitted lustre shine
> The treasured birthright of the spreading line![25]

Those two poems nicely demonstrate the power of this extended Dissenting network of families, friends and tutors, stretching across the country and 'from age to age'; they also show the important role of women in these families. Yet these are not straightforward commemorations – Barbauld's image of these women and their descendants as Israelites, protecting their 'treasured birthright', also shows how fiercely Rational Dissenters could construct and defend their family narratives. There was, perhaps, still a communal memory of persecution at work, the descendant of that described by Barbauld in her 'Thoughts on the Devotional Taste, on Sects, and on Establishments' (1775) where she describes the infancy of a religious sect, when its members are still inspired by the 'living spirit of devotion':

The social principle mixes with the flame, and renders it more intense; strong parties are formed, and friends or lovers are not more closely connected than the members of these little communities.[26]

Eighteenth-century Dissent still kept those familial, friendly 'little communities' alive. As at Kibworth, a family was often at the heart of a Dissenting school or academy. Anna Letitia Jennings had helped her husband at Kibworth and then become landlady to Doddridge; in turn, Doddridge was assisted in running his Northampton Academy by his wife Mercy, and John Aikin senior's wife, Jane, who had already helped Doddridge, similarly took in the pupils as boarders.[27]

At Warrington Academy, where John Aikin senior moved in 1758, the same familial atmosphere was a source of some pride. The Annual Reports of the Warrington Academy, for example, lay stress upon the way in which tutors and students 'live together in the highest Friendship and Harmony'.[28] William Turner, in the *Monthly Repository*, described the pastoral care offered to Warrington students by John Aikin senior, who 'had frequent small parties to drink tea with him, when he was accustomed quite to unbend, and enter with them into the most free familiar conversation'.[29] This picture of the Dissenting tutors is corroborated by the idealized image offered by Lucy Aikin, daughter of John Aikin, junior: 'they and theirs', she writes, 'lived together like one large family'.[30] Commenting on this phrase 'free familiar conversation', Anne Janowitz shows that it might be used as a model for thinking about provincial Dissenting sociability in the late eighteenth century, exemplified by the special atmosphere of Warrington Academy, where pedagogy ran alongside familial and friendly sociability. Here, as Janowitz discusses, 'tutors aimed to incarnate the ideal of social intercourse conceived of as informal, familiar and amiable, teaching the virtues of "candid manners" and an "active mind"'.[31]

In this volume, we extend this investigation of pedagogy and familiar sociability back into institutions such as Kibworth, tracing the connections between such provincial schools and the better-known Dissenting academies. Uncovering the records and memoirs of Kibworth pupils such as John Coltman, Wykes shows that Kibworth pupils had a thorough grounding in classical and modern languages, including French and Italian, as well as the study of geography. The way in which this innovative curriculum was delivered was equally important: Aikin's style of teaching also reflected what he had himself learned from the Dissenting academies. His students were encouraged to experiment 'pretty freely in general reading', and his 'familiar theological lectures' were remembered by pupils.[32]

That word 'familiar' is a key one. In this context it implies a sense both of 'pertaining to one's family life, private, domestic' and 'common, ordinary'. Indeed, both meanings were in play at the Dissenting academies, where the teaching style was characterized by familiar intimacy between teachers and students, and by teaching in 'ordinary' language – eschewing Latin, using techniques of discussion and exchange, and employing a much wider curriculum than the ancient universities. This reliance on familiar style can also be glimpsed in Dissenting literature such as Doddridge's *Family Expositor, or, A Paraphrase and Version of the New Testament*. One of his most popular works, this urges 'Heads of Families' to use the texts for 'Acts of Domestick Worship', and does so using a model of Christ not as 'polite *Orator*, yet more like a *Father* instructing his Children': 'perhaps if more of this familiar and condescending Method was practised in *our Sermons*', Doddridge suggests, 'the Souls of the People might be more edified'.[33] Here, again, familiar carries a double weight both of family intimacy and of ordinary language – both become a running theme in the Aikin family across the generations – and yet leads to something greater: the edification of 'the Souls of the People'. William McCarthy, in Chapter 3, shows the intense importance of the *Family Expositor* to Barbauld, suggesting that it might have been here that 'she first encountered representations of intense feeling, representations that, I surmise, first authorized her to experience her emotions'. Drawing on his years of research into the creative development and milieu of Barbauld, McCarthy shows how the complex of ideas she encountered in her Dissenting upbringing – from Doddridge to Elizabeth Rowe – shaped her energetic writing voice. It borrows from the Dissenting ethos in which she had grown up – but also, as McCarthy shows, transforms it into supple, emotional poetry and prose which had a lasting effect on its Romantic and Victorian readers.

To take one example, 'Washing Day', the poem she wrote (probably some time after 1783) remembering the house at Kibworth where she spent her childhood, opens up the language of poetry to the ordinary and domestic:

> The Muses are turned gossips; they have lost
> The buskin'd step, and clear high-sounding phrase,
> Language of gods. Come, then, domestic Muse,
> In slip-shod measure loosely prattling on
> Of farm or orchard, pleasant curds and cream,
> Or drowning flies, or shoe lost in the mire
> By little whimpering boy, with rueful face;
> Come, Muse, and sing the dreaded *Washing-Day*.[34]

Here we have the child's viewpoint on life at Kibworth 'Old House' and its washing-day upheaval, 'dirt and gravel stains', and 'linen-horse by dog thrown down', everyone at odds, the cat running scared from the kitchen, the child Anna driven away by the maids:

> All hands employed to wash, to rinse, to wring,
> To fold, and starch, and clap, and iron, and plait.

Yet it is also, of course, a very knowing subversion of poetic rule from a skilled, classically aware writer, relishing a relaxation into 'slip-shod measure' but at the same time alert to the literary possibilities of domestic language. Moreover, by the end of the poem, the domestic and familiar move out into the realms of imagination, as the child's soap bubble is linked to Montgolfier's 'silken ball' – a hot-air balloon of the type which Barbauld would enjoy seeing in London in 1784:

> Earth, air, and sky, and ocean, hath its bubbles,
> And verse is one of them – this most of all.

The poem becomes a bubble of speculation which holds in suspension woman's labour, the playfulness of the child and the aspirations of Montgolfier, yet does so playfully and lightly, in familiar language.[35] Indeed, this celebration of the ordinary might be set alongside the attempts of Wordsworth and Coleridge to forge a new style of conversational, familiar poetry. 'Washing-Day' was eventually published in the *Monthly Magazine* – edited by John Aikin (junior) – where poems such as 'Reflections on Having Left a Place of Retirement' also appeared.[36]

Another example of the way in which the Aikin–Barbauld language of the familiar and the domestic might open onto wider questions comes in a very regularly cited discussion by Barbauld of her family collaborations, in a letter to her brother of 1775:

I think we must some day sew all our fragments together, and make a *Joineriana* of them. Let me see: – I have, half a ballad; the first scene of a play; a plot of another, all but the catastrophe; half a dozen loose similes, and an eccentric flight or two among the fairies.[37]

In recent criticism this comment has taken on an almost emblematic significance. Daniel White takes this discussion of 'Joineriana' – a 'patch-work product of familial literary collaboration' – as his starting point for uncovering the dynamics of Dissenting family creativity.[38] Michelle Levy seconds White's findings with her discussion of Barbauld's 'domestic meta-phor of patchwork' to describe her texts, indicating 'both their homely origins as well as their basic functionality'.[39] But as both these critics point out, it is hard to categorize the Aikin–Barbauld brand of domesticity. On one level, Barbauld's image of 'Joineriana' works as an evocation of homely patchwork family production, non-threatening because it looks back to a traditional female activity. Certainly, the scene drawn by Lucy Aikin, and repeated by Henry Bright, of shared, sociable poetry reading in the Warrington Academy – 'it was their custom', she reports, 'to slip anonymous pieces into Mrs. Priestley's work-bag' before reading them out – seems to place domestic labour centre stage.[40] But there are some problems with this homely image. Indeed, as White points out, images such as the work-bag serve 'as much as emblems of representation as of practice'.[41] We might cite Harriet Martineau's comment, in the context of celebrating Barbauld's education, that Barbauld 'was not much of a needle-woman. There is a tradition that the skeleton of a mouse was found in her workbag.'[42] Moreover, the 'Joineriana' comment also alludes to a book which Barbauld and her brother must both have known, *Joineriana: or the Book of Scraps*, written by Samuel Paterson (1728–1802), bookseller and auctioneer. Paterson's *Joineriana*, published by Joseph Johnson in 1772 – the same year that he brought out John Aikin (junior)'s *Essays on Song-Writing* – is a curious work, a collection of musings on subjects as diverse as antiquaries, authors, booksellers and publishers, or bookmakers, whom he terms 'idle and unprofitable drone[s]'.[43] Given that Paterson filled, at different times, all of these roles, it is a droll and self-reflexive work, but it contains some serious musings on the nature of 'free-thinking': 'I am of opinion', writes Paterson, 'that it becomes every sensible man to be a Freethinker – nay more, that it is his duty, as a rational being', and he suggests that free-thinking in religion constitutes a 'lively sense of GOD's unbounded Mercy – our own Faith, and Hope, and Universal Love' as opposed to fear and superstition.[44] These ideas sound very close to Unitarian-leaning Dissent – they were, perhaps, a contributing factor in his friendship with Joseph Johnson – and, indeed, it was Samuel Paterson's book auction house, on Essex Street, off the Strand, which Johnson leased in 1774 in order to help establish the chapel which, under Theophilus Lindsey, would become the first avowedly Unitarian place of worship. 'Joineriana' might, therefore, convey a complex of ideas, as Barbauld alludes to someone who is deeply involved in Dissenting circles, and suggests how provincial Dissent might be linked to metropolitan enterprises. What at first seems to be a private domestic enterprise carries a larger public charge.

This is supported by the other allusion which lingers behind Barbauld's comment about 'sewing all our fragments together'. We could look back to the Virgilian epigraph she used for her 1773 publication of *Poems*, for instance:

HÆC SAT ERIT, DIVÆ, VESTRUM CECINISSE POETAM,
DUM SEDET, ET GRACILI FISCELLAM TEXIT HIBISCO.

which Guy Lee translates as:

To have sung of these things, goddesses, while he sat and wove
A frail of thin hibiscus, will suffice your poet.[45]

Behind this homely, patchwork domesticity stands the classically sanctioned trope of poet as weaver; Barbauld is deliberately taking part in a larger intellectual conversation, using a favourite text, Virgil's *Eclogues*, from which her brother also quotes extensively, and which also looks back to her father's teaching at Kibworth and Warrington. Barbauld may manipulate domestic imagery, but she does so on her own terms, informed and inflected by classical rhetoric. If the Aikin family's writing is about the home, it's also about finding a space for intellectual activity, even – or especially – as a female writer. That phrase, 'sew[ing] all our fragments', therefore, points up how difficult it is to arrive at a clear image of Aikin family ideology, which brings together the home, Dissent and wider intellectual exploration.

The same move outward from the domestic and familiar can be glimpsed in *Lessons for Children* (1778–9), designed with a family reader in mind – Barbauld's adopted son, Charles Rochemont, whom we last saw looking at Priestley's mouse. Stephen Daniels and Paul Elliott point out in their essay that both Barbauld and her brother show a similar alertness to pedagogic issues, and the experience of the child reader. *Lessons* is small, with large easily readable type, with a clear programme of development from 2 to 4 years old; Barbauld begins with a preface which shows a keen bibliographic sense, complaining about previous work for children which suffers from 'a want of good paper, clear and large type, and large spaces'.

Moreover, Daniels and Elliott show that, like John Aikin (junior)'s work, *Lessons for Children* seeks to inculcate the child's sense of his or her place as part of a larger community, and thus connects with the larger religious and civic ideals of the Aikin–Barbauld circle. First, the 2-year-old Charles is shown sitting, reading, in his mother's lap; as the books progress and the child begins to read more extensively, he is asked to consider his relation to others, to animals and to the world around him: 'a moral world is progressively unfolded through *Lessons for Children*', as Daniels and Elliott put it, 'through increasingly extensive excursions from home'. *Hymns in Prose* has a similar aim: the eighth Hymn, for instance, begins with an image of the labourer's cottage, and the family it contains, governed by the father. From this family we move outward to the village, the town, 'governed by a magistrate', the nation, ruled by a king, and finally the world, governed by God: 'All are God's family'.[46] The child is thus encouraged to think outwards from 'families of men' to 'nations of the earth' and to reason about how and why government is constructed. The same question informs Aikin's political writing, and Barbauld's later activism once she had given up the school at Palgrave and moved to London. In *Sins of Government, Sins of the Nation; Or, A Discourse for the Fast, Appointed on April 19, 1793* (1793) for example, Barbauld deconstructs the relationship between individual and nation, and in *Civic Sermons to the People* (1792), she suggests that listeners might inform their children about 'what a State is': the 'first society is called a Family. It is the root of every other society'.[47]

The relationship between family and society at large is a constant, illuminating theme for the writers in the Aikin–Barbauld circle. Most famously, the action of the celebrated children's work, *Evenings at Home*, collaboratively produced by Barbauld and John Aikin (junior) is structured around a scene of family reading, as the tolerant and endlessly instructive Fairborne clan pluck stories and dialogues written by family members and guests from the 'budget' and read them aloud to the children. Collaboratively written itself, the book encourages collaboration and shared reading, encoding a particular family ideology which reflects and promotes Dissenting ideals – a secularized version, perhaps, of Doddridge's emphasis on family reading.

The writing of the Aikin–Barbauld circle is rich in images of this kind of family-based intellectual sociability. Lucy Aikin's biographies, especially that of her father, contain wonderful descriptions of friendly and domestic reading, reporting, for instance, on her father's 'social and communicative habits of study'.[48] He often discussed his reading with the family; similarly, one of his writing habits was 'never to commit a single page to the printer without causing it to be previously read aloud by one of his family in his own presence, and in that of any other members of the domestic circle who could be conveniently assembled'.[49] Children's voices were also heard; William McCarthy's chapter in this volume analyses the contribution of 5-year-old Anna Letitia to a theological discussion between John Aikin (senior) and an older pupil. Lucy Aikin has a similar tale of how the child's voice might be encouraged and his or her self-confidence boosted within the family, 'it was the report, long after, of a lady who visited in our house at Warrington, that my voice was always heard in it, and that my papa never checked me, because he was so fond of me'.[50]

Yet this emphasis on family should not obscure the fact that the Aikins were also skilled in particular tasks, as well as collaboration. Part of what we hope to do with this book is to consider John Aikin's work outside his collaborations with Barbauld – to emphasize his work as a physician, for instance, and as a geographer, continuing and extending his father's interests at Kibworth and Warrington. He was among the first, as Kathryn Ready shows in her essay below, to 'think seriously about the literary physician as a historical phenomenon'. A practising doctor who worked in Leicestershire, Warrington and Yarmouth before moving to London, he also edited the *Monthly Magazine* and *The Athenaeum* and published extensively on a number of literary, geographical and historical subjects. His 1780 *Biographical Memoirs of Medicine in Great Britain from the Revival of Literature to the Time of Harvey* brings together his interest in the convergence of medicine and literature with the family fascination with biography. For Aikin, literature helped to imbue the physician with a holistic attitude – supported by Barbauld's poem 'Prologue to the Man of Pleasure by John Aikin'. This commemorates a play, sadly lost, which Aikin probably composed around 1771 when he was practising at Warrington, before a later move to Yarmouth. Aikin is shown excusing his play and claiming he has no literary abilities:

> Twas foreign from the task to him assigned
> To wake new feelings in the callous mind,
> With skill to set distorted judgments right,
> To purge the taste, and clear the mental sight.

Yet here medicine and literature are shown coming together – since surgeons 'set' bones, and prescribe purges. And Aikin did, in fact, see the two as supporting one another. Deriving, as Ready says, a special 'sense of authority from his position as a Dissenter', he seeks to minister to national ills in England – a stance evident in pamphlets such as his 1790 *An Address to the*

Dissidents of England on their Late Defeat and *The Spirit of the Constitution and that of the Church of England Compared.* It must be said, however, that his patients did not approve of their doctor's 'prescription for the ailing body politic', and the pamphlets cost him his Yarmouth practice in the early 1790s. But for Aikin, politics and medicine couldn't be kept separate; his position as a Dissenter informed his whole approach. Even his geographical writing, as Daniels and Elliott suggest in their chapter, owes a good deal to his Dissenting background; he sought to continue his father's pedagogy, which gave geography a central role, and to celebrate the work of Presbyterian writers such as Thomas Pennant and James Thomson, all the time working towards a liberal vision of Britain's place in a wider world. His language is accessible, clear and familiar, grounded, in the words of Daniels and Elliott, 'in empirical description' and aiming 'to reform teaching which focused on Latinate rhetoric not English reality, and to reconnect the word with the world'. The chapter also shows how John Aikin's is an interdisciplinary approach, in the sense that he sees each of his disciplines informing and furthering the others – his travels as a physician providing material for his geographical writing, for instance, and his 'geographical imagination' inextricably linked to his reformist sympathies and his literary sensibility. As Daniels and Elliott then show, he passes this onto his children, who worked in the same areas – geography and biography – and issued versions of their father's volumes such as *England Delineated.* As Ian Inkster's contribution also illustrates, this is a conversation which is continued across the generations.

Inkster begins by demonstrating the close links between Rational Dissent, intellect and industry, forged in the eighteenth century, continuing even through the political strife of the 1790s and the Napoleonic Wars, and evident in the circle around John Aikin's eldest son, Arthur, natural scientist and author. It was to the progressive atmosphere of Dissent and intellectual enquiry created by his father and grandfather, and his family association with Priestley, argues Inkster, that Arthur Aikin and his associates owed 'the cultural identity of intellectual Dissent, scientific enquiry and practical laboratory manipulation, a nexus not then found in any English university or in any English royal society'. Delineating the political and scientific micro-culture around Priestley and the senior Aikins, Inkster then shows how Arthur Aikin took their work forward into the nineteenth century. His first writings on geology were published in his father's *Monthly Magazine* and he went onto become a founding member of the Geological Society, and of the Chemical Society, and secretary of the Royal Society for the Encouragement of Arts, Manufactures and Commerce, where he instituted broader access and a series of popular lectures designed to open up issues of industry and manufacture to a wider audience. Indeed, his speech as secretary to the Royal Society of Arts, when he called for 'the art of design' to abandon the 'class of accomplishments' and be brought 'into the common and familiar use of ordinary life', demonstrates how closely he attempted to follow the Aikin–Barbauld line of pedagogy and social reform.[51] His research in mineralogy gave rise to his popular *Manual of Mineralogy* in 1814, and is celebrated in Aikinite, a sulfide mineral of lead, copper and bismuth, first found in the Ural Mountains in 1843, and named after him by E. J. Chapman, Professor of Mineralogy and Geology at University College, London. His skills in natural history are commemorated in the plant name *Aikinia*, a predominantly Asian species discovered by Nathaniel Wallich in 1832. These might be seen as the eventual fruit of the natural history observations encouraged in *Evenings at Home*, and nicely show how the Aikin family's name spreads out across the globe in different ways.

Arthur was the eldest of John Aikin's children; after him came Charles Rochemont (1775–1847), adopted by the Barbaulds, who would go on to become a surgeon and chemist. Continuing the family tradition of collaboration, he and his brother Arthur wrote a *Dictionary of Chemistry and Mineralogy* together in 1807, but Charles' particular interest was in vaccination, in which he would become an expert. He eagerly took up Edward Jenner's ideas, publishing a work on vaccination against cow pox in 1800 and becoming a vaccinator at the new National Vaccine Establishment in 1809 – again, we could see this as continuing a Warringtonian interest in scientific innovation, and in social reform, into the nineteenth century.

Moreover, as Inkster demonstrates, the achievements of Arthur and Charles Aikin pose something of a challenge to traditional historiographies of Dissent. Rather than seeing the repression of certain periods, such as the 1790s, as having had a negative impact on Dissenters, we might instead argue that it was precisely this 'non-fatal repression' which 'vastly stimulated the rate of commercial and technological change'. The containment of Dissent, furthermore, 'not only allowed but also induced associational experiment, intellectual enquiry and technological application' in particular circles, reducing the public cost of technological research and innovation, and giving Britain an edge over its rivals. A study of the tightly connected intellectual milieu of the Aikin–Barbauld circle of the 1780s and 1790s might afford insights, therefore, into a larger narrative of technological change and industrial revolution.

Meanwhile, the youngest brother, Edmund, became an architect, with a keen interest in Greek revival. He published numerous essays on architecture, although the only work of his which is still standing is the Wellington Rooms, fine neoclassical assembly rooms in Mount Pleasant in Liverpool. One of the reasons we know so much about these family members is John junior's youngest child, Lucy Aikin. Self-appointed family historian and biographer, she published – and supplemented – her father's and her aunt's work, and wrote a long biography of her father and a somewhat shorter, and rather more pointed, memoir of Anna Letitia Barbauld, whom she saw as overshadowing John Aikin's achievements. Lucy, too, continued the family business of writing children's books, and she was also a poet, whose *Epistles on Women, Exemplifying their Character and Condition in Various Ages and Nations* was published in 1810. It is a bold, challenging poem, which is recently attracting more critical attention, and a new edition, by Anne K. Mellor and Michelle Levy, who hail it as 'the first text in English to rewrite the entire history of western culture, from the Creation of Genesis through the eighteenth century, from a feminist perspective, explicitly defining the practices and consequences of a patriarchal social system'.[52] As Michelle Levy shows in Chapter 7 in this volume, Lucy Aikin is an innovative writer whose unique contribution to historiography has been little appreciated, partly because her series of *Memoirs*, in Levy's words, simply 'fail to conform to both earlier and later historical models'. Blending together different forms of historical writing, and incorporating details of domestic life, 'Aikin sought an intellectual and affective response for her readers, urging them to evaluate the systems of the past and their traces in the present day': a purpose which was, as Levy points out, informed by Lucy Aikin's own history, in terms both of her personal knowledge of the social and political position of Dissenters, and by her particular pedagogic and literary inheritance.

As family historian, Lucy was the promoter and editor of her father, producing a biography and a selection of his work in 1823, and, of course, of her aunt Barbauld. Her heavily selected collection of Barbauld's poems, and her memoir of her aunt, appeared in 1825, with a further selection, *A Legacy for Young Ladies*, published the following year. Her own 1864 *Memoirs*, also a family enterprise, since they were produced by her niece and nephew, Anna Letitia and Philip Hemery Le Breton, have also been important in shaping the posthumous reputation of the Aikin family, and in giving rise to other family narratives through the nineteenth and twentieth centuries. Anne Janowitz has described the Aikin family, with all its literary self-reflections, its layers of memoirs, collected letters and familial observations, as a 'reputation machine', working away through the nineteenth century and into the twentieth to present a powerful image of exemplary family life.[53]

This is not to say, however, that this is always a harmonious family tale. There are often undercurrents of tension, of conflict between families and generations. The Warrington Academy, for all its familial ideals, had serious problems with discipline; Gilbert Wakefield described the students as 'a set of wild and reckless boys'.[54] Within families, too, there could be tensions. The anecdote reported by McCarthy about Barbauld's precocious theological reasoning shows, as he suggests, both Aikin's liberal parenting and a challenge within the family. When, at 5 years old, Anna Letitia contributes her biblical knowledge to a dinner-table discussion, writes McCarthy, 'She was showing that she *ought* to have been in his class, for she was able to quote chapter and verse to the purpose; in fact, she was competitively showing him up by quoting an elementary verse that deflated his scholastic argument.' And he goes on to suggest that 'resentment of scholastic intellectual behaviour would become one of Barbauld's trademarks as a writer', possibly formulated in the heart of the family. Lucy Aikin, too, shows her resentment at intellectual behaviour in the family, complaining about her grandmother's unreasonable demands when she was a child. Spurred by the memory of Anna Letitia's precocity, her grandmother tried to teach Lucy to read, but ended by calling her 'Little Dunce'. This is the starting point for my own chapter, which suggests the way in which the Aikin family's formidable intellectual inheritance could be not a blessing but a burden. Lucy gets her own back, however, with her family biographies, which, while on the one hand promoting her aunt's writing, also suggest Barbauld's shortcomings. She appears in one of Lucy's memoirs as 'invincibly averse, from constitutional indolence, to any protracted effort', and instead, in Lucy's narrative, it is her brother, John, who is shown as the driving force behind family achievements, prompting Barbauld's work into print and behaving in a much more socially responsible way.[55]

There are, then, differences and conflicts across the Aikin family, and they could also be regarded with hostility or suspicion by others. Scott Krawczyk has given an entertaining overview of the negotiations between the two powerful literary dynasties of the Aikins and Edgeworths, as both advance different 'business models'.[56] A contemporary complaint about their family influence comes from Robert Southey, who regularly wrote for Arthur Aikin's *Annual Review*. Writing to C. W. Williams Wynn in September 1803, Southey notes in no very favourable terms a review he has recently completed of a volume of John Aikin's *General Biography* – 'one might as well review a dictionary'. Southey claims that because he had noted an omission, the review was turned over to someone else more sympathetic, and his work unprinted; 'So much for family interest', he concludes.[57] The poet Robert Bloomfield also complained at length about the arrogance of John and son Arthur at a dinner to which they were all invited:

I was anxious to see men so famous in the world of Books; But though Mr Rogers at whose table we met behaved with his usual kindness Dr A and Son would have known just as much of me had I been looking through a gimblet hole in the wainscot, and I should have made as good a figure in the company. Neither of them ask'd one question of any kind nor gave a moment's chance for poor Giles to mix his mud with the unceasing stream of erudition that flowd copiously for four hours.

He concludes by giving a very different perspective on the egalitarianism of the Aikins, adding, 'if a man invited to a neighbour's table finds there one inferior to him in knowledge and wealth, and takes care to let him see that he thinks so, my soul despises that man'.[58]

Both comments, however, also prove the power of the Aikin–Barbauld circle, moving outward from the 'world of Books'. In the extended Aikin family we witness, in the words of two eminent recent scholars, both 'the mobilization of the family, through writing, in the realm of political action', and the creation of a long-lasting ideology, whereby 'the family itself is the institution most capable of effecting profound national change'.[59] Anne Janowitz's closing piece responds to the essays on individual members of the Aikin–Barbauld circle in the volume, and speculates on the larger legacies of the family, tracing some possible narratives of change in which they might have unwittingly participated. These are diverse and inspirational. William McCarthy closes his chapter by summoning up the great power of Barbauld for nineteenth-century readers both here and across the Atlantic: 'What she made of Dissent went into the making of – to list just three things – Coleridge's poetry, New England's Unitarianism, and Britain's First Reform Act', he rousingly concludes. Ian Inkster shows how the distinct Dissenting micro-culture around Priestley and the Aikins in the eighteenth century informed nineteenth-century technological advance, and suggests some of the ways in which symbols of the culture of Rational Dissent, as the nineteenth century wore on, became 'increasingly those of a wider, liberal urbane society'. Janowitz then looks closely at the ways in which the values of Rational Dissent promulgated in the Aikin–Barbauld circle – and, particularly, in Barbauld's poetry as she struggles to articulate her differences with Priestley over the nature of religious devotion – may have shaped larger transformations of belief. Reading Barbauld's poetic, humanizing aesthetic in light of Charles Taylor's work on the gradual transformations of Protestantism and the emergence of secularization, Janowitz suggests that 'without intending to, Barbauld participates in a dialectic of Dissent, a process in which secular concerns emerge from within institutions and doctrines of belief as they engage with the new knowledge of the seventeenth and eighteenth centuries and the broadening of those secular institutions within Britain that lived alongside religious ones'. Janowitz's discussion of Barbauld's productive, frictive dispute with Priestley brings us back to our starting point: Bartolozzi's illustration for 'The Mouse's Petition', and its depiction of the poem as part of an ongoing conversation with Priestley. Through such exchanges, the Aikin–Barbauld circle helped to shape the culture – religious, political, scientific, educational, literary – of their period. Their ideas, both in theory and in practice, had a profound effect on the development of the nineteenth century. Both in the Bartolozzi engraving and in *Lessons for Children*, for instance, we saw Barbauld trying to inculcate ideas of community and empathy in Charles. Thirty years later, by now married to Gilbert Wakefield's daughter, Anne, he would be urging the adoption of vaccination, and would, eventually, be influential in the introduction of the first Vaccination Act. His work would be continued by his son, Charles Arthur Aikin, who was part of the committee set up to investigate and then pave the way for compulsory vaccination in 1853.[60]

This is a small example of the ways in which family connections might continue an ideal – in this case, of individual responsibility – through the generations, in changing political and social contexts. Looking at the family as a whole through the essays which follow, we might start to glimpse such continuations. There is still much more work to be done in relation to the family. This might be on material specifically related to its members, for example in terms of investigating the under-explored archival material of the Aikin Family Papers in the University of Rochester Library, or tracing the interdisciplinary work and legacies of the descendants: Edmund Aikin's elegant Wellington Rooms in Liverpool still lie semi-derelict, on English Heritage's national Buildings at Risk Register. It might also be in more abstract terms – what parallels might be drawn between Dissenting dynasties such as the Aikins and prominent Anglican families, or with continental families such as the Mendelssohns, for instance? The volume hopes to provide a starting point for such explorations, and to suggest some of the ways in which the Aikins both write and help to shape 'the poetry of history'.

NOTES

1. Image from the British Museum Collection Database; '1873, 0809.209' www.britishmuseum.org/collection, British Museum, online (accessed: 31/01/2011). Thanks to the Trustees of the British Museum for allowing its use.

2. See Barbauld's note to 'The Mouse's Petition', *Poems* (1792); reprinted in William McCarthy and Elizabeth Kraft (eds.), *Anna Letitia Barbauld: Selected Poetry and Prose* (Peterborough, ON: Broadview Press, 2002), 69–72. This will be cited as Barbauld, *Selected Poetry and Prose* throughout the collection.

3. See, for instance, Marlon Ross, 'Configurations of Feminine Reform: The Woman Writer and the Tradition of Dissent', in Carol Shiner Wilson and Joel Hafner (eds.), *Revisioning Romanticism: British Women Writers, 1776–1837* (Philadelphia, PA: University of Pennsylvania Press, 1994), 91–110 (98) and Mitzi Myers, 'Of Mice and Mothers: Mrs. Barbauld's "New Walk" and Gendered Codes in Children's Literature', in Louise Wetherbee Phelps and Janet Emig (eds.), *Feminine Principles in Women's Experience in American Composition and Rhetoric* (University of Pittsburgh Press, 1995), 255–88.

4. See E. P. Thompson, *The Making of the English Working Class* (1963 London: Penguin, 2002), 84–110 for his classic discussion of the phrase, 'The Free-born Englishman'.

5. David L. Wykes, 'Joseph Priestley, Minister and Teacher', in Isabel Rivers and David L. Wykes (eds.), *Joseph Priestley, Scientist, Philosopher, and Theologian* (Oxford University Press, 2008), 20–48 (44).

6. For more on the reputation and imagery of Priestley in the period, see Martin Fitzpatrick, 'Priestley Caricatured', in A. Truman Schwartz and John G. McEvoy (eds.), *Motion Toward Perfection: The Achievement of Joseph Priestley* (Boston, MA: Skinner House Books, 1990), 161–218; Malcolm Dick (ed.), *Joseph Priestley and Birmingham* (Studley: Brewin Books, 2005).

7. Barbauld, *Selected Poetry and Prose*, 69.

8. William McCarthy, *Anna Letitia Barbauld: Voice of the Enlightenment* (Baltimore, MD: Johns Hopkins University Press, 2008), 78.

9. Scott Krawczyk, *Romantic Literary Families* (New York and Basingstoke: Palgrave Macmillan, 2009), esp. chs. 1 and 2; Michelle Levy, *Family Authorship and Romantic Print Culture* (New York, NY and Basingstoke: Palgrave Macmillan, 2008), 22.

10. Gillian Russell and Clara Tuite, 'Introducing Romantic Sociability', in Gillian Russell and Clara Tuite (eds.), *Romantic Sociability: Social Networks and Literary Culture in Britain, 1770–1840* (Cambridge University Press, 2006), 4.

11. Noel Annan, 'The Intellectual Aristocracy', in J. H. Plumb (ed.), *Studies in Social History: A Tribute to G. M. Trevelyan* (London, New York, Toronto: Longman, 1955), 241–87 (243).

12. See, for example, Peter Laslett, *The World We Have Lost* (New York, NY: Scribner, 1966) and *The World We Have Lost: Further Explored*, 3rd edn, rev. (London: Routledge, 2002); Lawrence Stone, *The Family, Sex and Marriage in England 1500–1800* (Harmondsworth: Penguin, 1979); Leonore Davidoff and Catherine Hall, *Family Fortunes: Men and Women of the English Middle Class, 1780–1850*, 2nd edn (London: Routledge, 2002), 13.

13. Naomi Tadmor, *Family and Friends in Eighteenth-century England: Household, Kinship, and Patronage* (Cambridge University Press, 2000), 10; Adam Kuper,

Incest and Influence: The Private Life of Bourgeois England (Cambridge, MA: Harvard University Press, 2009).

14. Davidoff and Hall, *Family Fortunes*, xl.

15. Edmund Burke, *Reflections on the Revolution in France*, ed. L. G. Mitchell (Oxford University Press, 1993), 13; William Hazlitt, *The Complete Works of William Hazlitt*, ed. P. P. Howe, 20 vols. (London and Toronto: J. M. Dent), iv, 51.

16. See Robert Southey, *Life and Correspondence*, ed. Cuthbert Southey, 6 vols. (1849–50), ii, 275. Henry Crabb Robinson reports the comment by Coleridge, *Henry Crabb Robinson on Books and Their Writers*, ed. Edith Julia Morley, 3 vols. (London: J. M. Dent, 1938), i, 56; also related by Southey, *New Letters of Robert Southey*, ed. Kenneth Curry, 2 vols. (New York, NY: Columbia University Press, 1965), i, 498, with some slight alterations.

17. Matthew Arnold, *Culture and Anarchy and other Writings*, ed. Stefan Collini (Cambridge University Press, 1993), 70.

18. John M. Anderson, '"The First Fire": Barbauld Rewrites the Greater Romantic Lyric', *SEL*, 34 (1994), 719–38 (732).

19. Helen Thomas, *Romanticism and Slave Narratives: Transatlantic Testimonies* (Cambridge University Press, 2000); Richard E. Brantley, *Wordsworth's 'Natural Methodism'* (New Haven, CT: Yale University Press, 1975); *Coordinates of Anglo-American Romanticism: Wesley, Edwards, Carlyle and Emerson* (Gainesville, FL: University Press of Florida, 1993); Jasper Cragwall, 'Wordsworth and the Ragged Legion; or, the Lows of High Argument', in Eugene Stelzig (ed.), *Romantic Autobiography in England* (Farnham, Surrey: Ashgate Publishing, 2009), 179–94. Thanks to Richard Brantley for his discussion of this with me.

20. Anna Letitia Le Breton (ed.), *Correspondence of William Ellery Channing, DD, and Lucy Aikin, from 1826 to 1842* (Boston, MA: Roberts Brothers, 1874), 79.

21. McCarthy, *Barbauld*, 17.

22. John Seed, '"A Set of Men Powerful Enough in Many Things": Rational Dissent and Political Opposition in England, 1770–1790', in Knud Haakonssen (ed.), *Enlightenment and Religion: Rational Dissent in Eighteenth-century Britain* (Cambridge University Press, 1996), 140–68 (147).

23. Theophilus Lindsey, *A Sermon Preached at the Opening of the Chapel in Essex-House, Essex-Street* (1774), 20.

24. McCarthy, *Barbauld*, 5.

25. 'On the Death of Mrs. Martineau', Barbauld, *Selected Poetry and Prose*, 149–50.

26. 'Thoughts on the Devotional Taste, on Sects, and on Establishments', Barbauld, *Selected Poetry and Prose*, 223.

27. The tradition was continued by a Kibworth pupil, Thomas Belsham, whose sister Elizabeth moved with him to academies at Daventry and Hackney, and whose housekeeping he commended in his memoirs, recalling that 'by her cheerful and lively conversation and her good humour she was the idol of the students' (*Memoirs of the Late Reverend Thomas Belsham* (London: 1833), 694).

28. *A Report on the State of the Warrington Academy, by the Trustees at Their Annual Meeting*, 1 July 1762.
29. 'Historical Account of the Warrington Academy', *Monthly Repository of Theology and General Literature* (1813), 169.
30. H. A. Bright, *A Historical Sketch of Warrington Academy* (Liverpool, pr. T. Brakell, 1859), 15.
31. Anne Janowitz, 'Amiable and Radical Sociability: Anna Barbauld's "Free Familiar Conversation"', in Russell and Tuite (eds.), *Romantic Sociability*, 62–81 (62). As Janowitz points out, the ideal of the family could be disrupted, however: the reality of life at Warrington could be fraught, with frequent financial worries as well as disciplinary issues (*ibid.*, 68–9).
32. See David Wykes' comments on Thomas Cogan's education in this volume (Chapter 2); 'Biography: Memoir of the Late Dr. Cogan', *Monthly Repository*, 14 (January 1819), 1.
33. Philip Doddridge, *Family Expositor, or, A Paraphrase and Version of the New Testament. With critical notes; and a Practical Improvement of each Section*, 6 vols. (1739–56), 'Preface', 11, v; 1, 403–4.
34. 'Washing-Day', Barbauld, *Selected Poetry and Prose*, 144–7.
35. See Elizabeth Kraft, 'Anna Letitia Barbauld's "Washing-Day" and the Montgolfier Balloon', *Literature and History*, 4(2) (1995), 25–41, for an excellent discussion of various critical perspectives on the poem.
36. Or, as it appears in the *Monthly Magazine* for October 1796, 'Reflections on Entering into Active Life. A Poem which affects not to be POETRY', 732.
37. Lucy Aikin (ed.), *The Works of Anna Laetitia Barbauld. With a Memoir by Lucy Aikin*, 2 vols. (1825), 11, 9.
38. Daniel White, *Early Romanticism and Religious Dissent* (Cambridge University Press, 2006), 70. See also 'The "Joineriana": Anna Barbauld, the Aikin Family Circle, and the Dissenting Public Sphere', *Eighteenth-century Studies*, 32(4) (1999), 511–33.
39. Levy, *Family Authorship*, 22.
40. Bright, *Historical Sketch*, 14.
41. White, *Early Romanticism*, 75.
42. 'What Women Are Educated For', *Once a Week* (10 August 1861), 177; cited by White, *Early Romanticism*, 75. A rather startling counterpart to the image in our engraving of 'The Mouse's Petition'.
43. Samuel Paterson, *Joineriana: Or the Book of Scraps*, 2 vols. (London: J. Johnson, 1772), 1, 52.
44. *Ibid., Joineriana*, 1, 80–1.
45. Virgil, *The Eclogues*, ed. and trans. Guy Lee (London: Penguin Classics, 1984), 105–7.
46. *Hymns in Prose for Children* (London: J. Johnson, 1781), 59.
47. Barbauld, *Civic Sermons to the People. Number 11. From Mutual Wants Springs Mutual Happiness* (London: J. Johnson, 1792), 6. See Levy's discussion of the connections here with Locke; she traces a disagreement between Barbauld and Locke, arguing that although the two do come together in terms of the

importance of family as a building block for society, for Barbauld, 'there is no moment when men alone come together to form a society transcendent of their domestic ties' (*Family Authorship*, 28).

48. Lucy Aikin, *Memoir of John Aikin, MD with a Selection of Miscellaneous Pieces, Biographical, Moral and Critical*, 2 vols. (London: Baldwin, Cradock and Joy, 1823), 1, 201.

49. *Ibid.*, 1, 200.

50. Philip Hemery Le Breton (ed.), *Memoirs, Miscellanies and Letters of the Late Lucy Aikin* (London: Longman, 1864), xi.

51. *Literary Gazette*, 27 (Saturday, 26 July 1817), 56.

52. 'Introduction', by Anne K. Mellor and Michelle Levy (eds.), *Epistles on Women and Other Works by Lucy Aikin* (Peterborough, ON: Broadview, 2011).

53. Anne Janowitz, 'Memoirs of a Dutiful Niece: Lucy Aikin and Literary Reputation', in Heather Glen and Paul Hamilton (eds.), *Repossessing the Romantic Past* (Cambridge University Press, 2006), 80.

54. Bright, *Historical Sketch*, 28.

55. *Select Works of the British Poets, with Biographical and Critical Prefaces, by Dr. Aikin: A New Edition with a Supplement by Lucy Aikin* (London: Longman, 1852), 813.

56. Krawczyk, *Romantic Literary Families*, 95–134.

57. Robert Southey to C. W. Williams Wynn, September 1803, in Curry, *New Letters*, 1, 328–30.

58. Robert Bloomfield to George Bloomfield, 21 September 1803, in *The Letters of Robert Bloomfield and His Circle*, eds. Tim Fulford and Lynda Pratt, *Romantic Circles* (www.rc.umd.edu/editions/bloomfield_letters; accessed: 25/01/11). Thanks to Tim Fulford for alerting me to this reference and for discussing Southey's fractious relationship with Arthur Aikin. Southey and friends bore a long-lasting grievance against the Aikin–Barbauld circle after misattributing an unfavourable review of Charles Lamb's play *John Woodvil* in the *Annual Review* to Barbauld; see also Lucy Aikin's angry defence of her aunt against Southey's attacks in 'Southey and "The Aikins": His Injustice towards Mrs. Barbauld', *Gentleman's Magazine* (July 1850), 26–7. Thanks to Michelle Levy for pointing this out.

59. Krawczyk, *Romantic Literary Families*, 2; Levy, *Family Authorship*, 21.

60. See Deborah Brunton, *The Politics of Vaccination: Practice and Policy in England, Wales, Ireland, and Scotland, 1800–1874* (Rochester, NY: University of Rochester Press, 1988), 41. There is perhaps a certain irony in the Aikins' association with an Act which brought the liberties of the individual so sharply into question; another example of the ways in which family concerns, while remaining consistent in some ways, were given different expression through the changing social and cultural context of the nineteenth century.

CHAPTER 2

The Revd John Aikin senior: Kibworth School and Warrington Academy

David L. Wykes

John Aikin senior was the first member of an extraordinary eighteenth- and nineteenth-century provincial family of Dissenters to gain distinction, and is today largely remembered because he taught at the celebrated Warrington Academy, serving first as tutor in *belles-lettres* and then as theological tutor or principal. Aikin had earlier conducted an important school at Kibworth Harcourt in Leicestershire, the subject of much recent interest among scholars because it was at Kibworth that his children, John Aikin junior and Anna Letitia Barbauld, were born and began their schooling. Among his contemporaries Aikin also gained some celebrity as a scholar in languages and literature both classical and modern, but his failure to publish more than a couple of essays in the *Monthly Review* and a preface to his son's essays on Pliny means his scholarship has been little considered. Although Aikin's reputation is largely derived from his work as a tutor at Warrington Academy, it is clear his school was of regional significance, and that his contribution as a schoolmaster was at least as important as his role as a tutor at Warrington.[1]

AIKIN'S EDUCATION AND EARLY CAREER

John Aikin was born in London on 28 December 1713. His father, also John, a London linen draper, was originally from Kirkcudbright in south-east Scotland. Aikin was at first intended for his father's business, and after

I am grateful to Dr Simon Mills and Professor M. A. Stewart for their comments on this essay. I also wish to thank Mrs Sue Killoran, Librarian Fellow of Harris Manchester College, Oxford (hereafter HMCO), the Trustees of the Congregational Memorial Hall, London, Dr Margaret Bonney, Chief Archivist, Record Office for Leicestershire, Leicester, and Rutland (hereafter ROLLR), the University Librarian and Director, the John Rylands University Library, the University of Manchester, and Mrs Lynda Brooks, Librarian, Linnean Society Library, London, the Acting Manager, Liverpool Record Office, and the Archivist, Shropshire Archives, for permission to use and cite from the records in their keeping.

some time in his father's shop he was placed as a clerk in an overseas merchant house where he learned French, and indeed acquired a remarkable proficiency in the language as a result of living with a family where only French was spoken. Ill-health caused him to be sent to school in St Albans.[2] The school was kept in the old manor house of Newland Squillers, on the edge of the town, on the road leading to Hatfield and Hertford. The house 'had been let as a Boy's Boarding-School; and ... it was a very reputable school among the Dissenters, where the celebrated Dr. Doddridge, Dr. Aikin, and others, ministers, and other persons of that profession, received the rudiments of their education'. It seems likely that this was the Dissenter's charity school at St Albans which was a *cause célèbre* at the end of Queen Anne's reign. In May 1714 Dissenters were accused of also taking in church children and forcing them to attend the local Dissenting meeting – a hugely damaging charge just at the time when the Schism Bill was introduced into parliament.[3] The master was said to have 'once been upon the stage', and was fond of exercising his boys in dramatics. William Turner speculated that this gave Aikin 'an early taste for poetry, and also that force and clearness of enunciation, by which he was eminently distinguished'. Almost certainly through the influence of the local Dissenting minister in St Albans, Samuel Clarke, who was Philip Doddridge's friend and patron, Aikin was sent to Doddridge's Academy in Northampton in midsummer 1732 at the age of 19. At Northampton, according to his granddaughter Lucy, 'the bent of his mind towards learning so strongly manifested itself, that he obtained his father's permission to change his views and devote himself to the Christian ministry'.[4]

The earliest Dissenting academies were established following the Restoration of Charles II as a result of the 1662 Act of Uniformity, and were intended to provide Protestants dissenting from the Church of England with a higher education similar to that at Oxford and Cambridge from which they were largely excluded. These academies played a vital role in maintaining an educated ministry among the Dissenters. Many were open to both lay and ministerial students. The best gave their students the knowledge and skills to examine new ideas and arguments for themselves, and indeed to hold their own in disputes with their Anglican opponents. A number of tutors and students made major contributions to the development of ideas in theology, philosophy, literature and science during the eighteenth and nineteenth centuries. It is important to recognize, however, that considerable variations existed in the purpose, size and quality of the Dissenting academies. Scholars have tended to concentrate on the late eighteenth century and a few exceptional institutions, such as

Warrington Academy. Although the very best offered an education at least comparable to that provided by Oxford and Cambridge, many were much more modest both in their ambitions and in their achievements and offered a very uneven or incomplete education.

Doddridge's Academy, established in 1729 is considered one of the outstanding Dissenting academies of the first half of the eighteenth century, both for the quality of the teaching and for the breadth of the subjects taught. Doddridge taught both lay and ministerial students. The complete course for ministerial students lasted five years, though not all students followed the full course. Much of the first two years was taken up with studying the classics, but ministerial students began to learn Hebrew in the first year. Doddridge taught a wide range of subjects covering philosophy, logic, ethics, pneumatology (theory of the mind), divinity, ecclesiastical history, and preaching and pastoral care. Doddridge's method of instruction was also important. Students were expected to consider the arguments on both sides in matters of controversy, and were left to make their own judgements after reading the different authorities for themselves. Inevitably this form of instruction encouraged the questioning of existing interpretations and a willingness to consider controversial ideas. Doddridge's Academy had an excellent library of several thousand volumes, and students also had access to his own books.[5] In November 1733, while Aikin was a student at Northampton, Doddridge was prosecuted by the Chancellor of the Diocese of Lincoln for failing to obtain a licence to teach. The case was dropped after the Dissenting Deputies in London (who defended the rights of Dissenters) intervened with the government, and Doddridge obtained a prohibition to stay proceedings in the high court at Westminster. This is said to have been the last prosecution of Dissenters for teaching grammar school.[6]

Aikin was clearly rather a favourite of Doddridge, who was frequently a guest of the Aikin family when he stayed in London, though Aikin's attendance at Doddridge's Academy was not without difficulties. He became friendly with Jane, the daughter of Doddridge's old tutor John Jennings. At first Jane Jennings appears to have been welcome at the Aikin family home in London. But something more than a friendship developed between the two which met with opposition from Aikin's parents. Doddridge told his wife in July 1733 that he and Jane Jennings had experienced a very uncomfortable dinner at the Aikin household: 'It is impossible to tell you how much I was baited' by Mrs Aikin. By June 1734 Aikin's father was determined to send his son to a university in Scotland. In conversation with Doddridge he denied that the decision was prompted by any objection to Doddridge and his principles, or suspicion of his son's attachment to Jane Jennings, rather, he claimed, it was the result of his admiration for the Scottish universities. A few days later Doddridge was rather more optimistic and told his wife that he believed the son would return to Northampton 'if he manages dexterously'. He noted, though, that 'it is reported about town that his father removes him because I have debauched his principles'. A week later he was reporting that 'Mr Aikin is willing that his son should come and spend another year with us at least, or perhaps two'. In fact the son remained at Northampton for a further year, until midsummer 1735.[7]

Aikin was sent to Aberdeen to study divinity. The reasons why are puzzling. Glasgow would seem a more obvious choice since it had been patronized by English Dissenters since the late seventeenth century. It would also have been the local university for Aikin's father when he was growing up in Kirkcudbright. Furthermore the two colleges at Aberdeen, King's College and Marischal College, were both experiencing severe financial difficulties in the 1720s and 1730s. In addition very little divinity was being taught at either Glasgow or King's College. John Simson, the professor of divinity at Glasgow, had been suspended over doubts about his orthodoxy, and following the death of the professor of divinity at King's in 1733, there was no appointment to the chair until October 1735. There are few firm details about Aikin's studies at Aberdeen, excepted when he was appointed tutor at Warrington it was noted that he had 'pass'd a considerable time in Scotland, to improve his Critical Skills in Greek under Dr Blackwell, & his knowledge of Philosophy with other tutors', who unfortunately are not named. Thomas Blackwell (1701–57), professor of Greek at Marischal, was one of the major figures in the Scottish Enlightenment. According to Turner, whose account is not reliable, Aikin also came into contact with two other figures, Thomas Reid (1710–96) and David Fordyce (1711–51), who were subsequently to become leading figures in the Enlightenment. There is some evidence to support Turner's claim as in October 1739 Fordyce wrote to Aikin's old tutor, Doddridge, that he had sent him a copy of his 'Essay on Human Nature', 'which you have, perhaps, heard Mr Aikin mention'.[8] Doddridge was later to maintain an extensive correspondence with Fordyce, but before, in 1736, he received an honorary degree of doctor of divinity from Marischal College with the support of Blackwell and Fordyce, and the following year the same honour from King's College. It was from King's that Aikin received his degree. In July 1737 he was made a Master of Arts also by special decree as a favour. He was described as a 'Student in Divinity, having resided in the College for a considerable time past ... and given good testimony of his Proficiency in the Liberal Arts, and his regular and decent Behaviour, the University did unanimously agree for his farther Encouragement that he shou'd be graduate Master of Arts'.[9]

Aikin returned to Northampton to serve briefly as Doddridge's assistant in the Academy. In March 1738 Doddridge told his friend, Samuel Clark, that Aikin had received a call from the congregation at Market Harborough to be their minister which had been 'so pressing' that he 'thought it his duty to accept it'. Eighteen months later Doddridge informed Clark that 'Mr Aikin is disabled at Harborough, in consequence of the return of his spitting of blood'.[10] There are differing accounts of the exact nature of Aikin's illness. According to Aikin's granddaughter, Lucy, it was a disease of the lungs. Other accounts have Aikin injured as a result of a fall from his horse. Whatever the cause Aikin was unable to preach and he received an 'extraordinary supply' of £5 from the Presbyterian Fund Board following his incapacity.[11]

There is evidence that by this date Aikin's religious views had changed and that he had departed from strict orthodoxy. Doddridge, in response to Isaac Watts' criticism that he neglected the needs of London congregations preferring country charges for his students, told his friend Daniel Neal in London in November 1738 that 'Mr Isaac Wilkinson of Harbro were his Health confirmed or Mr Aikin of the same were his Orthodoxy unsuspected . . . are every one of them such Person as you want.'[12] The nature of Aikin's heterodoxy is unclear, but probably it involved some departure from strict Calvinism. He was not a Unitarian in this period. Twenty-five years later Priestley was to recall that at Warrington he and his fellow tutors, including Aikin, were all Arians, and they shared nearly the same opinions in religion and in other matters, Aikin alone holding 'some obscure notions' on the doctrine of atonement. At that date the only Socinian, or militant anti-Trinitarian, in the neighbourhood was John Seddon of Manchester, 'and we all wondered at him'.[13]

Prevented from preaching, Aikin was forced to abandon the ministry and turn to teaching, one of the few professions open to a man of learning educated in languages and the classics. He was first in partnership with Thomas Lee at East Farndon in Northamptonshire. Lee, a member of the Market Harborough Congregational Church, was conducting a school from at least 1733, when John Barker told Doddridge of his intentions of sending Thomas Steffe, a boy he was sponsoring for the ministry, to Lee's school. In 1737 the fees were 12 guineas a year.[14] In 1741 Aikin, while still living in East Farndon, married Jane Jennings. They moved to Kibworth Harcourt, in Leicestershire, about 5 miles north of Market Harborough, where Aikin opened his own school. John Jennings, Jane's father, had earlier conducted a notable Dissenting academy at Kibworth, which Doddridge himself had attended.[15]

JOHN AIKIN'S SCHOOL AT KIBWORTH, 1741–58

Even from the limited evidence that is available it is clear Aikin established an important school at Kibworth. It has been possible to recover the names of only twelve or possibly thirteen of his pupils, together with that of his own son.[16] A number were subsequently to distinguish themselves and have entries in the *Dictionary of National Biography*. They were Newcome Cappe, minister of the St Saviourgate congregation in York, whose 1776 fast-day sermon was passed around the benches in the House of Commons;[17] Thomas Cogan, one of the founders of the Royal Humane Society; Thomas Robins, theological tutor (in other words principal) at Daventry Academy; and also his successor, Thomas Belsham, who was subsequently theological tutor at New College, Hackney, and the leading Unitarian controversialist in the early nineteenth century; and John Simpson, Unitarian author and biblical critic.

From such a small sample firm conclusions are impossible, but some of the evidence is suggestive. The school appears to have had a regional reputation, at least among Dissenters. Geographically the pupils were drawn from, or had connections with, the East Midlands, especially Leicestershire and Northamptonshire. In turn Samuel Clark, Doddridge's friend and patron, was clearly the link explaining why Jabez Hirons was sent from St Albans. Even Cappe, whose widowed mother lived in Leeds, had connections with the East Midlands. Cappe's father had been minister at Lincoln before moving to the Presbyterian congregation at Mill Hill, Leeds. The only known exception is one of the later pupils, John Hall, who was from Sheffield.[18] The evidence for Aikin's earliest pupils suggests they were 15 or 16 when they entered. John Coltman, the son of a Leicester business-man, was 16 and stayed three years. Thomas Watson, from Kettering, was 17 when he left, Cappe 15, Hirons 17, and Richard Hodgson, the son of the minister at Lincoln, 15. Doddridge's own son was 14 in 1749, and judging from Doddridge's comments concerning Aikin's achievements, he had already been studying there a year or two at least. Interestingly the later pupils who have been identified were younger, 7 or 8 and 11 or 12. The evidence is too limited to be certain, but perhaps indicates that Aikin's school expanded to provide classes for younger boys.

A majority of the pupils who can be identified became ministers, but this is, in part, a result of the nature of the sources which favour the identification of those who went into the ministry, not least because of the tradition by the early nineteenth century of denominational periodicals providing detailed obituaries of even quite obscure ministers. William Turner in his account of Aikin suggested that lying close to the manufacturing districts of the East Midlands, the majority of pupils must have been intended for business. Nevertheless Aikin's school appears to have had a major role in giving boys a grammar education in the classics and ancient languages in preparation for studying at a Dissenting academy: principally Doddridge's, and later, after his death, Daventry and even Warrington. In July 1742, Doddridge suggested his friend Colonel James Gardner send his son, David, to Aikin's school, presumably because he was not sufficiently prepared by his previous schooling to enter the Academy. If David Gardner did attend, it was only for a short time, for later the same year he entered Doddridge's Academy at Northampton. As befits the son of a senior army officer, he was a cornet in Sir John Cope's Regiment of Dragoons by July 1747.[19]

There is little contemporary evidence relating to Aikin's school: in the main only a handful of references from Doddridge's correspondence. Some of the most important evidence is provided by John Coltman, the son of a Leicester manufacturer, who was sent to Kibworth on his sixteenth birthday in December 1743, only a year or so after the school opened. The school was sufficiently well established that at Kibworth, Coltman, according to his younger son, wore a school uniform consisting of a grey wig, purple velvet cap with gold tassel, and a plaid tunic or loose gown fastened with a leather belt, 'the whole having a picturesque if not [a] classical air'. A copy of the bill for Coltman's first year shows the subjects he studied included geography and French as well as Greek and Latin. The account came to £14 5s 3d, being £12 for board and teaching, and the remaining £2 5s 3d for books, pens, paper and ink. The books purchased were *Les Fables de la Fontaine*, a French classic, Cicero's *Orations*, Homer's *Iliad* and a 'Compleat System of Geography'.[20] There is evidence for the excellence of Aikin's instruction in languages, both ancient and modern. Doddridge sent his own son, Philip junior, to Aikin's school, and it is clear he thought highly of Aikin's teaching. In 1749 he said proudly that his son at the age of 14 'has made very uncommon attainments in Latin, Greek, French, and Italian, under the instruction of his worthy master, the Rev. Mr. Aiken, of Kibworth, once my pupil, and after that my assistant'.[21] A few years later, in December 1751, John Hodgson, minister of the Presbyterian congregation in Lincoln, told

George Benson that he intended to keep his son, Richard, with Aikin for another eighteen months, 'for I w^d have him a pretty good Master of ye Languages before he pursues Academical Studies' for the ministry at a Dissenting academy.[22] The teaching of languages does seem to have been a real strength of Aikin's school, not least because of Aikin's own deep knowledge and understanding.

What of Aikin's achievements as a schoolteacher? Much of course depends upon the ability and aptitude of the pupil, though a good master can draw out and encourage those abilities, just as a poor one can frustrate and stunt them. There is also the question of opportunity: the age at entry and the length of schooling, whether a boy was taught at an impressionable age and for how long. There is only incomplete evidence on the age of Aikin's pupils and the length of time they studied with him. Coltman was taught for three years, but Newcome Cappe and Belsham only for a year, though Belsham's course ended because of Aikin's appointment as a tutor at Warrington Academy. Coltman was 16, Cappe 15, but Belsham was only 7, while Cogan, who attended for two or three years, was 11 or 12 when he entered the school. Despite the shortness of his period of attendance, Cappe's widow recorded that 'he always looked back with peculiar satisfaction' on that period. 'Here he began, in earnest, that intellectual career in which he so much delighted.' The obituary in the *Monthly Magazine*, also possibly written by his widow, noted that he 'was accustomed to speak of that period of his life with great satisfaction ... on account of the progress he made under his kind and able tutor'.[23] The obituary for Cogan noted that it was under Aikin that 'he acquired a taste for classical knowledge, which never forsook him during the remainder of his life'. His attendance 'did not exceed two or three years; and he constantly lamented the shortness of his stay there, until the close of his life'.[24] Coltman's youngest daughter claimed that it was from Aikin that her father 'imbibed a taste for classical learning' which so characterized him in later life. According to Catherine Hutton, a close family friend of the Coltmans, it was at Kibworth that Coltman 'laid the foundation of those studious habits for which he was always remarkable'.[25]

Evidence survives for the profound influence Aikin and his teaching had on Coltman. Coltman is considered to have been among the most active and enterprising businessmen in Leicester during the late eighteenth century. He was responsible for a number of major initiatives resulting in the mechanization of worsted spinning, thereby removing a major bottleneck in the supply of yarn to the Leicester hosiery industry caused by the reliance on hand-spinning. Yet on close examination Coltman appears a paradox, possessing none of the drive and ambition usually associated with the successful businessman. Samuel, his younger son, claimed Coltman was 'considered a spirited and energetic manufacturer – one, ever ready to foster and encourage new inventions', but he also accused his father of neglecting his affairs by his love of study, which 'all through his life absorbed him more than is compatible with a strict attention to business'.[26] Coltman left Kibworth at the age of 19, rather late to enter on business. One explanation may be that he was intended for the ministry, but gave it up, possibly when his wealthy uncle, a London distiller, made him his heir. Among Leicester businessmen Coltman was almost certainly unique in having received a classical education; indeed his own sons' schooling ended at 16.[27]

Aikin clearly instilled a love of learning in Coltman. Coltman's eldest son told Aikin's granddaughter Lucy that his father had acquired from Aikin 'that love of reading which was ever after his delight and solace'.[28] Coltman was not only to continue his studies after leaving Kibworth, but to develop other scholarly interests, particularly relating to Roman antiquities. Among his papers is a memorandum book recording the dates and titles for a series of essays and notes he made between August 1747 and November 1751 on such subjects as 'enlarging the capacity of the mind' (15 August 1747) and 'Resolution in Logic is a branch of method' (4 November 1748), both clearly from reading Isaac Watts, and the geography of the *Iliad* (19 November 1751). There are also notes of his reading, ranging from astronomy and history to ecclesiastical and biblical history: John Flamsteed's *Historiae Coelestis* (1710) or catalogue of the stars, Samuel Pufendorf's bestselling *Introduction to European History*, first published in 1680, Laurence Echard's *A General Ecclesiastical History from the Nativity of Our Blessed Saviour to . . . the Emperor Constantine the Great* (1710), Thomas Stackhouse's *New History of the Bible* (1730), and more controversially William Whiston's *Historical Memoirs of the Life and Writings of Dr Samuel Clarke* (1730). Other entries in the volume take the form of entries in a commonplace book: a note from the *Evening Advertiser* (29 September 1755) on the number of hogsheads of tobacco sent annually to Britain from Virginia; an article on ambition from the *Northamptonshire Mercury* (2 October 1758); and a list of the popes. There is also a note of the number of slaves bought on the coast of Africa in 1768, perhaps illustrating an early awakening against the evils of the slave trade, for Coltman was later an active opponent. There are a handful of later entries, including a copy of a letter to Samuel Unwin jun. concerning the discovery of a Roman tessellated pavement at Dannetts Hall near Leicester dated January 1785.[29] During the period after he left Kibworth, Coltman used to meet weekly with a small group of friends to discuss literary and philosophical subjects of common interest. The other members of the 'Quadrumviate', as they named their group, were

Richard Pulteney, then an apothecary at Leicester, but later to become a celebrated botanist and the English publicist of Linnaeus; John Lewin, son of one of the leading hosiers in the town during the mid-eighteenth century; and the surgeon John Cogan, whose family were from Rothwell, though his relationship to the other Rothwell Cogans, including Aikin's pupil, is not clear. All four members of the 'Quadrumviate' were Dissenters. In addition, Aikin and Pulteney corresponded on botanical matters.[30]

Coltman was to develop the interests he had acquired in classical scholarship throughout his adult life. William Gardiner, who knew Coltman well, recalled that:

He had the reputation of being a first-rate classical scholar. He was an insatiable reader, and a noted antiquarian. His taste for the fine arts was as conspicuous as his knowledge of the learned languages, and his collection of coins, many of which were dug up in the parish in which he lived, was considered of great value . . . With the more learned he would adorn his conversation by citations from classical authors.[31]

Coltman's reputation 'as a friend to literature' meant that many of the scholars who visited the town came to see him. Coltman spent an afternoon in April 1762 with Pulteney in the company of Dr Richard Farmer (1735–97) of Cambridge. Farmer was then engaged on a history of Leicester, which was eventually abandoned on his appointment as Master of Emmanuel College in 1775. In 1787 Joseph Priestley, the celebrated scientist and theologian, visited Leicester. 'Mr Coltman accompanied the doctor into St Nicholas' churchyard, to view that great curiosity the Jewry wall.' Gardiner witnessed the occasion: 'for we two lads, John Coltman [jun.] and myself, sneaked behind the philosopher like two spaniels, and heard his opinion [correctly] that it was the remains of a Roman bath', rather than the popular belief that it was part of the Temple of Janus. When John Waltire, one of the many itinerant lecturers in natural philosophy or science in the late eighteenth century, came to Leicester, Coltman invited him to his house. Waltire's audience there for his lecture on mechanics included Coltman's own wife and also that of his friend Matthew Reid.[32] It was not simply that Aikin awakened an interest in Coltman in the classics, and in scholarly matters generally, but that Coltman had acquired the knowledge and skills at Aikin's school which enabled him to study those subjects for himself and advance his own learning.

Did Aikin have any influence on the religious development of the boys he taught? Earlier, Doddridge had feared Aikin's heterodoxy would make him unacceptable to many congregations. Did it impair the reputation of his school? There is no evidence on this latter point, but it is clear his heterodox views did influence some of his pupils. Cogan, who attended Aikin's school sometime between the ages of 11 or 12 and about 14 or 15, 'was accustomed to speak with peculiar pleasure of the familiar theological lectures' or addresses that Aikin 'was in the habit of delivering to his scholars on the Sunday evening; declaring, that he always looked forward to them with delight, and, though educated in the strictest Calvinism, owed to them his first religious impressions'; in other words the first changes in his religious opinions.[33] The development of Cogan's religious opinions as a young man caused precisely the difficulties that Doddridge had feared would compromise Aikin's ministry. At Kibworth Cogan had been encouraged to indulge 'pretty freely in general reading', suggesting, incidentally, that he had access to a well-stocked library, 'and the direction of his mind was afterwards turned towards controversial writings'. But Cogan's advanced views proved unpopular, so that when he went to candidate a number of congregations for their vacant pulpits, he did so 'without ever receiving a regular call or invitation'. This provoked a crisis and in the winter of 1758–9 Cogan decided to study medicine in Holland, leading eventually to the abandonment of the ministry in favour of medicine.[34] Not all of Aikin's pupils were influenced by their schoolmaster's heterodox views. Belsham certainly left the school still orthodox; it was only later, while theological tutor at Daventry that he adopted Unitarian opinions.

AIKIN AND WARRINGTON ACADEMY, 1758–80

In March 1758 Aikin was invited to become tutor in languages and *belles-lettres* at the recently established Warrington Academy. The Academy had opened in October the previous year, with the celebrated Hebraist John Taylor, as divinity tutor, and John Holt as tutor in mathematics and natural philosophy. Priestley later recalled that he had also been proposed as tutor in languages, but that Aikin, 'whose qualifications were superior to mine was justly preferred to me'.[35] Jenkin Jenkins (d. 1780), later divinity tutor at Carmarthen Academy, and Thomas Scott (1705–75), minister of St Nicholas Street meeting, Ipswich, who had earlier conducted a boarding school, were also considered. Scott was evidently thought too old: he had been a fellow student of Doddridge's at John Jennings' academy at Kibworth; and Priestley was judged too young. There were also concerns in Priestley's case about his speech impediment. Aikin was strongly recommended initially by the Birmingham inventor and manufacturer Dr John Roebuck (1718–94) who was a native of Sheffield. The Trustees at

Warrington also received testimonials from the author and translator, Samuel Dyer, a friend of Samuel Johnson, who had himself earlier refused the post, Job Orton, who had succeeded Aikin as Doddridge's assistant in the Academy at Northampton, Field Sylvester Wadsworth, who was briefly minister at Kibworth, and whose father had conducted an academy at Sheffield, and William Hawkes, minister of New Meeting, Birmingham, together with two members of his congregation, Joseph Smith and John Kettle. Roebuck, Dyer, Orton and Wadsworth had all been students at Doddridge's Academy: Orton had overlapped briefly with Aikin as a student, and Roebuck and Wadsworth were students when Aikin was Doddridge's assistant. This support for Aikin from Sheffield and Birmingham is perhaps further evidence of the patronage his school at Kibworth received. It is difficult to see otherwise how those who provided testimonials could have had practical knowledge of Aikin's abilities and learning.[36]

The Trustees were seeking to appoint a person well qualified in languages and *belles-lettres*, able 'to form the Youth to a just Taste, and to revive that branch of Learning, wch has been so much neglected, & especially in our Dissenting Schools'. They offered the post to Aikin because of his 'excellent Character for Learning & Virtue, & whose abilities as a Critick both in the Learned & Modern Languages are too publickly known to need to be mentioned'. They were however very uncertain that Aikin would accept the offer, for they feared 'his present situation may be too advantageous to permitt his removal'. The Trustees were only offering a salary of £100 a year, with 2 guineas for every lay student attending a course. They therefore sent one of their number, Philip Holland, to visit Aikin at Kibworth to try to persuade him. Despite the concerns of the Trustees, Aikin did accept, and he succeeded in disengaging himself from his school in time for the beginning of the academic year at Warrington in September 1758. The school was taken over by Stephen Addington (1729–96), minister at Market Harborough.[37] Turner suggests a major attraction for Aikin in relinquishing his school was the chance to give up taking boarders and thereby 'living more to himself', though the opportunities to enjoy the society of similar minded scholars was also appealing. Priestley, when he gave up his school on his appointment as tutor of *belles-lettres* at Warrington in succession to Aikin in 1761, did so because he believed it would be less demanding than conducting a school and also because he hoped it would extend his connections.[38]

Aikin was undoubtedly well qualified for his new post despite much of his previous experience of teaching being limited to the instruction of schoolboys. He had of course briefly assisted Doddridge in his Academy nearly twenty years earlier, as the Trustees of Warrington Academy themselves noted. No less a critic than the noted classicist Gilbert Wakefield observed that Aikin 'had an intimacy with the best authors of *Greece* and *Rome*, superior to what I have ever known in any *dissenting* minister from my own experience. His taste for composition was correct and elegant: and his repetition of beautiful passages ... highly animated, and expressive of sensibility.' In short, 'his intellectual attainments were of a very superior quality indeed ... Every path of polite literature had been traversed by him, and traversed with success'.[39]

Aikin was clearly a fine classical scholar, but one of his students, William Turner, also testified to his pedagogical skills. Aikin made each student in turn read a passage under his direction where he pointed out the significance of the work, corrected any errors, and cleared up any difficulties 'with uncommon clearness and precision'. His choice of books was also appropriate to the needs of his students. 'In history, for instance, he chose such portions of Herodotus, as might illustrate those parts of the Old Testament which were connected with Assyria and Egypt.' 'In reading the ancient poets, his extensive acquaintance with modern poetry enabled him to enliven his lectures with parallel passages, and his fine taste to dwell with peculiar delight [upon] ... those passages of either ancient or modern poets, which appeared most striking for noble sentiments or just reflections.' When his students included a number intended for the law 'he, more than once, read with them Justinian's Institutes'. Besides his lectures on the Greek and Roman classics, Aikin also gave lectures on grammar, oratory and criticism, and had two classes in French language. He also took over the lectures on logic and history previously given by John Holt, the tutor in natural philosophy and mathematics.[40]

On the death of Taylor in 1761 Aikin was unanimously chosen as theology tutor, and Priestley was chosen in his place as tutor in languages and *belles-lettres*. Initially Aikin does not appear to have found teaching his new subject easy, no doubt because of a lack of familiarity. Taylor had not been a success as theological tutor. He was old when he was appointed and he found it difficult to adapt to the demands of his new post. His time at Warrington was not made any happier by his disagreements with his colleagues and the Trustees. Taylor's death eased relations between the tutors and also with the Trustees, but the earlier disputes lost support for the Academy as Taylor's friends withdrew. There were also difficulties involving the students, which appear in part due to dissatisfaction with Aikin's theological lectures. In April 1762 Priestley met with all the divinity students over a dish of tea: 'I talked to them above an hour upon the state of the Academy, going over every particular. I inquired into all Mr Aikin's lectures.' The main critic among the students, John Palmer, was however 'generally the first to express his pleasure and satisfaction in them'. No doubt in response to the criticism, Aikin announced his intention of 'reading Dr Doddridge's divinity lectures, printed or not printed', and he enquired about the printing of the lectures in London, which was then in prospect. Doddridge's lectures were remarkable for the eighteenth century for the range of arguments and authors they covered across a wide selection of philosophical and theological subjects. As a result they were adopted by many Dissenting academies. Palmer was to express his displeasure with Aikin's plan, not because he was dissatisfied with Doddridge's lectures, but because he had already copied them out and would be 'sorry to be obliged to transcribe them now'.[41] Aikin was to use Doddridge's lectures for his own course, except in ethics, where he generally followed his own scheme, 'not, however, materially differing from that of David Fordyce, in the Preceptor'. In the fourth year Aikin made an important addition to his lectures by including a course on church history. Despite being criticized at first Aikin appears soon to have mastered his subject. Matthew Nicholson, the son of a Liverpool merchant, and a lay student in 1764, told his father 'The Moral Philosophy Lectures grow more and more entertain:[g] I should have been very sorry to have miss'd the oportunity of hear:[g] Mr Aikins Lectures on that subject.'[42]

Turner believed Aikin was hardly inferior to Taylor in his knowledge of Hebrew, and 'decidedly his superior' in the other ancient languages. Turner also considered it a considerable advantage that although Aikin had 'a very large and extensive acquaintance with theological works, on each side of every question, he had no system of his own construction to maintain', and having never written on controversial matters, he could with complete impartiality place all the available evidence on every side of the question before his students. According to John Simpson, who was an early student of Aikin's at Warrington having previously been a pupil at Kibworth: 'He stated the arguments on both sides of any disputed point, with great clearness and precision.' In any controversy he always avoided any declaration of his own opinions, encouraging his students to form their own. Both Rational Dissenters and Unitarians stressed the right of private judgement, since freedom of inquiry led in time to truth through rational investigation.[43]

Warrington has acquired the reputation of being the greatest of the Dissenting academies; indeed, as one of the leading educational establishments of the eighteenth century, according to some claims rivalling, even exceeding, Oxford and Cambridge. Historians have argued for the excellence of the education provided, the scholarship of the tutors, and, through the introduction of new subjects and methods of instruction, the innovative nature of the teaching, though in recent years a number of these claims have been qualified. In contrast the question of the contribution Warrington made to Dissent has received little consideration. Although evidence of the best that Dissent could achieve in terms of higher education before the nineteenth century, it did not fit the pattern of other eighteenth-century Dissenting academies. The Academy's reputation was founded on the excellence of its instruction in secular subjects: the teaching of science, languages and history. It did not compare with Daventry Academy, its main rival, in the teaching of theology, metaphysics or ethics.

There is further evidence for the secular nature of the Academy. Warrington educated significantly more students than any other Dissenting academy, just under 400 students between 1757 and 1782, a much higher total than either Daventry or Doddridge's Academy at Northampton, but in contrast very few were educated for the ministry. Only 53 students followed the divinity course at Warrington (fewer than one in seven), though the education of students for the ministry had been one of the main objects of the original founders. The reasons for the small numbers were largely financial. In June 1776 the trustees were unable to continue their divinity exhibitions. Only seven students who attended the Academy after that date entered the Nonconformist ministry. No other Dissenting academy had so high a proportion of lay students. By comparison, nearly three-fifths of the 254 students who attended Daventry were divinity students; a very similar proportion to that found at Doddridge's Academy. Of the 53 students who followed the divinity course at Warrington, 17 conformed or took holy orders, including 4 who had followed the lay course. It is clear that the Academy experienced difficulties in recruiting both students and subscriptions from Dissent. The Academy also did little to preserve the Nonconformist principles of those it educated. The sons of the Nonconformist gentry generally proceeded to Oxford or Cambridge and in time conformed to the Church of England. After the mid-1760s a significant proportion of the students educated at Warrington had no connection with Dissent as financial difficulties forced the trustees to be less selective. The five-year period between 1767 and 1771 saw a dramatic peak in the number of students from the West Indies, as well as an increase in the numbers from Ireland and Scotland. It was some of these students who were to cause the serious problems over discipline which eventually contributed to the closure of the Academy. Warrington Academy was an extraordinary achievement for

Dissenters, but in many respects it was more like a university rather than a Dissenting academy.[44]

CONCLUSION

It is clear that Aikin was an outstanding and influential teacher. While scholars have perhaps been aware of the extent of his scholarship, particularly in the classics, they have overlooked his pedagogical skills. Moreover Warrington has generally been seen as representing the most significant period in his teaching career, for the most part because of the high reputation of the Academy. On closer examination this conclusion is open to qualification. Despite the much admired innovations in teaching, particularly those introduced by Priestley, the contribution of Warrington to Dissent, the body it was established to serve and by whom it was largely maintained, cannot compare to the work of the other academies in this period, notably Daventry and Hoxton. It only educated a small number of students for the Dissenting ministry. There is also Aikin's contribution as a tutor at Warrington. He was an outstanding classical scholar, but he was only tutor in languages and *belles-lettres* for three years. By comparison he was theological tutor at Warrington, a subject he was much less qualified to teach, for nearly twenty.

In contrast to the generally accepted view that Aikin's years at Warrington were the most significant in his career, it can be argued that his school made the greater contribution to Dissent and education. While it is important to understand the crucial role of the Dissenting academy generally in maintaining an educated ministry and in producing some outstanding scholars, a much greater number from a broader section of society were taught at schools run by Dissenters than attended Dissenting academies. Furthermore because of the unusual amount of detail concerning one of his former pupils, John Coltman, there is sufficient evidence to examine Aikin's teaching, and not least the consequences of the learning imparted at his school. There is also enough evidence from other sources to help confirm Aikin's influence as an inspiring teacher, and, even to suggest that he helped change the religious opinions of some of those he taught. Much more still needs to be discovered about schools such as Kibworth and St Albans in preparing pupils in grammar education ready for entry to a Dissenting academy. Finally, perhaps John Aikin senior deserves to come out from behind the shadow of his two brilliant children. At least one modern author has made the editor of *Monthly Magazine* also the tutor of theology at Warrington.[45]

JOHN AIKIN'S PUPILS AT KIBWORTH ORDERED
BY YEAR OF ENTRY

1742

David Gardner, s. of Col. James
   Not clear if Gardner actually attended Aikin's school. Doddridge sug-
   gested to Gardner's father in July 1742 that he be sent to Aikin first,
   but he entered Doddridge's academy in 1742; a cornet in Sir John
   Cope's Regt of Dragoons by July 1747.
   (GFN 762, 772, 773, 1249)

Until 1744

Thomas Watson, b. at Kettering, c.1727; d. 5 Mar. 1793, aged 66
   Doddridge's Academy; minister, Coleford, Gloucestershire, 1748–55;
   Bridgwater, Somerset, 1755–93
   (Joshua Toulmin, *The Character and Reward of the Faithful Servant,
   considered and improved in a sermon, preached at Bridgwater, in the
   county of Somerset, on Lord's Day, March 10, 1793; on occasion of the
   much-lamented Death of the Rev. Thomas Watson* (Taunton [1793]), 26;
   Jerom Murch, *A History of the Presbyterian and General Baptist
   Churches in the West of England* (London, 1835), 179, 182, 185, 189;
   Dr Williams's Library, London, Walter Wilson MSS, A.8.63; Joseph
   Hunter, *Familiae Minorum Gentium*, ed. John W. Clay, 4 vols.,
   Harleian Society, 37 (London, 1894–6), 188; *Gentleman's Magazine*,
   74(1) (1793), 373–4)

1743–6

John Coltman, s. of Joseph of Leicester, hosier; b. 20 Dec. 1727; d. 1808.
   (ROLLR, 15 D 57/448, Samuel Coltman, 'Time's Stepping Stones', 66–7;
   Wykes, 'Reluctant Businessman', 71–85)

Until 1745

Jabez Hirons, s. of Jabez Hirons, grocer; b. St Albans, 11 Jul. 1728; d. 12 Dec.
1812.
   Hirons 'had his grammar learning partly under a respectable clergyman in
   Leicestershire, partly under Dr Aikin, at Kibworth, in the same county';
   entered Doddridge's Academy in 1745, where he remained for five years.

In 1750 he was appointed assistant to the Revd Samuel Clark, minister of St Albans, on whose death in 1751 he became minister, remaining until his own death in 1812. ('The Rev. Jabez Hirons', *Monthly Repository*, 8 (1813), 52–4; *Gentleman's Magazine*, 83(1) (1813), 84)

1748–9

Newcome Cappe (1733–1800)

'He was placed by his mother, in the same year (1748) with Mr (afterwards Dr) Aikin, at Kibworth in Leicestershire, where he remained one year; a period on which he always looked back with peculiar satisfaction. Here he began, in earnest, that intellectual career in which he so much delighted: he had a high respect for his tutor, by whom he was much distinguished' (*Discourses chiefly on Devotional Subjects, by the late Reverend Newcome Cappe. To which are prefixed Memoirs of his Life by Catherine Cappe* (York, 1805), xiii. See also *Monthly Magazine, or, British Register*, 11(1) (1801), 83; *ODNB*)

–1749

Philip Doddridge (1735–85)

1749: Our only son . . . is about fourteen, and has made very uncommon attainments in Latin, Greek, French, and Italian, under the instruction of his worthy master, the Rev. Mr. Aiken,* of Kibworth, once my pupil, and after that my assistant. (H, V, 532)

1747/8–50

Thomas Cogan, s. of John Cogan, surgeon and apothecary, b. at Rothwell, Northamptonshire, 8 February 1736; d. 2 February 1818; one of the founders of the Royal Humane Society.

(*Monthly Repository*, 14 (1819), 1–5, 74–6, 105; Carolyn D. Williams, 'Cogan, Thomas (1736–1818)', *ODNB*, www.oxforddnb.com/view/article/5813)

Until 1750

Thomas Robbins, s. of Richard, b. Keysoe, Bedfordshire, 1732; d. 20 May 1810.

Doddridge's Academy, 1750, removed to Daventry Academy in 1751; Minister, Stretton under Fosse, 1755–61; West Bromwich, 1761–75;

Daventry, assistant minister from 1775, then pastor until 1781; theology tutor, Daventry Academy, 1775–81, lost his voice and forced to retire.

'Being early inclined to literary pursuits and to the office of the ministry, among Protestant dissenters, had the principal part of his grammar education at Woolston, in Northamptonshire, which he finished under Mr. (afterwards Dr.) Aikin, who, for many years, kept a boarding-school at Kibworth, near Market Harborough. From thence, at the usual age, he removed to Northampton, where he entered on a course of academical studies under the superintendence of the great and good Dr Doddridge. But the doctor being removed by death within little more than a year after he began his course . . .' (*Monthly Repository* (July 1810), 362)

Until 1751

Richard Hodgson (*c*.1736–1816), s. of Revd John, minister of Lincoln, 1741–63/4 (*Monthly Repository* (1816), 243)

Daventry Academy, 1751–; Glasgow University; minister, Osset, Yorkshire, 1759–65, ordained 1762; Monton, 1765–71; Nantwich, 1771–99; Doncaster (with Long Houghton), 29 Sep. 1800– d. 18 Jan. 1816 aged 81 years: 'the smallness of the congregation there would often cause him a momentary concern'. 1808 'Old Presbyterian'. Described in his obituary as a 'Unitarian minister'. All his sons left dissent, except the youngest who is a Quaker. ('Obituary', *Monthly Repository* 11 (1816), 243)

John Hodgson: may keep his son with Mr Aikin until a year in the Summer 'for I w^d have him a pretty good Master of ye Languages before he pursues Academical Studies' (John Rylands University Library, Manchester, Benson MS 166, John Hodgson, Lincoln, 11 Dec. 1751)

Until 1755

Thomas Hutchinson, s. of Edward

b. [1734] at Clipston, Northamptonshire; after Aikin's school, matriculated Michaelmas 1755; admitted Fellow Commoner (age 21) at Christ's College, Cambridge, 1 July 1755.

(*Gentleman's Magazine*, 68(1) (1798), 539; *Biographical register of Christ's College 1505–1905 and of the earlier foundation, God's House 1448–1505* (Cambridge University Press, 1913), ed. John Peile, 11, 261)

Until 1756

John Hall, of Sheffield
Daventry, 1756–*c*.61; minister Stannington, Sheffield, 1761–*c*.79; English
Church, Rotterdam, 1779–*c*.1817
('Additions to the List of Pupils under Mr Aikin, while at Kibworth',
Monthly Repository, 8 (1813), 253–4)

1754–8

John Simpson s. of Nathaniel Simpson of Leicester, b. 30 Mar. 1746; d. 18
August 1812
Educated by Aikin at Kibworth, and later by Stephen Addington at
Market Harborough, 1758–60; Warrington Academy, 1760–5;
Glasgow, 1765–7; lived with his family in Leicester continuing his
private studies, until Apr. 1772 when he settled as joint minister at
High Pavement, Nottingham, with Revd George Walker.
(Alexander Gordon, 'Simpson, John (1746–1812)', Revd M. J. Mercer,
ODNB, www.oxforddnb.com/view/article/25586)

1757–8

Thomas Belsham, s. of the Revd James Belsham, b. Bedford, 15 Apr. 1750;
d. 11 Nov. 1829.
After a year at Kibworth removed to John French's school, first at
Wellingborough and then at Ware, 1758–66; Daventry Academy,
Aug. 1766–71.
From June 1757 to June 1758, I was at Kibworth under Dr. Aikin, and, for
the time of life, it was a year of pleasure and improvement. From July
1758 to June 1762, I was at Wellingborough, under Mr. French, a time
which I reflect upon with little satisfaction, having enjoyed little pleasure, and made little improvement. From July 1762 to August 1766, I was
at Ware, having removed thither with Mr. French. If possible, less
attention was paid to instruction here than at Wellingborough, and
my time was deplorably and irrecoverably lost. (*Memoirs of the late
Reverend Thomas Belsham*, p. 4; see R. K. Webb, 'Belsham, Thomas
(1750–1829)', *ODNB*, www.oxforddnb.com/view/article/2066)

NOTES

1. The most detailed account of Aikin is found in W. Turner, 'Historical Account
of Warrington Academy', *Monthly Repository*, 8 (1813), 161–72; see also Diana

K. Jones, 'Aikin, John (1713–1780)', *Oxford Dictionary of National Biography* (Oxford University Press, 2004) (www.oxforddnb.com/view/article/229). There are accounts of Aikin in the biographies of his children, notably Lucy Aikin, *Memoir of John Aikin*, I, 9–10, which appears to rely on Turner's 'Historical Account' for much of the early information; McCarthy, *Barbauld*, which provides new evidence on Aikin. There is a brief curriculum vitae for Aikin in the minutes of Warrington Academy: HMCO, MS Warrington 2, Minute book of Warrington Academy, 1757–75, p. 69 (March 1758).

2. HMCO, MS Warrington 2, 'Minute book', 69; Turner, 'Historical Account', 162; Aikin, *Memoir of John Aikin*, 9.

3. Turner, 'Historical Account', 162; *The Beauties of England and Wales; or Delineations Topographical, Historical, and Descriptive, of Each County*, ed. E. W. Brayley (London: J. Harris, 1808) VII, 104 n*; *Post Boy*, 25–7 May 1714; *Victoria County History: History of the County of Hertford* (1908), 2, 412–24.

4. Turner, 'Historical Account', 162; Aikin, *Memoir of John Aikin*, 9; Congregational Library, London, MS II. e. 43, Doddridge's cash book, 1730–4, fo. 95r.

5. For accounts of Doddridge's academy and his teaching, see Isabel Rivers, 'Doddridge, Philip (1702–1751)', *Oxford DNB* (Oxford University Press, 2004) (www.oxforddnb.com/view/article/7746); I. Rivers, *The Defence of Truth through the Knowledge of Error: Philip Doddridge's Academy Lectures* (London: Friends of Dr Williams's Library, 2003); *Calendar of the Correspondence of Philip Doddridge*, ed. G. F. Nuttall, Historical Manuscripts Commission, JP 26 (1979), xxii–xxv, 130–2, Doddridge to Daniel Wadsworth, Hertford, Connecticut, 6 March 1740/1 (Letter number (hereafter GFN) 663).

6. M. Watts, *The Dissenters: From the Reformation to the French Revolution* (Oxford University Press, 1978), 264.

7. John Rylands University Library, Manchester, Eng. MS 1209 (10, 14–16), Doddridge to his wife Mercy, 17 Jul. 1733, 15, 19, 25 Jun. 1734, printed in *Correspondence and Diary of Philip Doddridge*, ed. J. D. Humphreys (London: Colburn and Bentley, 1829–31) III (hereafter H, III), 121, 159, 161, 164, cf. GFN, 385, 413–14, 418; Congregational Library, MS II. e. 43, fo. 6v. The additional year can be deduced from the fees paid to Doddridge.

8. HMCO, MS Warrington 2, 'Minute book', 69 (March 1758). Turner states that Aikin studied with George Turnbull (Turner, 'Historical Account', 162–3), but as Professor M. A. Stewart points out, this is impossible. Turnbull left Aberdeen in 1727. I am very grateful to Professor Stewart for his comments on this section and for the information about the difficulties at both Aberdeen and Glasgow, thus saving me from a number of errors.

9. GFN, 469, n. 1; GFN, 565, David Fordyce, Newport Pagnell, to Doddridge, 3 Oct. 1739 (misdated 10 Apr. 1740 by Humphreys, see H, III, 442), I am grateful to Dr Simon Mills for this reference; *Roll of Alumni in Arts of the University and King's College of Aberdeen, 1596–1860*, ed. Peter John Anderson (Aberdeen, 1900), 194, Appendix A. 'Masters of Arts who were not Alumni of University and King's College'. I am grateful to Professor Stewart for pointing

out that the John Aikin awarded a Master's degree in 1744 by Marischal College cannot be the same person, as this was someone who was a regular student and attended the full course of study several years after Aikin had returned to Northamptonshire.

10. GFN 498 (25 Mar. 1738); GFN 561 (30 Aug. 1739); H, III, 331, 398. Both Lucy Aikin and Turner state that Aikin had just been chosen as minister of a congregation in Leicester (clearly the Presbyterian Great Meeting), but this seems unlikely and is presumably a mistake for Market Harborough. The minister at Leicester from 1730, James Watson, did not die until August 1741, the same day as his wife, after a short fever, aged 48: see Aikin, *Memoir of John Aikin*, 10; Turner, 'Historical Account', 163; McCarthy, *Barbauld*, 7, 557–8, n. 30; *Epitaphs in the Graveyard and Chapel of the Great Meeting Leicester*, ed., Alfred Henry Paget (Leicester: privately published, 1912), 33.

11. Aikin, *Memoir of John Aikin*, 9–10; H, III, 70 n*; MS OD69, Presbyterian Fund Board, III, 292 (11 Oct. 1739).

12. GFN 456, Doddridge to Samuel Clark, St Albans, 17 Apr. 1737; GFN 525, Doddridge to Daniel Neal, 17 Nov. 1738.

13. *The Theological and Miscellaneous Works of Joseph Priestley*, ed., J. T. Rutt, 25 vols. (London: G. Smallfield, 1817–35), I, i: 59; I. Rivers and David L. Wykes, *Joseph Priestley, Scientist, Philosopher, and Theologian* (Oxford University Press, 2008), 33. John Seddon (*c*.1719–69), minister of Cross Street, Manchester, is not to be confused with John Seddon (1725–70), minister of Cairo Street, Warrington, Secretary, later rector, of Warrington Academy.

14. Turner, 'Historical Memoirs', 163; Aikin, *Memoir of John Aikin*, 10; John Barker, Hackney, to Doddridge [Aug. 1733], H, III, 203; Doddridge to John Steffe, 8 May 1735 [late 1735], printed in *Congregational Magazine* (1822), 413–14; GFN: 389, 429, 441. Dr Williams's Library, London, New College, L1/10/35, Doddridge to Clark, 20 Jul. 1737. Lee's son, also Thomas, was an attorney, and after practising first in Market Harborough he moved to Birmingham in about 1760, where he was one of the leading Dissenters in the town.

15. For an account of Aikin's family at Kibworth and for the identification of the building in which the school was kept, see McCarthy, *Barbauld*, 7, 539–40, Appendix A.

16. See Appendix at the end of this chapter for details about the pupils who attended Aikin's school. It is unclear if David Gardner was sent to Kibworth.

17. Seed, '"A Set of Men Powerful Enough in Many Things"', in Haakonssen, *Enlightenment and Religion*, 162.

18. There is later evidence suggesting Aikin may have taught a number of boys from Sheffield; see Appendix at the end of this chapter.

19. Turner, 'Historical Memoirs', 164; letters between Philip and Mercy Doddridge, 2, 27, 30 Jul., 10 Aug. 1742, 1 Jul. 1747, GFN, 762, 770 , 773, 782, 1249.

20. ROLLR, 15 D 57/448, Samuel Coltman, 'Time's Stepping Stones – or Some Memorial of Four Generations of a Family – by an Octogenarian Member of the Same', 66–7.

21. H, v, 532.

22. John Rylands University Library, Manchester, Benson MS 166, John Hodgson, Lincoln, to George Benson, 11 Dec. 1751.

23. *Discourses chiefly on Devotional Subjects, by the late Reverend Newcome Cappe. To which are prefixed Memoirs of his Life by Catherine Cappe* (York: privately printed, 1805), xiv; *Monthly Magazine, or, British Register*, 11(1) (1801), 82–3.

24. 'Memoirs of Celebrated Men Who Have Died in 1817–1818', *Annual Biography and Obituary, for the Year 1819* (London, 1819), 111, 75; 'Biography: Memoir of the Late Dr. Cogan', *Monthly Repository*, 14 (January 1819), 1.

25. 15 D 57/448, 'Time's Stepping Stones', fos. 65, 67; [Catherine Hutton], 'A Sketch of a Family of Originals. By an Original, their Friend', *Ainsworth's Magazine*, 5 (1844), 57.

26. 15 D 57/449, 'Time's Stepping Stones', 2, ch. 14; David L. Wykes, 'The Reluctant Businessman: John Coltman of St Nicholas Street, Leicester (1727–1808)', *Transactions of the Leicestershire Archaeological and Historical Society*, 69 (1995), 74–5.

27. Wykes, 'Reluctant Businessman', 75.

28. Aikin, *Memoir of John Aikin*, 54 n*.

29. ROLLR, 15 D 57/451, John Coltman's memorandum or commonplace book. There is a note inside the front cover suggesting the vellum bound notebook was purchased on 10 Nov. 1746, presumably at the end of his final year at Kibworth. The last entry is dated 4 March 1801.

30. Wykes, 'Reluctant Businessman', 76.

31. William Gardiner, *Music and Friends: or, Pleasant Recollections of a Dilettante* (London: Longman, 1838), 1, 60–1.

32. Linnean Society Library, London, Pulteney MSS, Coltman letter 19, Coltman to Pulteney, 2 Jun. 1790; C. J. Billson, *Leicester Memoirs* (Leicester: Edgar Backus, 1924), 130–1; Gardiner, *Music and Friends*, 1, 63; C. H. Beale, *Catherine Hutton and Her Friends* (Birmingham: Cornish Brothers, 1895), 63.

33. 'Memoir of the Late Dr. Cogan', 1.

34. 'Memoirs of Celebrated Men', 75.

35. Rutt, *Theological and Miscellaneous Works*, 1, i, 47.

36. HMCO, MS Warrington 2, 52–75; Rutt, *Theological and Miscellaneous Works*, 1, i: 47; for Dyer, Orton, Roebuck, Scott and Wadsworth, see *Oxford DNB*.

37. HMCO, MS Warrington 2; 58, 62, 64–6. For Addington, see 'Addington, Stephen (1729–1796)', rev. M. J. Mercer, *Oxford DNB* (www.oxforddnb.com/view/article/152). Addington moved to London in 1781, when presumably he gave up his school in Leicestershire. He was tutor at Grove House Academy, Mile End, London, from 1783 until 1790.

38. Turner, 'Historical Account', 164; Rutt, *Theological and Miscellaneous Works*, 1, i: 47; Rivers and Wykes, *Priestley*, 32–3.

39. HMCO, MS Warrington 2; 64, 71; *Memoirs of the Life of Gilbert Wakefield*, 2 vols. (London: J. Johnson, 1804), 219–20. In considering Wakefield's praise, it should perhaps be noted that Wakefield's daughter married Aikin's grandson:

Charles Rochemont Aikin married Anne Wakefield on 20 August 1806. I am grateful to Mr Simon Martyn for this information.

40. Turner, 'Historical Account', 165.
41. *Ibid.*, 287; Joseph Priestley, Warrington, to John Seddon, London, 9 Apr. 1762, printed in 'Letters and Papers of Revd John Seddon, No. III', *Christian Reformer*, 10 (1854), 626. I owe this discussion of the use of Doddridge's lectures and the reference to Priestley's letter to Simon Mills, 'Joseph Priestley and the intellectual culture of Rational Dissent, 1752–1796', unpublished Ph.D. (University of London, 2009), 22–3, 40, 52 n. 155; the first edition of Doddridge's posthumously published *A Course of Lectures on the Principal Subjects in Pneumatology, Ethics, and Divinity*, ed. Samuel Clark, was published in 1763.
42. Liverpool Record Office, 920 NIC 5/8/7–9, Matthew Nicholson, Warrington Academy, to his father, Liverpool, [7], 8 Feb., 29 Apr. 1764; Turner, 'Historical Account', 167.
43. Turner, 'Historical Account', 166. For the identification of Simpson, see Shropshire Archives, 6000/15932, William Turner, Newcastle, to Richard Astley, Chesterfield, 16 Jun. 1812.
44. For a reassessment of the significance of Warrington, especially for Dissent, see David L. Wykes, 'The Contribution of the Dissenting Academy to the Emergence of Rational Dissent', in Haakonssen, *Enlightenment and Religion*, 132–4, 136.
45. Richard G. Terry, *Poetry and the Making of the English Literary Past* (Oxford University Press, 2001), 191.

CHAPTER 3

How Dissent made Anna Letitia Barbauld, and what she made of Dissent

William McCarthy

I begin with a few words of personal and national biography. When I visited England in 1988 to begin research for a new life of Anna Letitia Barbauld I was reviving a tradition of Americans making pilgrimage in her honour. Before me, in 1873, came Grace Ellis, New England feminist and advocate of women's education. She published two books about Barbauld, whom she regarded as nothing less than 'one of the great minds which belong to all time'. Fifty years before Ellis, in 1822 when Barbauld was still alive to receive him, came the leading voice of New England Unitarianism, William Ellery Channing. He had read Barbauld in childhood and revered her: 'I owe to her more than delight', he wrote to Barbauld's niece Lucy Aikin after Barbauld's death. Some fifteen years before him came another New England Unitarian, the Reverend Joseph Stevens Buckminster; and in 1812 Barbauld answered a fan letter from an American girl named Harris.[1]

My interest in Barbauld was thus congruent with Barbauld's reception in the early United States. She came to print there only thirteen years after her literary debut at home: her *Hymns in Prose for Children* in 1786, her *Lessons for Children* in 1788, the latter printed in Philadelphia by a grandson of Benjamin Franklin. For thirty years thereafter, editions of her books for children poured from presses in Boston, New York, Philadelphia and lesser towns.[2] New England Unitarian William Peabody could claim in 1826 that 'thousands look back [to *Hymns in Prose*] as the source of much happiness and devotion'. In a notebook remark about teaching manners to children Ralph Waldo Emerson recalled that 'Mrs Barbauld said, they should never remember the time when they knew not the name of God'. Emerson, aged 47 when he wrote this, was remembering *Hymns in Prose*. Bronson Alcott, father of the author of *Little Women*, taught religion to children in 1830s Boston and recorded what the children said about it. Seven-year-old Josiah Quincy read *Hymns in Prose* enthusiastically, and one day in class he 'burst out', 'Mr. Alcott! you know Mrs. Barbauld says in her hymns, everything is prayer; every action is prayer; all nature prays; the bird prays in singing; the tree prays in growing.'[3] Josiah understood *Hymns* better than many a later commentator on it.

Barbauld was welcomed in North America for her works for grown-ups also. Copies of her *Poems*, published to acclaim in London on the last day of 1772, crossed the Atlantic in the pockets of colonials who had business on both shores. Among her American readers was Thomas Jefferson (whom she was to meet in person in Paris in 1786). The first of her books to be reviewed in the States was her edition of the correspondence of the novelist Samuel Richardson, with a biography of him. 'The name of Mrs. Barbauld is justly placed among the most illustrious that have done honour to her sex', declared the Philadelphia reviewer of that book in 1804.[4] Her last major work, the poem *Eighteen Hundred and Eleven*, appeared in Boston and Philadelphia in the same year as its London publication; her *Works*, collected by Lucy Aikin in 1825, enjoyed two US editions in 1826.

Barbauld's North American welcome surely had to do with her being, at home in England, a Dissenter. For the political ideology to which the American revolutionaries had appealed was that of liberal Dissent, ultimately John Locke. As the president of Harvard College, Joseph Willard, wrote to Richard Price in 1788, British Dissenters 'are the strenuous assertors of religious liberty; and I look upon them to be very great supporters of the civil liberties of your nation'. Leading British Dissenters deplored the war to keep America. They saw it as an attempt to subject their fellow-Britons there to tyranny; one Dissenter, the Reverend Newcome Cappe, even declared the war against America a war against God.[5] In 1790, responding to parliament's rejection of a bill to repeal the Corporation and Test Acts – the two acts that denied avowed Dissenters the right to serve in a host of public offices and thus made them second-class citizens – Barbauld decried efforts 'to blend what God has made separate', Church and State.[6] What she and her liberal coreligionists wanted was something like the First Amendment to the new Constitution of the new United States: 'Congress shall make no law respecting an establishment of religion, or prohibiting the free exercise thereof.' Liberal Dissenters saw in the States, as they did in France in the dawn of the French Revolution, precedents for political reforms at home.

Their enthusiasm for the new United States may be said to have resembled the enthusiasm of Bolshevik sympathizers for the new Soviet Union in the 1920s: it had a utopian aspect. Thus the Reverend William Turner, Dissenting minister at Wakefield in Yorkshire, writing already in

1778 (only two years after the colonial declaration of independence) to his son at Warrington Academy:

Your best way will be to gather up . . . a good stock of the arts & sciences of this Country, & if you find a weight of despotism & wretchedness overwhelm this hemisphere, follow the course of the Sun to that country where freedom has already fixed her standard . . . & where the sciences & arts, wealth & power, will soon gather under her, & assist to adorn & strengthen her empire there.

Barbauld, too, could imagine the prospects of the new nation in utopian terms. 'Let them', she urged:

record the actions of their Washington, the purest character perhaps, that history has to boast of; let them enjoy their free, their unexpensive government, number their rising towns, and boast that persecution does not set her bloody foot in any corner of their extensive territories.

She knew better, of course, than to be always utopian. She also took a sceptical – and, inevitably, a more accurate – view of the United States:

Will they be wise by our experience, peaceable, moderate, virtuous? No: they will be learned by our learning, but not wise by our experience. Each country, as each man, must buy his own experience.[7]

But such sceptical moments seem to have been rare. Barbauld and other British liberals were enchanted by the new United States because it seemed to embody principles they were fighting for at home. Being a liberal Dissenter in Britain prepared Barbauld to sympathize with America, and to be sympathetically received in America.

That said, it must also be said that long before I began studying her both Barbauld and British Dissent had faded from the national memory, and from the awareness even of American academics. Among the many causes of that forgetting, the one that seems most pertinent to the present volume is that the academic study of British literature in America came to adopt the outlook and the canon of writers promulgated by the British universities around the end of the nineteenth century. Barbauld was right: the United States grew learned by British learning. But the outlook our academics acquired with British learning was essentially that of Matthew Arnold. In Arnold's mind literature was an elite 'humanist' club (see his essay 'The Study of Poetry') and Dissent a social embarrassment, like 'beer-shops' (his words).[8] So, for American academics, Dissenting British writers simply didn't make the club. The club's members included Wordsworth and Coleridge among the Romantics, Swift, Johnson and Burke for the eighteenth century; presented to us as normative, as simply 'great writers', they had all – with the exception of a certain John Milton – been conservative and anti-Dissent. Apart from Milton, in graduate-school courses forty years ago I never encountered a writer who was presented as, or indeed was, a Dissenter. (Milton was presented as a Puritan, which seemed noble.) When in 1983 I stumbled upon Barbauld by chance in the course of writing about somebody else, it was a bit like coming across an ancestor I didn't know I had.

Of the leading English literary figures of her day, Barbauld was the one most embedded in Dissent, a third-generation Dissenter on mother and father's side. Moreover, as the daughter and granddaughter of divinity teachers she was, as it were, a theorized Dissenter, fully conscious of Dissent's intellectual heritage and social position in all their nuances and ambiguities.

And of nuances and ambiguities there were plenty. As students of Dissent well know, British Protestant Dissent was fractured and fractious; Joseph Priestley exaggerated little when he said 'I never expect to see the Dissenters agree in any thing'.[9] Not obliged to pretend to believe a single doctrine, as the Church-of-England clergy were, eighteenth-century Dissenters contended among themselves for every theological view between damnation Calvinism on the right and Universal Redemption by an all-benevolent deity on the left. Their theological spread was matched by a political spread. There were 'presbyterian Tories' (William Turner's phrase), some of whom shocked their brethren in 1772 and 1773 by siding with the Church against Dissenting petitions to moderate the Toleration Act.[10] Socially, as that episode suggests, Dissent occupied an equivocal position vis-à-vis the establishment. Technically illegal but tolerated, Dissenters as long as they kept reasonably quiet could enjoy cordial relations with churchmen and even with courtiers – some of whom, up to 1790 at any rate, were quite liberal. Many Church-of-England parents sent sons to Warrington Academy, where Barbauld's father taught divinity. One of those sons, Rochemont Barbauld, whose father was a court preacher, went over to Dissent and married Anna Letitia. The Barbaulds went on to keep a school themselves, and numbered establishment children (even sons of aristocrats) among their pupils.[11] After her literary debut in 1773 Anna Letitia was wooed by the Blue-stockings, the circle of intellectual establishment women headed by Elizabeth Montagu and Elizabeth Carter who kept company with bishops and court ladies. She could have joined the Blue-stocking circle had she wished.

Thus Anna Letitia's social position was ambiguous: an outsider to the establishment by religion, she was invited inside for her talent – but invited by people who did not take seriously the concerns of her co-religionists. Elizabeth Montagu's letter inviting Anna Letitia's friendship discreetly cautions her against 'foolish animosities', by which Montagu may well have meant the failed 1772–3 Dissenting petitions to amend the Toleration Act. Montagu's circle aimed to practise a non-political ideal of 'sociability' – a sociability which, however, was premised on their allegiance to the politics of the establishment.[12] Anna Letitia and her brother, John Aikin, were well aware that the attitude of genteel establishment people towards Dissenters could include an admixture of condescension. Addressing his co-religionists after the 1790 failure to have the Test and Corporation Acts repealed, John Aikin diagnosed their social psychology:

You have so long laboured under the ridicule and aversion of your fellow-subjects, you have been so much accustomed to the scoffs of levity and the virulence of bigotry, that it is no wonder you have been formed to a general character of reserve and timidity, and that a false shame and awkward humility has hung about you, which has prevented you from maintaining your part with ease and spirit in the mixed commerce of society.[13]

If Aikin's language seems excessive, we must bear in mind that Dissenters had been a persecuted people – and were about to be again. The year after Aikin wrote these words, Joseph Priestley and a number of his co-religionists would be burned out of their houses in Birmingham by a 'Church-and-King' mob.

On the issue of religious freedom, Anna Letitia stood on the left; she had been brought up liberal by the Reverend John Aikin, and she became close friends with Joseph and Mary Priestley at Warrington in the 1760s. Politically, by 1811 if not earlier her views may have been republican: in a poem she wrote that year on George III's illness she consigns other kings (though not him) to 'burning thrones' in Hell. The liberal Dissent to which Barbauld adhered for almost her entire writing life identified itself as 'modern' and 'enlightened': as a liberal Dissenter she was *ipso facto* a voice of the British Enlightenment. An enquiring mind, temperamentally sceptical towards received views, distrustful of established power and devoted to the rights of conscience, she was as true a Dissenter as Priestley or Richard Price. She would have agreed entirely with Dissenter Andrew Kippis, explaining in 1772 why 'we dissent':

because we deny the right of any body of men, whether civil or ecclesiastical, to impose human tests, creeds, or articles; and because we think it our duty, not to submit to any such authority, but to protest against it, as a violation of our essential liberty to judge and act for ourselves in matters of religion.[14]

She might have added, indeed, 'in all matters of personal judgement'.

But she was also a woman, and the consequences of that tended to make her a dissenter (with a small D) within Dissent. For, just as male Dissenters suffered educational discrimination – they could not take degrees at Oxford or Cambridge without formally abjuring Dissent – so did women, even women within Dissent. At any rate, Anna Letitia did. Before he went to Warrington the Reverend John Aikin kept a school of his own in the Aikin home in Kibworth. Anna Letitia grew up surrounded by schoolboys but, being a girl, did not attend the classes her father held on the top floor of their house. And while her brother learned Latin as a matter of course, she had to wear down her father's resistance to her learning it.[15]

Being treated as a second-class citizen, educationally, by reason of her sex affected Barbauld's attitude towards academic Dissent and towards the uses of intellect by male intellectuals. An anecdote has come down to us of 5-year-old Anna Letitia and her father, which tells much about the intellectual behaviour she experienced growing up and about her response to it. One day her father and an older pupil got into a discussion of the passions, a discussion they continued at dinner in the child Anna Letitia's presence. Aikin brought it to what he must have thought a convincing close:

'You see, therefore, sir, that joy, accurately defined, cannot have place in a state of perfect felicity; for joy, supposes an accession of happiness.' 'I think you are mistaken, papa,' exclaimed a little voice from the opposite side of the table: 'Why do you think so, Laetitia?' 'Because, papa, in the chapter I read to you this morning in the Testament, it is said there is more *joy* in heaven over one sinner that repenteth, than over ninety-nine just persons that need no repentance.'[16]

The anecdote testifies to Aikin's liberal parenting: he took his daughter's objection seriously, and thus promoted her intellectual self-confidence. And that is important. Still, he did not admit her to his class; she just happened to be present at this dinner-table discussion. She was showing that she *ought* to have been in his class, for she was able to quote chapter and verse to the purpose; in fact, she was competitively showing him up by quoting an elementary verse that deflated his scholastic argument.

Resentment of scholastic intellectual behaviour would become one of Barbauld's trademarks as a writer. Thus, in an essay from around 1800 on the problem of working-class poverty, she lists the 'enjoyments of life' that were becoming ever more unequally distributed between the well-to-do and the working classes: good food, comfortable housing, stylish clothes, access to art and culture:

I know very well [she cautions, anticipating objections] that with philosophers these advantages are of little or no account; they can prove by many learned and logical arguments that external goods have nothing to do with happiness, which resides exclusively in the mind. We are therefore bound to believe that these gentlemen, though they appear to enjoy a good table, or an elegant carriage as well as their neighbours, in fact regard them with perfect indifference; for which reason I beg to be considered as only addressing those who share in the common feelings of mankind.[17]

'The common feelings of mankind': Barbauld fashioned her intellectual style in reaction against abstract, scholastic arguments of the sort she heard day in and day out growing up. Always she would anchor her ideas in what she took to be the real, material world and the ordinary people in it. A noteworthy innovation of her revolutionary reading primer for 2- and 3-year-olds, *Lessons for Children* (1778–9), was the complete absence from it of abstract 'Moral Precepts' such as 'Live well that you may die well', with which previous reading primers had sandbagged the hapless toddlers who were set to learn from them.[18] In *Lessons*, Barbauld drew her vocabulary instead from sights and sounds, flora and fauna of the country village where she wrote it, and the daily life of the child for whom she wrote it. Again, when classical scholar and religious controversialist Gilbert Wakefield published a manifesto denouncing public worship – churchgoing – as a relic of primitive religion unworthy to survive in the enlightened modern world, Barbauld defended communal worship by appeal to its universality throughout history and across cultures. However theory might look down on public worship, experience showed that worshipping in common was something that civilized people everywhere *did*. It must therefore satisfy a human need.[19]

She staked her own religion, too, on the common feelings of humankind – with the emphasis, here, on *feelings*. At Warrington in the 1760s she witnessed intense, exhaustive theological discussion. On Saturdays her father and his colleagues settled in over tea to question the composition of the deity and the nature of Christ's redemptive power, seeking to fathom Aikin's precise beliefs on these topics. It is significant that in her first publication after her marriage, when at age 31 she was at last out of her father's house, Barbauld dedicated to the Reverend John Aikin an essay on religion that severely criticizes theological discussion. Constant talk about God, she argued in that essay, trivialized God and deadened feelings of religious reverence, or devotion. Devotion, she argued, was the essence of religious experience; one should love God as one loves a beloved person. Modern Dissent, she argued, was too preoccupied with intellectual precision to satisfy the needs of the heart and the imagination; it had exchanged the zeal that sustained its persecuted ancestors for a spiritless scholasticism. It had renounced the clerical trappings, the rituals, the grand architecture, that warm the imaginations of ordinary churchgoers, and had nothing to offer in their place. Published in 1775, this essay, 'Thoughts on the Devotional Taste, on Sects, and on Establishments', shocked her friend Priestley and most other spokesmen for Dissent; to them, Barbauld appeared to have gone over to the Church, or even to Rome.[20]

She had not; this was an instance of her being a dissenter within Dissent. Her essay was in reality a plea for understanding, a plea against the all-male way of being religious that she had hitherto experienced. Barbauld's religious sensibility included a bent towards what the eighteenth century (and especially those who, like the Warrington tutors, called themselves 'Rational Christians') regarded as 'enthusiasm', the belief that one can enjoy intimate emotional relations with God. Anna Letitia wanted to believe exactly that, and she decried Warrington Dissenting behaviours that cast cold water on it.

Happily for her, because Dissent was fractured she could find sanction for religious emotion in other quarters within Dissent. One source of comfort was the religious poetry of Elizabeth Rowe, her elder by two generations; Anna Letitia publicized her allegiance to Rowe in 'Verses on Mrs. Rowe' in her 1773 *Poems*. Rowe was another Dissenter who had enjoyed general acceptance; she had counted bishops and aristocrats among her friends and admirers, as Anna Letitia took pains to notice in her verses on Rowe. Rowe's example could sustain her in her vocation of poet, too; in 'Verses on Mrs. Rowe' she called upon Rowe's blessing: 'Bright pattern of thy sex, be thou my muse'.[21]

But before she encountered Elizabeth Rowe, Anna Letitia must have encountered the Reverend Philip Doddridge. Her parents had known Doddridge personally (her father had been a pupil at his academy), but Anna Letitia would most likely have met him by way of a published work, his masterpiece *The Family Expositor* (1739–56). Her father subscribed for a copy of it, and surely Mr Aikin used the book in his family devotions. Thus Anna Letitia would have experienced it from infancy on; it must have worked its way into her nervous system. *The Family Expositor* is an introduction to and commentary on the New Testament. On every page it does three things. First it prints a segment of the Gospel text in the King James Version. Then it prints Doddridge's own paraphrase of that text. Lastly it prints what Doddridge calls an 'improvement'. The improvement proposes what may be learned from the Gospel passage. It 'consists [Doddridge says] of pressing Exhortations, and devout Meditations, grounded on the general

Design, or on some particular Passages', of the Gospel text it follows. Doddridge composed his improvements 'in an *Evangelical Strain*' (his words); the reader should be deeply moved by the sacred text, so that 'his Progress must often be interrupted with Tears of holy Delight, or with warm and perhaps rapturous Aspirations of Soul'. Accordingly, the improvements often model an emotional response to the Bible passage. They exclaim: 'May this plain and awakening Address be felt by every Soul that hears it!' 'Oh that we may stand the Trial!'[22] Memoirs of the Reverend John Aikin agree that he kept his feelings under tight control; Anna Letitia was brought up in an emotionally restrained household.[23] It could well have been in *The Family Expositor* that she first encountered representations of intense feeling, representations that, I surmise, first authorized her to experience her emotions – at least, those emotions that could be understood through religion.

Later she would meet with such representations again in the religious poems of Elizabeth Rowe. Like *The Family Expositor*, Rowe's devotional style was fervent, exclamatory:

> How strongly thou my panting heart dost move
> With all the holy ecstacies of love![24]

The rhetoric represents a 'spontaneous overflow of powerful feeling' (the phrase is Wordsworth's, but the concept, I am implying, long pre-dated him). Barbauld employed that rhetoric throughout her early poems – though she would surely have called it the natural language of emotion rather than a rhetoric. Eventually she came to regard emotion as the special province of women, and women's susceptibility to emotion as a mark of their superiority to men.[25] Her early poems ought to be read as personal utterances; so read, they show us a person of turbulent feelings who poured forth her feelings yet also yearned after inner peace. In her 'Hymn to Content' she prays to the 'Nymph' Contentment for release from the 'varying passions' that 'beat' upon her soul. Her 'Address to the Deity' also speaks of inner turmoil: 'the waves of grief' (which seem to have been frequent) and a 'headlong tide' of 'impetuous passion'. Her poems display emotional intensity by their verbal gestures. They supplicate: 'Oh! teach me', 'O come', 'O nymph approach!', 'O be it lawful now'. They burst out in joy or relief ('Yes, DELIA loves!'; ''Tis past!'), in enthusiasm ('Blest in thy friendships!'), in anger ('WISDOM, thine empire I disclaim, / Thou empty boast of pompous name!').[26] Authorized by Doddridge in *The Family Expositor* and by Elizabeth Rowe's sacred verse, Barbauld's youthful poems exclaim.

Her poems took the public by storm; Barbauld became overnight a literary celebrity and remained one of the leading British poets of either sex for a generation. Her poems went through six editions in twenty years; several became standard anthology pieces. So it should not be surprising to find her emotional style imitated in the work of her younger contemporaries. One such contemporary was Samuel Taylor Coleridge, who in his youth venerated Barbauld and whose youthful poems bear many a trace of hers. For example, her exclamations ('O be it lawful now', 'Oh! teach me') reappear in Coleridge lines such as 'O! teach our feeble tongues', 'O Spirit blest!', 'O! I have wak'd at midnight, and have wept'.[27] Afterwards, notoriously, Coleridge disclaimed his early admiration of Barbauld and took to ridiculing her. But it was from her exclamatory style that he had learned to make some of his greatest lines, lines such as:

> O Lady! we receive but what we give

and

> The very deep did rot: O Christ!
> That ever this should be![28]

I suggest, in short, that Barbauld found what she needed for her emotional development in Dissenting sources – *The Family Expositor*, Elizabeth Rowe – and that the poems she made with the aid of those sources inspired the next generation, the one that came to be called the Romantics. So the poetic genealogy would be Doddridge and Rowe to Barbauld to Coleridge.

Not that she intended her poems to transmit Doddridge or anyone else; in her poems she was serving her own needs. In another part of her work, however, Barbauld did intend to transmit something: in her teaching. Since she had grown up in a school, it was natural for her to take up teaching. Actually, Dissenting intellectuals such as her father often had to take up teaching to eke out their small ministerial incomes; when Rochemont Barbauld abandoned his career opportunities in the church he more or less condemned himself to schoolteaching, and his wife with him.[29]

The Barbaulds kept a school at the village of Palgrave in Suffolk for eleven years, and I estimate that some 130 boys aged 3 to 18 enjoyed their tutelage.[30] Their school had to teach basic skills such as arithmetic, of course; in that respect it must not have differed from any other village school. But the Barbaulds infused into their teaching principles of intellectual inquiry and citizenly ethics typical of Dissent, principles that governed the programme at Warrington Academy, where Joseph Priestley had taught a course on citizenship in the 1760s. Teaching itself figured for the Barbaulds as an act of citizenship: 'the true patriot', Rochemont Barbauld declared in a sermon on the subject, 'will gladly undertake a task whereby he may so essentially contribute to the welfare of his country'.[31] Not allowed by reason of her sex to perform any official act of citizenship herself, Anna Letitia saw teaching as a way for her to be an active citizen: through teaching, she could create the (male) citizens of the future. Palgrave School did produce some remarkable citizens, most famously Thomas Denman, who entered politics and went on to draft the 1832 Reform Bill. Denman passed less than three years at Palgrave in early childhood, but Barbauld's teaching so impressed him that he 'cherish[ed] her memory [Lucy Aikin said] most religiously'. To Barbauld's teaching Denman credited his elocution, love of literature, and political liberalism.[32]

At Palgrave School elocution, literature and liberalism formed a trio. Elocution was a political skill, for public speaking was still a prime tool of law- and policy-making. Barbauld taught elocution by way of literature, setting her pupils to recite swatches of poetry and drama at school examinations and herself writing pieces for them to recite. A few of the pieces she wrote for the school came to be published. One of them is a very short poem Barbauld is said to have inscribed on a marble – the kind of marble boys played with. The poem was written while Britain was fighting to keep a grip on its empire in North America:

> The world's something bigger,
> But just of this figure
> And speckled with mountains and seas;
> Your heroes are overgrown schoolboys
> Who scuffle for empires and toys,
> And kick the poor ball as they please.
> Now Caesar, now Pompey, gives law;
> And Pharsalia's plain,
> Though heaped with the slain,
> Was only a game at *taw*.[33]

In the midst of the war to keep America Barbauld's lines 'Written on a Marble' urged her pupils to regard war and empire as childish things that ought to be outgrown, like marbles. By contrast, at Eton College senior boys played soldier in an annual ceremony called 'Montem'; and if the Duke of Wellington were to be believed, the victors of Waterloo got their training on Eton's playing fields.[34]

At Palgrave Barbauld taught her youngest pupils the elements of religion (as schoolteachers were required to do by law). For that purpose she composed the work that was to carry her name across the oceans and exert incalculable influence far into the nineteenth century, *Hymns in Prose for Children* (1781). Although warmly received by readers as diverse in their views as Elizabeth Carter and Mary Wollstonecraft, *Hymns* dismayed some by its failure to teach original sin or other basic Christian doctrines.[35] It contains no catechism, never mentions the Bible, and does not even speak of Jesus until the eleventh of its original twelve hymns. It never mentions atonement or the Crucifixion. It never mentions Hell, and speaks of Heaven only at its very end.

What religion does *Hymns in Prose* teach? It aims to teach Devotion, love of the idea of God. It aims to weave that love (I use a favourite Barbauld metaphor) into the very texture of the child's mind, and as early as possible. It aims to achieve this result, Barbauld explains in her preface to *Hymns*:

by connecting religion with a variety of sensible objects; with all that [the child] sees, all he hears, all that affects his young mind with wonder or delight; and thus by deep, strong, and permanent associations, to lay the best foundation for practical devotion in future life.[36]

Once again, not doctrine but feeling is what she opts for. At the close of her 1775 essay, 'Thoughts on the Devotional Taste, on Sects, and on Establishments', Barbauld looked forward to the day when 'some free and enlarged genius' might remodel Christian worship.[37] She herself was that genius, and *Hymns in Prose* the remodelled worship. It is a liturgy consisting (in its original, 1781 form) of twelve 'hymns' that look a lot like psalms – and often sound like them, too. (Among literary people the psalms were prized as the most eloquent, poetic and moving parts of the Bible. '[I]n these divine songs', wrote Barbauld's Bluestocking acquaintance Hester Mulso Chapone, 'the spirit of true piety' combined with 'a rich vein of poetry' to enchanting effect.)[38]

Barbauld's liturgy can be exemplified from the second hymn. The 'we' who speak the hymn are the worshippers and their leader, originally Barbauld and her congregation of small boys.

Come, let us go forth into the fields, let us see how the flowers spring, let us listen to the warbling of the birds, and sport ourselves upon the new grass.
    The winter is over and gone, the buds come out upon the trees . . . and the green leaves sprout.
    The hedges are bordered with tufts of primroses, and yellow cowslips that hang down their heads; and the blue violet lies hid beneath the shade.
                                    . . .
    The young animals of every kind are sporting about, they feel themselves happy, they are glad to be alive, – they thank him that has made them alive.

They may thank him in their hearts, but we can thank him with our tongues; we are better than they, and can praise him better.

. . .

Therefore we will thank him for ourselves, and we will thank him for those that cannot speak.

Trees that blossom, and little lambs that skip about, if you could, you would say how good he is; but you are dumb, we will say it for you.[39]

Several strains of Dissenting thought and practice join in Barbauld's *Hymns*. Most basic was the Dissenting principle that congregations were free to compose their own liturgies – the condition of possibility for Barbauld to write *Hymns* in the first place. The idea, next, of encouraging children to associate God with nature and nature's works: the revered Isaac Watts had promoted that devotional practice.[40] Moreover, as can be seen in the hymn just quoted, Barbauld's devotional technique owes something to Philip Doddridge's 'improvements': the flower and the lamb – and, in other hymns a rose, the lion, the sun – become 'texts', as it were, that prompt meditation. Finally, a phrase Barbauld uses in her preface, 'habitual piety', recalls a sermon by Joseph Priestley that had deeply impressed her back in the 1760s, 'On Habitual Devotion'. Priestley's sermon urged its hearers to see God 'in every thing', and to see 'every thing in God'; the life of the person who did that would be a continual act of devotion.[41]

I have said that Barbauld opted for feeling over doctrine, but it is time to notice that her choice amounted to a doctrine – and was so perceived by those readers of *Hymns in Prose* who lamented its failure to teach about Sin and Damnation. Isaac Watts in his *Divine Songs* for children had taught about those subjects:

> There's not a Sin that we commit,
>   Nor wicked Word we say,
> But in thy dreadful Book 'tis writ
>   Against the Judgment-Day.[42]

Barbauld mentioned Watts in her preface to *Hymns*, remarking drily that his hymns for children were 'in pretty general use' but discreetly not remarking that her hymns opposed the Calvinism of his. (Some commentators have therefore mistakenly thrown Barbauld into the same Calvinist bin with Watts.)[43] The ethical philosophy underlying her hymns was that of Francis Hutcheson. Hutcheson, the liberal Presbyterian professor of moral philosophy in Glasgow (and not a Dissenter only because he never lived in England) had been the teacher of Dissenter John Seddon, who founded Warrington Academy and tried to run it on Hutcheson's principles.[44]

Hutcheson's principles were anti-Calvinist. Against the notion of total or near-total human depravity, Hutcheson argued that, on the contrary, a benevolent God had implanted in the human species a 'moral sense' very like the five physical senses. The moral sense could perceive good actions and delight in them; it tended naturally to lead to human affiliation and acts of mutual kindness, it made for social bonding, it drew us to love our creator. In Hutcheson, the social affections rippled outwards from their epicentre in the nuclear family to take in one's neighbours, one's country-men, one's species, the whole realm of created beings. This was a vision that moved Barbauld to her depths, and she wrote it into *Hymns in Prose*. Her eighth hymn leads the child from family cottage to village community to kingdom to world, each smaller form being a type of the larger until finally:

All are God's family; he knoweth every one of them, as a shepherd knoweth his flock: they pray to him in different languages, but he understandeth them all; he heareth them all; he taketh care of all; none are so great, that he cannot punish them; none are so mean, that he will not protect them.[45]

Not only did *Hymns* in Prose refuse to preach Sin and Damnation, but it shocked some conservatives by urging its child readers to take on the priestly office of mediators or spokesmen for their mute fellow-creatures: 'we will thank him for those that cannot speak', 'we will offer sacrifice for you'. Every child a Saint Francis? To proponents of Sin and Damnation this looked almost blasphemous; how could humans, who desperately needed a mediator themselves, presume to mediate for other creatures?[46] Today it looks attrac-tively like urging children to be responsible stewards of the Earth.

Nineteenth-century children learned much from *Hymns*. In Barbauld's biography I repeat anecdotes about children who, having apparently mem-orized *Hymns*, quoted bits of it on suitable occasions to their siblings. Young Mary Ann Galton took completely to heart the lessons *Hymns* taught about Nature and God: 'I cannot express the delight it often was to me to walk out alone and look at the beautiful hills, and wood, and water, or the flowers, and the happy birds, and insects, and to think that God had made them all in wisdom and in love.' Thomas De Quincey, the opium-eater, retained from his childhood reading of *Hymns* 'a deep impression of solemn beauty and simplicity'. An unnamed Victorian woman remembered how, as a girl, she used to find a quiet room and read *Hymns* aloud to herself, solemnly and reverently.[47] And we have seen testimony from New England Unitarians William Ellery Channing and William Peabody, and from 7-year-old Josiah Quincy of Boston.

The influence of a writer on later readers is seldom easy to document, but I close by offering a proposal. I've tried to suggest how Dissent made Anna Letitia Barbauld. What she made of Dissent, I propose, was a complex of thought and feeling that went into the making of nineteenth-century culture on both shores of the Atlantic. What she made of Dissent went into the making of – to list just three things – Coleridge's poetry, New England's Unitarianism and Britain's First Reform Act. Apart from John Milton, can we name another British Dissenting writer of whom so much can be said?

NOTES

1. Grace A. Ellis, *A Memoir of Mrs. Anna Lætitia Barbauld, with Many of Her Letters* (Boston, MA: Osgood, 1874), 338, 309; Le Breton, *Correspondence of William Ellery Channing*, 5; Joseph Buckminster (1784–1812), letter to John Aikin, 2 June 1809 (MS, Gratz Collection, Pennsylvania Historical Society); Barbauld to Miss Harris, [April 1812?] (Special Collections, Vassar College Library). Ellis' second book about Barbauld was published under her later married name, Oliver. My biography is *Anna Letitia Barbauld: Voice of the Enlightenment* (Baltimore, MD: Johns Hopkins University Press, 2008); the present chapter is distilled from it. Passages that first appeared there are reprinted here with permission of the Johns Hopkins University Press.
2. See d'Alté A. Welch, *A Bibliography of American Children's Books Printed Prior to 1821* ([Worcester, MA:] American Antiquarian Society, 1972), 16–22.
3. [W. B. O. Peabody] Review of *The Works of Anna Lætitia Barbauld*, *Christian Examiner*, 3(4) (1826), 310; Ralph Waldo Emerson, *The Journals and Miscellaneous Notebooks*, vol. XI, ed. A. W. Plumstead *et al.* (Cambridge, MA: Harvard University Press, 1975), 275–6; A. Bronson Alcott, *Concord Days* (1872; repr. Philadelphia, PA: Albert Saifer, 1962), 103.
4. 'European Literary Intelligence', *Literary Magazine*, 2 (1804), 532.
5. *The Correspondence of Richard Price*, vol. III, ed. W. Bernard Peach (Durham, NC: Duke University Press, 1994), 188; Newcome Cappe, *A Sermon Preached on Thursday, the twenty-ninth of July, MDCCLXXXIV, the late Day of National Thanksgiving* (York, 1784), 21.
6. Anna Letitia Barbauld, *An Address to the Opposers of the Repeal of the Corporation and Test Acts*, in Barbauld, *Selected Poetry and Prose*, 280.
7. William Turner, quoted in McCarthy, *Anna Letitia Barbauld*, 472; Barbauld to Maria Edgeworth, 25 October [1823], in Anna Letitia Le Breton, *Memoir of Mrs. Barbauld, Including Letters and Notices of Her Family and Friends* (London: George Bell, 1874), 185, and to Judith Beecroft, 14 November 1818, in *The Works of Anna Lætitia Barbauld*, ed. Lucy Aikin, 2 vols. (London: Longman, 1825), II, 100.
8. Arnold, quoted in William McCarthy, 'A "High-Minded Christian Lady": The Posthumous Reception of Anna Letitia Barbauld', in *Romanticism and Women*

Poets: Opening the Doors of Reception, Harriet Kramer Linkin and Stephen C. Behrendt (eds.) (Lexington, KY: University Press of Kentucky, 1999), 172 (and see also 187, n. 14). On Arnold's influence in the American university's understanding of 'humanism' see Gerald Graff, *Professing Literature: An Institutional History* (University of Chicago Press, 1987), 3–7. On Arnold as a literary elitist see Northrop Frye, *Anatomy of Criticism* (Princeton University Press, 1957), 21–2.

9. Joseph Priestley to Theophilus Lindsey, May 1772, in *Theological and Miscellaneous Works*, I, i, 173.

10. Turner, MS Letterbook (Unitarian College Archive, John Rylands Library of Manchester University), 136; Minutes of the Protestant Dissenting Ministers of the Three Denominations (MS 38.106, Dr Williams's Library), 12 May 1772, 10 June 1772 and 28 May 1773.

11. For a list of known pupils, see William McCarthy, 'The Celebrated Academy at Palgrave: A Documentary History of Anna Letitia Barbauld's School', *Age of Johnson*, 8 (1997), 279–392.

12. Elizabeth Montagu to Anna Letitia Aikin, 2 February 1774, in Le Breton, *Memoir of Mrs. Barbauld*, 38. See Emma Major, 'The Politics of Sociability: Public Dimensions of the Bluestocking Millennium', *Huntington Library Quarterly*, 65(1–2) (2002), 175–92.

13. [John Aikin,] *An Address to the Dissidents of England on their Late Defeat* (London: J. Johnson, 1790), 24.

14. Barbauld, 'On the King's Illness', in *Selected Poetry and Prose*, 158; Andrew Kippis, *A Vindication of the Protestant Dissenting Ministers, with Regard to their Late Application to Parliament*, quoted in *Monthly Review*, 47 (1772), 103–4.

15. Aikin, 'Memoir', *Works of Anna Lætitia Barbauld*, I, vii.

16. Catharine Cappe, 'Memoirs of His Life', in Newcome Cappe, *Discourses Chiefly on Devotional Subjects*, 2nd edn (York, 1816), xxii–xxiii.

17. Barbauld, 'Thoughts on the Inequality of Conditions', *Selected Poetry and Prose*, 346–7.

18. *The Child's New Play-Thing: Being a Spelling-Book Intended to Make the Learning to Read a Diversion Instead of a Task,* 8th edn (London, 1763), 23.

19. Barbauld, *Remarks on Mr. Gilbert Wakefield's Enquiry into the Expediency and Propriety of Public or Social Worship* (London: J. Johnson, 1792); see discussion in McCarthy, *Anna Letitia Barbauld*, 314–18.

20. On this, and on the following paragraph, see discussion in McCarthy, *Anna Letitia Barbauld*, ch. 7.

21. Barbauld, *Selected Poetry and Prose*, 97.

22. Doddridge, *Family Expositor*, vol. I, Subscribers' List and v; vol. III, viii; vol. I, 100.

23. 'In his life he was rigorously virtuous, and, when I knew him, under a self-government, as perfect as participation of human weaknesses can well allow' (Wakefield, *Memoirs of the Life of Gilbert Wakefield*, I, 217–18); quoted approvingly by William Turner, 'Historical Account of the Warrington Academy', *Monthly Repository*, 8 (1813), 171.

24. Elizabeth Rowe, 'Seraphic Love', in *The Poetry of Elizabeth Singer Rowe*, ed. Madeleine Forell Marshall (Lewiston, NY: Edwin Mellon, 1987), 223.

25. See Barbauld, 'An Enquiry into those Kinds of Distress which Excite Agreeable Sensations', *Selected Poetry and Prose*, 205.

26. *Ibid.*, 89–90, 42, 43, 90, 93, 100; 'Delia. An Elegy', *The Poems of Anna Letitia Barbauld*, ed. William McCarthy and Elizabeth Kraft (Athens, GA: University of Georgia Press, 1994), 72; Barbauld, *Selected Poetry and Prose*, 98, 97, 79–80.

27. Samuel Taylor Coleridge, 'Anthem for the Children of Christ's Hospital', 'Monody on the Death of Chatterton', and 'To a Friend', in *The Poems of Samuel Taylor Coleridge*, ed. Ernest Hartley Coleridge (Oxford University Press, 1912), 5, 15, 79. See also McCarthy, *Anna Letitia Barbauld*, 645, n. 28.

28. Coleridge, 'Dejection: An Ode', and 'The Rime of the Ancient Mariner', in *Poems of Coleridge*, 365, 191.

29. On teaching as an economic expedient for Dissenting ministers, see John Seed, 'Unitarian Ministers as Schoolmasters, 1780–1850: Some Notes', *Transactions of the Unitarian Historical Society*, 17 (1979–82), 170–6.

30. McCarthy, 'Celebrated Academy', Appendix III.

31. Rochemont Barbauld, *The Duty of Promoting the Welfare of the Rising Generation: Represented in a Sermon preached at St. Thomas's, Jan. 2, 1792. For the Benefit of the Charity-School, in Gravel-Lane, Southwark* (London, 1792), 13.

32. Aikin, *Memoirs, Miscellanies and Letters of the late Lucy Aikin*, ed. Philip Hemery Le Breton (London: Longman, 1864), 274; Sir Joseph Arnould, *Life of Thomas, First Lord Denman, formerly Lord Chief Justice of England*, 2 vols. (Boston, MA: Estes & Lauriat, 1874), 1, 6.

33. Barbauld, *Selected Poetry and Prose*, 109.

34. 'Account of Eton Montem', *Monthly Magazine*, 7 (1799), 268.

35. Carter, a staunch Churchwoman, thought parts of *Hymns* 'amazingly sublime' (*A Series of Letters between Mrs. Elizabeth Carter and Miss Catherine Talbot, from the Year 1741 to 1770. To which are added, Letters from Mrs. Elizabeth Carter to Mrs. Vesey, between the Years 1763 and 1787*, ed. Montagu Pennington, 2 vols. (London, 1808), II, 346). Wollstonecraft recommended *Hymns* in *Thoughts on the Education of Daughters* and reprinted part of Hymn VIII in *The Female Reader*. Conservative Anglican Sarah Trimmer praised *Hymns* warmly but urged doctrinal reservations: see below, n. 46. An 1840 edition of *Hymns* edited by 'the Wife of a Clergyman' added hymns about 'the fall and consequent depravity of man' to make up for Barbauld's doctrinal deficiencies (quoted in *Christian Reformer*, 8 (1841), 39).

36. Barbauld, *Selected Poetry and Prose*, 238.

37. *Ibid.*, 234.

38. Hester Mulso Chapone, *Letters on the Improvement of the Mind*, in *The Works of Mrs. Chapone*, new edn (Edinburgh, 1807), 22.

39. Barbauld, *Selected Poetry and Prose*, 239–40.

40. See Isaac Watts, *A Treatise on the Education of Children and Youth*, 2nd edn (London, 1769), 16.

41. Barbauld, *Selected Poetry and Prose*, 238; Priestley, 'On Habitual Devotion', in *Theological and Miscellaneous Works*, XV, 105, 106. According to Priestley, Barbauld was present when he delivered this sermon, and he claims she composed her 'Address to the Deity' immediately afterwards (McCarthy and Kraft, *Poems of Anna Letitia Barbauld*, 221).
42. Isaac Watts, 'Song IX. The All-seeing God', in *Divine Songs Attempted in Easy Language for the Use of Children* (1715; ed. J. H. P. Pafford (Oxford University Press, 1971)), 161. Watts insisted that children 'are naturally inclined to do Evil' and can be redeemed only through the intercession of Jesus Christ (*Treatise on the Education of Children*, 11).
43. Watts' Calvinism 'echoes through the [18th] century, most notably in the work of Anna Laetitia Barbauld, Dr John Aikin, Hannah More, and the Tractarians' (Margaret Kinnell, 'Publishing for Children, 1700–1780', in *Children's Literature: An Illustrated History*, Peter Hunt (ed.) (Oxford University Press, 1995), 28). The same confusion seems implied by children's author E. Nesbit's placing Barbauld at the head of an army of hateful and terrifying 'Book People' (*Wet Magic*, 1913, repr. London: Ernest Benn, 1958, 188), and by another writer's contemptuous reference to 'the harsh moralizing tracts of the Barbaulds and Trimmers' (Peter Coveney, *Poor Monkey: The Child in Literature* (London: Rockliff, 1957), 13). In fact, Barbauld differed doctrinally as widely from Trimmer and More as she did from Watts.
44. See 'Brief Memoir of Rev. John Seddon, of Warrington, with Selections from His Letters and Papers. No. 1', *Christian Reformer*, NS 10 (1854), 225, 230–1.
45. Barbauld, *Selected Poetry and Prose*, 249. See Francis Hutcheson, *An Essay on the Nature and Conduct of the Passions and Affections, with Illustrations on the Moral Sense* (1728; ed. Aaron Garrett (Indianapolis, IN: Liberty Fund, 2002)), 15–29, and *Philosophiae Moralis Institutio Compendiaria, with A Short Introduction to Moral Philosophy* (1747; ed. Luigi Turco (Indianapolis, IN: Liberty Fund, 2007)), Bk 1, 'The Elements of Ethicks'.
46. Sarah Trimmer, *Guardian of Education*, 2 (1803), 47.
47. See Barbauld, *Selected Poetry and Prose*, 240; McCarthy, *Anna Letitia Barbauld*, 217.

CHAPTER 4

'And make thine own Apollo doubly thine': John Aikin as literary physician and the intersection of medicine, morality and politics

Kathryn Ready

In her poem 'To Dr. Aikin on his Complaining that She Neglected Him, October 20th 1768', Anna Barbauld celebrates her brother John's prospective career as a literary physician. Drawing on the classical identification of Apollo as the deity who gave humanity poetry and medicine, she confidently predicts:

> So shall thy name be grac'd with fairer praise
> Than waits the laurel or the greenest bays:
> Yet shall the bays around thy temples twine,
> And make thine own Apollo doubly thine.   (86–9)[1]

From Aikin's own writings it appears that he had a strong and sustained investment in the character of the literary physician. Indeed, he seems to have been among the first to think seriously about the literary physician as a historical phenomenon. He identifies the appearance of the literary physician in early modern Europe as a product of the Renaissance 'revival of literature'. In his view, the appearance of the literary physician signalled an important historic shift in the field of medicine, towards an approach that was at once more holistic and scientifically sounder than in previous eras. This is a view at striking odds with recent scholarship and perceptions of the narrowing focus of medicine during the Enlightenment. As a literary physician, Aikin regularly blurred disciplinary boundaries, particularly those between medicine, morality and politics. Much writing of classical antiquity posits a direct analogy between medicine and morality, vice and disease, routinely extended into politics through the idea of the body politic. Aikin develops his own cure for what he sees as an ailing contemporary British body politic by bringing together ancient assumptions concerning the main causes of disease: moral, physical and political, with Enlightenment philosophy and medicine, and with the reformist politics of eighteenth-century liberal Dissent.

Educated at home and later the Warrington Academy, he was one of a number of graduates who went on to study medicine.[2] Indeed, this liberal Dissenting academy has been seen as substantially contributing to eighteenth-century medicine as a whole.[3] At age 15, Aikin began an apprenticeship to apothecary-surgeon Maxwell Garthshore, at Uppingham in Rutland, during which he sometimes assisted his father's friend, Leicester apothecary Richard Pulteney. This apprenticeship ended when Garthshore and Pulteney both decided to pursue degrees as physicians at the University of Edinburgh. After taking over Pulteney's practice for a few months, Aikin studied medicine at Edinburgh from 1764 to 1766, leaving without gaining a degree. He soon went on to another apprenticeship, this time to the surgeon Charles White in Manchester, where he had access to a large infirmary and the opportunity for medical experimentation and research. In 1769 and 1770, he completed his surgical apprenticeship in London under William Hunter (an Edinburgh graduate who was by this time physician to Queen Charlotte, Fellow of the Royal Society and Professor of Anatomy to the Royal Academy, and who had built a London anatomy theatre and museum, which would become famous for training some of the best surgeons and anatomists of the day). After an initial start in Chester, he moved his surgical practice to Warrington in 1771, and in 1774 he began lecturing part-time at the Warrington Academy on anatomy, physiology and chemistry. Lectures were reportedly designed both to prepare students with a professional interest in these subjects and to appeal to those who were engaged in 'a course of liberal education'.[4] Aikin apparently took special interest in mentoring future medical students.[5] While at Chester and Warrington, he was part of a group of medical men (including Matthew Dobson and John Bostock from Liverpool, John Haygarth from Chester and Thomas Percival from Manchester) who met four times a year to discuss medical subjects. When the academy ceased operations in 1783, he applied for a doctorate in medicine at the University of Leyden, successfully defending his thesis, '*De Lactis secretione in puerperis*', in the summer of 1784.[6] Hearing of a vacancy at Great Yarmouth in Norfolk, he decided to relocate there. Dissatisfied with the number of the available clients, he left after a year for London. Four months later, he was successfully petitioned to return to Yarmouth, which had recently been left without any physician. Word of his authorship of two controversial political pamphlets published anonymously in 1790, *An Address to the Dissidents of England on their Late Defeat* and *The Spirit of the Constitution and that of the Church of England Compared*, cost him his Yarmouth practice several years later. He settled in London in 1792, developing a decent London medical practice, which he maintained until 1798, when, suffering from ill health, he turned it over to his son Charles.[7] He subsequently recovered, but spent the rest of his life (until his final decline following a stroke in 1817) engaged in writing projects of various kinds.[8]

His medical publications are numerous, including 'An Essay on the Ligature of Arteries', which appeared in White's *Cases in Surgery with Remarks* (1770); a translation of Claude Pouteau's *Mélanges de chirurgie* (1760); *Observations on the External Use of Preparations of Lead* (1771); *Thoughts on Hospitals* (1771); *A Sketch of the Animal Economy* (1781) (later printed in an expanded Latin version); enlarged 1784 and 1791 editions of William Lewis' *An Experimental History of the* Materia Medica (1761); and *A Manual of* Materia Medica (1785). As well, Aikin contributed to John Haygarth's *A Sketch of a Plan to Exterminate the Casual Small-Pox from Great Britain* (1793).

However, medical writings make up only one portion of a sizable writing and translating corpus. In the course of his lifetime, Aikin's publications covered the developing scientific fields of biology, chemistry, geography and geology, among others, as well as fields that would now be considered part of the humanities and social sciences, such as classical studies, economics, education, history, literature, philosophy and politics. Aikin also continued to produce imaginative writing and literary criticism and was significantly involved in contemporary periodical culture as an editor.

Medicine and literature frequently converge in Aikin's writings and editorial projects. His medical writings are marked with literary flourishes. The original title page of *Thoughts on Hospitals* features an epigraph from Horace.[9] In 1795 Aikin edited John Armstrong's *The Art of Preserving Health* (1744) and in 1796 Matthew Green's *The Spleen, and Other Poems*, the former a medical themed poem by a medically trained writer and the latter by someone with a lay interest in medicine (as well as an obvious favourite of Aikin's).[10] The year 1796 also saw the publication of Aikin's edition of Oliver Goldsmith's poetry. Both *The Art of Preserving Health* and *The Spleen* later appear in Aikin's *Select Works of the British Poets* (1820), along with selections from literary physicians Abraham Cowley, Mark Akenside, Tobias Smollett and Goldsmith. Like Samuel Johnson, who took a keen amateur interest in medicine, Aikin often comments in his literary biographies on health problems and includes an attributed medical cause of death. In his critical writings, he pays attention to literary representations of the medical profession, as, for example, in the essay 'On the Province of Comedy' (1773), where he observes that '[a] good-natured physician can never be angry at Moliere's most laughable exhibitions of the faculty, when he reflects that the follies ridiculed . . . had a real existence; and, by being held up to public derision, have been a great measure reformed'.[11] As we shall see, medical language figures significantly outside Aikin's medical writings.

The *Biographical Memoirs of Medicine in Great Britain from the Revival of Literature to the Time of Harvey* (1780) marks a particularly noteworthy convergence of medicine and literature (anticipated in the opening epigraph from the Italian physician-poet Fracastorius, a translation of one of whose poems Aikin includes in his *Poems* of 1791). Essentially, it stands as a record of Aikin's thoughts on the historical phenomenon of the literary physician (in which context it makes a significant contribution to eighteenth-century medico-historical writing).[12] Aikin represents the 'revival of literature' as having produced the character of the literary physician, not possible during the Middle Ages because of the unreliable knowledge that physicians had coming to them from ancient sources. In his view, the Fall of Constantinople in 1453 and the consequent 'dispersion of several learned men skilled in the Greek language' served to free medicine 'from the mixture of Arabian folly and extravagance by a direct application to the purer sources of the Greeks', and physicians 'were not less benefited by the acquisition of those ornamental parts of literature, which dispelled the barbarism of their language, and formed that union of the character of the polite scholar with that of the physician, which they have ever since, so much to their credit, maintained'.[13]

One of the implications here is that from the 'revival of literature' onwards physicians might in some measure generally be considered literary, whether engaged in imaginative writing or not, because their writing reflected the liberalizing and refining effects of the West European re-acquaintance with the classics. While some might argue that, properly speaking, Aikin better fits the broader category of physician-writer than that of literary physician, this distinction would not have meant much to him.[14] What we would now call literary writers, including literary physicians, were not bound by such distinctions in the eighteenth century, exploring within their literary writing any number of subjects in the humanities, social sciences and sciences, as the eighteenth-century literary physician Erasmus Darwin famously attests with his poetic popularization of Carl Linnaeus' system of taxonomy in botany.

In the *Biographical Memoirs* Aikin celebrates the contributions of physicians to a variety of fields, with those to literature inspiring particular pride. Of the physician-poet John Phreas, he writes that a 'circumstance perhaps more to his credit than any other, is that he was requested by a noble Italian to write an epitaph for the tomb of Petrarch, to supply the place of a

barbarous one before inscribed upon it'. He includes admiring notice of
Thomas Linacre's contributions to Latin grammar and composition and
praises John Kaye or Key, alias Caius, for succeeding 'Linacre in uniting the
first honours of literature with those of medicine'.[15]

Underlying the *Biographical Memoirs* is an assumption that the 'revival of
literature' substantiated a holistic approach to medicine, where the physician was called to minister to the soul or mind as well as to the body. The
medieval physician John Giles is credited as 'learned in physic and divinity'
and for offering patients 'comfort . . . for body and soul'. Yet he is presented
as an exception. Aikin cites Geoffrey Chaucer's portrait of the physician
in *The Canterbury Tales* (*c.*1400) as illustration of the typical limitations
of medieval physicians. As he deduces, from 'the sarcasm thrown out
concerning . . . [the physician's] unacquaintance with scriptures, we may
judge that he did not, like many of that and an earlier age, unite the clerical
with the medical character'. After the 'revival of literature', however, physicians regularly unite 'the several characters of physician, naturalist, and
divine'. Aikin suggests that the Reformation helped particularly to popular-
ize the character of the physician-divine.[16]

In 'To Dr. Aikin', Barbauld celebrates her brother's own holistic approach
to medicine (which she suggests here as given weight by the eighteenth-
century culture of sensibility). She imagines Aikin not only treating illness
and tending wounds with 'skillful care', but also able to 'soothe the fears and
anguish of the mind; / Join to the sage advice, the tender sigh; / And to the
healing hand the pitying eye' (77–9). Beyond that, she anticipates:

> . . . thy art thy friendship shall prevail
> And cordial looks shall cure, when drugs would fail:
> Thy words of balm shall cure the wounds of strife,
> And med'cine all the sharper ills of life.   (80–3)

There is corroborating evidence from Aikin himself that he saw the physician
in precisely such terms. For example, in volume 1 of *Letters from a Father to a
Son* (1793–1800), he counsels his son Arthur as a ministerial candidate based
directly on his own professional experiences dealing with the bereaved.

It is important to underscore that Aikin did not regard the new liberal
and literary character of the physician and more holistic approach to healing
as incompatible with advances in medical knowledge that had been made
through the Scientific Revolution and, more particularly, the study of
anatomy. From the *Biographical Memoirs* it appears that he saw medicine
lacking a firm scientific foundation previous to the 'revival of literature'. In
fostering 'a spirit of rational inquiry', the 'revival of literature' had served, on

the one hand, to give the physician a breadth of interest, a literary character, and a holistic attitude he had tended to lack before. On the other hand, it had served to accelerate the progress of medico-scientific knowledge. Medieval physicians experimented haphazardly on patients and dispensed many cures according to astrology. Aikin disdains 'the folly and extravagance of some of the chemical sect, particularly Paracelsus, who treated with contempt the writings of the venerable father of physic' (that is, Hippocrates) and who perpetuated 'absurdities' as a result of their uncritical commitment to an 'empiric' method.[17]

Adamant that the most venerable classical authority must remain open to challenge, he particularly welcomes the displacement of humoural theory (originating with Hippocrates and considerably elaborated by Galen), approving those such as Thomas Moufet or Muffet, who disputed Galen's 'fanciful reasonings' by appealing to 'our own senses'.[18] Yet the way forward for Aikin is not to forget the Ancients, as becomes clear in his account of William Harvey.[19] According to Aikin, Harvey 'enlightened the world with the investigation of a law in the animal œconomy, of such fundamental importance, as justly to place his name in the highest rank of natural philosophers'. The chronicle of Harvey's medical studies at the University of Padua highlights his tutelage under the famous anatomist Fabricius ab Aquapendente. Yet Aikin characterizes Harvey as simultaneously 'literary', laying 'a proper foundation of classical learning' at grammar school and then spending six years at Cambridge 'in those academical studies which are prepatory to a learned profession'. He praises Harvey's writings as fully 'capable of supporting that classical reputation, which has adorned the character of so many English physicians'.[20]

From Aikin's point of view, there was obviously no historical tension between the humanities and the sciences, which he (like many Enlightenment historians) saw as having progressed side by side.[21] Aikin's interpretation of the history of medicine runs strikingly counter to the understanding of the history of medicine that has developed during the twentieth century. G. S. Rousseau has influentially argued that post-Cartesian Enlightenment medicine was characterized by a new preoccupation with the body at the expense of the mind (closely associated with the soul throughout the eighteenth century). One result was that 'health and art' were 'bifurcated into separate categories'.[22] 'Before then', Rousseau argues, 'health was not even a consciously articulated category, as pain and suffering were the given condition of mortal life'.[23] Such a vision of the history of medicine would have baffled Aikin, who saw no such break.

Both the Dissenting academies and the Edinburgh medical school have often been mischaracterized as prioritizing the sciences at the expense of the humanities, and particularly the classics (with, in the latter case, obvious implications for a holistic approach to medicine). Dissenting academies such as Warrington continued to place substantial emphasis on the classics.[24] Scottish medical schools might well have provided a more effective practical and scientific training in medicine than that of Oxford and Cambridge. Reportedly, the Scottish trained physician was likely to 'have had experience ... treating a range of medical conditions; he would have been skilled in a variety of techniques; he would have been given a systematic, academic introduction to the main branches of medicine; and he would probably have had a commitment to experimental method'.[25] Edinburgh offered 'instruction not only in all the main branches of medicine, but also in anatomy and surgery, botany, chemistry as applied to pharmacy, and midwifery'.[26] In contrast, the Oxford or Cambridge medical graduate would have been 'familiar with medical texts from a range of countries' thanks to his command of Latin, and 'in the absence of much practical instruction he might have developed strong interests in the theory of medicine' and its potential contribution to medical and general scientific knowledge.[27] Oxford and Cambridge placed greater emphasis on the classics than the Scottish universities (and, with it, the theories of Hippocrates and Galen). Nevertheless, this characterization of the difference between Scottish and Oxford or Cambridge educated physicians appears somewhat misleading. A practical and scientific emphasis would have been counterbalanced by 'the attractions of Edinburgh's teachings in philosophy and the human sciences'.[28] Ex-Warringtonian Percival and his fellow Edinburgh medical graduate John Gregory both touted the benefits of a liberal education for medical students and achieved their own fame as literary physicians. Moreover, as Lisbeth Haakonssen points out, a 'characteristic feature of Edinburgh medicine was its concern with the extent and nature of the interaction between mind and body'.[29] Edinburgh medical professor William Cullen's research particularly 'encouraged new thinking about the body and consciousness which enlarged the map of mind–body relations' and the displacement of humoural theory by the language of nerves.[30] The work of Cullen and his colleague Robert Whytt on the importance of the nervous system as a point of crossover between the mind and body can be seen as feeding into the culture of sensibility (along with that of contemporaries such as David Hartley) and a holistic approach to medicine.[31] Haakonssen notably describes Gregory as combining 'the virtues of the 'rational' physician with those of "the man of feeling"'.[32]

Fundamentally connected to the classical holistic approach to medicine was the analogy between medicine and morality, something which informs

Barbauld's 'Prologue to *The Man of Pleasure* by John Aikin', likely composed around 1771, for a play possibly performed privately at the Warrington Academy. Initially, Barbauld disclaims the relationship between medicine and literature. She has her brother excusing his play's deficiencies on the grounds '[t]hat plays and recipes had no relation' (21) and that

> Twas foreign from the task to him assigned
> To wake new feelings in the callous mind,
> With skill to set distorted judgments right,
> To purge the taste, and clear the mental sight.   (23–6)

However, as William McCarthy and Elizabeth Kraft point out, these lines sustain an implicit parallel between Aikin's twin vocations of medicine and literature. 'Surgeons *set* broken bones, *clear* the eyes of obstructions, and prescribe *purges* for the bowels.'[33] Developing this parallel further, Barbauld goes on to report that her brother had drawn 'up this prescription; / A two-act sermon 'tis by his description' (45–6) in response to the 'tempting poison' (30) too often 'wrought' by 'the Comic muse' (29). Her subsequent attempt to reassure the audience that 'he / Has gilt the pill, and calls it comedy' (49–50) indirectly underscores the analogy between medicine and morality.[34]

A classical education at Warrington, encompassing particularly the writings of Plato, Aristotle and Seneca (reportedly the first to claim 'to be the physician who can heal the ills of a man's soul as a doctor heals those of his body'), and any teachings Aikin received in Hippocratic medicine either at Warrington or Edinburgh, would have exposed him to a long tradition of correspondences between morality and medicine.[35] Rejecting the conception of disease as divine punishment, Hippocrates believed that disease could be traced to imbalances in the mind, the body or the environment, and that a physician must properly attend to both a patient's mental and physical state. His theory of humours provided a medical foundation for an ethic of moderation that was quickly picked up in classical moral philosophy, which preached moderation as fundamental to both a virtuous and a healthy life. As he himself declares in 'Epistle to the Rev. W. Enfield LLD' (1791), Aikin was a consistent advocate of 'temperance', which he calls in the *Letters* 'the grand prophylactic'.[36] In evaluating Armstrong, he approves the recommendation of 'temperance' and condemnation of 'luxury' of diet, while complaining that this recommendation is at odds with Armstrong's advocacy of 'the occasional debauch as a salutary spur to nature'.[37] He praises Green's 'corporeal regimen . . . against the Spleen consist[ing] of temperance and exercise'.[38] He sees Green's prescription as rooted in 'an easy good-humoured philosophy, resembling that of HORACE in his gay but sober mood, and comprising the best practical Epicurean system that has, perhaps, ever been sketched out'.[39] Horatian satire arguably marks the most famous classical literary expression of the ethic of moderation. Its influence on Aikin's *Poems* is unmistakable. Hippocrates' classification of humours itself bequeathed a powerful medico-moral language to literature, giving rise to its own literary genre in the form of the comedy of humours (elements of which originate with Aristophanes and were carried forward to Plautus and Terence, and ultimately to Ben Jonson and George Chapman). Aikin cites Jonson in his essay on comedy and addresses the subject of character types with specific reference to two familiar humoural personalities: 'the sanguine' and 'the splenetic'.[40]

Without a surviving text, it is of course impossible to say how Aikin developed the analogy between morality and medicine in the *Man of Pleasure*.[41] With his political writings it is a different story. In *Food for the National Penitence* (1793), Aikin explicitly affirms that a 'state of vice is a state of disease'. The same text makes transparent use of the classical analogy of the body politic. 'A nation ... being composed of individuals', Aikin observes, 'it may be said that it is the aggregate of their prevailing vices which forms the vicious character of the whole body'.[42] Aikin compares the diagnosis and treatment of individual and national vices, noting that 'national faults' are at once easier to identify than 'the faults of particular men', because they 'are something more fixed and uniform, proceeding from causes of general operation', and harder to treat, since they 'cannot be removed without changes of circumstances easily extensive'.[43]

Aikin goes on to consider the particular situation of contemporary Britain, drawing on the moral and political discourse often referred to as classical republicanism or civic humanism (although the question of terminology, and particularly the meaning of the term 'republican', remains fraught, and the understanding of the relationship between classical, early modern, and eighteenth-century political thought, a matter of ongoing debate). Evidently, the continuing relevance of classical republicanism in Western European political life was itself another product of the 'revival of literature'. At this particular historical juncture, he notes, Britain enjoyed unprecedented 'internal prosperity', 'almost uninterrupted peace at home', 'political liberty, greater than has been transmitted to any other people', and a global commerce that had made its merchants richer than those of 'ancient Tyre'. As he cautions, however, 'from the earliest ages of the world, down through each successive period, it has been found, that a similar state of prosperity is productive of vices which tend to the destruction of their parent'.[44]

Aikin warns that if Britain fails to 'cure' its state of vice or disease, God will attempt some difficult 'remedial process', citing America's victory in the

War of Independence as a warning that had been hitherto ignored. He accuses the British of 'overweening confidence . . . pride, arrogance, ostentation, luxurious indulgence, and insatiable avidity'. 'The excessive opulence of the few', he declares, 'stimulates the desires of the many'. The result is a general and constant demand for 'new inventions . . . political corruption contaminates every wholesome principle in the state . . . Principles are deserted and ridiculed; independence is sunk to an empty name; and all rush into servitude, for the sake of present advantages, blind to their lasting interests, careless for posterity'.[45]

Those familiar with the discourse of classical republicanism will register Aikin's use of the term 'independence' here. For classical republicans, patriotism and virtue (the latter defined as the sacrifice of self-interest to the public good) both demanded independence, since someone who depended on another was assumed to be susceptible to bribery and therefore to the possibility of acting in the interest of some person or party rather than that of the public as a whole. Luxury was the great evil for classical republicans precisely because it was seen as impeding the ability to work for the public good. Like many who condemned luxury from Plato onwards, Aikin identifies the rise of luxury with that of commerce and judges the current prevalence of luxury as evidence of a diseased state.[46]

So much for the diagnosis. As it turns out, Aikin's prescription is fairly predictable. In keeping with the writings of classical antiquity, he prays for the restoration of a 'spirit of equity, and moderation'. What has less precedence is the connection to Dissenting politics. Although this political pamphlet was published anonymously, one can see Aikin exploiting his authority here at once as physician and Dissenter. Aikin signals his position as a Dissenter in his condemnation of 'all interested opposition to the spread of religious truth, all debasement of the spirit of religion by allying it with state-policy, and making it subservient to party views'. This position equally comes through in his censure of those whose prioritization of 'utility' over 'truth' and assumption that the 'purpose [of religion] is chiefly to awe the minds of the vulgar' make them hostile to 'free inquiry' in religion.[47] Throughout this political pamphlet, a cure for the ills of the body politic is consistently tied to the reformist causes that Dissenters prominently espoused, including the American Revolution and abolition.

By this point, Aikin had already drawn on the discourse of classical republicanism to warn against the diminishing moral credibility and authority of establishment physicians.[48] The main problem, as he saw it, was with the Royal College of Physicians. As Aikin acknowledges, this institution had once served as a much needed regulatory body. Linacre, one of its founding members and first presidents, was responding to the problems that arose when too many medical practitioners were 'illiterate monks' and 'empirics' licensed by bishops with little medical knowledge. As such, Linacre was acting both in 'the interests of his profession, and of mankind in general'.[49] Aikin would elsewhere emphasize that only those who are qualified as physicians can properly judge the 'efficacy' of a medicine.[50] In the *Biographical Memoirs*, he praises Caius for his 'zealous attachment to the dignity and interests of this society'. However, he goes on to question whether Caius' success in upholding 'the rights and privileges of the College . . . in the reign of Elizabeth, against the surgeons' was entirely beneficial to the public, and he seconds John Woodall's 'sensible and modest defence of surgeons prescribing diet and medicines to their patients in certain cases'.[51] It appears that Aikin regarded the college as having become increasingly preoccupied with safeguarding its membership's interests to the detriment of the public good. Licensing was no longer determined strictly according to merit, and licenses were often denied to qualified practitioners. As such, the college had outlived its usefulness and was now, in fact, impeding medical progress and patient welfare.

Aikin would later cite the institutional evolution of the college as an example of how consideration for the public good can be overwhelmed by a 'corporation' and 'monopolizing spirit'.[52] Evidently, he was particularly sensitive to the problems with the licensing system because of his own position vis-à-vis the college. While he could apply to become a licentiate and gain 'the right of practicing', he could not become a college Fellow and gain 'collegiate powers and emoluments' without an Oxford or Cambridge degree, unobtainable to him as a Dissenter.[53] Licentiates generally had a much harder time making a living than Fellows. As Noel and José Parry note, 'the market for medical services in England during this period continued to be dominated at the higher end . . . by fellows of the Royal College of Physicians' and few 'of the licentiates could earn a living exclusively by giving medical advice'.[54] The college was a source of general resentment and condemnation at the Scottish universities.[55] In 1794 Aikin supported the attempt by the licentiates to assert the 'right, on the principles of the original charters, to be admitted to all professional honours on due examination'.[56] He added his name to a list of petitioners and was disappointed when the Court of King's Bench sided with the college. This gesture of public support cost him his borrowing privileges at the college, one of the reasons cited for his ultimate discontinuation of a sequel to the *Biographical Memoirs*.[57] As Aikin's daughter Lucy pointedly emphasizes, 'Into this cause, as into the question of the abolition of the Test Act, he entered without any personal interests whatever, but simply from that hatred of every thing unfair and inequitable which was his leading principle and almost his ruling passion.'[58] Thus, she underscores the obvious parallel that her father saw between the 'corporation spirit' of the college and that of the establishment as a whole. The college's monopoly over 'collegiate powers and emoluments' had direct parallels to the establishment monopoly over various civic offices. The insistence that Aikin's dedication to the reform of the medical profession was not motivated by 'personal interests' notably answers a frequent charge that in championing reform rational or liberal Dissenters such as the Aikins were motivated by personal or party rather than by public interests and illustrates a characteristic liberal Dissenting counter-strategy.[59] Branded as disloyal factionalists, liberal Dissenters sought to claim for themselves the classical republican title to independence and commitment to the public good. In *Spirit of the Constitution* Aikin explicitly characterizes Dissenters as 'the firm friends of freedom, without any interests separate from those of their country'.[60] In his view, it was the members of the clergy who were guilty of acting out of 'interest' in seeking to perpetuate the union between Church and State.[61] Lucy Aikin presents the Dissenting physician as fundamentally guided, like liberal Dissent itself, by the desire to serve the public good (in implicit contrast to the establishment physician).

In the *Letters*, John Aikin returns to the connection made by moralists between 'maladies of the body and mind', noting that it was 'nothing new to regard all mental vices and defects as so many *diseases* of that part of our frame'.[62] Yet he observes 'that something still remains to be done in the practical application of the doctrine' and 'that it is of importance, both with respect to the successful treatment of mental diseases, and to the preservation of our tranquillity under a view of the evils of life, that this resemblance should be strongly impressed on our thoughts'. Too often, in his opinion, people assumed that 'trifling and casual remedies' were sufficient to eliminate 'mental vices and defects'. Medicine taught that 'the resolute application of *opposites*' was necessary in such cases, to counteract 'the power of habit'.

To support this point, Aikin invokes 'the scholastic controversies concerning liberty and necessity'.[63] The beginning of this particular philosophical debate has been traced to John Locke's *An Essay Concerning Human Understanding* (1690). This debate preoccupied two prominent rational Dissenters and friends of the Aikin family, Joseph Priestley and Richard Price. Reduced to its simplest form, it addressed the relationship between motive and choice and whether people are free to make choices or not. Libertarians (including Samuel Clarke, Price and Thomas Reid) argued that motives cannot determine the choices we make, even when they seem to dictate morally one particular choice over another. Instead, motives serve as opportunities for people to act as agents in making specific choices. Necessitarians (including Anthony Collins, Hartley and Priestley) argued that motives can and do determine choices.[64]

Perhaps thinking of David Hume, who warned that most controversies over liberty and necessity stemmed from confusion over terminology, Aikin acknowledges that debates on this subject, 'when carried to their utmost degree of abstraction', become 'mere logomachies'. Nevertheless, he makes the point that engagement in such debates often has 'practical effects upon common minds'. To his mind, those who place too much faith in liberty become overconfident 'in the efficacy of the feebler aids to morality, such as precept and argumentation'. Aikin appeals to experience for evidence 'of the actual existence of a moral necessity; – that is, of such an overbearing prepollency of motives tending to one point, that in no one instant of a man's life could he be supposed capable of a course of action different from that he has really adopted'. Part of the experience that he is appealing to is as a physician, as he goes on to argue that 'the process of fixing . . . character' is 'as regular and unalterable' as 'that of . . . bodily constitution'. He cites the example of a child born to criminal parents who is destined 'by the all powerful force of education and habit' to assume 'the character of a ferocious beast; certain to end his life by violence, if it be not sooner cut off by the consequences of intemperance', and another example of 'the heir to a large entailed estate' whose typical upbringing will turn him into nothing 'else than a low-minded, brutal, tyrannical debauchee'.[65]

These examples show the way in which his vision of the relationship between medicine, morality and politics was coloured again by his Dissenting background. In his *Address to the Dissidents*, Aikin celebrates the status of Dissenters as part of 'the most virtuous, the most enlightened, the most independent part of the community, the *middle class*'.[66] In contrast to many conservatives who believed in the principle of paternalism, and the need for reform of manners to happen from the top down, liberals such as Aikin saw all reform campaigns (of manners included) as most effectively spearheaded by the middle classes (with Dissenters among the obvious leaders). Thus, he again tacitly draws a sense of authority from his position as a Dissenter, which he openly acknowledges and justifies in various ways throughout the *Letters*.

Significantly, however, the medico-moral philosophy that he develops here is equally informed by the deepening pessimism evident in the rational

Dissenting community during the 1790s concerning the prospect of social and particularly political reform. As Aikin insists:

The physician knows that certain modes of living will infallibly bring on certain diseases, which will descend from parents to children, and can never be extirpated as long as the original causes prevail. The moralist may equally foretel certain vices as the consequences of certain conditions and manners in society, which will prove unconquerable while circumstances remain the same. The morbid tendency in both cases is too strong to be counteracted by common remedies. Nothing but a total change of habit, effected by means equally powerful and long-continued with those which bred the malady, can work a cure.

This passage underscores the importance of controlled surroundings in curing disease and vice. In the case of the criminal poor, the only hope is for those who 'have made themselves the objects of legal punishment'.[67] This is the great insight with which Aikin credits his friend, prison reformer John Howard, who believed that, properly managed, prison could achieve rehabilitation.

Aikin has less hope for reform elsewhere, looking to 'those *grand remedial processes*, which are probably within the moral plan of Providence' for 'the reformation of a whole people, and especially of the higher classes'. He reiterates his apprehensions concerning the impact of 'prosperity' and 'opulence' in producing vanity, arrogance, luxury, and sacrificing 'honour' and 'justice' for the 'gratification' of 'increased wants and desires'. The image of disease comes up once more in Aikin's description of a nation that has 'arrived at that state in which, according to the energetic expression of the Roman historian, they can neither bear their vices nor the remedies of them'.[68] He anticipates the need for 'some signal catastrophe' to serve as such a cure.[69]

This deepening pessimism regarding social and political reform was mirrored elsewhere in Aikin's assessment of the progress being made in medicine (perhaps not surprising given the way in which rational Dissenters often connected progress in the sciences with reform in politics). In 1794 Aikin complained that the 'project of curing diseases by artificial airs has caused a little discussion, but does not seem to excite much expectation. Animal electricity has furnished some food for the physiologists, but I believe will not end in the discovery of any new law of nature.'[70] By 1798 he was professing himself 'absolutely shocked at the little advance that has been made in the healing art, in really important points, within our memory'.[71] Part of this pessimism about medicine may have sprung from a sense of frustration over the failure of various eighteenth-century medical improvement campaigns. As Andrew Cunningham and Roger French note, liberal Dissenting physicians such as Aikin made up a disproportionate number of eighteenth-century medical reformers.[72] As a close friend of Haygarth's, Aikin would have seen the politics-based resistance Haygarth encountered to his efforts to promote inoculation because he dared associate with Dissenters (resistance that offered further illustration of the evils of establishment factionalism and, more specifically, of the moral limitations of establishment physicians, Haygarth excluded). Inoculation significantly comes up in the *Letters*, where Aikin laments that as with 'the inoculation of the small pox . . . [the truth] confers indisputable benefits on those who receive it; yet too few will probably ever receive it to produce striking effects upon the whole species'. If Aikin's expectations for reform had been disappointed, he could still hope for an easing of tensions between the establishment and Dissent through the promotion of candour, which he likewise compares to inoculation, calling it 'the best preservative against virulence and acrimony in controversial debates', tending 'to heal those wounds on social comfort, which bigotry is perpetually inflicting'.[73]

Both during his lifetime and after his death, Aikin's general reputation as a man of letters has tended to overshadow his achievements in the field of medicine. This literary reputation has been eclipsed, in turn, by that of his more famous sibling, as Lucy Aikin recognized with some dismay, presenting her father to the world, in the words of Anne Janowitz, 'as a neglected poet and martyr to the talents of his sister'.[74] Certainly, John Aikin made a number of noteworthy contributions to medicine. His research on the transmission of fevers, written up in *Thoughts on Hospitals*, pre-dates, as Betsy Rodgers notes, that of Howard, and undoubtedly influenced him, and, it seems equally likely, influenced Haygarth, who published *Observations on the Population and Diseases of Chester* in 1774.[75] Of *Thoughts on Hospitals*, John F. Fulton writes that the 'book clearly bears the stamp of Charles White's influence, but there are signs of originality and independence throughout which seem not to have been referred to by the historians of English medicine'. Fulton contends further that the application to medical practice of the 'belief that wound infection is due to a viable agent transmitted by the air, or by direct contact' is 'the greatest single advance in medicine that was made by the Warrington group'.[76] As a collaborator with Haygarth in the ongoing research into and promotion of methods to eradicate smallpox Aikin equally deserves notice. Charles Aikin would pick up this particular cause and become prominent in pioneering early nineteenth-century efforts to provide free vaccination for the poor, through which he earned the patronage of Edward Jenner. Finally,

John Aikin's activity as a literary physician arguably itself ought to be regarded as a contribution to medicine as much as it was to letters, at a moment in history when medicine was being increasingly compartmentalized. If *Food for the National Penitence* offers a prescription for the ailing body politic straight from classical antiquity, we can see Aikin developing a much more novel cure in the *Letters*. Building on contemporary philosophical debates over liberty and necessity, Aikin produces a medico-moral discourse that strikes as a genuinely original contribution to eighteenth-century medical moral and political thought.

NOTES

1. Selections from Barbauld's poetry, line numbers and dates of composition and publication come from McCarthy and Kraft, *Poems of Anna Letitia Barbauld*.
2. Out of a total of 393 Warrington graduates, William Turner lists 22 who afterwards pursued medicine: Thomas Percival of Warrington; Aikin; Samuel Farr of Bristol; William Acklom of Welton, Yorkshire; John Taylor of Bolton; Timothy Bentley of Leicester; Edward Rigby of Warrington; John Bostock of Liverpool; Snowden White of Derby; Robert Dukinfield of Manchester; Philip Meadows Martineau of Norwich; John Wadsworth of Sheffield; Caleb Hillier Parry of Cirencester; John Vize of Clonmell; Dickson of Taunton; Moorhouse of Skipton; George Daniell of Yeovil; Thomas Crompton of Derby; Philip Holland of Bolton; Richard Codrington of Bridgewater; Edwood Chorley; and Peter Crompton of Derby. William Turner, 'Historical Account of Students Educated in the Warrington Academy', *Monthly Repository of Theology and General Literature*, 9(100–5) (1814), 201–5, 263–8, 385–90, 525–30, 594–9. Among these, the identification of Bentley's later professional career is only tentative, and the total has been variously stated as twenty or twenty-one. Turner seems not to have known about Warrington student Benjamin Vaughan's medical studies at Edinburgh and later founding of the Maine Medical Society in America.
3. Charles Webster and Jonathan Barry note that 'Warrington-educated doctors played a leading role in provincial medical affairs' and that this role 'extended to the wider fraternity of dissenting medical practitioners'. Charles Webster and Jonathan Barry, 'The Manchester Medical Revolution', in Barbara Smith (ed.), *Truth, Liberty, Religion: Essays Celebrating Two Hundred Years of Manchester College* (Oxford: Manchester College, 1986), 168. John F. Fulton recognizes the Warrington Academy as a major reason that 'many of the most important contributions to English medicine and science in the 18th century came from a rather restricted geographical district in and about the county of Lancashire' ('The Warrington Academy (1757–1786) and Its Influence upon Medicine and Science', *Bulletin of the Institute of History of Medicine*, 1(2) (1933), 50–80 (51)). Warrington graduates Percival, Farr, Rigby, Bostock and Parry all earn entries in the *ODNB* for notable achievements in medicine, with Percival making the

most widely celebrated contribution as author of the *Medical Ethics* (1803). According to McCarthy, Martineau was a pioneer of lithotomy (*Barbauld*, 229). Turner indicates, in addition, that Taylor had a notable career as a physician in Bolton, and Bostock briefly at Liverpool before his early death. He cites White as an eminent physician at Nottingham and Chorley at Doncaster, Holland as receiving praise as a physician in Hull from John Alderson in *An Essay on the Nature and Origin of the Contagion of Fever* (1788), and Peter Crompton as becoming a 'well-known advocate of parliamentary reform'. See Turner, 'Historical Account of Students Educated in the Warrington Academy', 9: 204, 263–4, 264, 529, 598.

4. William Turner, 'Historical Account of the Warrington Academy', *Monthly Repository of Theology and General Literature*, 8(85–94) (1813), 577.

5. If 1774 is indeed when Aikin started teaching at Warrington, the students he might have helped train for medicine would be Daniell, Thomas Crompton, Holland, Codrington, Chorley and Peter Crompton. While Holland and Chorley achieved some distinction in medicine and Peter Crompton in politics, Turner only says of Daniell that he graduated from Edinburgh and settled at Salisbury, of Thomas Crompton, that he studied under Percival and died as a medical student at Edinburgh, and, of Codrington, that he likely graduated from Edinburgh. Among those Aikin helped privately to prepare for medicine were two of Percival's sons, although one ultimately chose the Anglican ministry and the other died prematurely.

6. Turner's date is 1783. The date of cessation is sometimes given as 1782. Warrington Academy's remaining assets were not redistributed until 1786.

7. After his adoption by the Barbaulds, Charles Aikin attended their Palgrave school for boys, apprenticing first to Martineau and then to the surgeon Peter Holland of Knutsford, Cheshire before going on to Edinburgh. He graduated in 1795 and earned a diploma from the Company of Surgeons in 1799. My source here is Betsy Rodgers, *Georgian Chronicle: Mrs Barbauld and Her Family* (London: Methuen, 1958).

8. In addition to Lucy Aikin's *Memoir of John Aikin* and McCarthy's biography of Barbauld I draw here from Marilyn L. Brooks, 'John Aikin', *Oxford Dictionary of National Biography*, vol. 1 (Oxford University Press, 2004), 485–6.

9. For the original lines and the translation, see *Horace: The Odes and Epodes*, ed. and trans. C. E. Bennet (Cambridge, MA: Harvard University Press, 1952), 14–15.

10. *The Spleen* was first published posthumously in 1737, with a preface by Richard Glover.

11. John and Anna Aikin, *Miscellaneous Pieces in Prose* (London: J. Johnson, 1773), 13. The authorship of individual pieces in the collection is unattributed. Lucy Aikin identifies Barbauld's contributions in *Works of Anna Lætitia Barbauld*, xiii–xiv. I have here claimed 'On the Province of Comedy' as Aikin's, without dismissing the possibility that it is a collaborative production. Barbauld and

Aikin's collaborative mode is discussed in some detail in White, 'The "Joineriana"', 511–33 and Levy's *Family Authorship*.

12. Some other examples of eighteenth-century medico-historical writing are John Friend, *The History of Physick from the Time of Galen to the Beginning of the Sixteenth Century* (1725–6); John Coakley Lettsom, *History of the Origins of Medicine* (1778); Benjamin Waterhouse, *A Synopsis of a Course of Lectures on the Theory and Practice of Medicine* (1786); Samuel Davidson, *The History of Medicine* (1791); John Mason Good, *The History of Medicine so Far as it Relates to the Profession of the Apothecary* (1795); and Richard Walker, *Memoirs of Medicine* (1799). Aikin shows considerably greater interest in the impact of the 'revival of literature' on the field of medicine and in the historical phenomenon of the literary physician than these other writers. Walker is one of the few even to mention the early modern Renaissance. Craig Ashley Hanson briefly discusses Aikin's emphasis on the 'humanist model' in the *Biographical Memoirs* and his embrace of 'a thoroughly Renaissance conceptual framework', as 'he dates the earliest attempts to recover the ancient medical accomplishments of the Ancients to the fall of Constantinople' in *The English Virtuoso: Art, Medicine, and Antiquarianism in the Age of Empiricism* (Chicago, IL and London: University of Chicago Press, 2009), 52–3.

13. John Aikin, *Biographical Memoirs of Medicine in Great Britain from the Revival of Literature to the Time of Harvey* (London: J. Johnson, 1780), 22.

14. For example, Maureen McNeil carefully distinguishes between different kinds of eighteenth-century physician-writers, observing that the 'literary scene was blessed with the contributions of medical men such as John Arbuthnot, John Aikin, Mark Akenside, Sir Richard Blackmore, Oliver Goldsmith and Tobias Smollett ... Physicians also made their mark in the field of philosophy. John Locke, who wielded such a vital influence over the course of eighteenth-century philosophy, was medically trained ... Into countless other fields the medically-trained ventured with remarkable success: Nehemiah Grew ... into botany, George Fordyce ... into agriculture, Hans Sloane ... and John Hunter ... into natural history, and James Hutton ... into geology' (*Under the Banner of Science: Erasmus Darwin and his Age* (Manchester University Press, 1987), 125). Of Aikin, Fulton observes that no other eighteenth-century English medical practitioner, 'unless perhaps Richard Mead, carried higher the tradition of the scholar physician' ('The Warrington Academy (1757–1786)', 50–80 (66)).

15. Aikin, *Biographical Memoirs*, 26, 103. Although his career did not fall within the period covered by the *Biographical Memoirs*, famous literary physician Thomas Browne receives at least passing mention (*ibid.*, 284). It appears that Aikin later wrote an unpublished life of Browne (*Memoir of John Aikin*, 22).

16. Aikin, *Biographical Memoirs*, 6, 19, 80.

17. *Ibid.*, 172–3. On the conflict between the 'empiric' and the 'rational' or 'dogmatical' methods that came out of rival interpretations of Hippocrates, see Lester S. King, *The Medical World of the Eighteenth Century* (University of Chicago Press, 1958), 32. The Edinburgh medical school seems to have

encouraged combining the 'empiric' and 'rational' to avoid the weaknesses of each method.

18. Aikin, *Biographical Memoirs*, 171.

19. As Roy Porter chronicles, the 'dream of Renaissance humanists was to restore medicine to its Greek purity, but a counter-view gained ground in the seventeenth century as the "moderns" confronted the "ancients": medicine could thrive only if the deadweight of the past were cast off'. Nevertheless, as he himself points out, 'while experimental philosophers gloried in being "moderns," in clinical medicine much of the ancient heritage remained intact' (*The Greatest Benefit to Mankind: A Medical History of Humanity* (London and New York, NY: W. W. Norton, 1997), 201, 229). Aikin can notably be generous even of ancient medical theory, in acknowledging Harvey's debt to some discoveries of Galen's.

20. Aikin, *Biographical Memoirs*, 284, 285, 325. Evidently, the history of the University of Padua was closely tied to both the 'revival of literature' and to the Scientific Revolution (which Aikin never identifies as a separate intellectual movement, and whose status as a separate intellectual movement remains an object of controversy today). The beginning of Padua's rise to international fame coincided with that of the 'revival of literature'. Padua continued to be a great centre for classical learning after Harvey (one of his teachers was a renowned Aristotelian, Cesare Cremonini). It was additionally the alma mater for figures regarded as central to the Scientific Revolution, notably Nicolaus Copernicus and Andreas Vesalius, the latter helping to establish its reputation in anatomy.

21. For more on Enlightenment attitudes concerning the relative progress of the humanities and sciences, see David Spadafora, *The Idea of Progress in Eighteenth-century Britain* (New Haven, CT: Yale University Press, 1990), ch. 2. Aikin's *Essay on the Application of Natural History to Poetry* (Warrington: W. Eyres for J. Johnson, 1777) further highlights this sense of the compatibility between the humanities and sciences.

22. G. S. Rousseau, 'Medicine and the Muses: an approach to literature and medicine', in Marie Mulvey Roberts and Roy Porter (eds.), *Literature and Medicine during the Eighteenth Century* (London and New York, NY: Routledge, 1993), 23–57 (33). See also *Enlightenment Borders: Pre- and Post-Modern Discourses Medical, Scientific* (Manchester University Press, 1991). Roberts and Porter stress that if 'a bifurcation between literature and medicine began to occur in the eighteenth century, a disaffection developing in the face of increased professional specialisation, the process was slow and partial. Before 1800, medical writers did not commonly disown the literary text, nor vice versa' (*Literature and Medicine during the Eighteenth Century*, 1).

23. Rousseau, 'Medicine and the Muses', 33.

24. During Aikin's student days at Warrington, the three elected tutors were John Taylor in divinity, John Holt in mathematics and natural philosophy and John Aikin the elder in languages and *belles-lettres*, with the latter replacing Taylor as tutor of divinity in 1761 and Joseph Priestley engaged for *belles-lettres*.

According to Turner, all four tutors were profoundly knowledgeable of the Greek and Roman classics and quoted substantially from classical sources in their lectures ('Historical Account of the Warrington Academy', 8: 87–8, 165, 171–2, 227).

25. Neil Vickers, *Coleridge and the Doctors 1795–1806* (Oxford University Press, 2004), 20.

26. Ivan Waddington, *The Medical Profession in the Industrial Revolution* (Dublin: Gill & Macmillan, 1984), 14.

27. Vickers, *Coleridge and the Doctors*, 20.

28. Porter, *Greatest Benefit to Mankind*, 290.

29. Lisbeth Haakonssen, *Medicine and Morals in the Enlightenment: John Gregory, Thomas Percival, and Benjamin Rush* (Amsterdam and Atlanta, GA: Rodopi, 1997), 200.

30. Haakonssen, *Medicine and Morals in the Enlightenment*, 201. One must also note the general respect paid at Edinburgh to the example of Herman Boerhaave, who originally studied divinity and championed a holistic approach to medicine against what he saw as the negative impact of Cartesian philosophy. For more on Boerhaave and the Edinburgh medical school, see Andrew Cunningham, 'Medicine to Calm the Mind: Boerhaave's Medical System, and Why It Was Adopted in Edinburgh', in Andrew Cunningham and Roger French (eds.), *The Medical Enlightenment of the Eighteenth Century* (Cambridge University Press, 1990), 40–66. Aikin sent an article he had written on Boerhaave to Haygarth in 1800 (Aikin, *Memoir of John Aikin*, 131).

31. For more on eighteenth-century medicine and the culture of sensibility, see G. J. Barker-Benfield, *The Culture of Sensibility: Sex and Society in Eighteenth-century Great Britain* (Chicago, IL and London: University of Chicago Press, 1992), ch. 1.

32. Haakonssen, *Medicine and Morals in the Enlightenment*, 70.

33. McCarthy and Kraft, *Poems of Anna Letitia Barbauld*, 252.

34. White takes a similar point from Aikin's essay on comedy, remarking that it 'treats the comic genre as a curative moral agent that corrects communal vices and other shortcomings by holding them up to ridicule' ('The "Joineriana": Anna Barbauld, the Aikin Family Circle, and the Dissenting Public Sphere', 521).

35. John Wiltshire, *Samuel Johnson in the Medical World: The Doctor and the Patient* (Cambridge University Press, 1991), 158. Wiltshire narrates the history of this tradition through the Ancients and into the writings of Francis Bacon, and, ultimately, Johnson. As Turner notes, a recurring focus of interest for Aikin's father at Warrington was 'natural religion and ethics'. We are told that whichever 'plan he pursued, he amplified upon his written notes, by copious extemporary enlargements, enlivened by quotations of the most spirited passages of the ancient poets and moralists' and included in his curriculum 'the philosophical and ethical treatises of Plato, Aristotle, Epictetus, Marcus Antoninus and Max. Tyrius' and 'the philosophical and moral treatises of

Cicero and Seneca, Tacitus, the two Plinys and Quintilian' ('Historical Account of the Warrington Academy', 8: 165, 167, 165).

36. John Aikin, *Letters from a Father to his Son*, 2 vols. (London: J. Johnson, 1793–1800), I, 188.

37. John Armstrong, *The Art of Preserving Health*, ed. John Aikin (Walpole, NH: Thomas & Thomas, 1808), 9.

38. Matthew Green, *The Spleen, and other Poems*, ed. John Aikin (London: Thomas Cadell and William Davies, 1796), xii.

39. *Ibid.*, ix.

40. John and Anna Aikin, *Miscellaneous Pieces in Prose*, 14.

41. While the play's title calls to mind sentimental comedy, remarks in 'On Comedy' mitigate this impression. If the assessment of sentimental comedy is less harsh than Goldsmith's in *An Essay on the Theatre* (1773), there is a like desire to recapture the wit, without the viciousness, of what Goldsmith calls 'laughing comedy' (*ibid.*, 21). Barbauld's references in her 'Prologue' to purging and bleeding, both medical treatments originally derived from humoural theory, hint at a possible debt to the comedy of humours. David Garrick notably invokes medical language in the prologue of *She Stoops to Conquer* (1773), offering Goldsmith's play as 'five draughts *prepar'd*' (36) to cure the excesses of sentimental comedy. Oliver Goldsmith, *Collected Works of Oliver Goldsmith*, ed. Arthur Friedman, 5 vols. (Oxford: Clarendon Press, 1966), v, 103. This is my source for Goldsmith throughout.

42. John Aikin, *Food for National Penitence* (London: J. Johnson, 1793), 6, 4. While it has been argued that the concept of the body politic essentially died in eighteenth-century political writing, the persisting influence of classical republicanism can be seen as infusing at least some ongoing life into it.

43. *Ibid.*, 4.

44. *Ibid.*, 5–6 (6).

45. *Ibid.*, 7, 8 (8).

46. John Sekora remains a standard source on the classical and biblical origins of luxury as an idea and its history into the eighteenth century. He notes the persisting use of 'some metaphor like contagion' to characterize the spread of luxury (*Luxury: The Concept in Western Thought, Eden to Smollett* (Baltimore, MD: Johns Hopkins University Press, 1977), 49). Other eighteenth-century literary physicians to connect luxury with disease include Goldsmith, notably in *The Deserted Village* (1770), ll. 387–94. In Smollett's *The Expedition of Humphry Clinker* (1770), which Sekora discusses at length, Matthew Bramble's fears about catching disease are closely related to his fears about the impact of luxury. Yet Aikin's liberal Dissenting perspective differentiates him from both Goldsmith and Smollett.

47. Aikin, *Food for National Penitence*, 16, 12, 14.

48. Aikin did recognize that classical republican language was not entirely appropriate to characterize the modern medical professional. In ancient times, to preserve the 'honour' of independence people performed services for no other

reward than the title of 'patron'. Similar services would be provided in a modern economy by a professional who was hired or contracted by a client for a fee, with physicians curing people '*for pay*' (*Letters*, II, 181). As such, no physician could claim, properly speaking, to be independent, since he generated an income by contracting his skills and therefore needed to maintain a satisfied client base. Nevertheless, a physician could display independence in his attitude towards established medical authority and, at least to some extent, in his dealings with patients. Aikin seems to have believed that British physicians had historically shown greater independence in both of these respects than foreign physicians (see *Letters*, I, 33–4 and II, 337; *Biographical Memoirs*, 257).

49. Aikin, *Biographical Memoirs*, 30–1.
50. Aikin, *Letters*, II, 138.
51. Aikin, *Biographical Memoirs*, 106, 106, 242.
52. Aikin, *Letters*, II, 19–20.
53. *Ibid.*, 20. There were exceptions, as in the case of Akenside. While licentiates were only officially allowed to practise within seven miles of London, rules were not much enforced. Unlicensed physicians practised everywhere in England, especially in the north. Regardless, for many it was the principle rather than the practice. In his article in Cunningham and French (eds.), *Medical Enlightenment of the Eighteenth Century*, David Harley offers an excellent overview of some of the major professional disputes in eighteenth-century medicine.
54. Noel Parry and José Parry, *The Rise of the Medical Profession: A Study of Collective Social Mobility* (London: Croom Helm, 1976), 104.
55. Haakonssen, *Medicine and Morals in the Enlightenment*, 16. In 'An Enquiry into the Present State of Polite Learning in Europe' (1759), Goldsmith privileges an Oxford or Cambridge over an Edinburgh education, insisting that while Edinburgh cultivates a disposition for learning and good preparation for professional life, only Oxford and Cambridge provide actual learning and inspire greatness (*Collected Works*, I, 333–4).
56. Aikin, *Memoir of John Aikin*, 102.
57. *Ibid.*, 104.
58. *Ibid.*, 103.
59. Eighteenth-century liberal Dissent has often been cited as arising out of Presbyterianism, although Isabel Rivers challenges a straightforward division of early eighteenth-century Dissent into the 'rational and evangelical ... identified ... with Presbyterianism and Congregationalism' respectively, noting that 'in the period up to the beginnings of the Evangelical Revival in the 1730s and 1740s these tendencies were concurrent and interconnected'. She goes on to state that by 'the end of the century there was a gulf between rational dissent on the one hand and evangelicalism in its various manifestations on the other' (*Reason, Grace, and Sentiment: A Study of the Language of Religion and Ethics in England, 1660–1780*, 2 vols., *Volume II: Shaftesbury to Hume* (Cambridge University Press, 2000), 165, 204). In general, rational

Dissenters were marked by more liberal political views than evangelical Dissenters, a number of which opposed the repeal of the Corporation and Test Acts out of fear that this would encourage the spread of hetero-doxy. For more on this subject, see Rivers and Wykes, *Priestley*, 10.

60. John Aikin, *The Spirit of the Constitution and that of the Church of England, Compared* (London: J. Johnson, 1790), 14.

61. G. M. Ditchfield points out the efforts of other rational Dissenters to distance the repeal movement as a whole from allegations of party interest. He finds compelling confirmation that voting on the issue of repeal was not initially divided along party lines, although it was increasingly so following the French Revolution ('The Parliamentary Struggle over the Repeal of the Test and Corporation Acts, 1787–90', *English Historical Review*, 89 (1974), 551–77; 'Debates on the Test and Corporation Acts, 1787–90', *Bulletin of the Institute of Historical Research*, 50(121) (1977), 69–81).

62. Aikin, *Letters*, I, 174. Elsewhere, Aikin picks up the analogy between med-icine and morality in urging his son that 'one whose office it is to apply *medicine to the mind*, must, as well as the physician of the body, conquer his reluctance to give temporary pain, for the sake of affording lasting benefit' (*ibid.*, I, 12).

63. *Ibid.*, I, 174–5, 177.

64. For this summary I am indebted to James A. Harris' *Of Liberty and Necessity: The Free Will Debate in Eighteenth-century British Philosophy* (Oxford: Clarendon Press, 2005). Ruth Watts sees Aikin specifically influenced by Hartleyan associationism in his frequent analogies between physical and mental disease and view that 'bad characters are almost inevitably created out of bad conditions' (*Gender, Power and the Unitarians in England 1760–1860* (London and New York, NY: Longman, 1998), 41).

65. Aikin, *Letters*, I, 177–81.

66. Aikin, *An Address to the Dissidents*, 18.

67. Aikin, *Letters*, I, 181–2 (182).

68. *Ibid.*, 182–3. The phrase Aikin seems to be thinking of is 'quibus nec vitia nostra nec remedia pati possumus perventum est', translated as 'when we can endure neither our vices nor their cure' (*Livy*, ed. and trans. B. O. Foster, vol. I (New York, NY: G. P. Putnam's Sons, 1925), 6–7).

69. Aikin, *Letters*, I, 183.

70. Aikin, *Memoir of John Aikin*, 102.

71. *Ibid.*, 129. Richard H. Shryock writes that 'medicine had long been viewed as the scientific field *par excellence*. In the eighteenth century, however, one encounters the view that this field was failing to keep pace with the physical sciences' ('The Rise of Modern Scientific Medicine', *Studies in the History of Science* (Port Washington, NY: Kennikat Press, 1941), 55).

72. Cunningham and French (eds.), *Medical Enlightenment of the Eighteenth Century*, 3. In the same collection, see also Adrian Wilson, 'The Politics of Medical Improvement in Early Hanoverian London', 4–39; Francis M. Lobo,

'John Haygarth, Smallpox and Religious Dissent in Eighteenth-century England', 217–53.
73. Aikin, *Letters*, 1, 233, 94.
74. Anne Janowitz, 'Memoirs of a Dutiful Niece: Lucy Aikin and Literary Reputation', in Glen and Hamilton, *Repossessing the Romantic Past*, 81.
75. Rodgers, *Georgian Chronicle*, 55.
76. Fulton, 'The Warrington Academy (1757–1786)', 50–80 (68).

CHAPTER 5

'Outline maps of knowledge': John Aikin's geographical imagination

Stephen Daniels and Paul Elliott

In the memoir of her father John Aikin, published in 1823 shortly after his death, Lucy Aikin wrote of *England Delineated* (1788), a textbook 'for the use of young persons', that 'few of his works were executed with more pleasure to himself than this':

> [G]eographical and topographical pursuits were always congenial to his taste; in its least attractive forms, knowledge of this kind was welcome to his mind, and when embellished by the charms of eloquence and poetry, a source of high delight. I have often witnessed the admiration with which he perused the description of the site of Constantinople, and the other geographical delineations traced by the masterly hand of Gibbon; and the enthusiasm with which he dwelt upon the splendid *panoramas* of the ancient world exhibited by Milton in his Paradise Lost, and Paradise Regained.[1]

And commenting on her father's *Geographical Delineations, or a Compendious View of the Natural and Political State of all Parts of the Globe* (1806), a more advanced text aimed at those finishing their education, she noted 'that it is a leading object of this performance to communicate those enlarged views respecting the globe and its divisions, with their various occupations, which may rightly be called *the philosophy of geography*'. While the material was compiled from a range of sources, it was shaped by a style expressing the '*soul* and *spirit* of the work'. 'Leaving abstruse theories and difficult problems on one hand, and dry details on the other', the author sought 'a middle course' in which 'the useful and the agreeable' combined to trace '*outline maps* of knowledge'.[2]

The research for this chapter was funded with support from an AHRC research project 'A Place in the Nation: Geography, Education and Citizenship in Georgian England'. The authors wish to thank the following for their comments on earlier drafts: Emma Major, Robert Mayhew, Julie Sanders and Charles Withers.

This chapter focuses on *England Delineated* and *Geographical Delineations* as cultural texts to consider the character and scope of John Aikin's geographical imagination. We explore Aikin's formulation of geography as an educational discipline, raising the subject from its elementary role in Locke's pedagogy to a form of lifelong learning. This involved extending the scope of the subject, drawing on erudite works which surveyed the natural and social relations of land and life and charted the development of the habitable world, deploying a range of writings, notably topographical poetry and natural history. We consider exchanges between Aikin's writings and those of other members of his family circle, particularly with his sister, Anna Letitia Barbauld, and children, Lucy and Arthur Aikin. Geography will form the perspective as well as subject of this chapter, in considering the significance for his writings of the places where John Aikin lived and worked.

WARRINGTON

Trained for a medical career, from early adulthood John Aikin pursued the literary career at which he eventually made a good living. Lucy Aikin's memoir emphasizes the limited employment opportunities her father faced as a practising physician, although, as Kathryn Ready (Chapter 4 in this volume) points out, his literary and medical vocations were intertwined, with we might add his geographical vocation, in a concern with the relations of environment and health. In and from Warrington, Aikin cultivated an intellectual circle, including tutors at Warrington Academy (where he did some occasional lecturing) notably Joseph Priestley, William Enfield and John Reinholt Forster, his sister, Anna Letitia, and, more widely, members of the liberal intelligentsia based in Manchester and its region.

At Warrington's Eyres Press, Aikin supervised the production of Thomas Pennant's influential *Tours* of Scotland and later editions of his *British Zoology*. Pennant counted Aikin's father John as an authoritative source on both landscape and literature in his network of correspondents, notably topographical poetry and antiquarian and industrial sites in Lancashire, and the son sustained the correspondence, sending Pennant information on natural history, particularly birds.[3] Pennant's authority is cited in a number of John Aikin the younger's own writings. The *Tours* of Scotland are repeatedly referenced in Aikin's translations of Tacitus' works which focus on northern Europe, in matters of soil, climate and domestic virtue, its ancient cultural geography providing a genealogy for modern Protestant civility.[4] Dedicated to Pennant, Aikin's *An Essay on the Application of Natural History to Poetry* (1777) is a manifesto for the renovation of descriptive poetry 'which has degenerated into a kind of phraseology'.[5] Not only had authors turned away from observing and describing the natural world, but they lagged behind developments in natural philosophy, from botany to astronomy, their verse insulting any 'person of liberal education'.[6] Aikin offers an approved canon of ancient and modern works, including botanically reliable passages from Virgil's *Georgics* and Milton's description of the Garden of Eden, 'that piercing and intelligent survey through real objects'.[7] Above all the book upholds the work of Scottish Presbyterian poet James Thomson (1700–48) – Pennant referred to him in *British Zoology* as 'the naturalist's poet' – and calls for 'a second Thomson to arise'.[8] Thomson's long poem *The Seasons* (1730) is at the centre of Aikin's *Essay*. With its global range and local detail, and an aerial vantage point, from high latitudes, *The Seasons* may be read as transcending many of its proprietorial and party political viewpoints (notably the landscape gardens of Whig noblemen), and realigning the axis of European historical geography from a southern to a northern empire of knowledge. The defining trope of poetic imagination in Thomson's poem is not merely aerial but ornithological, 'the migration of birds' affording 'uncommon scope for grand and original painting in natural history [and] copious matter for philosophical and moral reflexion'.[9] Aikin's book was published by Joseph Johnson, of St Paul's Churchyard, London, who issued works by various members of the Warrington circle, notably Priestley in his list of liberal and reformist texts.

Some of the principles of Aikin's *Essay*, including its focus on birds and circling bird's-eye views, and the wings of 'fancy' as a vehicle of geographical knowledge, are evident in the first published work by his sister Anna Letitia. 'By his persuasion and assistance', Lucy Aikin notes in the memoir of her aunt, 'her Poems were selected, revised, and arranged for publication: and when all these preparations were completed, finding that she still hesitated and lingered – like the parent bird who pushes off its young to their first flight, he procured the paper, and set the press to work on his own authority'.[10] Published by Johnson in December 1772, with a date on the title page of 1773, they earned immediate critical acclaim, making their author a national literary figure. One of the long poems *The Invitation* focuses on the waterways between Manchester and Liverpool, including the astonishing sight of a new aqueduct at Barton Bridge:

> The traveller with pleasing wonder sees
> The white sail gleaming thro' the dusky trees;
> And views the alter'd landscape with surprise,
> And doubts the magic scenes which round him rise.
> Now, like a flock of swans, above his head
> Their woven wings the flying vessels spread   (67–72)[11]

Miscellaneous Pieces in Prose (1773), a collection of moral and literary essays jointly authored by John and Anna Letitia Aikin, explores the claims of rational and affective values in the pursuit of knowledge. 'The Canal and the Brook, a Reverie' describes an allegorical landscape based in actuality, the conjunction of the Duke of Bridgewater's canal crossing the aqueduct over the brook which was diverted into an underground passage. The dialogue between the Genius of the Canal and the Deity of the Stream is not merely between the claims of beauty and use, taste and commerce, but between the enduring power of the slow and weedy brook to fertilize meadows and afford botanists 'a pleasing speculation of the works of nature' and the temporary influence of the canal and its infrastructure to hasten wealth and commerce before they become as useless and ruinous as 'monuments of Roman grandeur'. A brook and cottage, sites which are confined and limiting in much picturesque discourse, are in these essays, as elsewhere in Aikin family writings, an extrovert domestic landscape, the threshold of a searching geographical imagination, at once finely detailed and wide ranging, analytical and devotional.[12]

PALGRAVE

The next collaborative venture between the Aikin siblings was set in train by Anna Letitia's marriage to Warrington alumnus Rochemont Barbauld and his taking up a ministry in the village of Palgrave in Suffolk on condition that the congregation sponsor a boys' school. This was a progressive, boarding academy, well situated on the Suffolk–Norfolk boundary for the educational catchment of East Anglia's Dissenting community, and drawing in pupils from further afield in Britain. These came from various denominations, from parents who wanted a liberal education for trade and the professions, including, it turned out, the literary profession a number of former pupils pursued. Following the example of Dissenting academies, and particularly Priestley's teaching at Warrington, and of its canonical texts such as Isaac Watts' *The Knowledge of the Heavens and the Earth*, Barbauld developed geography as a complementary subject to history as a framework of learning and citizenship. She did so as both an elementary and erudite subject, with an emphasis on geography as a graphically literary rather than mathematical discipline, extending its performative aspect from practising with instruments in the class or field, to reciting verse and putting on plays.[13] Lucy Aikin noted that her aunt relieved the dryness of a study 'seldom rendered interesting to children, by so many lively strokes of description, and such luminous and attractive views of the connexion of this branch of knowledge with the revolutions of empires, with national manners, and with the natural history of animals, that these impressive lectures were always remembered by her auditors less among their tasks than their pleasures'.[14]

A surviving fragment of notes on the Islamic world indicates the range of her lectures, with references to a series of works in Latin, from translations of the medieval scholar Ismael Abulfeda, 'skilled in medicine philosophy & Poetry, but chiefly known by his hist[l] and geograph[l] works', to a 'lately pub[d] . . . Geo[y] of Egypt' by J. D. Michaelis. Barbauld found little use for standard teaching books. She made use of literary and historical texts, maps, field study, and, particularly, poetry, which she found 'impresses both geography and history in a most agreeable manner upon those who are fond of it'. Among the regular parcels of texts she ordered from Joseph Johnson's shop in 1783 were '12 Thompson's [sic] seasons, small & cheap edition, but good type'. Barbauld wasn't the first geography teacher to use verse as a way of memorizing geographical facts, but she did so as a way of increasing accomplishment in language as well as empirical knowledge, in short rhyming stanzas: 'Animals, and their Countries', 'India', 'Lapland', 'Canada' and 'Constantinople'.[15]

In 1777, after three years of marriage, and with no prospect of children with whom 'to follow our own plans and schemes of education', the Barbaulds adopted John Aikin's third child Charles, a 2-year-old, to raise as their own. Barbauld turned the adoption to account by publishing a series of primers, *Lessons for Children* which were issued in four volumes covering the ages 2 to 4, issued between 1778 and 1779, which kept pace with the boy's growth. Published by Joseph Johnson at 6 pence each volume, *Lessons for Children* introduced a number of innovations explained in the preface to the first. The books were designed for 'the eye of a child' and were small enough to fit a child's hand, using '*good paper, a clear and large type, and large spaces*'. Unlike primers which jumped from words to scripture, a moral world is progressively unfolded through *Lessons for Children*, through increasingly extensive excursions from home. Along the way the child learns its bearings with a compass in the garden, assesses topography, estimates perspective and scale, observes the stars above its head and the rocks and minerals beneath its feet. Various symbolic systems, including maps, are introduced and tested through ground truths, as are connections of near and far, the local and global, the cornfields and pasture which provide the child's breakfast of bread and milk, the vines and canefields his raisins and sugar. The overall effect of *Lessons for Children* is to describe a cosmopolitan countryside, in interchangeable images of the book and of nature, feeding body and mind, of the open page and the open landscape as lettered spaces of learning, and a progressive province of citizenship.[16]

John Aikin's authorship of geographically framed teaching texts was prompted by the ages of his own children and the lessons he gave them at home, including those based on botanic observations that turned the 'plodding rounds of business into excursions of pleasure' and a seasonal account he kept of names and habitats of plants.[17] *The Calendar of Nature* (1784), dedicated to his 'dear sister', is modelled on the opening lesson of *Lessons for Children of Three Years Old*, 'where, in a very entertaining manner, you give a brief description of the several months, formed of some of the most striking circumstances attending each'.[18] Whereas the 'little boy' of Barbauld's text stays close to home, walking no further than the garden and neighbouring fields to build up his vocabulary, the 'young persons' of Aikin's, 10 to 14 years old of both sexes, are given a wide ranging survey of the circumstances of the seasons, albeit offering more of a national than an international vision of the natural world. This draws on a compilation of 'English books' including works of natural history, rural economy and topographical poetry, notably Thomson's *The Seasons*, to produce a pastoral vision of rural community, one threatened by the mean and narrow world of enclosure. So the 'pleasing harvest-scene' of Thomson's poem 'is beheld in its perfection only in the open-field counties, where the sight can take in at once an uninterrupted extent of land waving with corn, and a multitude of people engaged in the various parts of the labour. It is a prospect equally delightful to the eye and the heart, and which ought to inspire every sentiment of benevolence to our fellow creatures, and gratitude to our Creator.'[19] Here is a bookish view of the world, even in places a nostalgically fanciful one, but one that sought to ground language in empirical description, to reform teaching which focused on Latinate rhetoric not English reality, and to reconnect the word with the world. On the page, and on the ground, *The Calendar of Nature* is a world of substance, space, structure and shape, of typography on the page as well as topography on the ground, as it takes its readers across social and religious boundaries in matters of language as well as landscape, introducing them to 'words of every rank and denomination'.[20] As a scientific text on the weather, the book proved somewhat unreliable at the time it was published. 'My poor *Calendar* has appeared at an unfortunate time for its credit', Aikin wrote to his sister as he observed 500 ships at anchor waiting for an unseasonable wind to change, 'and I doubt it will be reckoned as fallacious as [the satirical almanac] Poor Robin'.[21]

YARMOUTH

John Aikin left Lancashire in 1784. Many of his intellectual circle had departed Warrington (the Academy was closed in 1783) and he was finding it impossible to establish a medical practice, in part, he reckoned, because the density of large manufacturing towns restricted rather than opened up opportunities, promoting narrow and factional interests and attracting 'men of established reputation'.[22] He submitted a thesis, on infections in childbirth, for a doctor's degree to the University of Leyden, the leading European centre of anatomy, and setting out for his examination compiled a diary of the road and boat trip through the towns and country-side of Flanders and Holland. This noted details of topography, natural history and economy and visible denominational distinctions, for example the combination of religious glamour and commercial gloom in Catholic Antwerp.

Learning of the departure of one of the two physicians in Yarmouth, and the promise of patronage, Aikin moved his family to the town. Yarmouth seemed more remote than Warrington, as the region was suffering from the decline of its textile industry as that of Lancashire was rapidly developing, but the port was visibly connected with northern Europe (Dutch fleets filling the harbour), and the countryside and coast offered a rich harvest of natural and social observation, from the habitat of plants, to the dwellings of the poor. Aikin kept up his connections with Lancashire, corresponding with colleagues in Liverpool and Manchester (where he was elected to the newly established Philosophical and Literary Society upon reading a paper on the effects on health of passing winter in high northern latitudes). Aikin's sister left East Anglia as he arrived. Having made sufficient money from teaching and text books, the Barbaulds quitted the school at Palgrave to travel through France but brother and sister kept up a close correspondence (which Aikin planned to publish) exchanging letters of topographical description, and with it rational and affective perspectives on the scenery. In one letter describing the grottoes of Auxelles, which 'had the appearance of a most magnificent Gothic church', sister told brother that had he been there, 'you would have seen it with a more philosophical eye', and would have been able to explain the process of petrifaction.[23] Aikin continued to write for publication, at first in a small way, submitting pieces to the *Gentleman's Magazine* on English maritime plants and an 'Apology for Literary Physicians', and then in 1788 authoring *England Delineated*.[24]

'England Delineated'

The 'principal object' of *England Delineated*, as the preface puts it, is 'to make my young countrymen better acquainted than they are usually found to be with their native land'.[25] If this was a conventional preamble to topographical texts of the time, Aikin's geographical instruction was more liberally than loyally patriotic. Like many Dissenters, Aikin's attachment to the Hanoverian regime, and its foreign wars, was put into question by the progress of hostilities with the American colonies. Initially 'an ardent rather than discriminating lover of his country', according to his daughter's memoir, Aikin became 'a strenuous supporter of the cause of civil liberty, in whatever quarter of the world her banner was displayed'.[26] The mid-1780s witnessed a growing, non-sectarian consensus that England's geography, particularly its prudently managed agrarian landscapes, displayed liberal and affective virtues for all the world to see. In 1785 Joseph Johnson published *The Task*, a long poem by the evangelical Anglican William Cowper, hymning the virtues of cottage and gardens – well stocked with books as well as plants – as the epicentre of panoramic terrestrial and celestial knowledge, and a vantage point from which to survey the virtues and vices of the world. Aikin asked his Chester friend, William Haygarth if he had read Cowper: 'If you have, you will join with him in saying "England, with all thy faults I love thee still, my country!" [. . .] Yes, I do think upon the whole ours a very tolerable country, nor would I quit it even to be a Dutch or American republican.'[27] It was an opportune time to publish *England Delineated*. Government and monarchy were unpopular after the debacle of the American war and calls for limited civil and political reforms were attracting considerable support. The culture of Rational Dissent, with its capacity to articulate a range of liberal opinion, was highly influential, notably through Joseph Johnson's expanding list of publications, which ranged from children's primers to adult periodicals and included among its authors sober evangelicals, political radicals and latitudinarian Anglicans.[28]

The market for geographical works was lucrative and rapidly expanded with both general and specialist works. These included books and magazine articles of many kinds, travels, local topography, global geography, also atlases, globes and maps in many forms from jigsaw puzzles and games to sewing samplers.[29] Teaching texts catered for both commercial schools and for more humanist curricula; many were written by headmasters of a range of schools whose differences in regional location and denominational politics were projected in the geographies they described.[30] There was a close connection, sometimes an overlap, with the market for history, with authors such as William Guthrie and John Pinkerton compiling texts in both subjects.[31] Texts travelled, with translations from French works, and versions customized for the North American market. Quality control was an issue for many reviewers with new editions of expensive erudite works criticized for careless transcriptions of information and statistics, and crude cut-and-paste production. Many teaching texts were subject to little revision in the light of changes in the world or attempted to make their reliable findings appealing to young people. In 1783 Johnson published a fourteenth edition of a standard text, Dufresnoy's *Geography for Children*, a book first published a half century earlier in French and English, and whose catechism of facts and moral digressions remained almost unchanged, even in an English version which gave priority to Britain.[32] When geography books were made more appealing, they gave the impression that the subject was facile, more entertainment than instruction. Robert Davidson's *The Elements of Geography* (1787) reckoned geography was 'the easiest Science in the world', requiring 'no more Time or Pains than to play a Game at Marbles every Day'. He advised his readers to read 'one Page a Day, with a Sixpenny Map of the Globe' and to 'persuade your parents to reward your Diligence with a dissected Map of England, which you may put together in five Minutes'.[33]

As the preface to Aikin's *England Delineated* put it, while there were increasing numbers of 'Tours through England, and accounts of English Geography' they were mostly:

works of a very low order in literature, abounding with gross faults both of plan and execution ... Tedious descriptions of objects, either absolutely trivial in themselves, or interesting only to readers of a particular turn; relations become totally erroneous through length of time, and transmitted, unchanged, from one successive compilation to another; weak and illiberal partialities, local and national, with inelegancies and vulgarisms of every kind; – these are defects from which none of them that I have seen can be called tolerably free; and which certainly render them little proper to be put into the hands of youth.[34]

England Delineated was carefully designed for its age group, easy to hold and easy on the eye too, spaciously printed with short paragraphs. Its title, too, was carefully chosen, since the term 'delineation' assumed a strong currency in the eye-witness culture of the eighteenth century, in the documentation and display of a number of sites of the material world, including the body, artefacts, buildings, landscapes and regions, and a convention that enlightened knowledge was map-like, a spatial display of clearly ordered information.[35] This distinguished Aikin's production from others available. Richard Gough's 1780 review of geographical descriptions of Britain, for instance, had found many wanting, with few based on newly observed evidence, and some unintelligible. The bulk of county topographies comprised 'incorrect pedigrees, futile etymologies, verbose disquisitions, crowds of epitaphs, lists of landowners, and such farrago, thrown together without method, unanimated by reflections, and delivered in the most uncouth and horrid style'; in this wilderness of words, there was little evidence of 'the face of the country'.[36] The last book entitled *Geography of England* had been issued anonymously in 1744 and 'done in the manner of' Gordon's *Geographical Grammar* first issued in 1704. This dealt with counties in alphabetical order, with the bulk of material on their ecclesiastical and legal history and prehistory, large sections on Oxford and Cambridge Colleges, and scarcely anything on commerce or current affairs.[37] Until such time as there was 'an accurate and comprehensive account of the present state of these kingdoms', undertaken as a collaborative project, Aikin's *England Delineated* offered 'a general view of each county [in England and Wales] with respect to its geography, products natural and artificial, commerce, towns, and other principal objects, as might impress upon the mind a distinct notion of its discriminating character and relative consequence'.[38] The book was a framework, for work in progress, an outline map of knowledge to be filled in with further information by the young reader as they learned more from other sources about the places concerned.

There were no actual maps in *England Delineated*, perhaps because cartography of adequate quality could not be affordably included; the descriptions of physical features, rivers, coasts, hills and so on were left 'somewhat diffuse' to encourage reading 'with a good map in hand'. Taking the illustrative role of maps, and impressing topography on the reader, are frequent passages of English poetry associated with particular places, by Milton, Drayton, Cowper, Akenside, Gray and Pope, and most frequently, by John Dyer. The states of cultivation, trade and manufacture had undergone so many rapid changes in the preceding years that as well as consulting 'some of the most modern' tours through particular districts and histories of towns and counties – for example by Arthur Young – Aikin requested written information from people residing in various parts of the country, although the response rate varied and coverage was uneven. Thus the account of the county of Gloucester was 'almost entirely as it is printed' the work of Robert Bransby Cooper of Dursley, lately a resident of Yarmouth. Similarly, the accounts of Welsh counties and southern coasts borrow 'freely' from the published and unpublished tours of Thomas Pennant.[39] The view of Norfolk, with an especially detailed account of the country around Yarmouth, its saltmarsh, broads, creeks and channels, is clearly based on Aikin's own observations.

Two subjects which dominate many topographical texts of the time are conspicuously absent from *England Delineated*: antiquities and aristocratic seats. Historical matter is restricted to relatively recent, reliably authenticated events that by their association with some particular place 'might be forcibly impressed upon the memory of a young reader'. These were largely sites of struggles for English liberty, such as Runnymede, Cromwell's birthplace Huntington and civil war battlefields. The few castles that get a mention are those renovated in peacetime for modern uses, such as Bamborough, 'remarkable for the humane purpose' of 'the reception and relief of shipwrecked mariners'. Another instance of Aikin's subtly reformist geography is provided by his quotation – taken from its transcription in Pennant's *The Journey from Chester to London* (1782) – of the verse by Foxite Whig Richard Fitzpatrick, inscribed 'on a column where the old castle stood' at Ampthill, Bedfordshire to commemorate the place where Catherine of Aragon sojourned during her divorce:

> Yet Freedom hence her radiant banner wav'd,
> And Love aveng'd a realm by priests enslav'd;
> From Catherine's wrongs a nation's bliss was spread
> And Luther's light from Henry's lawless bed.

If noblemen's parks and pleasure grounds are largely overlooked, some useful aristocratic projects are singled out, especially in the Midlands and the north, notably the Duke of Portland's woodland plantations of Nottinghamshire and the Duke of Bridgewater's canal scheme in Lancashire.[40]

The book's focus is on works which developed England's favoured resources of fertile lands, navigable waterways and frost-free ports. While 'no country has a smaller proportion of land absolutely steril and incapable of culture', it was one developed by a progressive history of woodland clearance, marshland drainage and animal and vegetable domestication and improvement. 'Favoured by nature', the country was 'greatly indebted also to industry; for, if this powerful spring were to slacken, the wild wood, the tangled thicket, and the pathless morass, would again cover the land'. While there were tracts of lofty mountains, barren moors and heaths, these only served to highlight 'so many agreeable scenes' of cultivation and pasture, particularly in the open-field regions. Moreover many mountainous regions 'contribute greatly to the wealth and advantage of the whole, by the mineral treasures with which they are amply furnished' and former moorland and heathland was being improved and cultivated.[41]

The sequence of counties in *England Delineated* foregrounds the country's progressive geography. It begins with a group of six in the north, including the modern industrial power bases of Lancashire and Yorkshire and the four bordering Wales, including the traditional agrarian heartland of Herefordshire as well as the mining and metalliferous districts of Shropshire. Rivers and waterways, especially new canal networks, carried readers across county boundaries. A unifying principle is provided by frequent extracts from John Dyer's poem *The Fleece* (1757), which traces Britain's wealth through wool as it follows the fleece from the pastures of the Welsh borderland to the manufactories of Yorkshire, to the export of bales from London throughout the globe. The extract on the title page moves from the 'spacious flocks of sheep' which adorn Britannia's paradise to 'towns superb of busy trade / And ports magnific'. Key passages from the poem are quoted in accounts of twelve counties, representative of all eight of the book's regions: Yorkshire, Herefordshire, Leicestershire, Worcestershire, Gloucestershire, Cambridgeshire, Surrey, Wiltshire, Devon, Montgomeryshire, Cardiganshire and Brecknockshire. Yet while Aikin cites Dyer's hymn to fen drainage, he nonetheless provides a remarkably sympathetic view of the 'fenny country' in its 'native state' – a place of 'fish and water-fowl', notable especially for its many birds.[42]

County culture is further undercut by the treatment of many county towns, the very topos of unreformed governance, despite the commercial importance of some places. Hereford's role as a major river port for a region extending into Wales is overlooked; it is an 'ancient decayed place' symbolized by its recently collapsed cathedral, 'in danger of speedy ruin'. Leicester is harshly judged, its industrial performance in textiles contrasted with the rich sheep farming of the county; the town is 'much fallen off from its former magnitude', with its trade 'nearly stationary; which may be a good deal imputed to a want of that spirit of improvement which has so much advanced many other trading places'. Not all flourishing commercial towns are praised unreservedly. If Manchester's centrality in the cotton trade is the focus of an industrial region extending in various directions, over many counties, as far as Furness, Derby and Halifax, it is lamented that one of the main branches of Liverpool's commerce, part of the transatlantic trade for cotton, is the traffic in human slaves. The county structure of the book had, as the text admitted, the effect of reducing the importance of London and precluding an adequate account of metropolitan transactions.[43]

England Delineated was issued in six subsequent editions. The 'considerably improved' third edition of 1795 included information, some statistical, from the Board of Agriculture's new *General Views* of each county and some additional passages of poetry, for example on Glamorgan's 'health inspiring gales' by the Unitarian bard Edward Williams, whose *Poems* had been published by Johnson the previous year.[44] The book was printed on larger pages and included 'outline maps' of each county, as well as the country as a whole, showing main towns and principal physical features such as hills, forests and waterways, including canals. *Scotland Delineated* by the literary scholar Robert Heron, first published in Edinburgh in 1791, was intended as a companion volume: 'ENGLAND has lately been delineated by an able hand; and the present work is an attempt to complete the description of our Island, on a plan somewhat similar.' Drawing on the Scottish tours of Thomas Pennant, as well as up-to-date maps and surveys, the book was intended to increase knowledge of northern Britain, unknown territory for 'many of the inhabitants of England, and not a few even in the metropolis of Scotland'.[45]

LONDON

Aikin was effectively exiled from Yarmouth by his response to two events which deepened sectarian divisions throughout the country. He warmly welcomed the outbreak of the French Revolution and authored two pamphlets fiercely criticizing the Commons' rejection of the bill to repeal the Corporation and Test Acts which excluded Dissenters from full citizenship. With one exception, Aikin was shunned by the town's Anglican clergy 'whose literary acquirements and polished manners' had made them his favourite company; the Tories who controlled the corporation and much of the town's commerce withdrew from supporting his practice, and invited another physician to the town.[46] In 1791 Priestley reported that Dissenters in Yarmouth were procuring arms to protect their property. Early in 1792 the Aikin family left for the City of London, for Broad Street, at the apex of the zone extending north-east through Hackney and Stoke Newington where Dissenters were culturally prominent. Joseph Priestley had already moved to Hackney, upon the opening of the Dissenting academy of New College which enrolled Arthur Aikin among its first intake of students. The Barbaulds were now living in Hampstead where Rochement had taken the ministry of the chapel on Rosslyn Hill and Anna Letitia took private pupils, girls and boys. She resumed her literary career and divided political opinion by publishing *Civic Sermons* which extended the patriotic vision of her children's books.[47]

John Aikin started a medical practice but devoted much of his time to literary pursuits which proved financially a better prospect. 'A physician well introduced and connected told me the other day, that out of a practice of £500 he was obliged to pay £200 for his carriage ... my *booksellers* will never expect me to visit them in my chariot.'[48] Aikin published a volume of his poems, biographies and topographies, including an improved edition of *England Delineated* and a *Description of the Country from Thirty to Forty Miles round Manchester* (1793), a liberal vision of the city and its region as a 'circle of country' covering much of north-west England, articulated by its network of waterways and the circulations of commerce.[49]

Aikin authored two works of liberal education and conduct. *Letters from a Father to His Son* (1793) examines what a progressive 'attachment to country' means in an England infected by the 'little spirit' of local and national loyalism, and explores the degree to which country 'can be regarded in the abstract, as a kind of geographical idea personified', or a mobile form of patriotism vested in a people not a place, such that we might 'owe nothing to England, but ... every thing to Englishmen'.[50] *Evenings at Home* surveys the grounds of learning and citizenship for a younger constituency through reading aloud.

Published by Johnson in six volumes from 1792 to 1796, *Evenings at Home* proved the most influential – and commercially successful – of Aikin's educational works. Patterned on a popular series of instructional stories by the educationalist Stéphanie Félicité Ducrest de St-Aubin, comtesse de Genlis, *Vieilles du Château* (issued in English as *Tales of the Castle*), *Evenings at Home* offered a polite version of home education and was in turn published in France in a French translation in 1797 as *Les Soirées à la Maison*. While the name of the village in *Evenings at Home* is a natural-sounding Beachgrove, the home is a 'mansion-house', and the family are called Fairborne, although this could denote a spiritual rather than social ancestry. Some of the Fairborne children are educated at home, others sent to school (like those of the Aikin household) and the book describes a holiday pastime with their many friends who come to the house, reading fables, stories or dialogues written during the year, ninety-five in all, to be read on thirty evenings to the assembled company, a notionally communal form of authorship. So popular was this instructional entertainment in the neighbourhood that the Fairborne family were urged to 'lay it open to the public'.[51] Despite or perhaps because of its sensational success as a publication, *Evenings at Home* initially divided pedagogical opinion in Britain. In the *Guardian of Education*, the periodical she founded to police suspect textbooks, Sarah Trimmer found the nature appreciation of *Evenings at Home* subversively non-scriptural. However, the work outlasted the sectarian divisions of the period, going on to be issued in thirteen editions in Aikin's lifetime, and remaining in print until the early twentieth century.[52]

According to Lucy Aikin, *Evenings at Home* disclosed 'the whole theory and practice of the author, as far as education is concerned; besides affording notice of his opinions on many highly important topics'. These included current affairs like the increasingly bloody war with France and the slave trade. The whole of *Evenings at Home* 'may be regarded as a commentary upon his two favourite ideas – of teaching *things* rather than *words*; and of early presenting to the mind capacious and diversified views of the great empire of knowledge'. In short pieces which encourage curiosity, observation and reasoning, and conversational exchange, there is a good deal of natural history, some chemistry and mineralogy – especially that informing manufacture – sympathetic sketches of the livelihood of peoples through the world, and homilies on heroic conduct, especially of civil as opposed to military exploits: 'The morality which they inculcate is not that of children merely, but of men and of citizens; it is lofty but not visionary, correct, yet glowing; it forms the mind to discrimination, while it engages the youthful feelings in the cause of truth, of freedom, and of virtue.'[53]

In the first volume of twenty pieces the contributions of John Aikin and Anna Letitia Barbauld are about equal; from volume three John Aikin is the sole author, although all continued to be issued under joint authorship. Lessons for girls tend to be set in the garden, carriage or library, whereas those for boys range more widely, with excursions, sometimes undertaken solely by themselves. There are various sources of ecumenical imagining, a devotional fable based on the Homeric hymn to a self-sustaining Mother Earth as well as rational narratives of resource transformation and peaceful commercial and cultural interdependence, such as the founding myth of Pennsylvania. If the globe forms, as it were, the public sphere of citizenship, the locus of Enlightenment is Europe. In 'A Globe Lecture' papa teaches 'Lucy' about the natural and cultural implications of the world's climatic zones. Human difference was not a matter of race, a man was a man, whether black or white, but the temperate zone was highly favourable for the growth of enlightened societies. If Europe was small compared to other continents, it was the most civilized, containing 'the prime of mankind'.[54]

The longest and most well-known piece, 'Eyes, and No Eyes; or, The Art of Seeing', recasts the trope of the idle and industrious schoolboy as a ramble by two friends across heathland, meadows and cornfields, a recognizably

Norfolk landscape probably drawn from recollections of the Aikin family's sojourn in Yarmouth.[55] Robert considers the ramble very dull, having 'scarcely met with a single person. I had rather by half gone along the turnpike road'. He leaves behind observant William, 'always stopping to look at this thing and that!', who is deeply fascinated by everything from mistletoe to marl pits. A barren place to Robert, the heath alone has been richly interesting to William; in its various parts, high and low, dry and marshy, William has noticed several varieties of plants, some of which he brings home in a handkerchief, as well as several birds, many new to him, and a dead adder killed by turf cutters as they went about their work. The summit of the heath, marked by a windmill, has not only afforded an extensive prospect of the countryside, in which he has counted churches, houses and plantations, but also revealed the ditches and mounds of what look like an ancient British camp. Robert asks his teacher Mr Andrews for a copy of Carey's county map to take next time, 'by which I shall probably be able to make out most of the places'; the teacher is so pleased he promises to accompany the boys next time with his pocket telescope. Extensive overseas travel, we are told, does not necessarily broaden the mind, often the opposite. Mr Andrews has known sailors returning from all quarters of the globe who could 'tell you nothing but the signs of tippling houses they frequented in different ports', to say nothing of the proverbially vacant young noblemen taking the Grand Tour 'without gaining a single idea worth crossing the street for', whereas 'the observing eye and inquiring mind finds matter of improvement and delight in every ramble in town or country'.[56]

In 1796 with Richard Phillips and Joseph Johnson, Aikin launched a new periodical, the *Monthly Magazine and British Register*. This set out to propagate 'liberal principles ... which have been either deserted or virulently opposed by other Periodical Miscellanies'.[57] The magazine offered a mixture of writings: reports on inventions and improvements in practical science, public health, farming and manufacturing, reviews of recent literature, especially travel writing, in French, German and Spanish as well as English, including Humboldt's observations on the Americas, new maps plotting the course of military operations in Europe and Egypt, letters on current affairs, and statistics on population and trade from throughout the world. The magazine also provided a platform for new topographical writings on Britain, including pedestrian excursions which cut across the grain of conventional picturesque tourism, in both register and locations. So great is the geographical coverage of the *Monthly Magazine* that the index of each volume reads like a gazetteer. The Aikin family contributed many pieces to the *Monthly Magazine*. Anna Letitia Barbauld produced poetry, and essays on education which emphasize practice over precept, the circumstantial over the theoretical. The publishing careers of Aikin's children were launched in the *Monthly Magazine*. In its first volume of 1796 it issued extracts from a tour Arthur Aikin took that summer of the mountains, mines and manufacturing sites of north Wales and Shropshire, a tour published by Johnson as a book the following year.[58]

Aikin's own 'Description of the Country About Dorking' was published in the *Monthly Magazine* in 1798, written in the spring of that year when he spent four months recuperating from serious – he thought terminal – illness, which left him unable to walk far, and also 'deeply wounded by "the desolating prospects which the late train of human affairs had presented to the lover of mankind"'.[59] Here in the Surrey downland he searched out the country air to convalesce – and more enriching prospects. Joined on occasion by the Barbaulds, he recovered his health sufficiently to make excursions, on foot and by carriage, to celebrated beauty spots such as Norbury Park and Box Hill as well as searching out lesser-known places. He enjoyed the 'liberty of wandering without obstacle or question through the most cultured scenes' and from elevated vantage points, with the aid of a telescope and map, he scanned as far as the coast. Following shortly after the publication of William Gilpin's account of this locality, the essay gave Aikin the opportunity to further challenge the narrowing of picturesque aesthetics. His vision of landscape deepens and widens the appreciation of its making and meaning, with a knowledge of geological structure and topography – including the role of chalk streams in driving mills and drenching meadows – opening out the locality with philosophical speculation on its prospects.[60]

Similarly, in the opening essay of *A Legacy for Young Ladies* (1826), a posthumous selection of unpublished pieces by Anna Letitia Barbauld edited by Lucy Aikin, such downland countryside is offered as a model of geographical knowledge. The essay takes the form of a letter written to one of the female pupils she was tutoring in Hampstead. The narrator falls asleep in her carriage from Surrey to London and dreams she is travelling through 'an unknown country', and is met by a pilgrim-guide who introduces her to various allegorical magicians personifying forms of knowledge. The first question that Geography asks her is whether she likes panoramas. On replying that she finds them entertaining, she is taken to an eminence and encouraged to look around: 'I did so and beheld the representation of the beautiful vale of Dorking, with Norbury Park and Box-Hill to the north, Riegate [sic] to the east, and Leith tower, with the Surry [sic] hills to the south.' After she has admired the beauty and accuracy of this painting, a vast curtain is drawn up and the view extended to all sides, along the Thames to Oxford and west into Wales, north to York Minster, south to the coast of France, 'with its ports blockaded by our fleets', over Paris and down the Loire. The Atlantic opens to view, as does the Mediterranean, as far east as the Bosphorus, north to the plains of Siberia, south to the Nile Delta, 'and the view extended further and further till the panorama took in the whole globe', the plains of Tartar, and the savannahs of America: 'I seemed to have put a girdle about the earth, and was gratified with an infinite variety of objects, which I thought I never could be weary of contemplating.' Just as visitors to contemporary metropolitan panoramas embarked upon a global tour, so the dreamer travels from Surrey through Europe and the wider world, interlinked through waterways and the oceans by British trade and naval supremacy.[61]

STOKE NEWINGTON

Upon his return from Surrey Aikin moved from Broad Street to the suburban village of Stoke Newington: the 'very Elysian field of non-conformity' as Lucy Aikin called it.[62] Aikin retired from his practice as a physician, except for ministering occasionally to the poor, and did not stray far from his garden, with its aviary and rockery, other than to take a walk in the local countryside: 'Literature was his sole regular occupation, and the domestic scene almost his only sphere of action'.[63] In 1802 Anna Letitia Barbauld moved to Stoke Newington, taking the house opposite John Aikin's, when her husband was appointed minister at Newington Green. John Aikin lived comfortably on the basis of an unexpected bequest from one of his childhood friends, Richard Pulteney, a fellow physician and even keener botanist, and the proceeds from an increasingly productive literary life. The course of the French Revolution, and domestic reaction to it, which saw Joseph Johnson imprisoned and Priestley driven into exile in Pennsylvania, saw Aikin affirm England as a patriotic landscape, whose topographical particulars offered an empirical, anti-theoretical, version of liberal reform. During the brief Peace of Amiens in 1802, he confessed he had not wished to follow some of his friends on a visit to France:

I have now settled into a conviction that England is the best country in the world . . . I am cured of all theoretical ideas of reform . . . we do inhabit a charming country, – that is the truth of it, – and I wish I could visit every part of it . . . The present ardor and unanimity in defence appears to me highly honorable to the national character . . . I confess I wish we had a clearer cause, upon paper, for our hostilities; but the sacred duty of defence against an inveterate foe can never be questioned.[64]

The reform of geography as a form of education became an Aikin family enterprise. As founder editor of the *Annual Review* (1803–8), Arthur Aikin sought to raise the threshold of book reviewing with substantial essays and to include a section on school books. This section regularly bemoaned the standards of textbooks on geography, 'this important topic', chiefly for their tendency to 'burden and harass the memory' with facts, some wrong or pointless. One author evinced 'the most deplorable ignorance of the science which he has undertaken to demonstrate', another sacrificed accuracy for brevity: 'the answer to "What is meant by the diameter of the earth", is "Its thickness"', and 'of Lapland, the only thing mentioned is, that it is divided into three parts'.[65]

The review essay in the section on *Geography* in the first issue of the *Annual Review* was devoted to one book, *Modern Geography*, by the Scottish author John Pinkerton. *Modern Geography* ran to over 1,600 pages in two quarto volumes, with a series of detailed maps. First issued in 1802, when 'Europe at length reposes in universal peace', *Modern Geography* offered a new system for a new century, charting historical–geographical change with the most reliable and recent information. It followed French and German traditions of geographical erudition in its literary and historical range. The sources on Britain included the 1801 census of England and Wales, unpublished papers on mineralogy and botany by Arthur Aikin, as well as copious references to topographical works by Thomas Pennant and John Aikin.[66]

The review essay on *Modern Geography* was authored by Palgrave school's former pupil and the Aikin family's favourite literary son, William Taylor. Taylor declared that geography had now overtaken history as a form of learning:

The one introduces us to the living world, and teaches the arts of intercourse with men: the other leads us by torch-light into catacombs and proses over the pedigree of carcases. The one is all eye, ear, hand, instructing us every instant about important realities: the other is memory or dream rehearsing ideal transactions. Nor is geography alone superior in the intensity, it is also in the diffusiveness of its utility. Here and there a statesman, or a general, borrows from history some precedent of legislation, or some plan of a campaign: but the travels of opulence which polish rulers into philanthropy, and the speculations of commerce, which distribute plenty among myriads, apply to geography for their road book and their chart.[67]

Arthur Aikin collaborated with Pinkerton on a new one-volume, octavo edition of *Modern Geography*, making it affordable and appropriate for schools and young people. First published in 1803, the abridgement involved reducing some of the scientific detail and revising the coverage, cutting material on Asia and making Europe, Africa, America and the West Indies more prominent.[68] This edition was also issued in Paris in a French translation. In the preface to an edition of 1806, written when hostilities had resumed, Pinkerton noted that 'the present abridgment, even at a period of violent animosity, has been preferred to their own elementary books on geography, and adopted in their colleges and academies'.[69]

Lucy Aikin's singular contribution to geographical education was written for Phillips, the leading publisher of school texts and atlases, and comprised a translation of Jauffret's *The Travels of Rolando*, issued in 1804. The four volumes offered a course of geography through following, with the aid of good maps, the adventures through Africa and Asia of a boy from Provence asked by his father to seek his fortune when the family had lost theirs in floods, and inspired to go abroad by the travellers' tales in his father's library. Aikin's preface essays the book's virtues: its form will make it 'more captivating than most geography texts, and more authentic and morally reflective, as well as cheaper, than most volumes of travels':

> Geography, as it has usually been taught, is to every child, one of the most irksome of his studies. It requires from him the most fatiguing exercise of memory and attention, and of its future utility he can scarcely form an idea. To the eye of a naturalist and philosopher, a map of the world is one of the most entertaining and interesting of objects. He peoples it with towns, cities, empires, – the past, the present and the future . . . 'till Contemplation has her fill.' But what is the same map to the eye of a child? What, but a barren waste, a trackless sea, – an unmeaning medley of letters, lines, and flourishes, – of blue and red, green and yellow? Surely then he who plants this waste – steers through this sea and decyphers these flourishes – deserves well both of instructor and pupil, by rendering their mutual task easy to one, pleasant to the other.[70]

Lucy Aikin remained in her father's house for his lifetime, assisting with his writings as well as undertaking her own, especially poems, and contributing to other aspects of the household economy. 'I have written four new lines and planned a great many more', she wrote to her mother in November 1805, 'The Geography is all printed but the index, which my father has made and pasted, with my help. I have weighed out all the bullace and sugar for preserving, with my own hands.'[71] The Geography is John Aikin's *Geographical Delineations, or a Compendious View of the Natural and Political State of all parts of the Globe*, published in 1806.

'Geographical Delineations'

The object of *Geographical Delineations*, according to the preface, was not to supersede 'the common elementary books on Geography' by giving basic principles, which the readership was assumed to know already, 'young persons of both sexes, at the period of finishing their education' and 'those of mature years, who are destitute of time and opportunity for copious research'. Nor was it to supersede 'the more complete systems of that branch of knowledge', notably new editions of Guthrie's *Universal Geography* and Pinkerton's *Modern Geography*. Rather the object of *Geographical Delineations* was to afford:

in a moderate compass, and under an agreeable form, such a view of every thing most important relative to the natural and political state of the world which we inhabit, as may dwell upon the mind in vivid colours, and durably impress it with just and instructive notions. In the prosecution of this design I have been guided by two leading considerations respecting each country – what nature has made it, and what man has made it [. . .] Both together have as much as possible been brought to conspire in forming the characteristic strokes of the sketch.[72]

The quotation on the title page of *Geographical Delineations* (one of the few literary extracts in the text) is from Book III of Milton's *Paradise Regained*, six lines beginning 'Fertile of corn the glebe . . .' In a critical essay prefacing an edition of Milton's poetical works published by Johnson in 1801, Aikin had sought to revise the public reputation of *Paradise Regained* as a poetic decline from *Paradise Lost* by pointing out that although it lacked dramatic action it contained 'many pleasing sketches of natural scenery', for example, the conversations between Satan and Christ during the temptation in the wilderness, as the Saviour calmly refuses 'to seek wealth / For empire's sake, nor empire to affect / For glory's sake' (Book III, 44–6). The passage glossing *Geographical Delineations* is quoted as a panoramic set piece of historical geography (Book III, 259–64), describing the moment when Christ is taken to the mountain top and beholds 'so large' a prospect; this takes in 'huge cities' as well as fertile fields and barren deserts, and allows him to behold the historical rise and fall of empires, including the battle-fields where successive dominion is decided.[73]

Following the convention of systematic geographical texts such as Guthrie's and Pinkerton's, predicated on stadial theories of cultural progress, and the likely readership market of the book, Europe was given priority in *Geographical Delineations*. Europeans would rightly regard their part of the globe as 'the centre of all relations and comparisons' for 'It is in Europe alone (that part of America which may be called European excepted) that the human mind is in a progressive state; that improvement of every kind is assiduously cultivated; and that the principle of liberal curiosity is active.' For the reader who chooses not to dip into the book with the aid of the index, but to read from the beginning of the section on Europe, in the northern lands of Scandinavia, 'we shall begin our tour from the north that we may enjoy the satisfaction of seeing the face of nature gradually improve upon us in our progress'.[74] It does so until the journey reaches Great Britain, 'the greatest commercial nation that the world ever beheld', then passes through its imperial rival France, and ends in the ruins of former stages of progress in Italy and Greece.[75]

Britain is defined by its English-speaking peoples who have 'held the torch of mental illumination to all Europe'.[76] Freed from the county framework of *England Delineated*, and linked to global flows of commerce, London assumes a powerful significance in *Geographical Delineations* as 'the metropolis of the British empire' and global cities elsewhere in Britain, such as Manchester and Glasgow, figure prominently too.[77] Most commercial developments in Britain are welcomed as signs of improvement apart from conspicuously monied ones, for example, as expressed in the rise of fashionable resorts. The Scottish church and universities are given due praise and the text is better disposed than *England Delineated* to the main cathedral and college towns, variously described as 'stately', 'agreeable' and 'venerable'.[78] It is a familiar, patriotic picture of Britain at this stage of the Napoleonic Wars, subscribed to by much of polite society, and underscored by its portrayal of France which had 'filled such a space in the history of the age'.[79] An agreeable nation 'within its ancient limits', France's successive annexations of the revolutionary period have created an alarmingly expansionist state, ruling over thirty million people, which only 'the naval supremacy of Great Britain' is keeping in check.[80] *Geographical Delineations* offers a hydrological view of the world, focused on the state of bodies of water (frost bound or free, marshy or drained, flowing or stagnant) with the ocean as the medium of 'sociability [and] universal communication'. The degree of improvement is connected to religious or political regimes, long-term denominational cultures, or recent events, such as the invasion of Switzerland and Holland. Most lands beyond Europe are resistant, if not hostile, to progress. Islam was 'utterly adverse to learning and philosophy', encouraging 'bigotry [in] every nation professing it'.[81] Land-based empires were limited, Turkey for example exhibiting 'an aversion to the sea'.[82] India was crippled by the caste system. Africa was the source of commercial slavery whose evils Europeans had aggravated. As outposts of enlightened English culture, the greatest prospects were offered speculatively by the lands that became Australasia – 'a new empire rising'[83] – and substantially by the United States. Philadelphia took its place as the centre of a culture in which government most favoured liberty, 'a professional man and a merchant are esteemed the highest grade in society', learning is well diffused and 'the common bond of citizen is found fully sufficient to secure that agreement by which civil society is held together'.[84]

Lucy Aikin reckoned that her father's general aim – to 'seek in a middle course the useful and the agreeable combined' – was more 'completely accomplished' in *Geographical Delineations* than any other work.[85] The book received a predictably approving notice in the review section on school texts in the *Annual Review*. But the fact that, unlike many of Aikin's educational works, *Geographical Delineations* did not go into a second edition indicates it was not a commercial success in Britain. Its 'middle course' may then have been less marketable.

A one-volume American edition of *Geographical Delineations* was published in 1807 in Philadelphia, and advertised as 'greatly superior' to the English one, because it included additional sections setting out geographical principles and terminology as well as greatly expanding the section on the United States and contracting that on Europe. Incorporated as part of the wider geographical grammar of nationalism in American education, this edition cuts phrases about the United States as a 'transplanted Europe' and Britain holding 'the torch of mental illumination'. Published before the war of 1812, it noted that the United States was 'happily detached from the scene of European contestation'. Notes on yellow fever in Philadelphia are omitted, as is condemnation of slaveholding and optimism about commercial and industrial progress in the Spanish American colonies. The revisions included material on the cultural gains of political independence, including geographical intelligence such as Jedidiah Morse's geography books and Benjamin Rush's medical books which challenged European views of the New World.[86]

In Britain the school version of Pinkerton's *Modern Geography*, reissued in 1806, may have proved a rival to *Geographical Delineations*, as for the less theoretically inclined did successive editions of Guthrie's *Geographical Grammar*. In a rapidly changing wartime world, magazines kept better pace with the latest geographical intelligence. Joseph Johnson died in 1809, but the company trading under his name continued to issue Aikin's most popular texts, including a new edition of *England Delineated* in the same year, and in subsequent years long poems by Lucy Aikin, *Epistles on Women* (1810), and by Barbauld, *Eighteen Hundred and Eleven* (1812).

Epistles on Women, Exemplifying their Character and Condition in Various Ages and Nations privileges the vantage point of a private modern English woman of learning, the 'polisht privacy' which inherits from literary and genetic fathers the capacity to comprehend history on a global scale:

> Come then my friend; my devious way pursue
> Pierce every clime, and search all ages through;
> Stretch wide and wider yet thy liberal mind,
> And grasp the sisterhood of womankind.

Drawing on various sources, including Gibbon, John Aikin's translations of Tacitus and the Transactions of the Missionary Society, the poem charts the condition of women from Greenland to Tahiti to 'Afric's palmy shore'. Lamplit progress is discerned from the robust 'German matrons' in Tacitus 'From Elbe and Weser, or some unknown North' through the 'visionary maids' in the lives of saints such as Catherine of Sienna to 'the gaze, so fond, so mild, / Some English mother bends upon her child'. This is opposed to 'the animated glance / Shot by the dames of gay seductive France'; English women, on the contrary, are 'Bright daughters of a land renowned, / By Genius blest, by glorious Freedom crown'd'.[87]

Eighteen Hundred and Eleven looks, less complacently, to the future. Barbauld's poem offers a new view of the theme of the westward passing of empire, in which Britain is displaced from its position of privilege. It was written in and for a critical period of the war – a difficult one for liberals – when there was no prospect of victory for protagonists who had each trampled on the cause of freedom, when military and civilian casualties in Europe reached horrific levels and Britain was close to famine. Milton's prospect of cornfields and olive groves, as quoted on the title page of *Geographical Delineations*, is shown to be 'bounteous in vain' with harvest fields turned into battlefields and the plundering of crops by invading armies. Also 'fruitful in vain' is the matron, the familiar wartime figure of the widowed wife and mother, who pores over a newspaper:

> To learn the fate of husband, brothers, friends
> Or the spread map with anxious eyes explores,
> Its dotted boundaries and penciled shores,
> Asks *where* the spot that wrecked her bliss is found,
> And learns the name but to detest the sound.

The virtues of commerce, knowledge and freedom leave the land fit only for future American tourists to visit for its sites of lost liberal civilization, such as Runnymede, neoclassical Edinburgh, Newton's Cambridge and cosmopolitan London. The Genius of progress flies west to America, not to the United States (in 1811 drawn into war with Europe) but further south:

> On Andes' heights he shrouds his awful form;
> On Chimborazo's summits treads sublime . . .
> Spreads his broad hand, and bids the nations rise.[88]

The location reflects the influence of recent writings by Alexander von Humboldt. Barbauld was enthralled by Humboldt's description of his climb of Chimborazo with his instruments which confirmed it was far higher than Mont Blanc, the highest then measured in the world.[89] The views of the 'marvellous country' offered a new prospect for 'the peopled earth', here described in the translation by Helen Maria Williams which Barbauld admired:

Those villages which proclaim the industry of a mountainous people; those pastures, covered at the same time with herds of lamas, and flocks of European sheep; those orchards bounded by hedges of duranta and barnadesia; those fields cultivated with care, and promising the richest harvests; hang, as it were, suspended in the lofty regions of the atmosphere.[90]

John Aikin forecast correctly that *Eighteen Hundred and Eleven* 'will not please those *patriots* who think their country just in all her projects' and it proved to be the last of Barbauld's published writings.[91] For the rest of the war John Aikin largely confined himself to editing and short biographical pieces. In a letter of 1813 to Thomas Roscoe, quoted in Lucy Aikin's memoir, he tells how he perused one of Roscoe's political essays on 'the cause of virtue and patriotism' with 'melancholy pleasure':

the late political events have, I confess, deprived me of all expectation of seeing better principles prevalent in this country; whilst the general state of the world has as little allowed me to indulge hopes of melioration elsewhere; and were I not obliged in consequence of my engagement in Dodsley's *Annual Register* to attend to public events as they are passing, I think I should shut up my mind to everything but old books, and old and new friends.[92]

The end of the war, and lessening of religious factionalism, served to restore John Aikin's public. These were 'golden days for us', Lucy Aikin recalled. New editions of *Evenings at Home* with a new sequence of volumes for older children attracted a devoted readership from a range of families, of all denominations. These were largely edited by Lucy Aikin, although she found the legacy unwelcome: 'They want me to write for young people, a thing to which I have no great stomach. Of the two, I believe I had rather amuse men and women than instruct children.' With the demise of Joseph

Johnson, a new publisher offered £100, 'which we think pretty good', noted
Lucy, to produce a new version of *England Delineated*.[93]

Written with the assistance of Arthur Aikin (John Aikin was now very
infirm) *England Described*, as it was now entitled, was issued in 1818, and as
an adult's rather than children's book. It was updated with new information, drawing on thirty years of published topographical writing on the
country. The information, much denser than the original, overwhelms
the passages of poetry which once stood out on the page. Now missing
from the title page, and buried in the rest of the text, Dyer's *The Fleece* loses
its profile as a running commentary for the text; in this role it is replaced by
the summary tables from the 1811 census. *England Described* went beyond
the 'limitation of the plan' of *England Delineated* by including 'distinguished *country seats*' and 'remarkable *remains of antiquity*', sites which
dominate an index once reserved for main towns. This did not necessarily
represent a cultural retreat, for some topographical works cited, notably
those of John Britton, democratized knowledge of antiquarian and aristocratic landscapes as a form of popular learning and entertainment. The
stated reason for the changes implied a change of real or imagined location
for the text, from library and schoolroom to coach and carriage. The
'increasing fashion for domestic travelling' during the war years demanded
a different kind of geography; with an up-to-date road map, *England
Described* 'furnish[ed] a desirable companion for the tourist'. The text
may have been overtaken by events. Although published in the post-war
depression, when the evidence of decline and suffering was all too apparent
to observers, progress is evident everywhere in the England of *England
Described*. Liverpool no longer profits from the slave trade, Leicester has
regained 'the spirit of improvement', from being of 'little consequence' in
England Delineated. Hertford in *England Described* is 'a respectable and
improving place' and not only has Hereford's cathedral been restored but
the 'ancient decayed place' of 1788 visibly benefits from other developments,
including a new gaol, infirmary and glove manufactory.[94]

GEOGRAPHY AT HOME

John Aikin never pretended to be a singularly original mind in the Aikin
circle of family and friends. He was a collaborative and enterprising figure,
his skills of editing, translation, compilation and commentary, and his
capacity to assimilate a vast range and amount of information to produce
a prolific number of works, written in accessible prose for various ages, were
the foundation of his literary achievement. Geography, like his other

favourite genre, biography, offered a way of combining 'entertainment and instruction', charting a 'middle course' between the 'elegancies of polite literature' and 'rational enquiry'.[95]

Designed to be an authoritative account of John Aikin's life and work, Lucy Aikin's memoir of her father charts this 'middle course' more largely in his career, the quiet 'unfoldings of character and sentiment' in a path of life that deliberately avoided large cities and the clamour of public life. While his life is therefore spared the distractions of 'the bustle of incident, or the splendor of description' to make an 'instructive and acceptable piece of biography', the impact of political controversies receives less attention.[96] So Aikin's life and work is at once a campaign to advance from province to metropolis, to break into the world of London and build a productive and profitable literary career, and also a retreat from a bustling and politically turbulent world. He moves from a major Lancashire river port to a minor Norfolk seaport and finally to a suburban, residential village, reducing his practice as a physician, although sustaining a discursive connection in his writing between the worlds of health, environment and literature and the practical choice of places to dwell and visit. Throughout, Aikin maintains as the locus of his learning and work a lettered and civilized home, full of family exchanges, and an enlarged domestic vision of geography as the home of mankind. While his life was always shaped by Dissent, culturally the course of this moderate and moderating sensibility is less a Puritan straight and narrow path than an Anglican *via media*. This was a cultural rather than denominational form of Englishness, to be found in the geography of the country beyond the axis of the country house and the parish church and learned through the contours of the landscape, including its commercial circulation. In developing geography as a literary as well as educational discipline, particularly in *England Delineated*, Aikin realigned the spatial, mathematical framework of many geography textbooks to accommodate genres of landscape writing, notably the poetry of place. It is a geographical imagination which can range globally and speculatively but is grounded in the local and empirical particularities of the England that Aikin knew familiarly, through its landscape and literature, as he endeavoured, against the grain of some established topographical traditions, to reconstruct a more liberal vision of the country and its place in the world.

NOTES

1. Aikin, *Memoir of John Aikin*, I, 199.
2. *Ibid.*, I, 123, 245.

3. See the letters from John Aikin the elder and younger to Pennant; Pennant Papers, Warwickshire Record Office CR 2017 TP 3/18; TP 33/2–3; 14; TP 154/1–7; TP 155/1–4.

4. *A Treatise on the Situation, Manners and Inhabitants of Germany and the Life of Agricola by C. Cornelius Tacitus* (Warrington: W. Eyres for J. Johnson, 1772).

5. John Aikin, *An Essay on the Application of Natural History to Poetry* (Warrington: W. Eyres for J. Johnson, 1777), 5.

6. *Ibid.*, 31.

7. *Ibid.*, 48.

8. *Ibid.*, 120. Pennant's citation of Thomson as 'the naturalist's poet' is in the index of the volume on birds of *British Zoology* (London: Benjamin White 1768), 530. On Pennant's praise for Presbyterian culture, see Robert Mayhew, *Enlightenment Geography: The Political Languages of British Geography 1650–1850* (Basingstoke: Macmillan, 2000), 143–51. McCarthy, *Anna Letitia Barbauld*, 108–9, 581.

9. Aikin, *An Essay on the Application of Natural History to Poetry*, 131–2.

10. Aikin, 'Memoir', *Works of Anna Lætitia Barbauld*, I, xii.

11. *Poems* (London: J. Johnson, 1773), 17. The transformation parallels a passage by Arthur Young on an imaginative scheme to extend an aqueduct across 'a boisterous arm of the sea: – To exhibit a navigation afloat in the air, with ships of a hundred tons sailing full masted beneath it. What a splendid idea!' *Extracts from Mr. Young's Six months tour through the north of England* (London: London Magazine, 1772), 22–3.

12. John and Anna Aikin, *Miscellaneous Pieces in Prose*, 79–87. See Harriet Guest, *Small Change: Women, Learning, Patriotism, 1750–1810* (University of Chicago Press, 2000), 335. On Barbauld's devotional tastes, see White, *Early Romanticism*, 34–60.

13. Harry Robinson, 'Geography in Dissenting Academies', *Geography*, 36 (1951), 179–86.

14. Aikin, 'Memoir', *Works of Anna Lætitia Barbauld*, xxvi.

15. McCarthy, *Anna Letitia Barbauld*, 165–86. This revises the account in McCarthy's 'The Celebrated Academy at Palgrave: A Documentary History of Anna Letitia Barbauld's School', *Age of Johnson*, 8 (1997), 279–392 (298–303, 326). This earlier article includes a discussion of her children's work, lectures and pedagogy (*ibid.*, 298–303) and has a valuable appendix of primary source material, including her 'fragment of a lecture (?) on Islamic history, c.1780' (*ibid.*, 326) and requests for teaching material such as '12 Thompson's seasons' (*ibid.*, 335).

16. William McCarthy, 'Mother of all Discourses: Anna Barbauld's *Lessons for Children*', *Princeton University Library Chronicle*, 60 (1999), 196–219; Emma Major, 'Nature, Nation and Imagination: Barbauld's Taste for the Public', *English Literary History*, 74 (2007), 909–30.

17. Aikin, *Memoir of John Aikin*, 36. For details of his teaching and observations, see *ibid.*, 28–9, 39–41.

18. John Aikin, *The Calendar of Nature* (Warrington: W. Eyres for J. Johnson, London, 1784), v.

19. Aikin, *Calendar of Nature*, 55.
20. *Ibid.*, vi.
21. Aikin, *Memoir of John Aikin*, I, 101.
22. *Ibid.*, I, 64.
23. Aikin, *Works of Anna Lætitia Barbauld*, II, 30–1.
24. Aikin, *Memoir of John Aikin*, I, 41–78.
25. John Aikin, *England Delineated, or a Geographical Description of Every County in England and Wales with a Concise Account of Its Most Important Products, Natural and Artificial* (London: J. Johnson, 1788), iii.
26. Aikin, *Memoir of John Aikin*, I, 45, 46.
27. *Ibid.*, I, 116. On the cultural consensus on nature and landscape, see Emma Major, '"Nature, Nation and Imagination"; Robert Mayhew, William Gilpin and the Latitudinarian Picturesque', *Eighteenth-century Studies*, 33 (2000), 349–66.
28. Helen Braithwaite, *Romanticism, Publishing and Dissent: Joseph Johnson and the Cause of Liberty* (London: Palgrave Macmillan, 2003).
29. Jill Shefrin, '"Make It a Pleasure and not a Task": Educational Games for Children in Georgian England', *Princeton University Library Chronicle*, 60 (1999), 251–75.
30. Mayhew, *Enlightenment Geography*, 168–92; Robert J. Mayhew, 'Geography in Eighteenth-century British Education', *Paedagogica Historica*, 34 (1998), 731–69; Charles W. J. Withers, 'Eighteenth-century Geography: Texts, Practices, Sites', *Progress in Human Geography*, 30 (2006), 711–29; Paul Elliott and Stephen Daniels, '"No Study so Agreeable to the Youthful Mind": Geographical Education in the Georgian Grammar School', *History of Education*, 39 (2010), 15–33.
31. Mayhew, *Enlightenment Geography*, 168–92.
32. [Nicholas Lenglet Dufresnoy], *Geography for Children*, 14th edn (London: J. Johnson, 1783).
33. Robert Davidson, *The Elements of Geography Short and Plain* (London: T. Wilkins, 1787), 7–8.
34. Aikin, *England Delineated*, iv.
35. Sam Smiles, *Eyewitness: Artists and Visual Documentation in Britain, 1770–1830* (Aldershot: Ashgate, 2000), 23–46; Stephen Daniels and John Bonehill (eds.), *Paul Sandby. Picturing Britain* (London: Royal Academy, 2009).
36. Richard Gough, *British Topography. Or, an Historical Account of What has been Done for Illustrating the Topographical Antiquities of Great Britain and Ireland*, 2 vols. (London: T. Payne and Son, 1780), I, xxi–xxii.
37. *The Geography of England: Done in the Manner of Gordon's 'Geographical Grammar'* (London: T. Dodsley, 1744).
38. Aikin, *England Delineated*, v.
39. *Ibid.*, vi–x.
40. *Ibid.*, 31, 187.
41. *Ibid.*, 13, 22, 13–14.
42. *Ibid.*, 203–5.

43. *Ibid.*, 103, 135, 244–55.

44. *Ibid.*, 393.

45. Robert Heron, *Scotland Delineated, or a Geographical Description of every Shire in Scotland, Including the Northern and Western Isles* (Edinburgh: James Neill, 1791), 1–2.

46. Aikin, *Memoir of John Aikin*, 1, 131.

47. *Ibid.*, 89–93; McCarthy, *Anna Letitia Barbauld*, 291–369.

48. Aikin, *Memoir of John Aikin*, 1, 186–7.

49. John Aikin, *A Description of the Country from Thirty to Forty Miles Around Manchester* (London: John Stockdale, 1795), 1–14.

50. Aikin, *Letters*, 303–15 (307, 312).

51. John Aikin and Anna Letitia Barbauld, *Evenings at Home, or the Juvenile Budget Opened*, 6 vols. (London: J. Johnson, 1792–6), 1, 1–3.

52. See White, 'The "Joineriana"', 511–33; Aileen Fyfe, 'Reading Children's Books in Late Eighteenth-century Dissenting Families', *Historical Journal*, 43 (2000), 453–73.

53. Aikin, *Memoir of John Aikin*, 1, 157–9.

54. *Evenings at Home*, VI (1796), 123–44 (141).

55. A story particularly remembered by John Ruskin, Charles Kingsley and Jane Loudon: see Fyfe, 'Reading Children's Books', 465.

56. *Evenings at Home*, IV (1794), 93–4, 100, 109.

57. *Monthly Magazine and British Register*, 1 (1796), preface [n.p.].

58. *Ibid.*, 15–18, 104–7, 191–4; Arthur Aikin, *Journal of a Tour through North Wales and Part of Shropshire* (London: J. Johnson, 1797). See H. S. Torrens, 'Arthur Aikin's Mineralogical Survey of Shropshire 1796–1816 and the Contemporary Audience for Geological Publications', *British Journal for the History of Science*, 16 (1983), 111–53.

59. Aikin, *Memoir of John Aikin*, 1, 212. Aikin confides his fears of not surviving the trip to Dorking, in a letter to Thomas Pennant, 30 March 1796, Pennant Papers CR 1017/TP 155/4.

60. John Aikin, 'Description of the Country about Dorking', in Aikin, *Memoir of John Aikin*, 1, 311–29. William Gilpin, *Observations on the Western Parts of England relative Chiefly to Picturesque Beauty* (London: T. Cadell, 1798), 7–42.

61. Barbauld, 'True Magicians', *A Legacy for Young Ladies. Consisting of Miscellaneous Pieces in Prose and Verse. By the late Mrs. Barbauld* (London: Longman, 1826), 1–17 (3–6). On the popularity of panoramas, see Ralph Hyde, *Panoramania! The Art and Entertainment of the 'All-Embracing' View* (London: Trefoil Publications, 1988).

62. Le Breton, *Memoir of Mrs. Barbauld*, 81. See Ana M. Acosta, 'Spaces of Dissent and the Public Sphere in Hackney, Stoke Newington, and Newington Green', *Eighteenth-century Life*, 27 (2003), 1–27; McCarthy, *Anna Letitia Barbauld*, 405–6.

63. Aikin, *Memoir of John Aikin*, 1, 213.

64. *Ibid.*, 1, 247–8.

65. *Annual Review*, 7, for 1808 (1809), 62.
66. John Pinkerton, *Modern Geography* (London: T. Cadell and Davies, 1802).
67. *Annual Review* 1, for 1802 (1803), 437–48 (439). Reprinted in *A Memoir of the Life and Writings of the Late William Taylor*, 2 vols. (London: John Murray, 1843), II, 47–52.
68. Pinkerton, *Modern Geography*.
69. Pinkerton, *Modern Geography*, 2nd edn, rev. (London: T. Cadell and Davies, 1806), vii.
70. Lucy Aikin, *The Travels of Rolando*, 4 vols. (London: Richard Phillips, 1804), I, ii–iv.
71. Quoted in Le Breton, *Memoirs, Miscellanies and Letters*, 82.
72. John Aikin, *Geographical Delineations, or a Compendious View of the Natural and Political State of all parts of the Globe*, 2 vols. (London: J. Johnson, 1806), I, iii–iv.
73. *The Poetical Works of John Milton, from the text of Dr. Newton: with a critical essay by J. Aikin*, 4 vols. (London: J. Johnson, 1801), I, 35.
74. Aikin, *Geographical Delineations*, I, 7–9.
75. *Ibid.*, I, 190.
76. *Ibid.*, I, 184.
77. *Ibid.*, I, 192.
78. *Ibid.*, I, 195.
79. *Ibid.*, I, 223.
80. *Ibid.*, II, 231, 238.
81. *Ibid.*, II, 310.
82. *Ibid.*, II, 314.
83. *Ibid.*, II, 400.
84. *Ibid.*, II, 314. Discussion of Philadelphia, 319–20.
85. Aikin, *Memoir of John Aikin*, I, 246.
86. Aikin, *Geographical Delineations*. On American nationalism in geographical pedagogy, see Martin Bruckner, 'Lessons in Geography: Maps, Spellers and other Grammars of Nationalism in the Early Republic', *American Quarterly*, 51 (1999), 310–43.
87. Lucy Aikin, *Epistles on Women, Exemplifying their Character and Condition in Various Ages and Nations. With Miscellaneous Poems. By Lucy Aikin* (London: J. Johnson, 1810), 16–17, 23, 59, 54, 79.
88. Anna Letitia Barbauld, *Eighteen Hundred and Eleven* (London: J. Johnson, 1812). Text here from McCarthy and Kraft, *Selected Poetry*, 162, 173.
89. E. C. Rickards, 'Mrs Barbauld and her Pupil', *Murray's Magazine*, 10 (1891), 706–26 (725).
90. Alexander von Humboldt, *Researches Concerning the Institutions and Monuments of the Ancient Inhabitants of America*, trans. H. M. Williams, 2 vols. (London: Longman, 1814), I, 232.
91. McCarthy and Kraft, *Selected Poetry*, 160. Aikin, *Memoir of John Aikin*, I, 258.
92. Aikin, *Memoir of John Aikin*, I, 258.
93. Le Breton, *Memoirs, Miscellanies and Letters*, 113–14.

94. John Aikin, *England Described, being a Concise Delineation of Every County in England and Wales* (London: Baldwin, Cradock and Joy, 1818), iii–vi, 147, 258–9, 174.

95. Marten Hutt, 'Maintaining "The Dignity of a Liberal and Learned Profession": John Aikin's *Biographical Memoirs of Medicine in Great Britain* (1780)', *Transactions of the Unitarian Historical Society*, 31 (1998), 302–10.

96. Aikin, *Memoir of John Aikin*, I, vi.

CHAPTER 6

'Under the eye of the public': Arthur Aikin (1773–1854), the Dissenting mind and the character of English industrialization

Ian Inkster

The first condition of having to deal with somebody at all is to know with whom one has to deal.

Georg Simmel, 1908

The Philosophers . . . are getting up what they are pleased to call a New Aristocracy – an Aristocracy of Science [which] is to be the enemy and ruler of the old one.

David Robinson, 1825

PROLOGUE IN 1833

At the great public dinner of March 1833 held at Freemason's Tavern, London, to mark the centenary of the birth of the exemplary Dissenting philosopher Joseph Priestley,[1] leading among the nineteen stewards representing the nation's 'Cultivators of Chemical Science' was Arthur Aikin Esq., FLS. Among the 120 diners were most of the notable Dissenting philosophers of the metropolis, including Arthur's brother Charles Rochemont Aikin as well as his close chemical associate W. H. Pepys. At 60 years of age Arthur Aikin was firmly ensconced among the foremost chemists of the decade of reform.

Something repeatedly stressed throughout the Priestley commemoration was the notion that the earlier period of 'political and theological strife' had passed away, indeed was now replaced by one of greater understanding and intellectual tolerance. By focusing upon the 'independence of dogma and of preconceived notions' that characterized Priestley himself, the assorted savants pointed to the relative liberalism that allowed intellectual association and discourse within a Dissenting culture even at a time of extended political crisis and warfare.[2] Although the Home Office had indeed attempted to crack down on such freedoms during the early 1790s and after the end of the Napoleonic Wars, this could now be forgotten in a spirit of progressive liberalism and victorious intellectual endeavour.[3] A former pupil of Priestley – as had been his father – Arthur Aikin centred on his own direct debt to the great philosopher while 'employed in assisting Dr Priestley in his laboratory when he removed from Birmingham to Hackney'.[4] We may thus fairly claim that Arthur Aikin stood at the epicentre of those associations and networks that linked the worlds of Dissent, intellect and industry. Furthermore, as was illustrated in later remarks made at that dinner by Aikin's collaborator W. H. Pepys, these two and several other practising chemists owed directly to Priestley the cultural identity of intellectual Dissent, scientific enquiry and practical laboratory manipulation, a nexus not then found in any English university or in any English royal society.[5] In this chapter we wish to explore the particular micro-culture of Dissent and intellectual enquiry established by Arthur Aikin's father and grandfather, and its later elaborations by Arthur and his brothers in their work on geology, chemical applications, medicine and architecture.

UNITARIANS IN THE GREAT SOCIETY:[6]
ARTHUR AIKIN AND HIS CIRCLE

As Thompson so vividly summarized in 1963, the 'intellectual history of Dissent is made up of collisions, schisms, mutations; and one feels often that the dormant seeds of political radicalism lie within it, ready to germinate whenever planted in a beneficent and hopeful social context'.[7] Such a context was urbanizing England between 1789 and 1793, during which time Arthur Aikin was coming of age, the son of a leading Dissenter who had emerged among the leadership of a new, provincial political radicalism.

It is probably impossible to overstress the mutual dependency tradition of rational Dissent, especially from the 1770s and in the arrangements of the academies.[8] This is caught well in a letter of December 1789 from the Revd William Enfield (1741–97) of Liverpool (a tutor at Warrington between 1770 and 1783) to the Rev.d Nicholas Clayton (1730–97) at Nottingham: 'I am sure you are as delighted with the great events that are passing in favour of liberty, and have read Dr Price's sermon with rapture. I trust you and I will still live to see glorious times: if the French succeed, as I think they must, we shall certainly grow wiser; for success is a wonderful enlightener.'[9] It should be noted that neither man was in his flush of youth, Clayton at 59 and Enfield at 48 years of age – the subject of their political rapture, Richard Price was then 66 years of age with only two more to live.[10] Young scholars such as Richard Bright (1754–1840) could not have managed at Warrington

Academy without extensive Dissenting familial ties. Networks of family and informal fostering of young scholars similarly supported William Shepherd (1768–1847) – a lifelong friend of the Aikin family, from the days at Hackney with Arthur to correspondence in the 1840s with Lucy Aikin[11] – and other associates of the Aikins.[12] In turn, William Shepherd as Unitarian minister at Gateacre, Liverpool, brought support of radicalism to the familial level – adopting the daughter of Jeremiah Joyce and acting as a kindly guardian to the children of Gilbert Wakefield (1756–1801, tutor at Warrington, Nottingham and Hackney) when he was imprisoned during 1799–1801.[13] So it was that the immediate effect of the French Revolution on the Unitarians[14] of the English provinces was likely transmitted from parents to their offspring as a matter of course.

John Aikin, 'strenuous supporter', in his own words, of American independence from 1778 and of civil liberty in 'whatever quarter',[15] by the 1790s regarded 'candour' as the key term of rational Dissent, and followed Priestley in urging Dissenters 'to think with freedom . . . to proceed with vigour'.[16] In June 1788 in the *Gentleman's Magazine*, Aikin had moved beyond the radical fashion concerning rights, going on to consider that philanthropy might be seen in terms of the rights of the poor, they had a claim to some freedom of choice, this being dubbed by Brown a form of social enlightenment.[17] In that year the initial activity of the Philanthropic Society was led by a coterie of Aikin and such London men as George Adams (1750–95, scientist and instrument maker), Robert Young (of Warwick Court, a science lecturer), James Sims MD (1741–1820), Thomas Skeete MD (medical lecturer), Revd Dr George Gregory (1754–1808, author and theologian), J. C. Lettsom MD FRS (1744–1815, Quaker physician) and William Wilberforce MP (1759–1833).[18] By 1791 the group was meeting in St Paul's Coffee House.[19] This was just as John Aikin moved to London from Yarmouth in 1791 as a result of the financial pressure stemming from his authorship of republican pamphlets. As he wrote in a letter to Thomas Percival:[20]

It is some time since an opposition on party grounds declared itself against me here: and as the whole business of the place is but an very immoderate competence, I was resolved not to sit down contented with a part of it, and amongst people who had violated their engagements with me. I have therefore determined again to settle in London and my friends are now looking out for a house for me . . . The honour done me by the Manchester [Literary and Philosophical] Society is very grateful to me. I shall be very happy on future occasions to contribute anything in my power to their amusement, and shall be proud of the credit of appearing before the world in such respectable company . . . I am sorry to learn that there has been a defection from the Society. If the cause of it was purely party difference, I lament that letters and science at least are not kept sacred from their intrusion.[21]

In this manner Aikin joined a society of London activists who exemplified rational Dissent and its extended network and larger public platform. A good example of the new setting for the Aikin family were the Wednesday evening popular lecture courses on political matters, natural theology and related subjects that were given from Salters Hall, by such leading Unitarians and Presbyterians as John Evans (1767–1827), Hugh Worthington (1752–1813), and Drs Winter, Phillips and Lee throughout the period of the revolution and wars.[22] In late 1792 the Friends of the People at Stoke Newington – where Richard Price was minister until he died in 1791[23] – sent a message of support to the French Convention, that is, just after the September Massacres, putting radical Unitarian opinion (particularly that associated with Hackney) at least for a time on a par with the London Corresponding Society or the Society for Constitutional Information.[24] Remaining in fear of outrage, Priestley was in Hackney from September 1791 until April 1794,[25] erecting a new laboratory in his substantial house in Clapton – then a village of Hackney parish – an increasingly savant neighbourhood with, nearby, Dr Richard Price, G. C. Morgan (1754–98, a Hackney tutor and scientific writer), Thomas Belsham, Gilbert Wakefield and Abraham Rees, with New College just 200 yards away and five minutes' walk from the Gravel Pit Meeting House.[26] With support from the London Dissenting coteries, including the practical assistance of young Arthur Aikin, by November of 1793 Priestley was back experimenting and publishing in chemistry despite his separation from the 'Lunars', disputing over phlogiston, as well as publicly quarrelling with the Royal Society on their rejection of Thomas Cooper[27] from the fellowship.[28]

By the time Aikin had left for this London micro-culture he had clearly become a leader among the politically radical Unitarians of centres such as Warrington or Liverpool, William Enfield (1741–97) – earlier a tutor at Warrington – applauding his 'elegant pen. You possibly saw his satirical lines *Now or Never*; and his pamphlet on the *Influence of the Establishment on the Civil Constitution*; another piece is sent to the Press, which states plain truths very boldly.'[29] Enfield and others ran to the press to support Aikin, placing articles in such establishment forums as the *Gentleman's Magazine*.[30] Writing to James Currie at Liverpool in November 1790, Aikin himself expressed the position of the rational Dissenters and their distaste at Burke's famous reply to the republicans:

The spirit of the times in this country does not surprise me. I have long been led to conclude from my conversation with mankind that those who love and understand true liberty among us are a very small portion, and almost confined to the body of Dissenters and free speculators in matters of religion. But whether they increase or diminish, whether they are objects of respect or hatred, I join with you in declaring that I am ready to run all fortunes with them.

Throughout these months Aikin was worried by 'the attacks of warm and angry foes'.[31] This was rational enough. There was a real danger for Unitarianism in the early 1790s. Thus the Revd Thomas Fyshe Palmer, friend of both Joyce and Shepherd (see below), a graduate of Queens' College, Cambridge who turned increasingly Unitarian during the 1780s was arrested in September 1793 for his *Address to the People*, and transported to New South Wales in February 1794.[32] More mildly, in Liverpool in 1792 leading Unitarians were placing great emphasis on both physical danger and a need to coalesce: 'I wish every Dissenter through England would, like Walker, provide firearms and defend his house, and have some idea of getting such a resolution passed here and printed.'[33]

One focus of life for the Aikins in London was the Hackney New College, dubbed by William Cobbett writing as Peter Porcupine in 1798 'a most convenient and successful school for treason'.[34] Here in fact was boasted a 'comprehensive and liberal education' for all denominations. The curriculum of the three-year course included the history and principles of law and government, mathematics, astronomy, natural and experimental philosophy, chemistry, logic, ethics, and for students who stayed beyond the normal years, courses were designed depending on their needs. Domestic care was provided by Thomas Belsham and Dr Abraham Rees (1743–1825) at fifty guineas per annum, but foundation students were free.[35] From 1791 Priestley's regime emphasized the liberality, inexpensiveness and efficiency, discipline and morality of education at Hackney, and that the rational Dissenters 'as the friends of reformation have nothing to expect from *power*, or *general favour*, but look for every species of abuse or persecution that the spirit of the times will admit of'. Power will yield to knowledge, and only freedom of thought may contribute to the 'flourishing state of science, arts, manufactures and commerce . . . the abolishing of all useless distinctions'.[36] Liberalism was extended to the teaching methods at Hackney, with much insistence on student participation and intervention, based on a Hartley-style association of ideas,[37] with studies 'unclogged by any subscription to articles of faith'.[38] His *Heads of Lectures on Experimental Chemistry* published in 1794 just prior to his departure for America, were those that Priestley delivered to New College, and began with a preface that situated him 'in the neighbourhood of the New College at Hackney, an institution that does honour to the Dissenters', and stressed the uniqueness in England of the education taught there. The special emphasis here on both manufactures and arts, where 'genius' was necessary but knowledge more tacit and tactile than in more classical fields, was precisely that of John Aikin in his *Letters* to his son of this time, and seemingly of enormous influence in determining the path that Arthur Aikin took during the subsequent years.[39] So too were there explicit statements of the closed group, familial culture of rational Dissent, with emphasis on the marginal and threatened position of Hackney and the need for its students to demonstrate their love of peace and good order but to think as liberally as they chose and to at all times address their vision to the 'reasoning' portion of society.

By 1791 William Shepherd was identifying reason and Dissent as a critical combination for all society. Writing anonymously and in the guise of a dialogue as 'Search' whose Establishment protagonist was 'Tightbound', Shepherd admonished his opponent for appealing to supposed learned opinion and for forgetting that there:

is within you a principle called *Reason*, which is, to yourself, of authority superior to that of all the learned men in the world; because it judges of their arguments, and determines concerning their propriety. This principle is of such authority, that when you know its decisions, you will follow them in spite of any opposition. Why, then, in cases of religion, cases of the greatest consequence, should you not consult this judge, why should you blindly, and without examination, follow the decisions of any man, or set of men?[40]

As we shall see, this was precisely the message of John Aikin to his son Arthur in 1791 when he argued that not 'to insist on the great advancements in arts and science which have originated from *natural philosophy* [. . .] what man of enlarged ideas will deny, that the *philosophy of the human mind*, of *law*, of *commerce*, of *government*, of *morals*, and, I will add, of *religion*, have greatly contributed to any superiority this age may claim over former periods?'[41] This was parallel to his sister's insistence some two years later, on the liberating values for children of science, industry and business, at the expense of the tales and fables so defended by Charles Lamb.[42]

ARTHUR AIKIN IN AN URBANE CULTURE
OF TECHNOLOGY AND INDUSTRY

Alongside such young men as Jeremiah Joyce or William Shepherd, Arthur Aikin was exposed to a curriculum at the New College that over a three-year course mixed Newtonian mathematics and calculation of chances and annuities, metaphysics and ethics, with astronomy, natural and experimental philosophy, and chemistry through the persuasions of such teachers as Richard Price, Abraham Rees and G. C. Morgan and a library well stocked with the natural theology and natural and experimental science of Priestley, Emerson, Percival, Boerhave, Gregory and Whiston. Priestley's thirty-six-lecture course in chemistry set out to establish that all 'arts and manufactures are derived from science ... Every thing we are capable of doing by means of the steam-engine is derived from our knowledge of the properties of water in steam'.[43] Hardly surprisingly, then, in the late 1790s the brothers Arthur and Charles Aikin combined to deliver twenty-eight to forty lecture courses from their house and general dispensary on Aldersgate Street near Foster-Lane on Chemistry and Chemical Manufactures. In their courses of 1799 delivered from 4 Broad Street Buildings, the brothers offered the 'principal application to the more common arts and manufactures', including sixteen lectures on general chemistry and mineralogy plus fifteen on the chemistry of the vegetable kingdom and a further twelve on the chemistry of the animal kingdom. Such courses included coverage of heat/caloric, repetitions of Rumford's experiments and those on atmosphere of both Priestley and Lavoisier that found air 'to consist of Oxygenous and Azotic gasses'.[44] The Aikins focused entirely on practical and even industrial applications of chemistry in gunpowder, medicine, bleaching, dyeing, cement, whitening silk, metallurgy, glass etching, assaying, engraving, artificial gems and soldering of metals. Beyond this, treatments included mining, stamping, waging, smelting of metals, and most detailed applications in metallurgy and mineralogy. Lectures embraced the utility of metallurgy and metals in glass making, enamelling, alloys, ink manufacture, pewter, type-founding, fireworks, gilding, construction of philosophical instruments, silvering mirrors, electrical machines, dyeing, refining of gold and silver, glazing pottery, as a pigment and colouring agent, calico printing, adulterating wines, sheathing ships, manufacture of boilers and civil engineering structures. In organic chemistry much was made of applications of compounds to pickling, dyeing, metallurgy, perfumes, drying oils, chocolate, lemonade, candles, dressing wool, varnishes, manufacture of soap, paints, antiseptics, medicine, manufacture of bread; preparation of glue, isinglass, leather-dressing, candles; manufacture of lamp-black and bone-ash; assaying; tanning and calico printing. The chemistry–mineralogical fusion was common enough by this time. Babington's regular lectures on elements of chemistry and mineralogy at his home on Basinghall St embraced similar experiments and apparatus[45] as did Samuel Varley's twelve lectures on chemistry at Hatton House, Hatton Garden.[46] Interestingly, active engagement in such courses did require that the student construct some individual laboratory equipment and develop experimental expertise, desiderata that were increasingly required in the scientific culture of London, and as specified in the works – published in several editions in London – of Europeans such as Axel Frederic Cronstadt and E. M. Da Costa.[47] By the time of the Aikins' public courses it was accepted that any study of mineralogy was dependent on practical instruction and teaching based on a relatively simple collection of laboratory equipment.[48]

A formative influence on Arthur Aikin as an exponent of applications of science was his membership of the Askesian Society of London from 1796 to 1807, a small group of savants whose prime concerns lay in chemistry, mineralogy and geology, who together provided him with research programmes, lifelong working relations with W. H. Pepys and others concerned in scientific applications, and association with such leading figures as Humphry Davy and William Allen.[49] Directly, the Askesian provided Arthur presidency of the British Mineralogical Society, and thus an influential position within the nascent Geological Society. By 1801 Allen and Aikin were actively engaged as a team in the working and purifying of metals, producing amalgams of iron and mercury and reguli of tungsten from chlorides of zinc and other salts.[50] Furthermore, Pepys and the Aikin brothers were important as providers of technical expertise and equipment for other members of the group, although much of the chemical analysis remained centred on the Plough Court Laboratory.[51] With Arthur Knight, Aikin provided analyses of mineral specimens from all over, was a member of the committee of apparatus, and with Pepys and Professor Marc Pictet experimented on galvanic troughs in 1801.[52] Work on tungsten by European chemists confirmed the Askesian experiments of Allen and Aikin on specific gravity.[53] By 1803 Charles Rochemont Aikin was advertising from Broad Street Buildings his Portable Chamber Blast Furnace, and there appears to have been something of a demand for his and Arthur's furnaces for chemical experimenting that required only small space and few facilities.[54] There can be little doubt that the Askesian provided a platform for Arthur Aikin's emergence as a leading figure within London's scientific community, from support of Jenner's vaccination technique in 1802,[55] the continued public lectures of both Aikin brothers at Aldersgate St,[56] presidency of the Mineralogical in 1802, editorship of the intended *Annual Review and History of Literature* from 1802, as well as his contributions to *Rees' Encyclopaedia* alongside his brother, Humphry Davy, William Nicholson and others of the London savant community.[57] Of these perhaps the British Mineralogical Society, which saw its major function as assisting 'both the miner and the mine owner in the analysis and reduction of substances', was closest to Arthur Aikin's heart, with both Aikins doing practical analysis.[58] Membership brought Arthur into regular, everyday contact with such scientists and technicians as William Babington, Humphry Davy and Richard Phillips.[59] It was against this immediate background that the Aikin brothers produced their *Dictionary* in two volumes in 1807.[60]

Arthur and Charles Rochemont produced an eminently applied work. Thus the extensive entry on iron provided critical commentary on the analysis and assaying of ores of Howard, Klaproth, Proust and others, and that on steel and its chemical analysis recognized the importance of carbon content in manufacture, with finer cast steel containing more carbon than softer steel or bar iron. In contrast the seven volumes of the *Annual Review* edited by Arthur from 1802 were aimed at critical coverage of all worthy books, when 'we shall be found the friends of good order, of domestic quiet'.[61] Under Arthur the reviews were huge in number and arranged in themes including history/politics/statistics, medicine, general science, mathematics, experimental philosophy, mineralogy and natural history. Unsurprisingly, good coverage was given the works of the Aikins and Barbaulds, of William Frend on evening amusements and astronomy, his own and his brother's *Dictionary*.[62] The review of the latter allowed Arthur to advertise widely the furnaces and equipment of Pepys, as well as John Cuthbertson's *Practical Electricity and Galvanism* and Chaptal's *Chemistry Applied to Arts and Manufactures*. In contrast, Aikin used volume 7 for 1809 to attack Nicholson's single-volume *Dictionary of Practical and Theoretical Chemistry*, as old-fashioned and too slight and lacking in any emphasis on 'actual practice'.[63]

Arthur Aikin's post-Askesian work centred on his activities in the Geological Society from 1807 and as Secretary of the Royal Society of Arts between 1817 and 1839. He was instrumental in establishing what might best be termed 'network research' via the questionnaire that he and Greenough compiled for Fellows of the Geological Society in 1808 as an exercise in 'democracy of the intellect', successfully collecting a variety of local information on specimens and deposits, an exercise that has been seen as important in turning it into a flourishing national body,[64] and as an early instance of 'radical empiricism'.[65] Arthur Aikin used the Geological as a forum for the establishment of a mineral chemistry as a basic foundation of geology but not ever at the expense of a broad-based avocation of geology.[66]

In 1814, the two brothers used the opportunity of a further edition of their *Dictionary*[67] to provide a very detailed supplement and copious reading and rendering of very recent work up to 1813. Especially covered were the French chemists (particularly Thenard and Gay-Lussac), but also the work of Dalton, Davy, Wollaston, Thomson, Bostock, Brande and Henry, as well as the Germans, with detailed reproduction of empirical results and applications, and much on mineral analyses. Arthur never abandoned this stress on practical applications. In the Guy's Hospital lecture courses of the 1820s, designed for but not confined to medical students, the focus remained on arts and manufactures 'whether useful or ornamental'; and emphasized laboratory instruction to 'fix in the memory' and to 'apply them with readiness'.[68]

Arthur Aikin served as Secretary to the RSA (1817–39), a period of decline in funds in the face of something of a contradiction between the much increased industrial production and patenting of the nation at large and the slow regulatory and tortuous character of the RSA itself. Despite this Aikin was seemingly a good secretary, instrumental in changing the RSA from a premium-awarding society to one of serious discussion. In this regard he was probably the main reformer, stressing the publication of inventions and technical discoveries and the dissemination of useful information on industrial arts, lectures and investigative meetings on industrial technology.[69] In his address to the 1,700 members of the RSA he described its prime purpose as the general communication of knowledge and the giving of status to those who most deserved it. It is honour that is the essence of reward, which shall encourage the 'meritorious inventions of ingenious men': there can be no patent of infallibility. His complaint – characteristically – concerned the insufficient communications in the area of chemical applications to mining and industry, to which he added a plea that art of design be taken over by the RSA as it was not properly in the care of the Royal Academy, and should be studied alongside more practical pursuits. In contrast, he applauded the very successful Committee of Mechanics, by far the most active and composed of 'men of real business' weekly examining and discussing various communications and artefacts.[70]

Between 1829 and 1838 Aikin delivered some forty papers to the RSA, published as a collection in 1841.[71] These ranged from chemical analyses of pottery and the fur trade to engraving and etching and, mostly, metallurgy. Aikin's penchant was to combine mechanical and chemical analyses with minute details of 'certain niceties or dexterities of manipulation'. The etching lectures allowed him to illustrate his more general rule that 'the fewer hands a work of art passes through to its completion the better, for no human can be employed in any work (except that of uniform mechanical routine) without leaving on it the impress of the intellect by which that hand was directed', a position very close to that of the later ideas and practices of William Morris and the Arts and Crafts movements. The biggest RSA study was that of 1837 on iron metallurgy, which detailed Coalbrookdale methods (Darby–Reynolds), Carron smelting from the 1760s, statistics up to 1826 of cast iron production, details of the furnace work of Mushet, Coste and Perdonnet of Glasgow from 1829 sources, Glasgow manufacturing details, and minute comparisons of iron produced in different parts of Britain. Aikin described in detail the method of preheating blast furnace air (hot blast), thus allowing use of raw coal, especially in Scotland where coal loses most in coking. He describes the experiments at Clyde Ironworks of 1829 and 1833, comparing these with hot blast performances at Staffordshire. In his coverage of bar iron manufacture Aikin uses the manuscripts of Major James Franklin of the East India Company on manufacture of iron in India, and refers to specimens and expert accounts from central India. The account of Swedish and Norwegian iron manufacture gives Berzelius' chemical analyses of bar iron refining and puddling, while his descriptions of practice in Shropshire are based on his own observations in surveys and trips together with the chemical explanations of Cort, Beddoes and Messrs. Bradley Forster and Co. of Stourbridge, Staffordshire.

THE MESH OF DISSENT: UNITARIANS AND THE FUNCTIONS OF SCIENCE

It may be argued that Arthur Aikin's concern to apply scientific experimental methods to matters of technology followed from a Dissenting microculture in which the two main formative elements were his father John Aikin on one hand, and on the other the changing context for rational Dissent of the republican political juxtapositions of the 1790s decade. After the Birmingham riots it became more difficult to maintain a radical stance, as reactionary associations multiplied and proclaimed a new identification of reform and revolution. As one result, rational Dissenters turned increasingly towards intellectual association as a defence against the attack on their political associations, though even this tactic was by no means guaranteed to allay the social pressures and legal threats placed upon them.[72] As we have suggested above, it was precisely in the 1790s that rational Dissenters had 'explicitly defined the duty of Dissent to support and promote civil liberty'.[73] It should also be emphasized that at least during the early 1790s the leaders of the revolutionary movement among the working classes and artisans did admit to common cause and identity with the more middle-class Dissent.[74]

Importantly, the older alliances between the Presbyterian meeting houses and the urban elites had been fading in the 1760s and 1770s, as Dissent passed over into a more overt Unitarianism. In the apposite words of Ian Sellers, rational Dissenters then emerged as a segregated class, 'cut off from their compeers in France from the sources of civic honour and profit to which they imagined themselves entitled, and seeking further outlets for their talents than the mere accumulation of capital, at which ... they seemed so peculiarly adept'. By the 1780s such urban Dissenting sub-groups tended to be politically vocal across a range of issues from the national to the local. Thus in Liverpool, Sellers noted Dissenting political radicalism embracing an attack on the slave trade, the campaign for the repeal of the Test and Corporation Acts, a movement for free trade with the Indies, and an attack on the closed corporation of the town, to which response to the French Revolution would add a novel focus and a heated intensity.[75]

By the 1780s rational Dissenters were probably among the most active members of the various Revolution Societies that sprang up throughout England during that decade. Clearly, representative members believed that centres such as Warrington should somehow be maintained at all odds as 'seminars so much wanted and looked up to by the friends of liberty' as Josiah Wedgwood declaimed to his friend Richard Bright in 1784.[76] Even prior to the 1789 Revolution in France, many British Dissenters were seeing the promotion of agitation as something that was beneficial to the common good. In a lecture promoting the cause of passive resistance before the members of the Manchester Literary and Philosophical Society, Thomas Percival MD, FRS contrasted the 'calm of despotism' with those agitations arising from intellectual improvement that 'diffuse the love of our country, kindle the ardour of ambition, animate the spirit of enterprise, and call forth into public exertion many talents, which might otherwise have remained in obscurity'.[77] Of course, it is commonly enough known that rational Dissent was particularly located in the industrializing areas of south Lancashire, south Yorkshire and Derbyshire, an outcome of social marginality widely accepted, then and now. As John Gay summarized, the 'more ambitious and prosperous section of the community realized it was wiser to belong to the Church of England and throughout the century there was a steady trickle of those who had struggled and succeeded, from the Nonconformist chapel, to the parish church. To announce that you were joining the Church of England was often regarded as a proclamation of success.'[78] Families such as the Brights of Bristol moved rapidly on from a Warrington Academy initiation – thus the father Richard, who had been remarkably active in

Bristol during 1789 to 1790 in chairing Dissenting delegations fighting for a repeal of the Test Acts,[79] becoming then Sheriff and then Mayor of Bristol in 1792, his sons Henry (1784–1869) entering Peterhouse, Cambridge, called to the Bar and MP 1826–30; Richard (1781–1858) educated in medicine at Edinburgh, Berlin and Vienna, with a successful practice in Bloomsbury Square and at Guy's Hospital; Robert (1795–1869) entering mercantile business in Bristol and Liverpool, extending to both cotton and the railways and founding Bright Bros. of Melbourne, Victoria.[80]

During the 1790s any existing continuum of Dissent was finally severed by the varying response to the French Revolution and its immediate aftermaths. Many Unitarians, in particular, began to feel both socially isolated and culturally marginal, with a consequent need to reaffirm their own networks of congregation, academy and association, as we have witnessed directly above in the person of John Aikin. But examples may be multiplied. A fine example of both the sense of isolation and the notion that the spread of 'light and knowledge' would eventually ensure change, was provided in a pamphlet by 'A Dissenter' (almost certainly Anna Letitia Barbauld) in March 1790, addressed to all those opposing the repeal of the Corporation and Test Acts, and identifying all Dissenters as 'citizens':

It is you, who by considering us as Aliens, make us so. It is you who force us to make our dissent a prominent feature in our character … If we are a party, remember it is you who force us to be so … You have refused us; and by so doing, you keep us under the eye of the public, in the interesting point of view of men who suffer under a deprivation of their rights. You have set a mark of separation upon us … but it is in our power to determine whether it shall be a disgraceful stigma or an honourable distinction … If our rising seminaries should excel in wholesome discipline and regularity … you will entrust us with the education of your youth … If our writers are solid, elegant, or nervous, you will read our books and imbibe our sentiments … If we enlighten the world by philosophical discoveries, you will pay the involuntary homage due to genius … If we seek for fortune in the track which you have left most open to us, we shall increase your commercial importance … we shall be bound together by mutual esteem and the mutual reciprocation of good offices … The minds of men are in movement from the Borysthenes to the Atlantic … The genius of Philosophy is walking abroad, and with the touch of Ithuriel's spear is trying the establishments of the earth … whatever is not built in the broad basis of public utility must be thrown to the ground.[81]

This was rousing but decidedly dangerous stuff, for our author went on to address the French: 'Be our model, as we have been yours … Go on to destroy the empire of prejudices, the empire of gigantic shadows, which are only formidable while they are not attacked'.[82]

More cautiously, here is James Currie of Liverpool to Priestley just after the attack on the Birmingham laboratory:

At a time when the friends of science and of freedom are recovering from their astonishment at the infamous proceedings in Birmingham, permit us to offer you our Congratulations on your escape from the savages there, and our anxious wishes for your future safety and health; [that] one who has so ably and so openly and so incessantly attacked the prevailing opinions should have become an object of dislike to the established priesthood [is] not only against the most respectable characters, but against knowledge and science themselves.[83]

It was in this key transition period that Arthur Aikin's father, John, addressed to him – at age 21 – most publicly his thirty *Letters*, written during 1792 to 1793. The context of the paternal advice and instruction can perhaps be defined on three levels. At that of the micro-cultural familial, this was the period of Arthur's higher education at Hackney College, his association with Priestley and training for the ministry, and not long after the escape of the family from Yarmouth to London. At the level of the Dissenting culture more generally, the letters were being written contemporaneously with the attack on Priestley in Birmingham during mid-1791 and the rise of a Church and King party that was distinctly opposed to all rational Dissent. We might recall, that it was Richard Price who in his sermon of November 1789 had instigated the intellectual debate on revolution that in turn began the hardening of political opinions and hastened Burke's reply.[84] Furthermore, at a third level of the national polity itself, war against France had converted infamous republicanism into culpable treason, and the trials of radicals that occurred (above and below) during these years served to associate in a most intimate fashion the culture of Dissent with that of insurrection, an association that bore juridical fruit in the Seditious Societies Acts of 1795 onwards.[85] But another context of the letters lies in the notion of Unitarians as the 'aristocracy of intellect'.[86] Long before 1798, Priestley and most Unitarians had taken up as a cultural and educational premise David Hartley's (1705–57) *Observations on Man*[87] – reprinted significantly enough in 1791 – which developed an associational psychological position, arguing that all complex or intellectual ideas arose from simple ones, these latter arising from sense data. So, an association of ideas could be seen as utilizing a Newtonianism of the mental and the social world, repeated sensations stimulating new ideas, a position to which both Arthur's father and his aunt Anna Barbauld most sincerely subscribed.[88] The notion that innate character may be modified by association led the way to radical notions of reform stemming from communities of spirit and action. It was this complexity of notion that John Aikin gifted to his son Arthur in 1792.

John began the *Letters* by emphasizing Arthur's education as based upon 'a varied and extensive plan, comprising many changes of discipline, and embracing a large field of instruction', as suited for an 'active and contemplative life'.[89] Following a basic associational view, 'all the branches of knowledge have a mutual connexion and dependence . . . reasoning consists in the comparison of ideas', suited to the great capacity of youth for 'prodigious acquisitions'.[90] There is thus conceptual as well as social justification for rejection of the classics and a consistent pursuit of ethics and theology, critical and polite literature, and the study of nature. This led John to his second main point – his son must not fall victim to prejudices and the false shame of 'being singular'. Indeed, the young Arthur should 'set a value on the circumstance of standing apart from the mass of mankind' and eschew the fear of offending, for this leads merely to an undue if polite assent, and a 'danger of subverting all our principles'.[91] The letters clearly represent a heartfelt plea for his son to exercise individual judgement based on principles of Dissent, scholarship and reflection, and against all social and cultural odds. Despite the setbacks of the radicals, John maintains his faith in progress and improvement as the inevitable outcome of rational Dissent. All those sceptical of this are either ignorant, weak or deriving selfish interest from the status quo – thus Burke bites the dust! Ignorant, because progress in science and arts does not oppose interests, for perfection is attainable in social institutions and in the 'regulations belonging to civil society'.[92] With the application of just reason – order, precision, concatenation and analysis – the complex and contradictory motives of men in society are systematized in law and governance. Arthur should resist all ironic sneers, polemical rhetoric and frothy insolence designed to counter such rationality, and strive for a candour and liberality 'beyond all petty distinctions of party and system',[93] reaffirming a Unitarian position that all the human race is approvable by a common Father. This is true within and between the sects themselves, as his defence of Barbauld's *Essay on Sects and Establishments* makes very clear.[94] On radical utterance in a time of conservative reaction, John treads a less than safe path, stressing that 'no attack on moral character is to be slighted' but that it is 'equally necessary to be circumspect in our actions, and spirited in self-defence'.[95] At the same time his highly individual notion of association leads to an argument from a defence of John Howard on criminal reforms,[96] where he draws an analogy with the illness of nations at large and the necessity for 'grand remedial processes', fairly close to an avant-garde advocating of at least social revolution. Clearly influenced by the recent move to London and the extremes of opulence and squalor, the half-million of poor surrounding him, John argues that the well-employed life is a major contribution towards mitigating or diminishing the evils of an 'absolutely unavoidable' inequality of circumstance. All remedial processes are just as natural and necessary as those that create inequality in the first place, this perhaps representing an early radical stance on the charity industries that were to emerge in the following century. Furthermore, a liberally reformed civil society based on self-interested good governance 'contains in it a levelling principle'.[97] John Aikin is perhaps at his most interesting in his judgement and advice on women. Very stridently condemned, akin to an 'unnerved frame of body, is that shrinking timidity of mind, and excessive nicety of feeling, which is too much encouraged under the notion of female delicacy', and which disguises the greater truth that women live a much tougher and uncertain life than do their menfolk, 'the man often runs abroad, the woman must stay at home and face the worst'.[98] In conclusion, the virtues and preferences of mind are not in any way gender based, education should adapt accordingly, even if the private sphere is the inevitable location of most women.[99] This formulation on the female mind and female education lies beyond even that of most female radicals of the 1790s and later years. Finally, John has much to say to Arthur concerning the relations of intellectual to innovative practical pursuits. In what may be seen as itself an application of associationism, John argued that from actually observing mechanism and other works of utility, 'though the inventor stands higher in the scale of genius than the improver, yet the workmanship of the latter will in many respects be more perfect than that of the former'.[100]

Furthermore, men's ideas progress 'by means of the expressions in which they clothed them – to view terms derived from sensible objects gradually transferred to intellectual notions, and simple energies receiving their successive modifications'.[101] So, simplistic mind–hand distinctions fail to recognize the reality of how science (as intellect) may be extended or applied to the manipulations of energy and mechanics as machines (technology).

When John penned a second volume of the *Letters* in 1798, written once more to Arthur – now 25 years of age – from Dorking and completed in Stoke Newington, he maintained all his former positions (volume 1 remained unexpurgated), but acknowledged at once the disillusions and regressions of the 1790s: 'What disappointment of elevated hopes! [...] what triumph of violence and injustice! ... shameless violations of all faith, equity and humanity!'[102] Throughout, John depicts the 1790s as dominated by the converts from reason to authority, a denial of those 'fundamental axioms respecting civil society, on which all improvements in government and political institutions were to be built'.[103] Despite this Arthur must preserve a 'free and independent mind ... making truth the great object of your researches', the best approach to which were now the direct propositions and deductions of Kepler, Newton and Leibnitz, in opposition to all intellectual authority.[104] He discounts all cases for respect except that within the family, concluding that 'arrogant claims of superiority are maintained to a degree subversive of all the principles of civil liberty'.[105] It seems that Aikin's letters to his son represent a micro-culture of rational Dissent that was hardly dimmed by reaction or oppression and that was codified in education and employment and direct social action. His clear stress on diversity of opinion and refusal of all restraints on private judgement raised the intellectual status of self-scrutiny, including that of women. The *Letters* accord well with modern analyses that characterize radical Unitarians as at once close-knit yet refusing of all the 'tyrannies that bound mind as well as man'.[106] Furthermore, the regressions of the 1790s seemed not to have generated political pessimism. It is surely certain that Arthur and his siblings took much of this strong position on board, but that during the early 1800s they translated such paternal advice into the search for applications of useful knowledge in technology and industry. This was a common enough transition. Another of this circle, Richard Knight (1768–1844) a close friend of Arthur Aikin at Hackney Academy before Arthur left in September of 1793 to enter the ministry at Shrewsbury, was almost certainly associated with him in assisting Priestley in setting up his laboraory in Clapton, and then became a fellow-Askesian with strong interests in industrial chemistry.[107] But we may not assume that this path was the only one possible or that there were not a variety of deviations from it. During the 1790s Jeremiah Joyce (1763–1816)[108] represented an excellent example of a close linkage of Dissent, radical politics and scientific expertise and entrepreneurship in the years of revolution, and is of particular note here as an older friend and fellow student of Arthur Aikin at Hackney New College from 1786.[109] Furthermore, during 1794 to 1796 William Shepherd was the strongest and most public supporter of Joyce during his imprisonment and other vicissitudes, despite his youth and relative vulnerability.[110] The two men remained close in later years.[111] With his early years as a journeyman glazier, Joyce serves for Goodwin as a good representative of a new group of ascendant radicals from humble backgrounds but with professional, intellectual skills such as the engraver William Sharp (1749–1824) or the schoolteacher and playwright Thomas Holcroft (1745–1809).[112] While at Hackney, Joyce received additional mathematical instruction from Dr Richard Price who introduced him to Charles Stanhope (1753–1816, FRS 1772, MP 1780), as a tutor.[113] At times confused with his brother, the Dissenting minister Joshua Joyce, Jeremiah the younger was both Secretary of the Society for Constitutional Information from April 1792 as well as Secretary to the Unitarian Society in London.[114] Apprehended by the authorities on 14 May 1794, just two days after Thomas Hardy, at his own treason trial Joyce defended radical political associations as educative and progressive and cited the life of Christ as exemplary for all 'friends to freedom'.[115] Upon his release from the Tower after twenty-three weeks he was treated by the Unitarian community as a heroic figure, invited to preach to congregations including those of Thomas Belsham at Hackney and George Lewis at Carter Lane.[116] From that time onwards Joyce lived under the political and financial patronage of Stanhope[117] and as an itinerant Dissenting preacher and popular exponent of experimental philosophy[118] and natural theology.[119]

We may suggest that the periodic increase[120] in what we might dub 'network connectedness' served to create cultural neighbourhoods for small groups of geographically dispersed Dissenting intellectuals, and it was these that emerged as the scientific and technical associations of industrialization.[121] At the more general level of analysis, the sociologist Robert Merton identified a sociological ambivalence 'found in the disjunction between culturally prescribed aspirations and socially structured avenues for realising these aspirations'.[122] Merton is postulating a contradiction between the cultural structures and the social structures of a society.[123] In their micro-society of rational Dissent, young men such as Arthur Aikin were educated progressively to aspire to the heights of a new world, just as the wider society impinged on such aspirations through restrictive legislation. We have argued here that such disjunctions formed around crisis times or short conjunctures such as 1791–8 or 1817–23 and stimulated the emergence of a new combination of social identity, rational enquiry and – at times – technological application.

CONCLUSION: DISSENT AND THE PUBLIC
COST OF INVENTION

The accepted historiography of English Dissent is that it was socially costly for the Dissenters themselves and to an extent costly for the development of an industrial, urban society. Thus in describing the turmoil of 1791, Stevenson points out not only that it was the intellectual Dissenters who 'bore the brunt of the riots', but that such a burden was aided and abetted by

Tory local magistrates.[124] Dinwiddy sees the politics and 'common intellec-tual concerns' of rational Dissent as resulting in the feeling that 'their interests were being adversely affected by the uncertainties of war and were being subordinated to the interests of people such as City financiers and West India merchants who had close links with the political establish-ment', which in turn led to Benthamite understandings of corruption, privilege and inefficiency among the liberal middle classes more generally, as pursued in such journals as the *Westminster Review* in the 1820s.[125] In the world of the Utilitarians, repressive treatment of rational Dissenters ran counter to the efficient running of the economy. Yet the other side of this coin might be of more interest to the historian of industrialization. It might be reasonable to argue that the precisely non-fatal repression of Dissent in England from the 1780s represented a political element that vastly stimu-lated the rate of commercial and technological change. As Holt insisted long ago, the new Unitarian congregations were most visible in the innovating industrial towns of Manchester, Birmingham, Nottingham, Liverpool, Sheffield, Leeds and Newcastle.[126]

Years ago Bert Hoselitz argued from a broadly Weberian position that individuals engaged in deviant economic activities might well lie 'at the margin of a given culture or [be] in a social or cultural position in which they straddle more than one culture'. Here we have converted this sort of overall functional perspective into a cultural microcosm that began with Arthur Aikin and his circle and ends with a claim about the character of technological change! However, this too seems to have been at least con-doned by Hoselitz when he argued that insights into social change may be sharpened if 'we take account not of changes affecting the society as a whole but of those affecting specialized sections or classes in the society'.[127] In effect, we might argue that the containment of Dissent among 'specialized sections' within the cultural associations of England served to reduce the public cost of technological change in early nineteenth-century Britain in comparison to other, potential rivals. With E. P. Thompson we might remember that such men as Priestley, Price, Frend and John Aikin '*did* enjoy liberty of conscience, they were not threatened by the Inquisition or the dungeon of the "Scarlet Whore of Babylon"'.[128] Palmer, it is true, took the trip to the Antipodes in 1794 but was immediately able to purchase good land, was 'treated with civility', and died wealthy in Guam in 1802 after a life of much adventure.[129] Others suffered irreparable harm from their periods of imprisonment.[130] But just as over time Dissenting communities dispelled or were partially absorbed into more established society, so too this was merely another side of a coin that saw the Dissenting 'universe of discourse' dispersed much more broadly within that established society.[131] The candour of Dissent might only be expressed or acted upon within an essentially civil society, and increasingly the society that emerged after the French wars was one both urban and urbane.[132] Rational Dissenters were Friends of the People, of Freedom, of Liberty and of Reformation, but also Friends of Science and of Good Order and Domestic Quiet. Such terms denoted symbols of the culture of rational Dissent that were increasingly those of a wider, liberal urbane society.[133] In contrast, by these years the otherwise competing French system had clearly fallen into a post-revolutionary haze of hierarchical administration, zealous regulation and imperial ambition, a mixture that did not bode well for the mathematics and natural and experimental philosophy that had led the European intellectual system prior to 1789. In distinct contrast, Britain was to continue to gain culturally and technologically from a form of tenuous control over Dissent that not only allowed but also induced associational experiment, intellectual enquiry and technological application among significant, dynamic and urbane groups of those who considered themselves to be beyond the pale of the Anglican establishment. The cost of this to the tax-paying public was zero.

An unintended consequence of the containment of Dissent in a precisely British mode was a precisely British industrialization. Of course, much else went into the conjuncture of the British industrial revolution, a globally significant watershed between the early modern and the modern that has been found impossible to convincingly colligate.[134] But it seems reasonable to suggest that an important element that increased the likelihood and lowered the cost of technological innovation in Britain during and beyond the later eighteenth century was the complex, only partially regulated configurations of Dissent, authority, useful knowledge and technological change.

NOTES

1. In 1760 Priestley (1733–1804) moved to Warrington under Dr Aikin the elder, was involved with Price and Franklin in London, and wrote his *History of Electricity* and became FRS. He then removed to Mill Hill Chapel, Leeds in 1767, wrote *An Essay on Government* (1768), and turned more precisely Unitarian. He was employed with Shelburne in scientific work and in London (1773–80). From 1780 Priestley was in Birmingham as minister of the New Meeting and a member of the small, elite Lunar Society and adopting a more radical religious position; his *Corruptions* (1782) embracing not only the Trinity but notions of original sin, predestination, the Atonement and 'the plenary inspiration of Scripture'. On 14 July 1791 the Birmingham riot against the

meeting house and the laboratory meant his removal to Hackney and then America in April 1794.

2. *Philosophical Magazine*, 2 (January–June 1833), 385–91 (385; 390).

3. Ian Inkster, 'London Science and the Seditious Meetings Act of 1817', *British Journal for the History of Science*, 12 (1979),192–6.

4. *Philosophical Magazine*, 2 (January–June 1833), 394.

5. Pepys owed the 'apparatus and the arrangement of my own laboratory' as well as research projects and individual experiments to Priestley; *ibid.*, 400.

6. The notion of cosmopolitan urbanites and their entry 'in the Great Society' is formulated initially and most clearly in Robert Merton, 'Patterns of Influence: A Study of Interpersonal Influence and of Communications Behaviour in a Local Community' (1948), reprinted in Merton, *Social Theory and Social Structure* (New York, NY: Free Press, 1968), 91–110.

7. E. P. Thompson, *The Making of the English Working Class* (London: Victor Gollancz, 1963), 36.

8. Note that John Aikin began delivery of a course on chemistry at Warrington Academy in 1773 at a time when it was going through one of its several crises, this one occasioned by student riots led by William Strickland, and an ongoing faculty quarrel between William Enfield and others. See, W. Strickland to Richard Bright, Boynton, 15 January 1773; J. Norman at Warrington Academy to Richard Bright, 20 February 1774, [Volume of MS Letters of Bright Family of Bristol and London, Bright Family Papers, Melbourne].

9. Enfield from Norwich to Clayton at Nottingham, 23 December 1789 [Nicholson Papers, Liverpool Record Office, 920 NIC. 9/12/4].

10. Clayton had been a minister at Benn's Garden Chapel, Liverpool, 1776–81 when he then succeeded John Aikin to the divinity chair of Warrington Academy, and was at this time pondering the foundation of a Dissenting academy in Nottingham: Enfield was the minister at Benn's Garden in the 1760s and later tutor and minister at Warrington; Price (1723–91), a major figure among rational Dissenters, had published *Review of the Principal Questions in Morals* as an attack on Hutcheson in 1756 and at the end of his life was famously denounced by Edmund Burke. See George E. Evans, *A History of Renshaw Street Chapel and Its Institutions, with some Account of the former chapels Castle Hey and Benn's Garden* (London: C. Green, 1887).

11. See William Shepherd from Gateacre, Liverpool to Walter Wilson (1781–1847), Bath, 3 December 1841 [MS Montagu Collection, Bodleian Library, Oxford, d21, fl 258–9].

12. A. and B. Heywood of Liverpool Correspondence with Henry Bright 1770–1 [Papers of Henry Bright, Section 1, vol. 11 of Bright Family MS Collection, Melbourne University Archives: 25f.].

13. Shepherd's birth was registered at Benn's Garden Chapel and he came from a local family of master shoemakers. After a spell at Daventry Academy he transferred to Hackney, where he seems to have been strongly influenced by Price and began a very close friendship with Joyce; see *A Selection from the Early Letters of Revd William Shepherd LLD* (Liverpool: H. Bradley, 1855), 1–39. For

Shepherd as a kindly guardian, see Wakefield from Dorchester Gaol to Shepherd at Liverpool, 7 October 1799. [William Shepherd MS Collection in 26 vols., Manchester College, Oxford, henceforth WS Collection], 11, fo. 127. Dr Crompton had introduced the two men when Shepherd was at Hackney around September 1798. For an introduction to this impressive archival collection, see Francis Nicholson, 'The MS of William Shepherd at Manchester College, Oxford', *Transactions of the Unitarian Historical Society*, 2 (4) (1922), 119–30.

14. This is most certainly not the place to dispute the use of the term Unitarian, except to say that individuals termed Unitarian in the present chapter were so self-labelled at that time or were identified at the time as having passed into a Unitarian doctrinal position. By these years the term included all those who recognized the 'Supremacy of the Father': thus *Arians* held that the Three are distinct and pre-existent Beings, but that the Son and Holy Ghost owe their existence to the will of the Father; *Socinians* held that the Father alone is the Most High God, that the Son is not pre-existent, the Holy Ghost is divine influence. The house of rational Dissent was built from many blocks but perhaps centred on the notion that 'whatever is obscure or inexplicable must be orthodoxy' (anonymous letter to the Bishop of Chester 1790) and that the duty of a Christian minister is to divulge the seeming mysteries of the scriptures, with reference to St Paul on what was loosely translated as 'liberty of speech'.

15. Anthony Lincoln, *Some Political and Social Ideas of English Dissent, 1763–1800* (Cambridge University Press, 1938), 25–6, quoting Aikin, *Memoir of John Aikin*, 1, 46.

16. Aikin, *Letters*, 1, 93 (the letters were compiled during 1792); Priestley, *A Letter of Advice to those Dissenters who conduct the Application to Parliament for Relief from certain Penal Laws, with various Observations relating to similar subjects* (1773), in Rutt, *Theological and Miscellaneous Works*, XXII, 455.

17. Philip Anthony Brown, *The French Revolution in English History* (1918; London: Frank Cass, 1965), 6.

18. *Times*, 26 June 1789, 1.

19. *Ibid.*, 9 July, 14; 17 September, 1791, 1.

20. Both men were associated with the rejuvenation of Warrington Academy in 1779: *Gore's General Liverpool Advertiser*, 13 August, 1 September and 13 October 1779.

21. J. Aikin, Yarmouth, to Dr Thomas Percival, Manchester, 17 December 1791 [MS Bound Volume, James Kendrick, 'Profile of Warrington Worthies, Autographs and Letters', n.d., Local History Collection, Warrington Public Library, Warrington].

22. John Evans, *A Sermon on the Decease of the Rev. Hugh Worthington of Salters Hall*, Islington (London: privately printed, 1813).

23. Gravel Pit Chapel first opened during 1716 as a result of a local dispute and split; the move from Arminian tendencies to Arian was not especially public or notable until the arrival of Price in 1770 from Newington Green, and

subsequent large congregations, support for America, massive Fast Day congregations and increased radicalism. See Alan R. Ruston, *Unitarianism and Early Presbyterians in Hackney* (Oxley: privately printed, 1980 [British Library: x.200/40127]).

24. R. V. Holt, *The Unitarian Contribution to Social Progress in England* (London: Allen & Unwin, 1938), 115.

25. Priestley's local life in Clapton was periodically made dreadful by local tradesmen etc., but he became dependent on a new local coterie of Belsham, Lindsey and others until his escape to America in April 1794. He was followed by Thomas Belsham who continuously expanded the congregation, he being a staunch Unitarian controversialist. See Ruston, *Unitarianism in Hackney*, 17.

26. Mike Gray, 'Joseph Priestley in Hackney', *Enlightenment and Dissent*, 2 (1983), 107–10.

27. Cooper (1769–1839) had withdrawn from the Manchester LPS – to which he had read his propositions respecting the *Foundations of Civil Government* on 7 March 1787, which made claim of justifiable revolution – because they did not publicly support Priestley during the 1791 riots.

28. Priestley, *Dedication to the Members of the Lunar Society of Birmingham* republished as appendix to *Heads of Lectures* 1794 dated Clapton 16 November 1793. Priestley, Kirwan, Boulton, Wedgwood, Watt and others all recommended Thomas Cooper to the Fellowship of the RS in two separate cases in 1792, undoubtedly for political reasons. The allegiances of Cooper in the late 1780s and 1790s with men such as Price, Priestley and Paine epitomized the configurations of rational Dissent and civil society.

29. Enfield from Norwich to Clayton, 22 March 1790 [Nicholson Papers, Liverpool Record Office, 920 NIC. 9/12/5].

30. As told by Aikin to James Currie, JA from Yarmouth to JC at Liverpool, 16 November 1790 [Currie Papers, Liverpool Record Office, 920 CUR, 55–7].

31. Aikin to Currie, 16 November 1790.

32. Mrs Ridyard, 'Notes on T. Fyshe Palmer' [WS Collection x, fo. 9, nd *c*.1802].

33. Samuel Heywood of Liverpool to Richard Bright, 20 December 1792 [Miscellany Volume of Letters, Brights of Bristol and London, Bright Family Papers, Melbourne].

34. Ruston, *Unitarianism in Hackney*, 18.

35. *New College 24th June, 1789* [printed handbill BL 4406.g.2 [134]].

36. Priestley, *The proper objects of education in the present state of the world: represented in a discourse, delivered on Wednesday, April 27, 1791, at the meetinghouse in the Old-Jewry, London; to the supporters of the New College at Hackney* (London: Johnson, 1791), 24, 34.

37. Priestley drew explicitly on Hartley's *Theory of the Human Mind*, in his own *Miscellaneous Observations relating to Education, More especially as it Respects the Conduct of the Mind* (Bath: R. Cruttwell, 1788), xii.

38. Joseph Priestley, *Heads of Lectures on a Course of Experimental Philosophy, particularly including Chemistry* (London, New College, Hackney: G. Smallfield, 1794), viii. The book is contemporary with Erasmus Darwin's evocation of a naturalistic

evolutionism in *Zoonomia*, vol. 1 (London, 1794). From around then, and led by such reviews as the *British Critic* or the *Anti-Jacobin*, a Pittite attack began on a range of scientific works that could be construed as anti-scriptural and the old English relaxation recognized by Willey ('the holy alliance between science and religion') had been destroyed by the later 1790s; Basil Willey, *The Eighteenth Century Background* (London: Chatto & Windus, 1946), 136; see Norman Garfinkle, 'Science and Religion in England 1790–1800', *Journal of the History of Ideas*, 26 (1955), 376–88.

39. Priestley had been pursuing this tack for some time, at Warrington Academy attacking older teaching of grammar and so on as unsuited to those who would 'fill the principal stations of active life': his position was that the new world depended not only on new content but on new style also: see his *An Essay on a Course of Liberal Education for Civil and Active Life* (London: C. Henderson, 1768), 2–3.

40. Anonymous [William Shepherd], *Every Man his Own Parson* (Liverpool: private printing, 1791), 15.

41. Aikin, *Letters*, 1, 47. See Roy Porter, *Enlightenment. Britain and the Creation of the Modern World* (London: Penguin, 2000), 154–5.

42. *Ibid.*, 352–3.

43. Priestley, *Heads of Lectures on a Course of Experimental Philosophy*, 2–4.

44. Arthur Aikin, *Syllabus of a Course of Lectures on Chemistry and Chemical Manufactures. By A. and C. R. Aikin* (London: Johnson, 1799), 1, 4.

45. *Times*, 13 July 1796.

46. *Times*, 21 November 1796.

47. A. F. Cronstadt, *An Essay towards a System of Mineralogy, translated from the Swedish by Gustav von Engerstrom to which is added a Treatise on the Pocket Laboratory, by the translator, including revisions and comments by E. M. Da Costa* (London: E. and C. Dilly, 1770). Da Costa operated from his General Office of Business, Arts and Trade in Cheapside, this book having originated in 1758 but since circulated in English, Swedish and German editions. In terms of the cultural status of such work at this time we might note that the booksellers Charles and Edward Dilly produced Boswell's *Life of Johnson*, and in addition to famous literary dinners held at their shop in the Poultry, were associated with such a variety of cultural leaders as Oliver Goldsmith and Joseph Priestley.

48. Frederick Accum, *A Practical Essay on the Analysis of Minerals* (London: printed for the author, 1804), i–ix; 4–24.

49. Ian Inkster, 'Science and Society in the Metropolis. A Preliminary Examination of the Social and Institutional Context of the Askesian Society of London', *Annals of Science*, 34 (1977), 1–32.

50. *Philosophical Magazine*, 13 (1802), 406–7.

51. E. C. Cripps, *Plough Court. The Story of a Notable Pharmacy 1715–1927* (London: Allen & Hanbury, 1927).

52. *Philosophical Magazine*, 10 (June–September 1801), 38, 370–1.

53. *Annals of Philosophy* (July–December 1815), 198–209.

54. *Philosophical Magazine*, 12 (October–December 1803), 166–9.
55. *The Star*, 19 March 1802, 1.
56. *Philosophical Magazine*, 11 (October–December 1801), 382.
57. *The Star*, 3 November 1804, 2.
58. *Philosophical Magazine*, 14 (January–March 1804), 85–90.
59. H. B. Woodward, *The History of the Geological Society of London* (London: Geological Society, 1907).
60. *A Dictionary of Chemistry and Mineralogy*, vols. 1 and 11 (London: W. Phillips, 1807).
61. Arthur Aikin (ed.), *The Annual Review and History of Literature*, from 1802, vol. 1 (London: T. Gillet, 1803), with preliminary prospectus.
62. Vol. 6 for 1808, 804–8, where it is argued to be principally 'a Laboratory Guide' and generally very empirically critical in order to try to resolve differences between such writers as Priestley, Klaproth, Kirwan or Vauquelin. The intention is not to teach crafts but show manufacturers 'what parts of [processes] offer the most reasonable probability of improvement' that is like a guide to intelligent investors or promoters; not merely a critical survey but with experiments and adding communications from friends, especially in areas such as metal smelting, manufacture of acids, etc.; the review notes the special feature on chemical apparatus and laboratories for younger chemists and how in each experiment much detail of apparatus is included.
63. *Annual Review*, 7 (1809), 683–6, 805–6.
64. D. E. Allen, *The Naturalist in Britain. A Social History* (London: Penguin 1978), 67. This may be seen as an extension of the cooperative information system initiated in the Mineralogical.
65. For discussion of which, see Rachel Laudan, 'Ideas and Organizations in British Geology: A Case Study in Institutional History', *Isis*, 68 (1977), 527–38; D. P. Miller, 'Method and the "Micropolitics" of Science: The Early Years of the Geological and Astronomical Societies of London', in J. A. Schuster and R. R. Yeo (eds.), *The Politics and Rhetoric of Scientific Method* (London: Reidel, 1986), 227–57.
66. Arthur Aikin, *A Manual of Mineralogy* (London: Longman, 1814). See Hugh Torrens in *British Journal for the History of Science*, 16 (1983), esp. 118–28.
67. *An Account of the Most Important Recent Discoveries and Improvements in Chemistry and Mineralogy, An Appendix to the Dictionary of Chemistry and Mineralogy* (London: W. Phillips, 1814).
68. John Bostock, Arthur Aikin and Alexander Barry, *Syllabus of a Course of Chemical Lectures delivered at Guy's Hospital* (London: E. Cox, 1827), vi–vii. Pages 27–63 were devoted to metals and metallurgy.
69. Derek Hudson and Kenneth W. Luckhurst, *The Royal Society of Arts 1754–1954* (London: John Murray, 1954), 172–6, 179–80.
70. Arthur Aikin, *An Address delivered on 27 May 1817 at the Annual distribution of Rewards of the Society for the Encouragement of Arts, Manufactures and Commerce* (London: T. Woodfall, 1817), 14, 20–1, 24–5. The secretary received a salary.

71. Arthur Aikin, *Illustrations of Arts and Manufactures* (London: J. van Voorst, 1841). For quotes and main points see: 318–22, 344–5, 283–9ff. Considerable attention is given to furnaces and iron ores of India, where they do not roast ore prior to fusion, using bamboo charcoal, and no lime or flux is then needed as silica provides potash, in small thin furnaces.

72. See Eric Robinson, 'The English "Philosophes" and the French Revolution', *History Today*, 6 (1956), 116–21; Ian Inkster, 'Seditious Science: A Reply to Paul Weindling', *British Journal for History of Science*, 14 (1981), 181–7.

73. Erik Routley, *English Religious Dissent* (Cambridge University Press, 1960), 165.

74. This is doubted or questioned often enough, but for contrast see D. I. Eaton (ed.), *Politics for the People* (London: Hogs Wash, 1794), vol. 1, pt 1, 1794, no. 5: 66–8 (where Quakers in particular are identified as 'republicans and levellers'); no. 11: 160–4; no. 12: 165; no. 13: 182–3. Several times arrested for seditious publishing, Daniel Isaac Eaton was a veteran of the revolutionary movement and a publisher of Tom Paine's *Age of Reason*, in 1795; see also Thompson, *Making of the English Working Class*, 97, 109, 124–9, 604–5.

75. Ian Sellers, 'William Roscoe, the Roscoe Circle and Radical Politics in Liverpool 1787–1807', *Transactions of Historical Society of Lancashire and Cheshire*, 12 (1968), 45–62 (47).

76. Josiah Wedgwood, Etruria to Richard Bright, 28 June 1784 [vol. 111, Bright Family Papers, Melbourne]. At this time Bright, Wedgwood and Priestley appear to have been planning to set up a new academy to succeed that of Warrington.

77. Thomas Percival, *A Short View of the Grounds and Limits of Taxes, addressed to the Manchester Literary and Philosophical Society* (Warrington: private printing, 24 March 1785) and *An Appendix to the Inquiry concerning the Principles of Taxation* (Warrington: Eyres, for T. Cadell, 1790), 20.

78. John D. Gay, *The Geography of Religion in England* (Basingstoke: Macmillan, 1971), 107.

79. Two printed leaflets dated 25 May 1789 signed Richard Bright, Chairman of Bristol committee; Richard Bright to William Russell, 10 February 1790; letters of William Rathbone of Liverpool and Richard Bright, 15–24 November 1792 [Bright Family MS, Melbourne].

80. Section XI of vol. 11 [Bright Family MS, Melbourne]. Richard identified Bright's disease.

81. A Dissenter [Anna Letitia Barbauld], *An Address to the Opposers of the Repeal of the Corporation and Test Acts*, 3 March 1790 (London: J. Johnson, 1790), 16, 21, 30–3. The references here seem to be to Ptolemy's allusion to the Polish river and the horned river-god Borysthenes; see Orianne Smith, '"Unlearned and ill-qualified Pokers into Prophecy": Hester Lynch Piozzi and the Female Prophetic Tradition', *Eighteenth-century Life*, 28(2) (spring 2004), 87–112. Milton represents Ithuriel as sent by Gabriel to search for Satan in Paradise, armed with a spear, the touch of which could expose the true form of each being, unmasking any falsehood.

82. Barbauld, *An Address to the Opposers of the Repeal of the Corporation and Test Acts*, 36–7.

83. Draft of proposals by Dr Currie to Dr Priestley [Currie Papers, Liverpool Record Office, 920 CUR, fl58 undated].
84. For which see in general J. C. D. Clark, *English Society 1688–1832* (Cambridge University Press, 1985), esp. 346–8; Richard Brown, *Church and State in Modern Britain, 1700–1850* (London: Routledge, 1991), 328–84.
85. Roger Wells, *Insurrection. The British Experience 1795–1803* (London: Alan Sutton, 1983).
86. A. C. Grayling, *The Quarrel of the Age. The Life and Times of William Hazlitt* (London: Phoenix Press, 2000), 5. Grayling is looking back to Noel Annan's concept of 'The Intellectual Aristocracy'; see Annan's essay in Plumb, *Studies in Social History*, 243.
87. David Hartley, *Observations on Man, His Frame, Duty and Expectations* (London: S. Richardson, 2 vols. 1749, repr. 1791, 1799).
88. Ruth Watts, *Gender, Power and the Unitarians in England 1760–1860* (Harlow: Pearson Education Limited, 1998), 35–6, 40–52.
89. All quotations here are from the single volume, *Letters from a Father to His Son* (London: J. Johnson, 1793), written 1792–3.
90. *Ibid.*, 2–3.
91. *Ibid.*, 9–11.
92. *Ibid.*, 41.
93. *Ibid.*, 94.
94. For which, see T. C. Kennedy, 'From Anna Barbauld's *Hymns in Prose* to William Blake's *Songs of Innocence and of Experience*', *Philological Quarterly*, 77 (1998); White, 'The "Joineriana"', 511–33.
95. Aikin, *Letters*, 1, 112, 114.
96. John Howard (1726?–1790), who published his *State of the Prisons* in 1777 and pursued the subject to the end of his life.
97. Aikin, *Letters*, 1, 212.
98. Aikin, *Letters*, 1, 339, 340.
99. For a general approach to the private and public spheres in 1790s England see Andrew McCann, *Cultural Politics in the 1790s. Literature, Radicalism and the Public Sphere* (Basingstoke: Macmillan, 1999), the overall excellence of which is somewhat marred by neglect of Unitarians/rational Dissent and of natural philosophy.
100. Aikin, *Letters*, 1, 34.
101. *Ibid.*, 36.
102. All quotations here are from the first edition of vol. 11 (London: Johnson, 1800), written 1798–9.
103. *Ibid.*, 7.
104. *Ibid.*, 11.
105. *Ibid.*, 175.
106. Joseph O. Baylen and Norbert J. Gossman, *A Biographical Dictionary of Modern British Radicals*, 3 vols. (Hassocks: Harvester Press, 1979–88), 1, 125.
107. L. B. Hunt and P. D. Buchanan, 'Richard Knight 1768–1844: A Forgotten Chemist and Apparatus Designer', *Ambix*, 31, pt 2 (1984), 57–67.

108. A recent biography of Joyce is somewhat disappointing, its author being content to itemize the varied, interlocking and progressive activities of his subject under three separated rubrics: John Issitt, *Jeremiah Joyce. Radical, Dissenter and Writer* (London: Ashgate, 2006). For a reliable itemizing of the published work of Joyce, see *Gore's Liverpool Advertiser*, 28 February 1822, 1; Robert Aspland, 'Memoir of the Late Rev. Jeremiah Joyce', *Monthly Repository*, 12 (1817), 697–704.

109. *Liverpool Mercury*, 27 December 1816, 3. The inscription on his tombstone in Cheshunt churchyard was a poem from the Liverpool Unitarian and radical scientist William Shepherd, part of which read 'Firm in his Country's and in Freedom's Cause / Braved the dread peril of perversed laws . . .'

110. See Shepherd, *Early Letters of Revd William Shepherd*, throughout ch. 4.

111. WS Collection, 111, Joyce to Shepherd, 25 November 1814, writing and vacationing together.

112. Albert Goodwin, *The Friends of Liberty: The English Democratic Movement in the Age of the French Revolution* (London: Hutchinson, 1979), 215–16.

113. Aspland, 'Memoir of the Late Rev. Jeremiah Joyce'. Another radical whose house was fired by a Tory mob, Chairman of the Revolution Society, the third Earl Stanhope was a scientist, patentee and innovator in stereotyping, the hand-press and logotypes. He published *Principles of Electricity* in 1779.

114. *Monthly Repository*, 11 (1816), 434–45. Notably, Jeremiah, Joshua and Hannah their mother (aged 90) all died within months of each other. See also J. Seed, 'Jeremiah Joyce, Unitarianism and the Vicissitudes of the Radical Intelligentsia in the 1790s', *Transactions of the Unitarian Historical Society*, 17(3) (April 1981), 97–108.

115. Jeremiah Joyce, *A Sermon Preached 23 February 1794, to Which is Added an Appendix, An Account of the Author's Arrest for Treasonable Practices* (London: privately printed, 1794), xii.

116. Jeremiah Joyce, *An Account of Mr Joyce's Arrest for Treasonable Practices* (London: Chevening House, 1795), 13–15, 24. At which time Joyce was employed as tutor to the sons of Lord Stanhope. He was released from the Tower upon acquittal on 29 November along with Hardy, John Thelwall, J. H. Tooke and others. At this time and until the later 1790s Joyce remained a financial and personal supporter of many imprisoned or impoverished political radicals: J. T. Rutt, 'An Account of Jeremiah Joyce', *Monthly Repository*, 12 (1817), 357–61.

117. WS Collection, 111, Stanhope to Joyce, 24 March 1801, fo. 297, wherein both remain 'Citizen': 'It is very important that, when the people begin to remonstrate, true informed *Principles* should be the Order of the Day'.

118. In particular see *Scientific Dialogues* (many editions 1800–43); the 1806–12 *Book of Trades*; *Dialogues on Chemistry* (1810–22); *Letters on Natural and Experimental Philosophy* (1810–22) and his contributions to *Rees' Encyclopaedia* and the *Monthly Magazine*.

119. In particular see contributions in thirteen numbers to *Monthly Repository* for 1815/16 and his works of 1795 and 1804 on Paley's natural theology.

120. We might briefly note an increase of Unitarian marginality after the failed Trinity Act of 1813, when the subsequent prosecutions of 1817 established the vanishing point for Unitarian property rights, and 'helped to isolate the Unitarians from the increasing number of the orthodox, and drive them outside the main body of Dissenters into their own association', perforce and against their own wish to near-deistic social positions. Ursula Henriques, *Religious Toleration in England 1787–1833* (University of Toronto Press, 1961), 209. For the deistic step of the 1790s, see Thompson, *Making of the English Working Class*, 26–54.

121. Elizabeth Bott, *Family and Social Networks* (London: Tavistock, 1971). We are suggesting that political crisis converted the Unitarian network from one that was relatively loose-knit to one that was close-knit. We are also suggesting that the fundamental areas for association changed from immediate neighbour-hoods (arbitrary) to more complex and symbolic intellectual associations, or what might be thought of as cultural neighbourhoods. This meant that the rational Dissenters as a cultural community became more exclusive in terms of membership yet more inclusive in terms of geographical location. For conceptions of this, see S. Greer, *The Emerging City: Myth and Reality* (New York, NY: Free Press, 1962).

122. R. K. Merton, *Sociological Ambivalence and Other Essays* (New York, NY: Free Press/Macmillan, 1976), 11.

123. See also his 'Social Conformity, Deviation, and Opportunity Structures', *American Sociological Review*, 24 (1959), 177–89.

124. John Stevenson, *Popular Disturbances in England 1700–1870* (London: Longman, 1979), 136–42.

125. J. R. Dinwiddy, *From Luddism to the First Reform Bill* (Oxford: Blackwell, 1986), 10–18 (11).

126. Holt, *The Unitarian Contribution*, 31.

127. Bert F. Hoselitz, 'Economic Growth – Non-Economic Aspects', *International Encyclopaedia of the Social Sciences* (London and New York, NY: Macmillan/Free Press, 1968), IV, 427.

128. Thompson, *Making of the English Working Class*, 35–6, original emphasis. On Frend's career under banishment from Cambridge and in subsequent years see Frida Knight, *University Rebel, the Life of William Frend 1757–1841* (London: Victor Gollancz, 1971), 173–308.

129. The *Monthly Magazine* carried much information on Palmer, who generally claimed to prosper at the 'despotic caprice' of the New South Wales colonial authorities; see also WS Collection, x, fo. 9, 11, 13.

130. Thus William Shepherd's assistant teacher Thomas Lloyd suffered permanently impaired health; see E. Axon (ed.), *Memorials of the Nicholson Family* (Kendal: printed for private circulation, 1928), 112. Others, such as William Winterbotham (1763–1829), the silversmith turned Dissenting minister and another close friend of Shepherd, received highly disproportionate sentences for seditious sermons, in his case four years' imprisonment plus a £400 fine (see *DNB*).

131. For the idea that social groups are bounded by their 'universe of discourse', see G. H. Mead, *Mind, Self and Society* (University of Chicago Press, 1967).

132. See especially the editor's contributions in José Harris (ed.), *Civil Society in British History: Ideas, Identities and Institutions* (Oxford University Press, 2003).

133. On symbols and the interaction between groups, see D. Rothstein, 'Culture Creation and Social Reconstruction: the Socio-Cultural Dynamics of Intergroup Contact', *American Sociological Review*, 37 (1972), 671–8.

134. For the British case in a global context see Ian Inkster, 'Potentially Global: "Useful and Reliable Knowledge" and Material Progress in Europe, 1474–1914', *International History Review*, 28 (2006), 237–86 and P. K. O'Brien, 'The Reconstruction, Rehabilitation and Reconfiguration of the British Industrial Revolution as a Conjuncture in Global History', *Itinerario*, 26 (2000), 118–36.

CHAPTER 7

'The different genius of woman': Lucy Aikin's historiography

Michelle Levy

In its composition, the objects in view have been perspicuity and order in narrative, selection of the most important circumstances, and a strict impartiality, exhibited not only in a fair and ungarbled representation of facts, but in the absence of every kind of colouring which might favour the purposes of what may properly be denominated *party*. This last intention, which has never ceased to guide the writer's pen, did not appear to him necessarily to preclude every expression of his feelings on points involving moral or constitutional questions.

John Aikin, *Annals of the Reign of King George the Third*[1]

In the study of history the different genius of woman I imagine will show itself. The detail of battles, the art of sieges, will not interest her so much as manners and sentiment: this is the food she assimilates to herself.

Anna Barbauld, 'On Female Studies'[2]

Lucy Aikin was best known in her lifetime, and for many decades thereafter, for her three, two-volume court histories, *Memoirs of the Court of Queen Elizabeth* (1818), *Memoirs of the Court of James the First* (1822) and *Memoirs of the Court of Charles the First* (1833). They were published by Longman, one of the leading presses of the day: their titles included the *Edinburgh Review* and their authors included Wordsworth, Coleridge, Southey, Moore and Scott. All of Aikin's histories sold well: *Elizabeth* was in its fourth edition in 1819, a year after its debut, and its eighth printing by 1869; *James* was in its third edition in 1823; and *Charles* was in its second edition within the first few months of its publication. The *Memoirs* were popular in America and the Continent as well: *Elizabeth* was first printed in America in 1821, with at least four more printings by 1870, and it was translated into German in 1819, Dutch in 1821 and French in 1827. *James* and *Charles* were both reprinted in America in the first year of their appearance. Lengthy, largely favourable reviews in the major periodicals of the day signalled the importance of the *Memoirs*.[3] The *Eclectic Review* spoke for many when it declared, in 1819, that with *Elizabeth* readers were 'put into possession of more correct information relating to those times, than they could obtain from any other single work'.[4] Fifteen years later, in 1834, an American reviewer summed up her achievement as follows: 'Aikin has done more to illustrate modern English history than almost any of the numerous and able writers, who, within the last fifty years, have turned their attention to the subject.'[5] Readers were impressed by Aikin's skill in marshalling a large body of material – gathered from both print and manuscript collections, in private hands and public institutions, scattered across the country – and transforming it into an entertaining, elegant and scrupulously objective narrative covering the period from Elizabeth's birth in 1533 to Charles I's death in 1649.[6]

In the past decade, there has been renewed interest in eighteenth- and nineteenth-century women's contributions to historiography – a function of the rising tides of feminism and historicism within the academy. Yet, despite the critical and popular success of Aikin's historical writing in her own day, and the revival of interest in women's historical writing in our own, her histories have rarely been the subject of careful scholarly consideration. Rosemary Mitchell is one of the few scholars to have acknowledged her contemporary significance: 'Lucy Aikin was the best-known woman scholar in this field: her studies of the courts of Elizabeth I, James I and Charles I, published between 1818 and 1833, led the way for the works of the Strickland sisters, Mary Anne Everett Green, Julia Pardoe (1806–62), Louisa Costello (1799–1870), and Martha Freer.'[7] Still, Aikin's memoirs are overlooked in important investigations, including Devoney Looser's study of the long eighteenth century, *British Women Writers and the Writing of History, 1670–1820* (2000) and Rohan Maitzen's *Gender, Genre, and Victorian Historical Writing* (1998).[8] They have been passed over in overarching treatments of the field: in seminal essays by Natalie Zemon Davis,[9] and in book-length treatments of the subject by Bonnie Smith (*The Gender of History: Men, Women, and Historical Practice*, 1998), Mary Spongberg (*Writing Women's History Since the Renaissance*, 2002), Miriam Burstein (*Narrating Women's History in Britain, 1770–1902*, 2004) and Lynette Felber (an edited collection, *Clio's Daughters: British Women Making History, 1790–1899*, 2007).[10] Periodization may in part be answerable for this neglect: Aikin's writing falling slightly too late for eighteenth-centurists, and slightly too early for Victorianists.

Greg Kucich, a Romantic literary scholar, has thoughtfully if briefly addressed Aikin's work in several essays by situating her writing within Romantic-era developments in feminist historiography.[11] Kucich reads Aikin's *Memoirs of the Court of Queen Elizabeth* through the lens of her earlier feminist retelling of women's history, *Epistles on Women, Exemplifying their Character and Condition in Various Ages and Nations* (1810). While I agree with Kucich that Aikin participates in the larger historiographical project of rejecting universal paradigms to concentrate on private life, Aikin's *Memoirs* cannot be so easily classed with the body of historical work devoted to women's lives, in so far as her works address the reigns of three sovereigns, only one of whom was female. Moreover, while I think there are useful insights to be derived from examining the *Epistles* and *Memoirs* together – a point to which I return at the end of this chapter – Aikin's innovations as a historian can only be grasped if her *Memoirs* are subject to a level of scrutiny that they have not yet received.

Indeed, the most salient reason for Aikin's *Memoirs* having been ignored is that they fail to conform to both earlier and later historical models. By her contemporaries, Aikin's *Memoirs* were most frequently compared to those of David Hume (*History of England from the Invasion of Julius Caesar to the Revolution in 1688*, 6 vols., 1754–62) and Catherine Macaulay (*History of England from the Accession of James I to the Elevation of the House of Hanover*, 8 vols., 1763–83).[12] Yet Aikin's histories reflect a considerable departure from theirs: whereas Hume and Macaulay wrote expansive political histories from a partisan perspective, Tory and Whig respectively, she focused on a much shorter period, and was consistently praised for her objectivity. By addressing a far briefer period of time within approximately the same scope as Hume, Aikin delved much more deeply into biography as well as social, cultural and legal history.[13]

At the same time that Aikin's three court memoirs are appreciably different from her immediate predecessors, they are also readily distinguishable from the tradition developed by her contemporaries and Victorian successors, that of 'women worthies', examples of which include Mary Hays' *Female Biography, or Memoirs of Illustrious and Celebrated Women, of All Ages and Countries* (1803) and Agnes Strickland's *Lives of the Queens of England* (1840–8), as well as similar works on female monarchs by Hannah Lawrance, Annie Forbes Bush, Martha Walker Freer, Mrs Matthew Hall and Mary Anne Everett Green.[14] These accounts of famous women 'had a polemical purpose: to disclose the range of female capacity, to provide exemplars, to argue from what some women had done to what women could do, if given the chance and the education'.[15] Aikin's *Memoirs*, by contrast, did not focus exclusively on the lives of royal women, and the women she does illustrate are rarely shown to be 'worthy'.[16] Even when writing her earlier history of women, *Epistles*, she explicitly rejects exemplarity in favour of the unexceptional, depicting women, almost exclusively,

as victims of male degradation and oppression.[17] Although she acknowledges the virtue and strength of many historical women, both within the
Memoirs and the *Epistles*, Aikin appears to have been suspicious of attempts
to separate women from men, at least for special treatment.

Another way of gauging the uniqueness of Aikin's historical method is to
consider her *Memoirs* in relation to pronouncements about historiography
that began to emerge in the early Victorian period, precisely at the moment
her *Memoirs* were drawing to a close. Attempts to define the discipline of
history arose chiefly as a response to the enormous popularity of the
historical novel; in order to separate historical fiction from history proper,
we find assertions being made that history 'proceeded according to rules of
form and content quite unlike the rules for fiction', and furthermore that 'it
was impersonal, grave, serious, methodical, strictly impartial, and concerned with large transformations and philosophical abstractions rather
than with concrete, personal details'.[18] Aikin, as we shall see, defies these
categories: her work is at once a highly serious endeavour, in its representations of the continual crises in which the nation was enveloped during
the sixteenth and early seventeenth centuries, and a species of 'lighter
literature',[19] in its effort to entertain readers as did novels; it is simultaneously methodical, employing a chronological approach, and digressive,
with repeated anecdotes and extended treatments of cultural, legal and
social topics; and, perhaps most significantly, it combines attention to the
large transformations of public history – above all the ongoing struggle to
reform both Church and State – and to the small 'concrete, personal details'
of individual lives – as she depicts the domestic history of the court as well
the lives of those affected by the repressive regimes under consideration.
Furthermore, though writing about historical rulers and administrations,
Aikin was inevitably inviting assessments of her own historical moment: as
Rohan Maitzen has remarked, 'historical description easily could, and often
did, become political prescription'.[20] By ingeniously blending together
different strands of historical practice, Aikin sought an intellectual and
affective response from her readers, urging them to evaluate the systems
of the past and their traces in the present day.

'BETWEEN POLITICAL HISTORY
AND HISTORICAL ROMANCE'

The significance and difficulty of Aikin's task was not lost on her contemporaries. In 1834, the *Edinburgh Review* noted that even though her
Memoirs had not been wholly successful, more than anyone else, she had

endeavoured 'to fill adequately that wide and ill-defined place which the memoir ought to occupy – a place intermediate between political history and historical romance'.[21] He continues:

It should have the truth and authority of the former [political history] – the detail and lively interest of the latter [historical romance]. It should convey to us the graphic exhibition of those characteristic trifles which the gravity of history will not stoop to notice. It should aim at rendering us intimately acquainted with the most eminent characters of the period it embraces, and make us live in former times. To attain this object successfully, demands more address, and a more careful selection of diversified materials, than is required by the narrator of political events.[22]

Aikin's mediation of these different historical modes may be traced, at least in part, to the Dissenting cultural values she inherited from her family, particularly her father and aunt. In her resolute support for a mixed monarchy – in which the sovereign's power is limited by the will of the people – and her powerful condemnation of the persecution of Nonconformists, Aikin speaks at once to the past and to the ongoing struggles of reformers and religious minorities. Her reflections on abuse of power, injustice in the administration of law, and violation of religious freedom during the reigns of the late Tudors and early Stuarts put into historical perspective the aspirations of Dissenters and liberals, long and anxiously awaiting the repeal of the Corporation and Test Acts and the reform of parliament (finally achieved during the period in which her court memoirs were written, in 1828 and 1832 respectively).

Though Aikin does not style herself as either a Tory or Whig, her memoirs are nevertheless highly critical of past regimes and, by implication, of the ongoing injustices still in want of reform. Her histories thus speak what Dan White has termed the 'new language of opposition' of 'a dissident middle-class'.[23] She achieves this oppositional stance largely by effecting another rhetorical strategy of Dissenters, that of resolving all political questions into ethical ones. Just as Dissenters had repeatedly presented their opposition to war, to colonial slavery and to their own marginalized status as moral issues, Aikin likewise treats efforts to curtail the privileges of Parliament, contravene the rule of law, impose cruel and unusual forms of punishment, especially torture, and persecute or inflict hardships on Nonconformists, as not merely contrary to the English con- stitution but in violation of basic moral principles. In doing so, she alights on the precise distinction established by her father in his foray into con- temporary history, *Annals of the Reign of King George the Third* (1816). For although her father embraced 'a strict impartiality', which his daughter felt to be 'the great historic virtue',[24] he nevertheless felt entitled to opine on 'moral and constitutional questions'. Aikin likewise empowers herself to cast stern judgements on her subjects, resulting in a history that is at once rigorously critical of England's former rulers and sufficiently evenhanded to preclude any charge of partisanship.

Informing Aikin's selection of the memoir genre is her rhetorical emphasis on ethics. Like her father and aunt's *Evenings at Home; or, the Juvenile Budget Opened* (1792–6), which urged even the youngest members of society to exercise their own capacity for moral judgement, even on the most pressing issues facing the nation, Aikin's attention to 'domestic history' seemed naturally to allow political questions to be transmuted into ethical ones.[25] Aikin privately acknowledged this to be her object, asserting that '[i]t is from intimate views of private life in various ages and countries that the moral of political history is alone to be derived'; and she expressed gratification when the 'moral tone' of her *Memoirs* was praised.[26] The *Ladies' Monthly Museum* noticed how Aikin's 'domestic history' allowed for the cultivation of moral judgement:

in the glare of history, we are apt to dwell on the consequences without perceiving the cause, and are frequently led to attribute excellencies to a character which never existed, and to overlook defects which we should do well to notice. In the bright pages of the former, the sovereign and the hero shine with undiminished lustre; but in the private chamber, they are divested of all adventitious advantages, and appear mortals, like ourselves. We probably find, in this minute inspection, a great deal to lessen, or at least qualify, our admiration, but we are enabled to form a juster estimate of the real character.[27]

Aikin in her private correspondence suggested that 'the chief utility of introducing biographical details largely into works of history' was not merely that it allowed her readers to judge individual conduct, but that they could discern whether individuals had been corrupted by their adherence to certain principles.[28] By enabling her readers to judge individual conduct and the principles that animated them, Aikin was fostering one of the most cherished tenets of Dissenting life: that all individuals had the capacity and right to form their own private judgements.[29]

Aikin's memoirs are also indebted to a feminist discourse familiar to her both through the writing of her aunt as well as that of her contemporaries, including her lifelong friend Joanna Baillie, as well as Charlotte Smith and Felicia Hemans, who had in their writing called attention to the private trauma that public events often inflicted on women, children and the family.[30] Barbauld had predicted that female writers would bring the 'different genius of woman' to historical consciousness: in her niece's histories, this is realized, as Aikin traces the effects of various social and political systems on individuals, families and by implication the nation. She also seeks to generate an affective response from her readers by turning their attention from large, unfathomable calamities to portraits of the suffering individual, a strategy rehearsed by her aunt in her poem 'The Caterpillar' and performed by many of the period's female writers.

Also like her aunt, Aikin did not wish to be viewed, particularly in her historical memoirs, exclusively as a female author. Barbauld, in her political writing, signed herself as 'an apparently ungendered "Dissenter" and "Volunteer"'.[31] She also resisted efforts to form associations exclusively with her own sex, whether to establish a girls' school or a women's journal.[32] It seems that, as a Dissenter, Barbauld was acutely aware that the urging of what she calls 'separate rights' (in 'The Rights of Women') could invite and even justify *un*equal treatment.[33] Aikin was similarly cautious: she made no special claims to be writing as a woman; she promised no special insight into the hearts of her female subjects, nor did she concentrate especially on the lives of historical women, though it may be that she devoted somewhat more attention to royal and noblewomen, who had been entirely overlooked in previous accounts.[34]

In one important respect, however, Aikin did address her readers as a woman – in her pledge to 'avoid . . . as much as possible all encroachments on the peculiar province of history'.[35] In a gesture evidently intended to disarm critics who might disapprove of a woman taking up political history,[36] Aikin proposes a plan that:

comprehends a detailed view of the private life of Elizabeth from the period of her birth; a view of the domestic history of her reign; memoirs of the principal families of the nobility and biographical anecdotes of the celebrated characters who composed her court; besides notices of the manners, opinions and literature of the reign.[37]

Yet, as at least one reviewer comments, the line 'between the office of the historian and that of the memoir-writer' is difficult to draw 'with any precision', and doubts whether 'her readers will perceive the distinction she imagines herself to have kept'.[38] Indeed, Aikin's claim to be working within a more confined genre than traditional history demands careful scrutiny: for Aikin's historical project was at once broader in scope, and more radical in its reach, than she claims. Attention to 'domestic history' in no ways evades 'the peculiar province of history', but, as Aikin knew, aims to transform it by shifting priorities and perspectives.

It is not improbable that Aikin deliberately misled in her prefatory remarks: we know that in seeking to promote her aunt's reputation, she occasionally misrepresented Barbauld's views on controversial social issues.[39] Her trepidation at penning Barbauld's memoirs may in part explain her motivations: 'But think of the age we live in! – think of the Quarterly Review, the Saints, the clergy, the tories & the canters, & tell me how we are to be at once safe & honest!'[40] Aikin's concern with reception is also at work in the introduction to *Epistles*, wherein she pleaded: 'Let me in the first place disclaim entirely the absurd idea that the two sexes ever can be, or ever ought to be, placed in all respects on a footing of equality.'[41] Barbauld had praised her niece's *Epistles* for their 'delicate . . . management', for having 'taken great care not to . . . say anything which a man jealous for the superiority of his sex . . . can reasonably object to'.[42] And yet, as her aunt undoubtedly realized, Aikin's disclaimer was 'a brilliant stroke of feminist irony', for she proceeds to establish how women's fundamental equality with men renders their oppressive treatment morally reprehensible.[43] Even decades later, while writing the *Memoirs*, Aikin privately conveys her ongoing commitment to the feminist ideals expressed in the *Epistles*, while at the same time acknowledging the need for caution in how these views are publicized: 'it contains many sentiments which I still cherish, and would give much to be enabled to disseminate'.[44] Similarly, in her *Memoirs* Aikin appeases readers whom she imagines might have been antagonistic to her aims only to seek a more radical refashioning of their very conception of history.

'THE DIFFERENT GENIUS OF WOMEN'

Barbauld's conjectures about 'the different genius of women' were well known to her niece and editor.[45] As her aunt had predicted, Aikin avoided '[t]he detail of battles, the art of sieges',[46] the traditional subjects of male history: Edward Gibbon, for example, had declared in *The Rise and Decline of the Roman Empire* that '[w]ars, and the administration of public affairs, are the principal subjects of history'.[47] Reviewers were quick to notice that with Aikin, there was a discernible shift in focus:

In the page of history, a disproportioned space is commonly allotted to the great political events which induce some sudden and marked change, *viz.* invasions, conquests, or defeats, powerful alliances abroad, or successful rebellions at home; while the influence of domestic institutions on the character of a country, or even that of its religion, laws, government, prevailing manners, and opinions, seems often to be regarded as an object of secondary moment, at which the writer is required only to glance.[48]

In *Elizabeth*, she assigns herself 'the humbler, but not uninteresting task, of tracing [the] effects' on individuals of 'public measures', cunningly implying that the latter may be of less interest, and import, than private history.[49] Indeed, privately she expressed the view that without the depiction of private life, which allowed for the assessment of public acts, there was no value to 'long tales of wars and conquests, and of one king deposing and succeeding another'.[50]

In her review of *The Life of William Roscoe*, Aikin similarly claims that the examination of private lives can powerfully elucidate public history: private letters, recording both opinion and events, 'may be regarded as running commentaries on the history and spirit of an age, more interesting, and more instructive in some respects, than any others'.[51] Although biography and letters may provide the 'means of estimating the character and principles of an individual ... we often gain, conversely, more insight into the real nature of a public measure ... from the sentiments of that individual, as thrown out in conversation or in familiar letters, than is to be obtained by the most assiduous study of official documents, Parliamentary speeches, or political pamphlets'.[52] For this very reason Aikin pays greater attention to private sources of information – to letters and journals – favouring memory over public record, the anecdote over the decree. She is thus able to draw upon 'a vast repertory ... of curious and interesting facts seldom recurred to for the composition of books of lighter literature'.[53]

The novelty of Aikin's historical method is also apparent in her refusal to represent armed conflict. Of the two major conflicts during the reigns under her consideration, the defeat of the Spanish Armada in 1588 and the various armed conflicts that punctuated the English Civil War, she has little to say. 'The memorialist of the court and character of Charles I', she writes, 'mindful of the just limitations of that theme, and anxious to escape as much as possible from the dry details of political debate, and the sickening ones of a fratricidal warfare, must here draw a firm and decided line', taking leave of the ongoing affairs of parliament, and 'declining also the detail of all military transactions in which the king was not immediately engaged'.[54] By focusing on other aspects of Charles I's reign, including the conduct of his administrators in the church and courts, she grants her readers leave to judge not merely the King's actions but also the principles that animated them.

Her cursory treatment of the threatened Spanish invasion embodies the desire to shift priorities in historical discourse. She passes over the battle itself, once again by reference to the design of the memoir: 'It is foreign from the business of this work to detail the particulars of that signal victory'.[55] She does, however, discuss the events leading up to battle, particularly the wider national response to the crisis, whereby '[a]ll ranks and orders vied with each other in an eager devotedness to the sacred cause of national independence'.[56] Celebrating their patriotic sacrifices, she nevertheless refuses to linger over 'the splendid tale of England's naval glory', devoting only the briefest mention to the outcome of the war in terms of prisoners taken and ships lost, pensions awarded and victories celebrated.[57] Instead, she elaborates upon what previous historians had failed to record, the emergence of the daily press: 'The intense interest in public events excited in every class by the threatened invasion of Spain, gave rise to the introduction in this country of one of the most important inventions of social life, – that of newspapers.'[58] For Aikin, one of the truly consequential outcomes of the war is the birth of a media that reports daily on events from a wide range of perspectives. The gradual emergence of a free press was, for obvious reasons, of the utmost importance to Dissenters: as Dan White has observed, liberty of 'the pulpit and the press' were centrally co-joined within Dissenting culture.[59]

Aikin also uses the occasion of the war as an opportunity to reflect on the Queen's private character. Despite praise for her steely resolve during the days leading up to the threatened invasion, Aikin is far more admiring of Elizabeth's refusal to use the war as a pretext for executing some of the country's leading Catholics, as was proposed by some of her advisers. The Queen's restraint at this juncture (to be contrasted with her subsequent persecutions) earns her high praise from Aikin, far more so than her martial courage. Aikin further insists upon the efficacy of such policy, explaining that the Queen's 'lenient proceeding ... was productive of the best effects', instilling loyalty on the part of the Catholics who remained at liberty, many of whom decided to fight against their church for their country and Queen.[60] Aikin will continue to connect toleration and national and domestic security on the one hand, and intolerance and unrest on the other, in an effort to draw the lessons of the past into the present. In doing so, she elucidates a relentlessly moral view of political history, claiming explicitly that freedom of conscience is at once a moral imperative and good policy, and implicitly what she owned only in private, that the 'great engine of civil and intellectual tyranny [is] a State religion'.[61]

'THE *MORAL* OF POLITICAL HISTORY'

It is in her treatment of the relationship between Elizabeth and Mary, Queen of Scots, that Aikin most pointedly engaged her readers in 'the *moral* of political history'. While Aikin was highly sympathetic to the challenges of Elizabeth's rule, paying particular attention to the insecurities of her early life at court and the terror she suffered while imprisoned in the Tower, she urges her readers to regard Elizabeth's transgressions with severity. She attempts to do justice to the Queen's reign, as had Hume, by commencing with a review of the 'legalized atrocity' characteristic of the reigns of her father and sister, for Elizabeth's 'fame has often suffered by inconsiderate comparisons which have placed her in parallel with the enlightened and humanized sovereigns of more modern days, rather than with the stern and arbitrary Tudors, her barbarous predecessors'.[62] Nevertheless, Aikin is no apologist for Elizabeth, and takes historical relativism only so far. Though the Queen is warmly praised for her courage during the threatened invasion, she is severely criticized for many other acts of her reign, above all the persecution of Puritans, and the imprisonment and execution of her cousin, Mary.

Aikin condemns the 'unwise and unauthorized detention of the queen of Scots', and denounces the 'arbitrary, unprecedented, [and] unjust' nature of her treatment generally.[63] She points out that Elizabeth's measures, rather than ensuring her safety, had the opposite effect, generating more mistrust and giving rise to fresh criminal conspiracies against her life. Her harshest censure against Elizabeth relates to her delays and prevarications in executing the sentence against Mary after her guilt in the conspiracy had been proved and sentence against her life had been passed, in the belief that 'an extraordinary parade of reluctance' would 'preserve to her the reputation of feminine mildness and sensibility'.[64] '[T]he sole result of her artifices', however, 'was to aggravate in the eyes of all mankind the criminality of the act, by giving it rather the air of a treacherous and cold-blooded murder, than of solemn execution done upon a formidable culprit by the sentence of offended laws'.[65] Aikin further condemns Elizabeth's hypocrisy after the execution; for the scapegoating of her secretary, William Davison, whom she had ordered to bring the warrant against Mary, and in the false claim to James, Mary's son, of her (Elizabeth's) 'perfect innocence in the tragical *accident* of his mother's death'.[66] Perhaps most damningly, and reflective of Aikin's ongoing attention to the inefficacy of intolerance and oppression, she contends that this act of executing her rival, 'the strongest and most extraordinary' of her reign, 'appears to have been productive of scarcely any assignable political effect'.[67]

Notwithstanding the 'infringement of morality committed by Elizabeth', 'which brought the blood of a sister-queen upon her head and indelible reproach upon her memory', Aikin by no means exonerates Mary.[68] Acknowledging that Mary was seeking to liberate herself from unjust detention, 'though with the destruction of her enemy and at the cost of a civil war to England', Elizabeth's wrongs cannot excuse Mary's 'many foibles, stained by some enormous crimes, and never under the guidance of the genuine principles of moral rectitude'.[69] Admonishing other historians who had taken a far more sympathetic view of the Scottish Queen, and staking her own position in the ongoing debates as to Mary's guilt or innocence, she intones: 'let not our resentment of the wrongs, or compassion for the long misfortunes, of this unhappy woman betray us into a blind concurrence in eulogiums lavished' on such an unworthy object.[70]

Aikin's endeavour to reduce all political questions to moral ones is strongly evident in her treatment of the two defining conflicts of the period under investigation: the struggle between the established religion and all other faiths, particularly during the reigns of late Tudors (Mary and Elizabeth), and the conflict between the monarchy and parliament, particularly during the reigns of the early Stuarts (James I and Charles I). (Of course, the ongoing nature of these political struggles would have been all too apparent to Aikin's readers.) For Aikin, the attempt to usurp the traditional privileges of parliament, contravene the rule of law, and persecute or impose hardships on those whose faith lies outside the Church of England is contrary not only to the ancient English constitution, but to basic principles of morality. Aikin, as we have seen, casts Elizabeth's decision to execute her rival and kinswoman as a moral transgression; she also evaluates the sovereign's interference with the 'known rights' of parliament, as well as that of her successors, as a moral offence. From Elizabeth's 'haughty and menacing' attitude to Charles I's relentless outrages against parliament, Aikin narrates what is in effect a 'whig history', assuming the existence and validity of parliamentary rights, and charting their greater recognition over time as at once inevitable and progressive. Parliament and the rule of law are the necessary protections against tyranny, and the *Memoirs* perpetually lament that both James I and his son flagrantly disavow these ancient institutions. Expressing scorn for James I's 'theory of regal prerogative', she condemns his lifelong attachment to the divine right of kings. So extreme was the King's belief in his own powers 'that he was constantly tempted to accuse his subjects of blasphemy and irreligion when they presumed to oppose his will, or call in question his lawless assumptions of authority'.[71]

With Charles I the threats to the ancient constitution reached an obvious crisis, the chief cause of which was his permanent proroguing of parliament: 'all of the invasions of right complained of had been carried on under shelter of the long intermissions of parliaments', with the King having 'openly declared his purpose of continuing to reign without them'.[72] Charles I's escalating assaults on parliamentary rule in effect sealed his fate: 'Charles speedily drew upon himself such unequivocal marks of resentment from all classes', rising to '[u]niversal indignation and complaint, and in some instances firm resistance', which eventually culminated in outright civil war.[73] Aikin's fulminations against these attacks on parliament were coloured by her anger over the delays in passing the first reform bill; Aikin is so overwrought by the crises precipitated by the House of Lords' rejection of the bill in late 1831 that she 'fear[s] its giving some tinge or some vices to my representation of the events of a former period of revolution'.[74] Although as we shall see, Aikin is ambivalent about the King's ultimate fate, she views the passage of a bill for triennial parliaments by the long parliament in 1641 as a triumphant moment: 'This grand security for the permanence of other reformations being thus obtained, the parliament proceeded to overthrow the whole machinery of arbitrary and illegal tribunals, which had proved so efficacious an engine for the purposes of the subverters of English liberty.'[75] She then lists the many reforms enacted by the long parliament, including the abolition of the Star Chamber and the right to seek redress for unlawful detention by way of habeas corpus. Aikin's history necessarily argues for the ongoing need to reform parliament, as the 'grand security' for all the other reforms still pressing upon Dissenters and liberals.

Notwithstanding Aikin's explicit support for the cause of parliament during Charles' reign, her discussion of the execution of the King is more ambivalent. She notes the irregularities of the proceedings – 'It is exceedingly remarkable that no legal advisers were assigned to the king by the court' – which she describes as 'the most unprecedented, judicial proceeding on record'.[76] In a summation disliked by some critics, she withholds her opinion: 'To pronounce any solid judgment, whether moral or political, respecting the sentence executed upon him, would require a discussion of alternatives which offered themselves to the choice of the party leaders of the time, of the aspects of affairs in their eyes, of their motives and ulterior designs, foreign from the character of this work, and to which the writer feels herself in many ways unequal.'[77] Here the moral complexities involved in evaluating the King's trial and execution seem to overpower Aikin, in so far as the necessity for the extraordinary proceedings against Charles could not be proved. In responding to a friend who felt she had showed a 'little want [of] indulgence to Charles', she expresses her 'regret that I forebore to sum up his character', explaining her reasons for doing so:

I shrunk from the task as a difficult, and in some sense dangerous one; for I should have made for him such allowances on account of education and the influences generally to which his situation exposed him, that the almost unavoidable inference would have been, that all kings must be, more or less, the enemies of liberty, of public virtue, of the happiness and progress of mankind. I have come as near this inference as I well could, by showing that Charles was absolutely suckled in falsehood and dissimulation, and that *as prince* he thought himself as much above the laws of social morality as those of the land.[78]

Although she refuses to sensationalize his end, she nevertheless sympathizes with him in his final moments, in his admission to being both a wrongdoer and a victim,[79] and in relating his pathetic parting from his children. Aikin's reluctance to reach a conclusion reflects her awareness of moral complexities involved in evaluating his life and end, and her refusal to endorse outcomes based on either party or hindsight.

In her comparisons of Queen Elizabeth and her sister, Mary I, Aikin offers similarly nuanced judgements about what for her is the most fundamental of all moral issues, freedom of conscience. Unlike Hume, for whom, 'Elizabeth appears clemency and moderation itself, when viewed as coming after her sister and father',[80] Aikin finds the sisters almost equally guilty in their attacks on religious freedom. Mary presided over 'a reign of terror':

The reestablishment ... of the Romish ritual and the papal authority, though attended with the entire prohibition of all protestant worship, was not sufficient for the bigotry of Mary. Aware that the new doctrines still found harbour in the bosoms of her subjects, she sought to drag them by her violence from this last asylum; for to her, as to all tyrants, it appeared both desirable and possible to subject the liberty of thinking to the regulation and control of human laws.[81]

By contrast to 'the genuine bigotry of her sister', Elizabeth was 'contented with a kind of negative intolerance', prosecuting only those who exhibited hostility against her government or church.[82] Her ecclesiastical policy was, therefore, based on 'compromise and political expediency' as opposed to faith, principle or concern for her subjects.[83] Furthermore, increasingly provoked by the Puritans, she became that 'incongruous and odious character of a protestant persecutor of protestants'.[84]

Not surprisingly, by far the greatest villain to appear in all three of Aikin's memoirs is Charles' archbishop, William Laud. Assailed for his 'complete intolerance of all protestant deviation from exact conformity, or uniformity, within the sphere of his authority', Aikin vilifies the archbishop for his attacks on Nonconformists. She is contemptuous of his attempt to turn parish priests informants, and praises those members of the established church who were reluctant 'to apply the scourge of persecution to brother protestants exemplary for their industry, their regular and inoffensive behavior, and their earnest piety'.[85] Even Catholics were treated with more tolerance than other sects: they could pay fines to celebrate mass which, though illegal, was connived at, whereas 'no similar indulgence [was] . . . extended to the religious services of protestant sectaries'.[86] Because most Nonconformists were ordained members of the official church, 'their deviations from conformity were easy and obvious' to detect and punish.[87] Her fullest condemnation of Laud, and of religious persecution generally, emerges in her delineation of the suffering of his victims, to be considered in the following section.

'A SINGLE SUFFERER'

In Anna Barbauld's poem 'The Caterpillar', the destruction (and rescue) of insects gives rise to a series of reflections about the nature, and operation, of sympathy. In the poem, the speaker explains that, though she had only recently 'crushed whole families [of caterpillars] beneath my foot', the sight of 'A single wretch, escaped the general gloom, / Mak[es] me feel and clearly recognise / Thine individual existence.'[88] Once she has physically examined the creature and felt its presence as a fellow being she can no longer 'hurt thy weakness'.[89] She proceeds to analogize her situation to that of a soldier, whose work of death and carnage is 'by no soft relentings stopped', except:

> . . . should one,
> A single sufferer from the field escaped,
> Panting and pale, and bleeding at his feet,
> Lift his imploring eyes, – the hero weeps;
> He is grown human, and capricious Pity,
> Which would not stir for thousands, melts for one
> With sympathy spontaneous.[90]

Barbauld's recognition of the greater capacity for sympathy generated by the appreciation of individuated, as opposed to mass suffering, is one that profoundly informs Aikin's historical representations.

In the opening pages of *Elizabeth*, Aikin describes all of the members of the court in attendance at the princess's christening, in part to introduce them to the reader, but also for a more profoundly affective end, to demonstrate 'how awfully large a proportion of their number should fall, or behold their nearest connexions falling, untimely victims of the jealous tyranny of Henry himself, or of the convulsions and persecutions of the two troubled reigns destined to intervene' before Elizabeth's.[91] With this synoptic approach, Aikin briefly describes the noble families only to point out how many of them ended their days on the scaffold or in captivity, in exile or penury. She does so to prefigure the despotism to come, to garner sympathy for the suffering that inevitably results, and to develop her readers' repugnance at the intolerable costs of tyranny.

The memoirs are punctuated with accounts of wrongful imprisonment, torture and death. Judicial torture in particular is singled out as especially pernicious, as at once inhuman and impolitic. Though her remarks are largely concentrated in *James*, she note how all of the monarchs under consideration resorted, at various times, to torture, notwithstanding that it had 'always, and in all circumstances, [been] contrary to the law of England'.[92] Extensively consulting and quoting from a manuscript collection 'of a late eminent ornament of the chancery bar, kindly communicated to me for the use of this work' she 'trace[s] with some minuteness the progress of this abuse', which contravenes one of the keystones of English justice.[93] She excoriates 'the anomaly truly barbarous' which sentenced women found guilty of high treason to execution by burning, a form of threatened torture that is used to extort a confession of sorts from Anne Boleyn.[94] Aikin denounces Boleyn's daughter, Elizabeth, for having resorted, 'to her eternal reproach', to torture more than 'any of her predecessors, or perhaps all of them put together' until 'compelled by public indignation to renounce it'.[95] She notes that of all James I's many abuses during his first session of parliament, the most offensive of all was 'his atrocious and most shameless assertion that torture itself might justifiably be inflicted on free-born Englishmen, at the will and pleasure of their sovereign'.[96]

Aikin, though she bears witness to the physical cruelty of torture, objects to it not only on this account, but because it is 'contrary to that sacred maxim of the English law, that no man is bound to accuse himself'.[97] Once torture is permitted, other abuses ineluctably follow, including the shameful practice of producing in court written depositions obtained through torture, thereby obviating the need for the witness's testimony and cross-examination. Thus was Sir Walter Raleigh tried and convicted of treason – the evidence against him consisting of a nobleman's unsigned and retracted statement, probably elicited through torture. The inequity of these unprecedented proceedings are lamented by Aikin in this rousing peroration:

> Better men and better patriots than Raleigh have sometimes fallen by that perversion of public justice which disgraces too many periods of the English annals; but none of those victims of iniquity, it may safely be affirmed, over whom the tears of liberty and of virtue have fallen the most copiously, have suffered by a sentence more illegal, more oppressive, more worthy to be branded with the note of infamy, that this extraordinary and memorable person.[98]

She is little concerned, it is to be noted, with the efficacy of torture; thus she does not assume Raleigh's innocence, which she considers as only merely possible. The chief injustice complained of is not the punishment of an innocent man, but the punishment of a man found guilty based upon a confession extorted by torture, which not only invades the dignity of the individual but threatens to destroy the entire system of criminal justice.

Aikin also notices another class of individuals subject to torture – those suspected of witchcraft and magic. James I is blasted for his revival of witchcraft persecutions, and particularly the infamous Lancashire trials of 1612, in which ten women and men were put to death based on evidence 'such as ought not to have been listened to on the most trifling charge ever obtruded upon the notice of a court of justice'.[99] She further recounts the many inexcusable trials held in James' 'favorite tribunal, the court of star-chamber', a court 'completely arbitrary, being bound neither by rules of law, nor even by its own precedents', as well as the similarly unprincipled court of high commission, 'that genuine Inquisition . . . through which the king exercised his jurisdiction as head of the church'.[100]

Aikin's comprehensive account of the corrupt administration of justice during James' reign extends even to the most forgotten victims of injustice. She attempts to trace 'the daily increasing abuses in the administration of justice' specifically because they bore so hard on the people, though, perhaps for that very reason, they have been 'too much neglected by the historians of the reign of James'.[101] She offers one example of James' shocking contempt for due process: shortly after he was named successor, James ordered a 'cutpurse' (a pickpocket) to be executed without trial. By 'perpetrating so wanton an outrage on the most venerated institution of the country, – trial by jury' for a trivial offence, 'men wondered what further innovations would ensue'.[102] She also recalls the grave punishments inflicted on Scottish clergy who protested his attempted abolition of

Presbyterian worship and discipline; and the unlawful detention of lawyers whose only offence had been the attempt to defend Puritans from unlawful detention.[103]

Her denunciation of illegal proceedings and corporeal punishment reaches its apotheosis in her representation of the proceedings against William Prynne, Henry Burton and John Bastwick for seditious libel during the middle years of Charles I's rule, in 1637. Aikin points out that although 'the language of all [their] tracts was violent and provoking in the extreme', to 'a church which felt itself strong in the reverence and attachment of the people, such railing accusations might with equal dignity and safety have been passed over in silence'.[104] The decision of Laud to proceed against the three of them, together, in the Star Chamber, is condemned as at once illegal and unwise, but it is the 'barbarous sentence' that warrants the most outrage.[105] As punishment, the men are ordered to pay the enormous sum of £5,000 apiece, to be set in the pillory and have their ears cut off, and to be imprisoned perpetually, without access to family or writing implements. Prynne, whose ears had already been cropped in satisfaction of a prior sentence, was ordered to have his ears cut closer, and to have his cheeks branded with the letters 'SL' (seditious libeller).

The execution of the sentence is described by Aikin in detail, who does so to generate sympathy for the sufferers and their families, to condemn 'the contrivers of an infliction which filled all impartial persons with horror and indignation', and to demonstrate the inefficacy of torture and cruelty.[106] For the men quickly become 'the three martyrs, as they were considered by themselves and by a great portion of the spectators'.[107] She further recounts the horrors and sympathies of the large crowds attending the pillorying of the men and their transportation to jail, and records the insult felt by the three learned professions, who felt the 'ignominy of the punishment inflicted on their respective members' (Prynne was a lawyer, Burton a clergyman, Bastwick a physician).[108] For Aikin, the near-universal sympathy felt for the sufferers is nothing less than a source of national pride: 'It is a generous characteristic of the English people, – and one which rulers have never found their account in overlooking, – to side with the weak and the persecuted. Mutilated, stigmatized, pilloried and ruined, the puritan confessors instantly became objects of sympathy, esteem, enthusiasm.'[109] Aikin concludes by reminding her readers that all of Laud's efforts to stifle dissent were frustrated, as additional libellous notes, directed chiefly at him, were tacked up through the city, whereas attempts to silence the prisoners also fail, their writings are smuggled out of prison and widely disseminated to an eager public.[110] As Puritan martyrs, the men are not forgotten, with their liberation in 1640 being one of the earliest acts of the long parliament, and their return to the capital greeted by a triumphal procession.

Aikin also enumerates a long list of men who fell victims to the persecutions of Laud: John Lilburn ('Freeborn John'), who was imprisoned and flogged during his lifelong trials in the Star Chamber, and who coined the phrase 'freeborn rights'; Archibald Armstrong ('Archy'), the king's fool, who was ignominiously discharged from the King's service for insulting the archbishop; and the unknown John Archer, a drummer who had participated in a mob attack against Laud's palace in Lambeth, and was tortured on the rack to name his companions. Aikin relies on a manuscript held in the British Museum, and surmises that the man was probably executed, though '[t]he circumstance is mentioned by no historian'.[111] It is in seeking to represent the lives of those who had been lost to history that Aikin's ambitions encounter the greatest frustration; similar obstacles had impeded her earlier attempt to write women's history in her *Epistles*. In the final section, I return to *Epistles* to consider how they informed the *Memoirs*, and how attention to the *Memoirs* sheds new light upon the *Epistles*.

'MENTIONED BY NO HISTORIAN'

Aikin's attempt to represent what no historian had before her thought fit to mention, has special resonance for her treatment of women's history. Notwithstanding the wide range of documentary sources that Aikin had at her disposal in preparing the *Memoirs*, virtually nothing recorded the lives of the lower classes and women. A few decades later, George Eliot would describe the 'unhistoric acts' of her heroine in *Middlemarch*, and by extension of most women, making the further claim that it was precisely this unrecorded history upon which 'the growing good of the world is partly dependent'.[112] For Eliot, the imaginative form of the historical novel – *Middlemarch* is set forty years before it was written – was necessary to recreate a faithful portrait of women's lives. Aikin likewise had elected to use the form of the epistle to represent the history of women's lives, poetic licence being mandated by the dearth of documentary materials describing women's existence in prior ages.[113]

By fictionalizing her *Epistles*, Aikin claims the right of women to retell their own history; and peremptorily dismisses the need to fashion women's history by slavish adherence to the existing record. Undoubtedly she would have been sympathetic to Jane Austen's similar gesture in *Persuasion*: 'Men have had every advantage of us in telling their own story. Education has been theirs in so much higher a degree; the pen has been in their hands. I will not allow books to prove anything.'[114] Aikin by no means ignores the record that does exist, as she densely annotates her epistles with references to a wide range of relevant sources. But the movement from the poetry of the *Epistles* to the prose of the *Memoirs*, from the exclusive focus on women's lives to that of court biographies, does not reflect any sharp transition in either form or subject. Instead, it is that with the *Epistles* the historical record is so scant, and, in the ancient and biblical periods, so mythical, that Aikin grants herself permission to reinvent the past. Thus she reimagines Adam not as a victim of feminine weakness but as a 'moping idiot', and will reconstruct female suffering from 'the Western wilds' of North America to 'Afric's palmy shore', from 'the Southern Main' to 'Chaldea's plains'.[115] Indeed, 'Aikin asserts, in every earlier or "primitive" society, women have been brutally abused, exploited, and degraded', and it is a view of women that is carried into her historical memoirs as even the most powerful women struggle in ways unknown to men.[116]

While the *Epistles* have been studied almost exclusively independently of Aikin's other work, including her major work of the *Memoirs*, examining the two alongside one another is a fruitful exercise: we find the *Memoirs* illuminate hitherto unnoticed aspects of the *Epistles* and, conversely, the methods and aims of the *Epistles* inform her project in the *Memoirs*. To begin, it is clear that reading retrospectively confirms what has already been strongly suspected about the *Epistles*: that the disclaimer of female equality is a sham. Consider, for example, her apparent submission to the superiority of men in the *Epistles*:

> I touch no sacred thing,
> But bow to Right Divine in man and king,
> Nature endows him with superior force,
> Superior wisdom then I grant, of course,
> For who gainsays the despot in his might,
> Or when was ever weakness in the right?
>
> Aikin, *Epistles*, 1, 39–44

Given her denunciation of the divine right of kings throughout the *Memoirs*, these lines must be read as heavily ironic. Echoing her claim in the introduction that men's greater authority and assumption of 'public and active offices' derives from their bodily strength, Aikin sarcastically disavows the corollary, that from 'superior force' flows '[s]uperior wisdom'.[117] Aikin's poem, when read with the *Memoirs*, thus explodes Aikin's attempt to characterize the claim for sexual equality as an 'absurd idea'.[118]

Additionally, attentive reading of the *Epistles* brings into sharper focus Aikin's object in the *Memoirs* in at least two respects. First, the description Aikin provides for her 'general plan' of the *Epistles* – 'To mark the effect of various codes, institutions, and states of manners, on the virtue and happiness of man, and the concomitant and proportional elevation or depression of woman in the scale of existence' – adumbrates the approach taken in her *Memoirs*, where she ascertains 'the virtue and happiness' of people under various historical regimes.[119] Aikin's statement also enunciates her belief that history must trace 'the effect of various codes, institutions, and states of manners' on individuals; and furthermore suggests that historical change results from individual activity that gradually and imperceptibly transforms these codes, institutions and manners, what Macaulay had called the 'noiseless revolutions' so 'rarely indicated by what historians are please to call important events'.[120] Aikin thus implicitly, and somewhat paradoxically for the author of royal biographies, rejects Carlyle's pronouncement that '[t]he history of the world is but the biography of great men'.[121]

Finally, Aikin's early foray into creative history signals her own recognition of the importance of storytelling in bringing the past alive, and it is in this respect as well that *Memoirs* can may be seen as a continuation of the *Epistles*. Despite the lament of one reviewer that her 'volumes, we fear, can scarcely hope to compete in popularity with the melo-dramatic sketches of the historical novelists – the magic lantern pictures of romance',[122] others disagreed strongly; her work was even criticized for being 'more like a romance, than a real history'.[123] This blurring of the lines between fiction and history was variously received: in 1822 there appeared in the *Edinburgh Review* a commentary on Walter Scott's *The Fortunes of Nigel* in which leave was taken of Scott's novel to praise Aikin's *Memoirs of the Court of James I* as 'a work as entertaining as a novel, and far more instructive than most histories. It is not only full of interest and curiosity, but is written throughout with the temperance, impartiality, and dispassionate judgment of a true historian, in a style always lucid and succinct, and frequently both animated and elegant.'[124] The *North British Review* heaped even more praise on Aikin in its review of *Memoirs, Miscellanies, and Letters of the Late Lucy Aikin*, flattering her with having invested her *Memoirs* with the vivifying spirit of Scott's novels, and with having initiated what Scott, according to Carlyle, had taught his generation, 'That the bygone ages of the world were actually filled by living men, not by protocols, state-papers, controversies and abstractions of men'.[125] The *Review* contended that

it should be remembered, and Miss Aikin must have the credit due from the fact, that she began to contemplate her work in 1814, before even the first of the Waverly Novels had appeared; years before Kenilworth had set the world mad about Queen Bess and the Earl of Leicester . . . So that the plagiarism of the topic, if any, was the other way. Miss Aikin could not have been set on the track of Elizabethan gossip by any historical fiction of Walter Scott's, but Scott may have been induced by Miss Aikin's book to think of Kenilworth as a subject.[126]

Notwithstanding the recognition she received from these reviewers, Aikin's contributions to historiography were soon forgotten. Although T. H. Lister's 1832 commentary in the *Edinburgh Review* on the *Waverly* novels appears only a decade after the review on *Nigel* praising Aikin, she is no longer mentioned even though what is said of Scott's novels could just as easily describe her innovations in historiography: 'Great changes in the condition and opinions of a people will silently and gradually take place, unmarked by any signal event . . . History has been hitherto too prone to note with eagerness only [the most striking events]; – avoiding, as if with disdain, the more difficult, honourable, and useful task, of tracing the progress of the former.'[127] Even among historians, Aikin's efforts were overlooked. In 1832, one year before the final instalment of her *Memoirs* appeared, Thomas Carlyle prophesized that: 'The time is approaching when History will be attempted on quite other principles [than it is today]; when the Court, the Senate and the Battlefield, receding more and more into the background, the Temple, the Worship and Social Hearth will advance more and more into the foreground'.[128] By speaking of this mode of history as one that belonged to the future, Carlyle effectively expunges Aikin's ongoing efforts to reshape history according to the very principles he describes. The irony would not have been lost on Aikin, who herself had undertaken the task of reanimating the lives of those obliterated from the historical record.

NOTES

1. John Aikin, *Annals of the Reign of King George the Third; From Its Commencement in the Year 1760, to the General Peace in the Year 1815*, 2 vols. (London: Longman, 1816), v.
2. Barbauld, *Selected Poetry and Prose*, 474–82 (480).
3. 'Review of Memoirs of the Court of Queen Elizabeth', *Monthly Review*, 87 (November 1818), 225–50; 'Review of Memoirs of the Court of Queen Elizabeth', *Eclectic Review*, 11 (February 1819), 105–26; 'Review of Memoirs of the Court of King James I', *Monthly Review*, 97 (March 1822), 225–47; 'Review of Memoirs of the Court of King James I', *Eclectic Review*, 18 (August 1822), 97–119; 'Review of Memoirs of the Court of King Charles I', *Monthly Review*, 2 (August 1833), 449–66; 'Review of Memoirs of the Court of King Charles I', *Eclectic Review*, 10 (December 1833), 461–79: 'Review of Memoirs of the Court of Charles I', *Edinburgh Review* (January 1834), 398–422.
4. *Eclectic Review* (1819), 106.
5. 'Review of Memoirs of the Court of King Charles I', *The Knickerbocker; or New York Monthly Magazine*, 3(2) (February 1834), 145–7 (145).

6. On Aikin's extensive use of public archives, and her involvement in an 1851 petition demanding that fees for consulting public records be waived for 'people engaged on serious literary or historical signatories', see Anne Laurence, 'Women Historians and Documentary Research: Lucy Aikin, Agnes Strickland, Mary Anne Everett Green, and Lucy Toulmin Smith', in Joan Bellamy, Anne Laurence and Gillian Perry (eds.), *Women, Scholarship and Criticism c.1790–1900* (Manchester University Press, 2000), 125–41.

7. Rosemary Ann Mitchell, '"The Busy Daughters of Clio": Women Writers of History from 1820 to 1880', *Women's History Review*, 7 (1998), 107–34 (121–2).

8. Devoney Looser, *British Women Writers and the Writing of History, 1670–1820* (Baltimore, MD: Johns Hopkins University Press, 2000); Rohan Maitzen, *Gender, Genre, and Victorian Historical Writing* (New York, NY and London: Garland, 1998).

9. Natalie Zemon Davis, 'Gender and Genre: Women as Historical Writers, 1400–1820', in Patricia H. Labalme (ed.), *Beyond Their Sex: Learned Women of the European Past* (New York University Press, 1980), 153–82; '"Women's History" in Transition: The European Case', *Feminist Studies*, 3 (spring–summer, 1976), 83–103.

10. Bonnie Smith, *The Gender of History: Men, Women, and Historical Practice* (Cambridge, MA: Harvard University Press, 1998); Mary Spongberg, *Writing Women's History since the Renaissance* (New York and Basingstoke: Palgrave Macmillan, 2002); Miriam Burstein, *Narrating Women's History in Britain, 1770–1902* (Aldershot: Ashgate, 2004); Lynette Felber (ed.), *Clio's Daughters: British Women Making History, 1790–1899* (Newark, DE: University of Delaware Press, 2007).

11. Greg Kucich, '"This Horrid Theatre of Human Sufferings": Gendering the Stages of History in Catharine Macaulay and Percy Bysshe Shelley', in Thomas Pfau (ed. and introd.) and Robert F. Gleckner (ed.), *Lessons of Romanticism: A Critical Companion* (Durham, NC: Duke University Press, 1998), 448–65; 'Romanticism and Feminist Historiography', *Wordsworth Circle*, 24(3) (summer 1993), 133–40; 'Women's Historiography and the (Dis)Embodiment of Law: Ann Yearsley, Mary Hays, Elizabeth Benger', *Wordsworth Circle*, 33(1) (winter 2002), 3–7. Kucich concentrates on Aikin's *Epistles* and, very briefly, refers to *Elizabeth*. She is briefly mentioned as a historian by Gary Kelly, 'Romanticism and the Feminist Uses of History', in Damian Walford Davies (ed.), *Romanticism, History, Historicism: Essays on an Orthodoxy* (New York, NY: Routledge, 2009), 163–80.

12. *Eclectic Review* (1819), 106 (citing Hume); *Monthly Review* (1818), 226, 236, 250 (citing Hume and Macaulay).

13. Each two-volume set of the three *Memoirs* reached about 1,000 pages (the volumes in order, were 488, 524, 424, 413, 464 and 544 pages, for a total of 2,857 pages), such that Aikin's six-volume history of the years 1533 to 1649 was slightly longer (in terms of total number of pages) than Hume's six volumes (his volumes in order were 473, 459, 402, 403, 424 and 446 pages, for a total of

2,204 pages). However, it appears that Hume's volumes were printed in a slightly larger format, so that the word lengths were likely comparable.

14. Maitzen, *Gender*, 8–9.
15. See Zemon Davis, '"Women's History" in Transition', 83.
16. For a detailed account of the preference held by many Victorians for Mary, Queen of Scots over Elizabeth, see Maitzen, *Gender*, 161–97.
17. Mellor and Levy, *Epistles on Women and Other Works*.
18. Maitzen, *Gender*, 6.
19. Aikin, *Memoirs of the Court of Queen Elizabeth* (London: Longman, 1818), 1, vii.
20. Maitzen, *Gender*, 3–4.
21. *Edinburgh Review* (1834), 399.
22. *Ibid.*
23. Daniel White, *Early Romanticism and Religious Dissent* (Cambridge University Press, 2006), 187.
24. Le Breton, *Correspondence*, 15.
25. For the development of this argument about Barbauld and John Aikin's six-volume miscellany for children, see Levy, *Family Authorship*, 21–2; 37–44.
26. Le Breton, *Correspondence*, 184.
27. 'Review of Memoirs of the Court of Elizabeth', *Ladies' Monthly Magazine* (March 1820), 155–6 (155).
28. Le Breton, *Correspondence*, 15.
29. See White, *Early Romanticism*, 10.
30. On the topic of war, for example, many women had attempted to depict its effects from a female perspective. Important examples include Charlotte Smith's *The Emigrants* (1793), Felicia Hemans' *The Records of Women* (1828) as well as Barbauld's own *Eighteen Hundred and Eleven* (1812).
31. Barbauld, *Selected Poetry and Prose*, 26.
32. For a detailed history of Barbauld's position, one that mitigates much of its presumed anti-feminism, see William McCarthy, 'Why Anna Letitia Barbauld Refused to Head a Women's College: New Facts, New Story', *Nineteenth-century Contexts*, 23(3) (2001), 349–79.
33. I develop this argument in *Family Authorship*, 42, 178–9.
34. It was observed that Aikin had shown Henrietta Stuart (Charles I's consort) as having 'had a much greater share than history usually assigns to her, in the overthrow of her husband's dynasty' (*Monthly Review* (1833), 453). As these comments indicate, Aikin was hostile towards the Queen for having provoked the nation with her overt support for the Catholic cause.
35. Aikin, *Memoirs of the Court of Queen Elizabeth*, 1, vii–viii.
36. On the increasing scrutiny of and hostility towards female historians in the Victorian period, see Maitzen, *Gender*, 6–32.
37. Aikin, *Memoirs of the Court of Queen Elizabeth*, 1, iv.
38. *Eclectic Review* (1819), 105.
39. See McCarthy, 'New Facts', and my discussion of Aikin having likely deliberately underestimated Barbauld's contributions to *Evenings at Home* in *Family Authorship*, 25–6.

40. Quoted by William McCarthy in 'A "High-Minded Christian Lady": The Posthumous Reception of Anna Letitia Barbauld', in Harriet Kramer Linkin and Stephen C. Behrendt (eds.), *Romanticism and Women Poets: Opening the Doors of Reception* (Lexington, KY: University Press of Kentucky, 1999), 165–91, 176.

41. Mellor and Levy, *Epistles on Women and Other Works*, 51.

42. McCarthy, *Anna Letitia Barbauld*, 500.

43. Mellor and Levy, *Epistles on Women and Other Works*, 26.

44. Le Breton, *Correspondence*, 128.

45. Aikin edited and published 'On Female Studies', in *A Legacy for Young Ladies* (London: Longman, 1826).

46. Barbauld, *Selected Poetry and Prose*, 480.

47. Edward Gibbon, *The Rise and Decline of the Roman Empire*, 8 vols. (London: Murray, 1887), I, 371.

48. *Monthly Review* (1818), 225.

49. Aikin, *Memoirs of the Court of Queen Elizabeth*, I, 145–6.

50. Le Breton, *Correspondence*, 79.

51. 'Review of *The Life of William Roscoe*', *Edinburgh Review*, 58(117) (July 1833), 65–86 (65). Aikin acknowledges this anonymous review as her own in Le Breton, *Correspondence*, 183.

52. 'Review of The Life of William Roscoe', *Edinburgh Review*, 65.

53. Aikin, *Memoirs of the Court of Queen Elizabeth*, I, iv–vii.

54. Aikin, *Memoirs of the Court of King Charles I*, II, 242.

55. Aikin, *Memoirs of the Court of Queen Elizabeth*, II, 230.

56. *Ibid.*, II, 210.

57. *Ibid.*, II, 230.

58. *Ibid.*, II, 232.

59. White, *Early Romanticism*, 19.

60. Aikin, *Memoirs of the Court of Queen Elizabeth*, II, 213.

61. Le Breton, *Correspondence*, 4.

62. Aikin, *Memoirs of the Court of Queen Elizabeth*, I, 46–7.

63. *Ibid.*, II, 106, 176.

64. *Ibid.*, II, 178.

65. *Ibid.*

66. *Ibid.*, II, 188.

67. *Ibid.*, II, 196.

68. *Ibid.*, II, 194, 196.

69. *Ibid.*, II, 195.

70. *Ibid.* Aikin may be rebuking Hume and his followers who, though accepting of Mary's likely guilt, nevertheless sympathetically portray the Scotch Queen by describing her many accomplishments and dwelling at length upon the pathetic scene of her execution.

71. Aikin, *Memoirs of the Court of King James I*, I, 189.

72. Aikin, *Memoirs of the Court of King Charles I*, II, 106.

73. *Ibid.*, II, 73.

74. Le Breton, *Correspondence*, 96–7.
75. Aikin, *Memoirs of the Court of King Charles I*, ii, 109.
76. *Ibid.*, ii, 595.
77. *Ibid.*, ii, 600.
78. Le Breton, *Correspondence*, 194.
79. Aikin, *Memoirs of the Court of King Charles I*, ii, 599.
80. *Eclectic Review* (1819), 106.
81. Aikin, *Memoirs of the Court of Queen Elizabeth*, i, 183, 221.
82. *Ibid.*, i, 322.
83. *Ibid.*, i, 319.
84. *Ibid.*, ii, 108.
85. Aikin, *Memoirs of the Court of King Charles I*, i, 377–8, 382–3.
86. *Ibid.*, i, 474.
87. *Ibid.*
88. Barbauld, *Selected Poetry and Prose*, 179–80, ll. 25–6.
89. *Ibid.*, l. 29.
90. *Ibid.*, 179–80, ll. 36–41.
91. Aikin, *Memoirs of the Court of Queen Elizabeth*, i, 6.
92. Aikin, *Memoirs of the Court of King Charles I*, ii, 70.
93. Aikin, *Memoirs of the Court of King James I*, ii, 159, 158–71.
94. Aikin, *Memoirs of the Court of Queen Elizabeth I*, i, 19.
95. Aikin, *Memoirs of the Court of King James I*, i, 270.
96. *Ibid.*, i, 397.
97. *Ibid.*, ii, 164.
98. *Ibid.*, i, 166.
99. *Ibid.*, ii, 169.
100. *Ibid.*, ii, 117, 110, 157.
101. *Ibid.*, i, 156.
102. *Ibid.*, i, 103.
103. *Ibid.*, i, 61, 303.
104. Aikin, *Memoir of the Court of King Charles I*, i, 488, 489.
105. *Ibid.*, i, 491.
106. *Ibid.*, i, 493.
107. *Ibid.*, i, 491.
108. *Ibid.*, i, 493.
109. *Ibid.*, i, 493–4.
110. *Ibid.*, i, 498.
111. *Ibid.*, ii, 70.
112. George Eliot, *Middlemarch* (London: Penguin, 1985), 896.
113. Aikin writes in her introduction: 'We have no records of any early people in a ruder state than some savage tribes of the present day' (Mellor and Levy, *Epistles on Women and Other Works*, 53).
114. Jane Austen, *Persuasion* (Peterborough, ON: Broadview Press, 1998), 243.
115. Mellor and Levy, *Epistles on Women and Other Works*, 63, l. 67, 66, l. 51, 62, l. 36, 67, l. 184.

116. *Ibid.*, 33. In 1838, Aikin also spoke about a 'project . . . to write something or other respecting us Englishwomen' but poor health, and perhaps the difficulty involved in addressing a public readership on this topic, frustrated her efforts (Le Breton, *Correspondence*, 309).

117. See Mellor and Levy, *Epistles on Women and Other Works*, 57.

118. Aikin's private correspondence confirms this reading: see Le Breton, *Correspondence*, 127–8.

119. Aikin, *Epistles*; see Mellor and Levy, *Epistles on Women and Other Works*, 53.

120. Quoted in Maitzen, *Gender*, 21 and 59 n.

121. Thomas Carlyle, *Heroes, Hero-Worship, and the Heroic in History* (New York, NY: Alden, 1888), 26.

122. *Eclectic Review* (1833), 461.

123. 'Review of *Memoirs of the Court of Queen Elizabeth*', *La Belle Assemblée*, 118 (January 1818), 326–9 (326).

124. 'Review of *The Fortunes of Nigel*', *Edinburgh Review*, 37(73) (June 1822), 204–25, 212–13.

125. Thomas Carlyle, 'Sir Walter Scott', *Critical and Miscellaneous Essays*, in H. D. Traill (ed.), *The Works of Thomas Carlyle*, centenary edn, 30 vols. (New York, NY: Scribner's, 1896–1901), v, 275.

126. 'Review of Memoirs, Miscellanies, and Letters of the Late Lucy Aikin', *North British Review*, 84 (June 1865), 166–7.

127. [T. H. Lister], 'The Waverley Novels', *Edinburgh Review*, 55 (April 1832), 61–79, 77–8.

128. Carlyle, *Critical and Miscellaneous Essays*, iii, 83.

CHAPTER 8

Lucy Aikin and the legacies of Dissent

Felicity James

I want to begin with a snowy journey, a bitter, cold, long trek across country from a child's viewpoint:

> My grandmother, her maid, my little brother, and myself, were packed in a post-chaise; my father accompanied us on horseback. It was Christmas week, the snow deep on the ground; the whole distance was two hundred and forty miles across the country, and we were six days in accomplishing it.[1]

This is the image with which Lucy Aikin begins her reminiscences, published by her nephew-in-law Philip Hemery Le Breton in 1864. She was 3 years old when her father, John Aikin junior, left Warrington Academy for Yarmouth, and the long journey across country, from one Dissenting stronghold to another, took its toll upon the family. 'The last night we arrived at my aunt's, Mrs. Barbauld's, house at Palgrave', she goes on, 'where my grandmother remained behind; she died in a few days of the cold and fatigue of the journey'. Yet in some ways this memorial of her grandmother turns out not to be an act of family piety – like the poetry written by Barbauld about her female ancestors – but an overdue redress, since the grandmother is primarily remembered not with fondness, but for having rebuked the infant Aikin:

> My father's mother, who lived in the house with us, made some attempts to teach me to read; the extraordinary precocity of my aunt and of my eldest brother had perhaps rendered her unreasonable in her expectations of progress; she called me 'Little Dunce'; the reproach sank deep, and its effect was certainly unfavourable; it did not rouse me to further exertion, for I had already done my utmost, and it filled me with a sense of incurable deficiency. How soon may the tender spirit of a child be broken, and its faculties permanently dulled by such treatment![2]

Already we have a sense of family history as vexed, as members are unreasonably compared to one another. The formidable intellectual inheritance of the Aikin family is shown to be a burden, as well as a blessing. For the Aikins, as Michelle Levy and Daniel White have explored, 'the home is part of the public sphere, and the family itself is the institution most capable of effecting profound national change', and in this volume different essays have demonstrated the ways in which such a family ethos was gradually con-structed across the generations.[3] In Lucy Aikin's writing, however, we see the pressure of having inherited this collective identity, as she attempts to maintain and continue family legacies while also negotiating a place for her own role as a woman writer. Lucy Aikin's vivid recollection of the smart of a childhood insult bears a close similarity to the *Autobiography* of Harriet Martineau, another Unitarian daughter, who also reports in detail childhood injuries and injustices which demonstrate the problems of establishing an identity within the larger family narrative. For Martineau release came through the collapse of the family textile business, allowing her 'a wholly new freedom' to write and publish; she further distanced herself through her later rejection of Unitarianism.[4] For Lucy Aikin, a junior partner in the family business of letters, independence was harder to achieve.

Although her work has endured a long period of neglect, Lucy Aikin was a successful author in the nineteenth century, and her writing – which ranged from poetry to fiction, writing for children, literary criticism and biography – is now once again attracting critical attention. As Michelle Levy discusses in detail in this volume (Chapter 7), it was for her work as a historian that Aikin was probably best known in her lifetime. She was, as Levy shows, an impressive and innovative historical writer; it is, however, her role as a family historian which I want to address in detail in this chapter. In many ways this overlapped with her historical writing, in which, to quote Levy, she combined 'attention to the large transformations of public his-tory – above all the ongoing struggle to reform both church and state – and to the small "concrete, personal details" of individual lives'. Her interest in the revelatory power of domestic and private history is evident in her family memoirs too, where she is eager to highlight the ways in which the Aikins' affective relationships connected with, and continued, their political and literary ideals. At the same time, however, she promoted her own larger image of the Aikin family, which could sometimes be at odds with the work of her immediate forebears.

She was the promoter and editor of her father – producing a biography and a selection of his work in 1823 – and, of course, of her aunt Barbauld. Her heavily selective collection of Barbauld's poems and her memoir of her aunt appeared in 1825, with a further selection, *A Legacy for Young Ladies*, published the following year. Aikin's own 1864 *Memoirs* – also a family enterprise, produced by her niece and nephew, Anna Letitia and Philip Hemery Le Breton – have also been immensely important in shaping the posthumous reputation of the Aikin family, and in giving rise to other family narratives, including Betsy Rodgers' 1958 *Georgian Chronicle: Mrs Barbauld and Her Family.*[5] Considering these layers of memoirs, collected letters, literary self-reflections and familial observations, Anne Janowitz has spoken of the Aikin family as a 'reputation machine', working away through the nineteenth century and into the twentieth to present a powerful image of exemplary family life.[6]

Except, as that opening image from Aikin's *Memoirs* shows, this family journey is not always straightforward; the legacies of Dissent can be complex and sometimes unwelcome. In this chapter, I want to focus on two interrelated aspects of Aikin's writing life and her treatment of her Dissenting inheritance; first, her negotiations with her femininity and her role as a female reader and writer, which I will explore with especial reference to her early poem, *Epistles on Women*; and, second, her presentation of her father and aunt as writers in her biographies, shaped by her double identity as female writer and heir to Barbauld and also by her sense of herself as her father's child. These latter aspects of the chapter take their cue from recent revaluations of Aikin's role as biographer and writer, in particular from Janowitz's exploration of the way in which her memoir writing 'interestingly reveals and conceals her own ambivalence about her father's and her aunt's literary vocations'.[7] Lucy, I argue, seeks to present a particular narrative of the Aikin family which to some extent resists Barbauld's achievements as a woman writer, placing them instead in a context of family creativity, and of her brother's encouragement.

FAMILY TRADITIONS

Lucy was born on 6 November 1781, youngest child of John Aikin and Martha Jennings, and heir to a long family tradition of Dissent. She could claim descent from an illustrious line of preachers and educators, since both her father and grandfather, distinguished in their own right, had married into the Jennings family; moreover, she herself was born at Warrington, into one of the centres of provincial Dissent and scholarship. Although she was too young to remember Warrington Academy directly, its intellectual atmosphere was imparted to her both through family friends such as John Howard and Joseph Priestley – Aikin never forgot Howard's kindness to her at 8 years old, and his 'interesting conversation with us children', nor the 'cheerful, even playful' Priestley – and through vigorous family attention to her mental development.[8] From earliest childhood, she was educated within the family, where, after that inauspicious beginning with her grandmother, she had a happier experience being instructed by her father, who taught her natural history when she accompanied him on his drives out to see his patients. Her literary and religious sensibilities were nurtured by early reading of her aunt's *Lessons for Children*, with what she later recalled as their 'spirit of poetry', and *Hymns in Prose*, which had a strong and lasting effect:

> the hymns gave me the idea of something bright and glorious, hung on high above my present reach, but not above my aspirations. They gave me first the sentiment of sublimity, and of the Author of all that is sublime. They taught me piety.[9]

As William McCarthy has already discussed in this volume (Chapter 3), this was no uncommon sentiment for nineteenth-century child readers; again, a parallel might be suggested with Harriet Martineau's memories of the *Hymns*, 'there were parts of them which I dearly loved:' she recalls in her *Autobiography*, 'but other parts made me shiver with awe'.[10] The effect was particularly acute for Lucy Aikin, however, as the only next-generation female, with writing ambitions of her own to boot. As my opening anecdote testifies, comparison with Barbauld was a constant feature of Lucy's development, further demonstrated by another story in the *Memoirs*, a quotation from a letter by John Aikin junior reporting on the precocity of the infant Lucy:

> We were talking of Cadmus, and I was saying I was not certain whether he lived before or after the Trojan war; when this chit of six years old decided the matter, by observing that she had heard her brother Edmund read in Pope's 'Homer' about a son of Cadmus fighting against the Trojans.[11]

Not only does this give a powerful image of the sort of shared family reading that characterized the Aikin home, it also demonstrates the pervasive influence of Barbauld's biography on that of her niece, since the story is a retelling of Barbauld's own childhood intervention in her father's theological discussion, as discussed by McCarthy in his chapter in this volume. Lucy Aikin is being schooled in a particular tradition of debate and exchange, where even the youngest members of the household are allowed a voice. In her biography of her father, for instance, Lucy Aikin records his habit of having family members read aloud his own work to him, when he 'not only permitted, but invited and encouraged, the freest strictures even from the youngest and most unskilful of those whom he was pleased to call his *household critics*'.[12] On the other hand, anecdotes such as this show that there were powerful expectations about how and what Lucy Aikin would achieve, her intellectual growth taking shape within the constraints of a larger family narrative. Similarly, Aikin remembers a turning point where she became aware of her own abilities – an early altercation with her brother George about a stolen piece of tart. Running to her parents to remonstrate about the injustice, Aikin was dismissed by her mother:

> But how many fold was I compensated when my father, who had listened with great attention to my harangue, exclaimed, 'Why Lucy, you are quite eloquent!' O! never-to-be-forgotten praise! Had I been a boy, it might have made me an orator; as it was, it incited me to exert to the utmost, by tongue and by pen, all the power of words I possessed or could ever acquire – I had learned where my strength lay.[13]

These childhood anecdotes are worth dwelling on since they give a powerful image of the ways in which Aikin's abilities were shaped within a family context, and bound up with her desire for parental approval. Later, she would record her 'proud delight' in having been educated solely within the family: 'my father taught me this, my mother that – one of my brothers informed me of such a thing – in short, not only the foundation-stone, but every other in the fabric of my mind and manners was laid by an honoured and a loving hand – no mercenary touched it!'[14]

This effusion comes in the context of 'a practical lesson in the art of custard-making': family education, for Lucy Aikin, was also deeply connected with domesticity. When discussing her later literary activities, she often takes pains to emphasize their place within her domestic achievements. The comment mentioned by Stephen Daniels and Paul Elliott, for instance, about Aikin helping her father with his geographical writing, records a moment of family collaboration firmly embedded in a domestic setting: 'The Geography is all printed but the index, which my father has made and pasted, with my help. I have weighed out all the bullace and sugar for preserving with my own hands.'[15] The pairing of the two activities is no coincidence: she is demonstrating her ability to move between two roles, 'her own hands' taking charge both of household chores and intellectual work. '[A]s literary characters must now and then descend from their altitudes', she tells Susannah Taylor in 1805, 'I have been several days hard at work upon parlour curtains, which are at length hung up, to the great glory and satisfaction of my mother and me.'[16] Elsewhere she offers numerous portraits of family life which combine domestic and literary production: her portrait of her father's '*household critics*', for example, or her image of her later life in Stoke Newington in a letter which describes her father writing biography, her mother and brother Arthur gardening, and herself stepping 'to the butcher's to order dinner' before settling down to write; in the evenings 'after tea we walk or sit down to our business till candle-light, when we meet with books, and work in the study; after supper we play whist for some time, I read Virgil to my father, and at eleven we march off to bed'.[17]

Yet even in the homely account offered by the *Memoirs* there are hints at the ways in which families might also exert a destructive power. Interspersed with the accounts of John Howard in the *Memoirs* are reports of his son's insanity and his paranoid fear of being poisoned at family tea parties; lurking behind the Aikin family anecdotes there is the memory of the attacks of mental illness experienced by Barbauld's husband Rochemont. In the grip of compulsion and violent delusions, he attacked his wife several times, on one occasion attempting to force her to drink laudanum, a situation from which she only escaped by throwing herself out of a window; as his aggression increased, the couple were forced to separate, and he committed suicide by throwing himself into the New River in 1808. Rochemont's illness is discreetly veiled in Lucy Aikin's memoir of her aunt, where he becomes 'a sufferer from the most melancholy of human maladies'.[18] Her own opinion of Rochemont, however, was far less sympathetic, as revealed by the multiple revisions of her manuscript, recorded by McCarthy in his biography of Barbauld. Her attraction to Rochemont Lucy Aikin dismisses as 'the illusion of a romantic fancy, not of a tender heart', the result of the 'baleful influence' of too much Rousseau. Had Anna Letitia Barbauld been more affectionate, Lucy continues – or rather, she qualifies, had her affections 'been ^early^ called forth by a more genial home-atmosphere, she could never have <given> ^allowed^ herself <up to the insane rhapsodies of constitutional insanity'. 'This is Lucy Aikin', McCarthy comments, 'nearly inarticulate with fury in her autograph "Family History", writing and crossing out and rewriting'.[19] She is writing too, as McCarthy points out, from a position of hindsight, informed by her father's perspective, well aware of the ways in which Anna Letitia had rebelled against the wishes of her parents in choosing Rochemont, and feeling anger towards her aunt's irresponsible sentiments of romance. Beneath the surface of family life, there might be dangerous currents of rebellion, violence and rage; Lucy Aikin's work, as we will see, registers some ways in which this might be contained and closed down.

LITERARY CAREER

Lucy Aikin began her literary career first in 1801 with an anthology of *Poetry for Children*, published by Joseph Johnson, and then in her own voice in 1810 with a quarto volume, *Epistles on Women, Exemplifying Their Character and Condition in Various Ages and Nations.* The *Epistles on Women* were also published by Joseph Johnson, and printed by Richard Taylor; they carried a dedication to Mrs Charles Rochemont Aikin. Everything about those details points back to family connection, and the way in which the work is embedded in the religious, intellectual and affectionate culture of the Aikin circle. The choice of publisher was an obvious one: Johnson was deeply committed to the Dissenting cause, financially, politically and socially.[20] In 1774, he had helped Theophilus Lindsey establish the Essex Street Chapel, and in the turbulent 1790s he had endured imprisonment as a 'malicious, seditious, and ill-disposed person' for selling Gilbert Wakefield's *A Reply to Some Parts of the Bishop of Llandaff's Address.*[21] Throughout the decades, his house and shop had functioned as a hub of a Unitarian intellectual network which stretched across the country, from Warrington to Norwich. Although Joseph Johnson had died the year before Lucy Aikin's book appeared, his two assistants continued to publish under his name, and so her first work was published under the same auspices as that of her father, taking its part in a line of family writings issued by Johnson for over thirty years, signalling its loyalties to the larger family of Unitarian Dissent from its very title page. Even the choice of printer, Richard Taylor, indicates a further connection to Unitarian culture, intellectual and familial. He offers a nice example, too, of the intersections between Dissent, science and industry which Ian Inkster's contribution to this volume highlights (see Chapter 6). Born into a Norwich family of manufacture and Dissent, Taylor's professional and intellectual interests coincided; he not only printed a wide range of scientific books and periodicals which featured science, including the *Monthly Magazine*, but was also a fellow of the Linnean society. His firm was also a powerful family institution, since Taylor took his natural son William Francis into the business; indeed, their company, Taylor & Francis, is still one of the leading publishers of scientific journals (among many other interests). As we will see, there were also familial and emotional bonds between the writer and the printer of *Epistles*, since all the Taylors were closely friendly with the Aikin clan.[22]

Simply on a bibliographic level, then, the book is meshed into a larger structure of Dissenting networks. While Lucy Aikin presents the 'Introduction' to her *Epistles* with 'all the diffidence and anxiety of a literary novice conscious of a bold and arduous undertaking' she has the weight of family tradition and support behind her, and is self-consciously continuing a family literary lineage. The dedication confirms the strength of these connections:

TO Mrs. CHARLES ROCHEMONT AIKIN, THE FOLLOWING EPISTLES, ORIGINALLY ADDRESSED TO HER BY THE SOLE APPELLATION OF FRIEND, ARE NOW INSCRIBED, TOGETHER WITH THE REMAINING CONTENTS OF THIS VOLUME, BY HER AFFECTIONATE FRIEND AND SISTER LUCY AIKIN.

Anne Wakefield, daughter of Gilbert, had married Lucy's brother, Charles, in August 1806. This dedication demonstrates the interlinking of the various Dissenting intellectual clans: Wakefield, who had been appointed as classical tutor at Warrington in 1779, had been close friends with both John Aikins, father and son. The exchange and friendship of the previous generations was confirmed in the intermarriages of the next. Furthermore, Charles, the second son of John Aikin, had been adopted by the Barbaulds at the age of 2, although the siblings had remained close, so the dedication also binds Lucy and her aunt's family together. The Dedication of the *Epistles* also finds a direct parallel in the Barbauld poem, 'Lines for Anne Wakefield on her Wedding to Charles Rochemont Aikin, with a Pair of Chimney Ornaments in the Figures of two Females seated with open Books'. The poem allegorizes the two figures as Science and Love, intellectual achievement and family affection which are brought together in the marriage. The two poems – Barbauld's short wedding-present tribute, and Lucy Aikin's 1,200 line *Epistles* – thus occupy a similar place in the family culture of gift-circulation and of women celebrating and confirming one another's achievements.

Lucy Aikin's poem itself is a bold and confident tribute to female power. Four books of heroic couplets recount the history of humanity from the Garden of Eden to 1750, linking the progress of civilization specifically to women and their achievements. Recent criticism has provided new insights into the feminist strategies of *Epistles*, poetical, political and historical, in terms both of Lucy's contribution to feminism and to historiography. Anne Mellor places it as a triumphant culmination at the end of her chapter on women's political poetry in *Mothers of the Nation*, 'a female-authored poem', she says, 'which more than any other mounted a demand for a social revolution, for the initiation of a women's movement which would overthrow the existing construction of gender and ensure the equality, perhaps even the social and political superiority, of the female'.[23] Kathryn Ready, who has examined its use of stadial theory in detail, has discussed the poem as a 'unique contribution to Enlightenment feminist thought', and this idea is supported by Kathryn Gleadle's suggestion that the poem functions as an important intermediary stage 'between the arguments of the Enlightenment anthropologists, and the radical unitarian feminists of the 1830s and 1840s'.[24] Without downplaying the significance of Lucy's writing, we should be aware of its possible tensions and conflicts, and read her feminism in light of her familial commitments. Michelle Levy, in this volume (Chapter 7), shows how the poem 'claims the right of women to retell their own history', and should be read alongside Lucy's own retellings of history in her series of court *Memoirs*.[25] Alongside this exploration of Lucy as innovative historian, I want to read the *Epistles* in light of her retellings of *family* history, affording us a slightly different perspective on her writing.

Epistles begins with an apparent rejection of 'the absurd idea that the two sexes ever can be, or ever ought to be, placed in all respects on a footing of equality'.[26] Instead, Lucy appeals for the recognition of separate spheres of women's achievements and pride in a specifically female identity: 'No! instead of aspiring to be inferior men, let us content ourselves with becoming noble women . . . but let not sex be carried into every thing'.[27] Yet this apparently demure preface conceals a subversive element. Having made the claim for two distinct, gendered spheres, Lucy fiercely attacks the ways in which men treat women. '[I]t is impossible for men to degrade his companion without degrading himself', she comments, before opening the poem with a severe indictment of the value placed upon ephemeral female charm: woman is a 'poor helpless passenger from love to scorn', not because of inherent failings but because men do not value female intellect. Lucy outlines the ways in which male constraints have created the attributes of femininity, only to tire of them: once beauty fades, the poem asserts, 'man contemns the trifler he has made'. As the historical narratives begin, the poem goes on to make a claim not simply for the equal intelligence of women, but for their superiority. Certainly that is the case with the portrait of Adam, listless and torpid, with 'fixt infantile stare', until Eve's appearance:

> Sure a new soul that moping idiot warms,
> Dilates his stature, and his mien informs![28]

Eden is presented rather as a state of mind or emotion than a place – 'Eden opened in the heart of Man' – and is defined primarily through equality of the sexes:

> *Equal* they trod till want and guilt arose,
> Till Savage blood was spilt, and man had foes.[29]

Crucially, 'want and guilt' do not belong solely to the female, and the ambiguous phrasing of 'Savage blood' leaves the nature of the savagery unspecified: 'Savage' could characterize the blood, Adam or Eve, or another force outside their equal realm. In the next epistle, however, depicting a distinctly un-Rousseauvian primitive state, women are the victims, not participants, in savage behaviour. Man is shown as a 'reckless hunter', 'of beasts the worst, / in want, in guilt, in lawless rapine nurst'.[30] 'Certainly Rousseau did not consult the interests of the weaker sex in his preference of savage life to civilised', Lucy comments dryly in her notes.[31] From this savage state we move to a pastoral setting, then into scenes from classical epic as Lucy rewrites Homer from the female viewpoint, suggesting a bleak picture of the condition of women in the Greek republic: 'Thy wives, proud Athens! fettered and debased'. We move gradually forward, through a survey of Hindu widows and Turkish harems, into a discussion of important women through history, and close by looking toward an enlightened future of intellectual equality, as she urges the 'sons of fair Albion' to 'unbind / Your barbarous shackles, loose the female mind'.[32]

The epistles move broadly along the lines of stadial, or four-stage, theory – where man is traced through four broad social stages, hunting and fishing; pasturage; agriculture; and commerce or manufacturing, and where a society's progress can be measured and determined by its treatment of women. Kathryn Ready has powerfully demonstrated Lucy Aikin's debt – and her contribution – to Enlightenment historiography including stadial theory, while pointing out that Aikin's application of this 'to understanding historical and geographical variations in the status of women is never formulaic'.[33] Stadial theory would later powerfully influence both Jane Marcet, whose *Conversations on Political Economy* Aikin would read in June 1817, when she tells her brother she is enjoying them in spite of herself, and Harriet Martineau, whose *Illustrations of Political Economy* explore, as Ella Dzelzainis has analysed, the 'feminist potential of . . . stadial theory'.[34] Lucy's, too, is a feminist version of stadial theory. Savage behaviour is, in her version of history, perpetrated by men, as when her savage 'monster-man' preys on womankind:

> Mark the grim ruffian roll his crafty glance,
> And crouching, slow, his tiger-step advance,
> With brandisht club surprise his human prey,
> And drag the bleeding victim bride away.[35]

This lack of empathy is contrasted with female self-sacrifice in the same epistle:

> Maternal Love! thy watchful glances roll
> From zone to zone, from pole to distant pole;

Cheer the long patience of the brooding hen,
Soothe the she-fox that trembles in her den,
'Mid Greenland ice-caves warm the female bear,
And rouse the tigress from her sultry lair.
At thy command, what zeal, what ardour, fires
The softer sex! a mightier soul inspires . . .[36]

Even in a savage state, therefore, female creatures are presented as having superior powers of empathy demonstrable in their behaviour towards their families, pointing the way towards a state of civilization later in the poem. Aikin's use and interrogation of Enlightenment historiography here reminds us that she is – as Ready, and Levy in her chapter for this volume (see Chapter 7), have shown us – actively reinterpreting women's history, and participating in a larger community of women writers such as Marcet and Martineau. Indeed, in October 1832, Lucy Aikin would read and greatly approve of Martineau's *Illustrations*. 'Know that a great new light has arisen among English women', she told William Ellery Channing, praising the principles of her political economy stories, and the 'grace', 'animation' and 'powerful pathos' of her narratives.[37] Lucy Aikin's own project, '[t]o mark the effect of various codes, institutions, and states of manners, on the virtue and happiness of man, and the concomitant and proportional elevation or depression of woman in the scale of existence',[38] therefore takes its place in a larger feminist appropriation of male narratives of history.

Yet Lucy's feminism picks its way carefully between family loyalties and feminine ideals. Recent work on Aikin has repeatedly returned to the implications of her treatment of femininity, maternity and domesticity. Anne Mellor discusses the way in which Aikin 'praises those women who carried the values of maternal love into the public realm', concluding that she closes *Epistles* by affirming 'the domestic affections as the noblest model for all public and private social relationships'.[39] Harriet Guest, meanwhile, reads a greater ambivalence into Aikin's emphasis on domesticity, uncovering its political charge by analysing her portrayal of Spartan women in particular detail: for Aikin, she argues, domesticity becomes 'the site from which an oppositional political discourse can be articulated'.[40] Ready, meanwhile, sees Aikin as striving to 'reconcile the republican and commercial models of femininity to promote women's education'.[41] All these approaches return to the ways in which Aikin expresses interest in some forms of dominant behaviour by women while simultaneously displaying a repeated distrust of women whose power is achieved or deployed in aggressive or 'relentless' ways, such as 'fierce Bonduca', or 'the dread Eliza', Elizabeth I. Instead, she reserves her highest praise for those women whose behaviour in the public realm is informed by their values of family love and devotion, such as Margaret Roper, pictured weeping, 'pale and shrieking', at the execution of her father Thomas More. This act of filial piety finds its own textual echo in the footnotes, which give an account of Roper's 'reverence and affection for her father' drawn directly from John Aikin's *General Biography*.[42] Both through her narrative of Roper and through her own practice, Lucy Aikin suggests that women's claim to immortality rests upon their relationship to the family, in filial or maternal affection. This, I argue, should be seen as a model for understanding her practice both as a writer and as a family biographer; women's achievements and ambitions, while they may be celebrated, must also be understood in relation to their familial role, an idea which gains special force in the context of Aikin family ideology. Ultimately it is the family which gives the woman strength, and which, perhaps, has more force than the woman herself.

We might look back to the ways in which Lucy herself had been educated, and her repeated placement of her literary work within a larger context of familial pride and domesticity. Her correspondence with female friends continues this pattern: for example, the letters she sent in the early 1800s to the family friend Susannah Taylor, mother of Richard Taylor, who would later print the *Epistles*. These letters, composed when she was already writing the *Epistles*, give interesting insights into the creation of this power-ful family-centred ideology. For a start, they represent not only a friendly exchange of letters, but the intersection of two major Dissenting family networks, which perhaps accounts for the slightly self-conscious tone adopted by Lucy. Susannah (1755–1823) was her mother's generation, wife of John Taylor, Unitarian hymn-writer and yarn manufacturer, the grand-son of John Taylor the Presbyterian divine. The Taylor clan provide a parallel with the Aikins. Related to or friendly with a wide range of other Dissenters – the Martineaus, the Opies, William Enfield, Henry Crabb Robinson – they and their descendants populate all sorts of branches of learning and intellectual exploration. Of Susannah's children, John Taylor (1779–1863) was a mining engineer, Edward Taylor (1784–1863) became Gresham professor of music, and Philip Taylor (1786–1870) was a civil engineer; Richard, printer and naturalist, was joined by his brother Arthur in the firm. Susannah's daughters Susan and Sarah were also highly edu-cated: Sarah (1793–1867), under her married name of Austin, was to achieve fame as a translator from the German, and Susan (1788–1853) was later to marry Henry Reeve (1780–1814), a renowned physician, student under Philip Martineau, who was the uncle of Harriet. Susan's son, Henry Reeve junior, was a translator, leader-writer of the *Times*, and, eventually, editor of the *Edinburgh Review*. As with the Aikin family, there is a powerful sense of an interconnected, intergenerational nexus of exchange between industry, exploration, European culture and journalism.

Lucy Aikin's letters to Taylor reveal a remarkable range of reading, placed within a circle of familial or friendly exchange, as in her discussion, in January 1803, of a 'lady's book society' she has set up with Barbauld. The feminism of this enterprise, however, is immediately qualified; even as Aikin asks Taylor to admire 'our spirit in setting up an institution into which not a single man is admitted, even to keep the accounts', she goes on to stress the essential femininity of the assembled women:

I must indeed whisper in your ear that it is no very easy matter to get the ladies to suspend their dissertations on new plays and new fashions to discuss the merits of books, and that sometimes it is rather difficult for the president, treasurer, and secretary, calling all at once to order, to obtain a hearing.[43]

This sense of careful negotiation between feminism and femininity appears too in her comments in the same letter on a 'singular work lately published': Mary Hays' six-volume *Female Biography or, Memoirs of Illustrious and Celebrated Women of All Ages and Countries* (1803). This remarkable work is now – like Lucy Aikin's historical writing – slowly being recognized as groundbreaking. Mary Spongberg terms it 'the first and perhaps the most important collection of women's lives': it is a lively, critical, wide-ranging rewriting of biography from a female perspective.[44] As such, it would seem to be a natural forebear for Aikin's own work. However, Aikin distances herself from Hays, whom she describes as a 'great disciple of Mrs Godwin'. She might well have been expected, therefore, to interest a woman such as Susannah Taylor, who is said to have danced round the tree of liberty in Norwich at the news of the fall of the Bastille. Certainly Susannah's husband's hymn, 'Trumpet of Liberty', was composed for the occasion, and sung at a public celebratory Revolutionary dinner on 5 November 1789. But despite these connections, and despite the similarity of their female-centred projects, Aikin distrusts Hays' 'zealous' feminism. Quoting Swift, she tells Susannah Taylor that 'Her arguments directly tend / Against the cause she would defend [. . .] Alas, alas! though Miss Hayes has wisely addressed herself to the ladies alone, I am afraid the gentlemen will get a peep at her book and repeat with tenfold energy that women have no business with anything but nursing children and mending stockings.' This gets to the nub of Aikin's problem with Hays: her feminism is too overt. Aikin's comments here anticipate Barbauld's better-known assertion to Maria Edgeworth in 1803 that 'there is no bond of union among literary women [...] Mrs. Hannah More would not write along with you or me, and we should probably hesitate at joining Miss Hays, or if she were living, Mrs Godwin.'[45] One reason for this hesitation is given by Lucy Aikin to Susannah Taylor: 'I do not think her book is written quite in an edifying manner neither – the morals are too French for my taste.' In *Female Biography*, the pious and the rebellious are placed side by side: close on the heels of Margaret Roper, for example (whose learning and intellect are praised as highly as her family piety), comes Madame Roland, to whom a large proportion of Hays' sixth volume is dedicated: 'heroine of the French revolution, and the martyr of liberty'.[46] While both authors exhibit interest in the ways in which women shape their history and historiography, Hays is drawn to defiant and independent characters. Aikin, on the other hand, treats 'the Character of Women' as a subject which 'is delicate and requires management', in Barbauld's words.[47] And while Aikin's book club is composed of ladies, female writing which, like Hays', remains spiky, rebellious and unrepentant, is still viewed with suspicion.

Meanwhile Aikin herself was negotiating similar problems as a writer, as revealed in a subsequent letter to Susannah Taylor.[48] She describes her slow progress writing the epic (this is 1805, so it would go on for some time yet): 'On the whole, I consider the Roman dames as the queens of their sex, but there are a few ugly facts against them which I do not well know what to do with. At one time they had a disagreeable habit of poisoning their husbands; but I don't think much of that', she adds saucily, 'for no doubt the men gave them provocation'. This leads her off into a story about a 'heroine' of Newington Green, a cook maid who stabbed the footman in a dispute; a story she implicitly parallels to the 'wild and lawless manners of the old Scotch Borderers', the 'valiant marauders' who seize her imagination when reading Walter Scott. It is perhaps significant that almost immediately after describing this imaginative violence and these rebellious, lawless characters – and an episode which brings them into the heart of domesticity – she moves into a spot of sentimental moralizing about family and home. Setting herself up – however playfully – as more prudent than Barbauld, 'who is at least forty years younger than I am' and given to gaiety and racketing, she rather cloyingly muses on her 'homebred satisfactions': her dedication to home and its 'revered inhabitants', exclaiming 'Oh! How could I ever bear to be separated from those who unite in themselves all the strongest titles to my gratitude and affection!'[49] Lucy Aikin's rhetorical appeal to the family is backed up by references to Taylor's domestic 'fireside circle', and an appeal to her daughter Susan to write. Potentially subversive, violent behaviour – from the Roman matrons, the cook's maid, or from reading Scott's lawless adventurers – is evoked, and then firmly closed down into the safety of family sentiment.

Like the *Epistles*, Aikin's letters to Taylor show a certain tension in nego-tiating the claims of family and feminism: both argue that a woman's power, social and literary, must be carefully negotiated and claimed through the family rather than as an individual. I want now to turn back to the concluding passages of *Epistles* to see this in action. Here, Lucy Aikin addresses a land of enlightened women readers, 'bright daughters of a land renowned', and looks forward to a time of equality between man and woman. But she is also addressing one particular daughter, the dedicatee Anne Wakefield. This national appeal is elided with the personal, since this evocation of future social and intellectual equality is also a portrait of Anne's future marriage:

> 'Tis yours to elevate, 'tis yours to bless;
> Your interest one with his; your hopes the same.[50]

These lines look back to Barbauld's poem 'The Rights of Woman' – often seen as an angry answer to Mary Wollstonecraft's *Vindication of the Rights of Woman* – and its closing call for 'separate rights' to be 'lost in mutual love'. Barbauld's is a difficult poem to read, particularly in relation to Wollstonecraft, since it carries a charge of knowing, sexually alert irony.[51] The possibility of irony, however, is lost in these closing stanzas of her niece's poem. Instead, the wider social ideal becomes identified with one particular inter-family marriage, so that the Aikin family is seen as the ultimate model for reform. The final verse of the poem gives us an image of 'Anna', Anne Wakefield, as intellectually and affectionately nourished within her family; her learning indistinguishably linked to fatherly love:

> (For not the Roman, not the Attic store,
> Nor poets' song, nor reverend sages' lore
> To thee a Wakefield's liberal love denied,
> His child and friend, his pupil and his pride).[52]

The image of learning and love coming together comes very close to Barbauld's poem, 'Lines for Anne Wakefield on her Wedding [. . .] with a Pair of Chimney Ornaments in the Figures of two Females seated with open Books'. The ornaments, Anne's daughter recalled, were Wedgwood ware, 'two beautiful little female figures seated on cushions, each with an open book on her knees, and in one hand a gilt flower cup to hold a candle'.[53] Here, one figure represents Science, in imagery very close to Aikin's poem:

> The stores of Rome and Greece I spoil,
> And feed my lamp with Attic oil;

While for my mistress I explore
The treasures deep of ancient lore.[54]

The matching figure represents Love, a feminine ideal identified by 'gentle deeds and rosy smiles', and thus allows an interpretation of the poem along gendered lines, with Charles representing Science and Anne Love. Certainly this was the way in which Anne's daughter would read it, recording in her *Memories of Seventy Years*, where the poem was first published, that: 'My father's lamp of Science burned long, my poor mother's lamp of Love was soon extinguished by the hand of Death.'[55] Yet Barbauld's poem in some ways resists that gendered reading. After all, the poem is addressed solely to Anne, and both the figures are female readers, sisters; the representation of Science clearly tells us she is gathering material 'for my mistress'. Marriage will unite Science and Love in Anne's own mind, perhaps – so that one figure might represent Anne Wakefield, and the other Mrs Charles Rochemont Aikin, before and after marriage. And this might also be where Barbauld's poem differs from that of Lucy Aikin. In the *Epistles*, Anne's wedding becomes symbolic of a much larger social ideal, as she is folded into a familial and historical narrative of progress. Barbauld's small poem, circulated in manuscript, is a more private enterprise, and also, I think, remains slightly evasive: it is both about the marriage and about Anne's growth as an individual. Subsequent readings, by Lucy Aikin and by Anna Letitia Le Breton, have turned it into a family narrative, rather than a female one.

BIOGRAPHIES

In my closing section, I want to move to perhaps the most obvious example of this sanitization in Lucy Aikin's biographies of Barbauld and her father, and to show how these are structured and to some extent constrained by the familial model. On the one hand, both biographies, especially that of her father, convey a strong sense of literary sociability and family creativity, and contain wonderful descriptions of friendly and domestic reading. Lucy Aikin reports, for instance, on her father's 'social and communicative habits of study'.[56] He often discussed his reading with the family; similarly, one of his writing habits was 'never to commit a single page to the printer without causing it to be previously read aloud by one of his family in his own presence, and in that of any other members of the domestic circle who could be conveniently assembled'.[57] The Aikin family is set up as a democratic powerhouse, with all invited to contribute. However, this also has the effect of absorbing individual voices, transforming them into part of a larger family narrative. I think this becomes a motivating factor in Lucy Aikin's representation of Barbauld in the memoir attached to her 1825 edition of her *Works*: a representation of her as feminized and conservative; ripe for Victorian appropriation. A representation, moreover, which would subsequently lead, as the critical tide turned against this Angel in the House, to her being reinterpreted as starchy, solemn, priggish and Whiggish. Aikin's portrayal of Barbauld as possessing 'a double portion of bashfulness and maidenly reserve', and her emphasis on her aunt's bloom, her beauty and her dark blue eyes certainly contributes to this effect.[58] More damaging still, as McCarthy has shown, is her partial, biased and deliberately misleading account of her reluctance to establish an academy for young ladies. Aikin reports her aunt's rejection of this plan in the *Memoirs* as 'a monument of her acuteness and good sense', or, in other words, her anti-feminism.[59] Replacing the letter in its proper context and redirecting it to its proper recipient, Rochemont Barbauld, William McCarthy has given a different interpretation of Barbauld's rejection of the plan for a female academy. The crux of the matter, in his rereading of the letter, is not Barbauld's modesty, but her defence of her identity and her time as an author: taking on a headmistress-ship would have dangerously encroached on her writing career. The feminized, unfeminist Barbauld thus presented by Aikin, who steers her well out of the choppy Jacobin waters of the 1790s into the calmer reaches of children's education, is a misrepresentation drawn from Aikin's anxiety about the ways in which her aunt had been vilified by the *Quarterly Review*: a 'surely honorable and protective' impulse, writes McCarthy.[60] This is true, and there is certainly a benign aspect to this rewriting. Yet its effect on the later reputation of Barbauld was significant; not least, in McCarthy's words, the irony:

in Lucy Aikin's having done for (or to) Barbauld textually what Barbauld herself felt had not been successfully performed upon her in life: rendering her conventionally feminine. And there is more than irony, there is something like historical tragedy, that in protecting Barbauld from attack by enemies who did not, in fact, attack her, Lucy Aikin laid her open, in the longer run, to attack by those who should – and, if properly informed, surely would – have been her friends.[61]

In closing I will suggest a further aspect of Aikin's negotiation with her aunt's legacy: not only that she wants to bring a more feminized Barbauld into step with post-1790s politics, but also, interconnectedly, that she is making an important claim for an alternative Aikin legacy, seeking to displace Barbauld from the forefront of their intellectual narrative, and emphasize her status as merely part of a larger family story. It is the same ideology which lies behind the *Epistles* – female power and female action celebrated not as the achievement of an individual, but within the family context. The effect of Aikin's censored letter, for instance, is both to emphasize Barbauld's feminine distrust of feminist undertakings, and also to show her as a product of the Aikin family, rather than as an individual, self-determining author. She also persistently shows her aunt as having to be encouraged and dragged from her torpor into literary production: she 'could seldom excite herself to the labour of composition', Aikin tells us, 'except on the spur of occasion', and presents her as having been constantly prompted by her brother.[62] In Lucy Aikin's biography of her father, Barbauld first appears as his 'beloved confident', not as an author in her own right, but lovingly encouraging the authorial ambitions of her brother. It is only well into the first chapter that her own writing is mentioned, and then it comes firmly under the auspices of her brother, as Aikin depicts her as having been prompted into poetry by John Aikin's 1772 *Essays on Song Writing*, and then encouraged into print by him:

He had the high gratification of aiding his sister in selecting, revising, and conducting through the press, her volume of poems, which the urgency of his entreaties had chiefly prevailed upon her to give to the world; – their success proved equal to their merit; and while it justified the judgment of her brother from the imputation of partiality, it swelled his heart with the purest emotions of delight and triumph.[63]

This is expanded in Aikin's *Memoirs* of Barbauld:

By his [John Aikin's] persuasion and assistance, her Poems were selected, revised, and arranged for publication: and when all these preparations were completed, finding that she still hesitated and lingered, – like the parent bird who pushes off its young to their first flight, he procured the paper, and set the press to work on his own authority.[64]

This is more than encouragement; more, even, than 'urgent entreaty'. This is Aikin bringing the poems into the world, 'like the parent bird'. He might not, indeed, be the author, but they are produced 'on his own authority'. This pattern is repeated when it comes to the appearance of their joint volume, *Miscellaneous Pieces in Prose*. While she admits in her biography of her father that 'the share of Mr. Aikin in this collection was considerably the smallest and least important', she also wishes it to be known that his Gothic tale of Sir Bertrand 'produced a considerable effect, and has been many times republished by the compilers of selections'.[65] But by the time this passage reaches the biography of her aunt, however, it has been expanded to underscore John Aikin's role as motivator and prime mover in the family's literary inheritance:

> her brother, who possessed all the activity and spirit of literary enterprise in which she was deficient, now urged her to collect her Prose Pieces, and to join him in forming a small volume.[66]

This, I think, goes further than wanting to reclaim Barbauld as feminine, bashful and modest: it also seeks to make a larger claim for the authority, and the authorial power, of John Aikin, and, in a wider sense, the Aikin family. As in the *Epistles*, women's power is shown as most effectively taking shape through their family relationships. Daniel White has spoken about the ways in which middle-class Dissenting women writers could strategically use 'their dual status as private family members and professional authors to enter public discourse from a tenuous but potentially privileged station': writing within the family model, he suggests, allows both protection and freedom for Barbauld, an intimate sphere which is also connected to a wider political and social world.[67] In Lucy Aikin's reading, it can also become a constraint, looking not outward to the wider world, but pointing conservatively inward, so that Barbauld's subversive voice is enclosed, and almost smothered, by her role as sister, mother, beloved children's teacher. We began with an image of the child's resentment at being compared to her precocious aunt and elder brother; this is, perhaps, her belated attempt to readjust the formidable Aikin family narrative.

NOTES

1. Le Breton, *Memoirs*, x.
2. *Ibid.*, x–xi.
3. Levy, *Family Authorship*, 21. See also White, *Early Romanticism*, esp. ch. 3, 66–86.
4. Harriet Martineau, *Autobiography*, ed. Linda H. Peterson (Peterborough, ON: Broadview, 2007), 126.
5. Betsy Rodgers (née Aikin-Sneath) (1907–98) was a descendant of John Aikin, an academic and historian who first specialized in German drama before writing her books on charity in the eighteenth century and on Barbauld. See obituary by Susan Lasdun, *Independent* (5 June 1998).
6. Anne Janowitz, 'Memoirs of a Dutiful Niece: Lucy Aikin and literary reputation', in Glen and Hamilton, *Repossessing the Romantic Past*, 80.
7. *Ibid.*, 93.
8. Le Breton, *Memoirs*, xii; 222.
9. *Ibid.*, xi.
10. Martineau, *Autobiography*, 55.
11. Le Breton, *Memoirs*, xiii.

12. Aikin, *Memoir of John Aikin*, 200.
13. Le Breton, *Memoirs*, xvii.
14. *Ibid.*, 87.
15. *Ibid.*, 82.
16. *Ibid.*, 133. Lucy's pride in her achievement might be set alongside Martineau's loaded comment that Barbauld 'was not much of a needlewoman' ('What Women are Educated For', *Once a Week* (10 August, 1861), 177), discussed in my 'Introduction'.
17. *Ibid.*, xxiv–xxv.
18. Aikin, *Works of Anna Lætitia Barbauld*, 1, xliv.
19. McCarthy, *Anna Letitia Barbauld*, 135. The transcription of the 'Family History' is McCarthy's, in which carats denote additions, and angle brackets deletions (see n. 34; 589).
20. See Braithwaite, *Romanticism, Publishing and Dissent*.
21. See Gerald P. Tyson, *Joseph Johnson: A Liberal Publisher* (Iowa City, IA: University of Iowa Press, 1979), 159–61.
22. W. H. Brock and A. J. Meadows, *The Lamp of Learning: Two Centuries of Publishing at Taylor & Francis* (London and Bristol, PA: Taylor & Francis, 1998). See also Jonathan R. Topham, 'Technicians of Print and the Making of Natural Knowledge', *Studies in History and Philosophy of Science*, 35(2) (2004), 391–400.
23. Anne K. Mellor, *Mothers of the Nation: Women's Political Writing in England, 1780–1830* (Bloomington, IN: Indiana University Press, 2000), 80.
24. Kathryn Ready, 'The Enlightenment Feminist Project of Lucy Aikin's *Epistles on Women* (1810)', *History of European Ideas*, 31 (2005), 435–50 (449); Kathryn Gleadle, *The Early Feminists: Radical Unitarians and the Emergence of the Women's Rights Movement, 1831–5* (New York, NY: St Martin's Press, 1995), 68.
25. While the merit of Aikin's poetry is still a subject for debate – see Janowitz, 'The Aikin Family, Retrospectively', Chapter 9 in this volume – a new edition of her poetry and prose by Mellor and Levy, *Epistles on Women and Other Works*, points the way towards an increased appreciation of the historical and literary significance of Lucy Aikin's work.
26. Aikin, *Epistles*, v.
27. *Ibid.*, vi.
28. *Ibid.*, 10.
29. *Ibid.*, 12.
30. *Ibid.*, 18.
31. *Ibid.*, 84.
32. *Ibid.*, 78.
33. Ready, 'The Enlightenment Feminist Project of Lucy Aikin's *Epistles on Women*', 440.
34. Ella Dzelzainis, 'Reason vs Revelation: Feminism, Malthus, and the New Poor Law in Narratives by Harriet Martineau and Charlotte Elizabeth Tonna', *Interdisciplinary Studies in the Long Nineteenth Century*, 19(2) (2006), 4.
35. *Epistles*, 17.

36. *Ibid.*, 22.
37. To Dr Channing, 15 October 1832, *Correspondence of William Ellery Channing*, 148.
38. *Epistles*, vii.
39. Anne K. Mellor, 'The Female Poet and the Poetess: Two Traditions of British Women's Poetry, 1780–1830', *Studies in Romanticism*, 36 (1997), 261–76 (275, 276).
40. Guest, *Small Change*, 18, 335–8.
41. Ready, 'The Enlightenment Feminist Project of Lucy Aikin's *Epistles on Women*', 449.
42. *Epistles*, 73; John Aikin, *General Biography; or Lives, Critical and Historical, of the Most Eminent Persons of All Ages, Countries, Conditions, and Professions*, 10 vols. (London, 1799–1815), VII, 208.
43. Lucy Aikin, letter to Susannah Taylor, 27 January 1803, in Le Breton, *Memoirs*, 124–7.
44. Spongberg, *Writing Women's History*, 115–18.
45. Barbauld, letter to Maria Edgeworth, August 1804, in Le Breton, *Memoir of Mrs. Barbauld*, 86–7.
46. Mary Hays, *Female Biography, or Memoirs of Illustrious and Celebrated Women, of all Ages and Countries Alphabetically Arranged*, 6 vols. (London: Richard Phillips, 1803), VI, 103. Hays has been criticized for her exclusion of Mary Wollstonecraft, and *Female Biography* seen as a departure from her earlier radicalism; I follow Gina Luria Walker, however, in seeing the work as a continuation and extension of Hays' feminist convictions (see Gina Luria Walker, *Mary Hays (1759–1843). The Growth of a Woman's Mind* (Aldershot: Ashgate, 2006), esp. 222–9).
47. Barbauld, letter to Lydia Withering, cited by McCarthy, *Anna Letitia Barbauld*, 500.
48. Lucy Aikin, letter to Susannah Taylor, 23 March 1805, in Le Breton, *Memoirs*, 127–30.
49. *Ibid.*, 128–9.
50. *Epistles*, 80.
51. 'The Rights of Woman', Barbauld, *Selected Poetry and Prose*, 130–1 (see also the headnote by the editors exploring the ironic potential of the poem).
52. *Epistles*, 81.
53. Anna Letitia Le Breton, *Memories of Seventy Years by One of a Literary Family*, ed. Mrs Herbert Martin (London: Griffith & Farran, 1883), 61; quoted in Barbauld, *Selected Poetry and Prose*, 150–1.
54. Barbauld, *Selected Poetry and Prose*, 151.
55. *Memories of Seventy Years*, 62; Barbauld, *Selected Poetry and Prose*, 151.
56. Aikin, *Memoir of John Aikin*, I, 201.
57. *Ibid.*, I, 200.
58. Aikin, *Works of Anna Lætitia Barbauld*, I, viii.
59. *Ibid.*, I, xvi.

60. McCarthy, 'Why Anna Letitia Barbauld Refused to Head a Women's College', 349–79 (365).
61. *Ibid.*
62. Aikin, *Works of Anna Lætitia Barbauld*, 1, xxxvii.
63. Aikin, *Memoir of John Aikin*, 1, 20.
64. Aikin, *Works of Anna Lætitia Barbauld*, 1, xii.
65. Aikin, *Memoir of John Aikin*, 1, 21.
66. Aikin, *Works of Anna Lætitia Barbauld*, 1, xiii.
67. White, *Early Romanticism*, 68.

CHAPTER 9

The Aikin family, retrospectively

Anne F. Janowitz

I

The chapters in this volume describe and evaluate many of the contributions that the Aikin family made to and through religious, intellectual,
literary and political practices in the eighteenth and into the nineteenth centuries.[1] The report from the conference where many earlier
versions of these essays were presented, 'The Dissenting Mind: The
Aikin Circle, *c.* 1760s to *c.* 1860s', opens by remarking on how many of
'that remarkably gifted provincial family of dissenters', the Aikins, are
given entries in the *New Oxford Dictionary of National Biography*.[2] Many
of the *New ODNB* entries are by contemporary scholars, including
Barbara Brandon Schnorrenberg, a distinguished women's historian, and
William McCarthy, Anna Barbauld's biographer. Over the last twenty years
researchers working on the Aikin family have produced a successful
example of network study, one of the most interesting methods for looking
at the cultural life of beliefs, ideas and texts that are written by and
circulate among a group of people – a contemporary method that blends
Namierism, women's history and contextual study.[3]

It is worth pointing out that these same Aikins had entries in the *Old
DNB* as well as the *New* – which might be used as evidence of their
importance throughout the nineteenth century. But in Leslie Stephen's
1885 *DNB*, the sources for that evidence derive almost entirely from the
series of memoirs of the family written by Lucy Aikin, daughter of John
Aikin, 'physician and author', sister of Arthur Aikin, 'chemist and scientific
writer', and Charles Rochemont Aikin, 'doctor and chemist', and niece of
Anna Barbauld, 'poet and miscellaneous writer', and all the articles are
signed A. A. B., Arthur Aikin Brodribb.[4] The obituary in *The Times* for
Brodribb, which praises his long service to that newspaper as a gallery
reporter at parliament, reminds the reader that, '[h]is grandmother, Susan
Aikin, was a granddaughter of John Aikin, M. D., a well-known writer in

his day and the brother of Mrs. Barbauld' (who, this sentence implies, remains well known).[5] Coteries require their own historians if they are to be known coteries, and if the Arthur Aikin Brodribb articles suggest that the Aikins wrote themselves into the *DNB*, it has been literary critics and historians of women and literature written by women, who have created our current interest in Anna Barbauld and her family.[6] The most recent instance is William McCarthy's summation of twenty years of research in his authoritative biography of Anna Barbauld, a discussion that combines feminist sympathy with attention to the range and power of Anna Barbauld as an Enlightenment poet.[7] Taken altogether the Aikin-related entries in the *Old* and *New DNB*, along with more detailed twentieth- and twenty-first-century studies, agree that the importance of their network of family and friends lies in their rootedness in the late eighteenth-century religious culture of heterodox, Rational Dissent, and their attachment, both intellectually and as an idealized geography, to the Warrington Academy, founded in 1757. One result of network studies has been that we can make the case that the Aikins' subsequent contributions to broader institutions of learning, literary and liberal practice reached a wider public than their marginal social and religious place (marginal even *within* Dissent) might have predicted.

The transit between the Aikins' individual intellectual and literary projects and the shaping of their collective public reputation was achieved chiefly through two important mechanisms. The first, which I have just illustrated by the 1885 *DNB* articles, was the Aikin reputation machine, which was elaborated and maintained through a series of periodicals that originated among liberal Dissenters, and through Aikin family memoirs. For about a hundred years this family observed itself and wrote about itself and did an impressive job of redescribing itself in response to earlier versions of their family's various intellectual commitments.[8]

The second chief mechanism for the advancement of the Aikins as a public family arose through and benefited from their engagement in a number of differentiated but contiguous contemporary concerns. Not only as a Dissenting family in the decades just prior to the lifting of sanctions against Nonconformists, and not only as a literary family in which Anna Barbauld's poetic vocation was emulated both by her brother, John, and her niece, Lucy, the Aikins participated in the reform and liberal modelling of modern life. The interests of the Aikins during their public lives from the 1760s – their commitment to ending the constraints imposed on Dissenters, to abolishing the traffic in human slaves, to enlarging the voting franchise, to supporting (up to a point) the French Revolution, and later the Reform Bill – were the campaigns that transformed discourses of sociability and sympathy into what would become the politics of liberalism. Political men, such as Thomas Denman, who drafted the Reform Bill of 1832, learned their sociable 'liberality' at Palgrave, the school run by Anna Barbauld and her husband, Rochemont, a school where, as William McCarthy puts it in this volume (Chapter 3), 'elocution, literature and liberalism formed a trio'. So, the Aikins in and after the Warrington years were engaged in an olio of secular and religious principles and projects.

After its closure in 1786, Warrington's reputation served as an emblem of what liberal pedagogy might rise to, 'distinguished by sound learning, just and liberal principles, and virtuous manners'.[9] The pedagogic goal had been to produce what Anna Barbauld called 'a well-tuned mind' in her *Poems* of 1773, the volume that introduced her to the metropolitan literary milieu.[10] The Warrington tutors aimed to incarnate an ideal of social intercourse conceived of as informal, familiar and amiable, teaching the virtues of 'candid manners' and an 'active mind'.[11] In a letter written in 1828, Lucy Aikin described her own roots in Warrington, and she makes the point that the practice there was as much social as it was religious. Writing that 'my excellent grandfather Aikin' had his colleagues 'begun to break forth out of the chains and darkness of Calvinism, and their manners softened with their system . . . in *manners*, the free dissenters, as they were called, came much nearer the [Established] Church than to their own stricter brethren, yet in *doctrine no* sect departed so far from the Establishment'.[12] The history of the Warrington Academy was mythologized and made widely available to Unitarians by a former student, William Turner. Twenty-five years after the Academy had closed, Turner's lengthy narrative was published in the *Monthly Repository*, the central periodical of the Unitarian intelligentsia.[13] The *Monthly Repository*, which Isobel Armstrong has shown to have been a decisive cultural influence in Victorian society, became, under the editorship of W. J. Fox, the great Unitarian/Benthamite journal for and the public archive of liberal Dissent throughout the nineteenth century.[14] The *Monthly Repository* was a periodical in which a 'democratic' form of poetics was promoted, not only in the criticism written by J. S. Mill and others, but in which Robert Browning was welcomed into the tradition with his dramatic monologues. These poems, which tested and stretched the five-beat verse line into something new, put the speech of all manner of men and women in the metre of the well-born speakers of its earlier history. Anna Barbauld published some poems and memoirs in the first series, edited by Robert Aspland. The *Monthly Repository* was similar in orientation to the London Dissenting publisher Joseph Johnson's earlier 1788–9

Analytical Review, and also to the journals edited by Anna Aikin's brother. John Aikin edited the *Monthly Magazine* from 1796 to 1806, and took an important step in turning Dissenting journals towards the larger liberal public by not offering much in the way of religious controversies, but rather, purveying the secular knowledge created from within the Dissenting community to the growing world of the informed middle-class reader. John went on to edit the *Athenaeum*, and his son Arthur took on the *Annual Review: A Magazine of Literary and Miscellaneous Information*, which lasted for six years.[15] The Aikins' publications were handled, for the most part, by Johnson, and he broadened his list from Dissent-related religious materials to a more political and, in the first years of the French Revolution, a more fully radical publishing programme. John Aikin and Anna Barbauld, along with former Warrington Tutors, including William Enfield and Gilbert Wakefield, also took up political issues more directly.

What is certain is that the Aikin family – active as Dissenters, reforming polemicists, liberal intellectuals and pedagogues – received and half-created character-types of their period that threaded together aspects of their religious, intellectual and literary projects detailed in the chapters of this collection. Unlike the eccentric and radical dramas of the Shelley–Godwin family's self-publicity and literary works, the Aikin publications and social ambitions belong to the Dissenting community's drive towards inclusion within civil society, grounded in Dissenters' increased financial and industrial power.[16] This regularizing was in step with the growth of public dissemination of science and scholarship, and promised a society of mutually tolerant liberal persons. Kathryn Ready's contribution in this volume (Chapter 4) shows us how John Aikin moved among disciplines and discourses and took on the figure of the 'literary physician', a type that bound together liberality and economic status, and that allowed him to understand Dissent in its bearing on secular concerns:

> In his *Address to the Dissidents*, Aikin celebrates the status of Dissenters as part of 'the most virtuous, the most enlightened, the most independent part of the community, the *middle class*'. In contrast to many conservatives who believed in the principle of paternalism, and the need for reform of manners to happen from the top down, liberals like Aikin saw all reform campaigns (of manners included) as most effectively spearheaded by the middle classes (including Dissenters). Thus, he again tacitly draws a sense of authority from his position as a Dissenter, which he openly acknowledges and justifies in various ways throughout the *Letters*.

I have argued elsewhere that John Aikin had a rivalrous and somewhat aggressive relationship with his more talented sister, as presented by Lucy

Aikin in her *Memoir* of her father; Ready, Stephen Daniels and Paul Elliott, in their discussion in this collection of the disciplinary contributions made by John Aikin to the understanding of landscape and geography, give him his due as a creative disciplinary thinker (see Chapter 5). Felicity James' chapter in this volume shows how very complex – both burdensome and authorizing – the legacy of a family can be to a woman of the third generation taking on the role of family publicist. One recurring theme in her writings on her father and on Anna Barbauld is Lucy's intimation that John Aikin has been undervalued in a world that spends too much time crediting his sister. She aims to establish his calling as a man of letters, and opens her memoir with a description of how he was 'imbued indelibly . . . with that love of letters which became at once the ornament and safeguard of his youth, and the occupation and solace of every succeeding period of his life'.[17] William McCarthy has plotted the steps by which John Aikin aimed to bring himself and Anna into the London literary world, the results of which detached Anna somewhat from her family and brought her into a less safe but more exciting world.[18] Philip Le Breton's memoir of Lucy Aikin reveals that Lucy herself felt defeated by her family's judgement. Referring to her grandmother, Jane Aikin, Lucy writes, 'She called me "Little Dunce"; the reproach sank deep, and its effect was certainly unfavourable . . . it filled me with a sense of incurable deficiency'.[19] But John remained a disappointed poet, though a vigorous proponent of reform and an impressive essayist.

Like father, like daughter? Michelle Levy makes a very strong case for the innovative aspects of Lucy Aikin as a historian, but leaves aside the problem of Lucy's bad poetry. When her volume of *Epistles on Women* and other miscellaneous poems was reviewed in the *Critical Review*, it was described as 'being stuffed with epithets and receding only from prose in the obscurity of their ideas and the strutting pomp of their diction'.[20] The *Epistles* have been rehabilitated in the twenty-first century, but primarily as documentary evidence in an argument about Lucy Aikin's feminism. Felicity James, bravely, does consider the poetic structure of the *Epistles*, and makes the excellent point that the poem's structure conforms to the then-popular stadial theory of history, a theory that was part of the eighteenth-century emphasis on progress and perfectibility. Her argument is very persuasive, and it presents us with the possibility that Anna Barbauld's *Eighteen Hundred and Eleven*, a ruin poem and a 'Westward the Course of Empire' poem, which was written around the same time as the *Epistles*, engages with Lucy's poem at the level of poetic genre – Barbauld's prophetic vision of the ruins of London offers a critical and clever counterposition to Lucy's poem of the stages of women's place in history understood to be closely tied to her emphasis on maternal power in familial relationships. James carefully maps the ways in which Lucy's deployment of the genre also raises questions about women's mediated relationship to power. I am tempted to think that aunt and niece talked about their opposing models of human change. Michelle Levy is also right to commend Lucy Aikin's innovative and well-written books of history, early versions of what is now called 'cultural history', and to take seriously her modification of the genres of history writing. Lucy's 1818 *Memoirs of the Court of Queen Elizabeth* was widely read and reprinted throughout the nineteenth century, going through six editions by 1874. She went on to write *Memoirs of the Court of James I* (1822) and of *Charles I* (1833). Aikin argued that there was a dearth of the *kind* of writing 'in that class which forms the glory of French literature – memoir'. She was not aiming to produce history, but to capture 'the biography, the literature, and the manners of the period'.[21]

So it is that, drawing on elements of literary writing by both John and Anna, as well as looking back on over fifty years of Aikin texts in 1822, the *Monthly Repository* crowns John Aikin MD with literary laurels, and calls him 'the head of a family which has perhaps done more than any other family in England for the promotion of knowledge and the gratification of the literary taste'.[22] With the label of 'literary', the Aikin family is shown to embody the social and cultural values of middle-class liberal life while their history as 'free' Dissenters and supporters of the French Revolution is not invoked. But the praise of Aikin as a literary man was a posthumous gift, for it appears only in his obituary.

II

On the basis of the works of John Aikin MD and Lucy Aikin, and despite the praise given to John Aikin at his death in the house journal of liberal Dissent, it is difficult to think of the Aikin family as individually so talented as they were collectively *exemplary* in the period. Dissenting men and women and the political tendency towards liberalism were moving in the same direction. This was a period in which, in the 1780s and 1790s, the Aikins responded to significant public issues, in the campaigns for the repeal of the Test and Corporation Acts, and in the first years of the French Revolution, when Anna Barbauld, in the voice of a 'citizen', greeted the defeat of Wilberforce's bill as an occasion on which to link the Dissenter's complaint, in the passionate language of the moment, to the revolutionary and democratic force sweeping Europe:

Agitated with new and strong emotions, they ['the minds of men'] swell and heave beneath oppression, as the seas within the Polar Circle, when, at the approach of Spring, they grow impatient to burst their icy chains; when what, but an instant before, seemed so firm, spread for many a dreary league like a floor of solid marble, at once with a tremendous noise gives way, long fissures spread in every direction, and the air redounds with the clash of floating fragments, which every hour are broken from the mass.[23]

In fact, it was Barbauld's ability to write passionately as a woman of letters which constituted the complex of the polemical and political reputation of the Aikins in the years around the Revolution, when Anna was called a 'Virago' by Horace Walpole, and the question of her being a Dissenter was half-obscured by her apparent Jacobinism. She never was a Jacobin, but like her fellow temporary radicals, was much closer to the Gironde. The negative publicity around her in the late 1780s and early 1790s was based on her politics, which would again diminish her status in 1812, when she published *Eighteen Hundred and Eleven* and was accused of lowering national morale in a war that had been going on since 1793. The collapse of radical support for the French Revolution was felt within the Aikin circle. Joseph Johnson was tried and imprisoned for publishing Gilbert Wakefield's excoriation of Bishop Llandaff.[24] Wakefield spent a year in prison and died soon after in 1801. Just after his release, John Aikin wrote a poem to Wakefield in the temper of anti-Jacobinism, in which he invited Wakefield to put aside his politics and return to a more private sphere: 'Cease then, my Friend, thy generous hopeless aim . . . And in the soothing voice of friendship drown / The groans and shouts, and triumphs of the world'. Wakefield replied in a poem, also published in Aikin's *Monthly Magazine*, in which he refused to follow the Aikins in retreat, vowing still to 'front the grim visage of despotic power, / Lawless, self-will'd, fierce, merciless, corrupt'.[25] What had been a friendship nurtured in the Rational Dissenting circle at Warrington became a political split, and the issues were based on political and secular concerns, however much they may also have a lineage in the Dissenting community's struggle for civil entitlements.

Nonetheless, I think we should consider Anna Barbauld's poetic vocation as the primary condition of possibility for the Aikin public reputation. Having begun with the *ODNB*, and pausing briefly in the 1790s, I want now to turn back to the moment when the Aikin circle became publicly known through Anna Barbauld's literary debut as the 'Miss Aikin' of *Poems* (1773), and was courted as a Bluestocking by Elizabeth Montagu, whom Dr Johnson called the 'Queen of the Blues'. As a woman of letters, Barbauld engaged in a wide range of writing: she inhabited successive epochs as a poet, an educationalist, a polemicist, an editor of the works of Akenside and a set of introductions to a fifty-volume edition of *The British Novelists*.[26] But in 1773 she was most responsive to, and inspired by, her immediate environment at the Warrington Academy, where she thought deeply and wrote her way into a poetic that would bring subjective religious experiences close to the poetics of sensibility, both for the sake of her beliefs and in order to temper the intellectual strictness of Rational Dissent. I think she was finding a way to come to terms with and yet maintain her own difference from the versions of both religion and natural philosophy that Joseph Priestley was developing; namely, a programme of rigorous interrogation of all religious doctrine, and a distrust of sentiment as a basis of religious certainty.

Though the recognition of her talents was not limited to her close community, Anna Barbauld was a conscious engineer of the image of her family in her poems written at Warrington, as well as through her educational programme at the Palgrave School, and she endorsed (with caveats) the principles of her religious community. As William McCarthy's subtitle to his biography claims, Barbauld was a 'voice of the enlightenment' and the Rational Dissenters were deeply influenced by Enlightenment philosophy in their critique of orthodox Christian doctrine. Perhaps most noticeably among the *Poems* (1773), Barbauld's 'The Invitation' serves as an advertisement for the value of the Warrington Academy as a place to educate young men. It was at Warrington that she lived from the age of 15 until 30, and it was there that she wrote most of the poems for which she was valued in the later eighteenth and early nineteenth centuries. But even before the publication of 'The Invitation', she wrote many poems that remained unpublished but circulated within the Warrington circle, and taken as a group they reveal her ideas of the benefits of a circle. For example, when visiting the Priestleys at home, she writes:

> Oft have I there the social circle joined
> Whose brightening influence raised my pensive mind,
> For none within that circle's magic bound,
> But sprightly spirits move their cheerful round.[27]

Barbauld praises the individual autonomy and group cohesion of the members of the 'social circle'; they are not 'bound' by a charm, but shaped through voluntary association and, notably, though ornamented by 'easy smiles', 'no dark unfriendly passions enter there'. The principle of such association connects sociability and morality: it is 'ev'ry social tye that binds the good'.[28] At the same time the vision of sociability that Barbauld created in her poems of family and friends appealed to 'polite society'. Barbauld's *Poems* were reprinted four times in 1773 and her reputation was soon established as a Bluestocking and as a new poetic voice. Her standing among the women of letters of the later eighteenth century is confirmed by her place in Richard Samuel's painting *The Nine Living Muses of Great Britain*, exhibited at the Royal Academy in 1779, where she is painted as a Bluestocking among equals. Elizabeth Montagu, Elizabeth Griffith, Elizabeth Carter, Charlotte Lennox, Elizabeth Linley, Angelica Kauffman, Catharine Macaulay, Anna Barbauld and Hannah More emblematized, for Samuel, the intellectual and artistic capabilities of the English Enlightenment. In her important study of the painting, Elizabeth Eger reports that the image had been widely distributed before its exhibition when it was published as a print in Joseph Johnson's ephemeral 'pocket memorandum' book for 1778.[29]

By 1779, however, when Anna and Rochemont Barbauld had established their school, it seemed to many in the London intelligentsia that as one of the 'living muses', Anna Barbauld was not living up to the promise of Miss Aikin's *Poems*. Eger's study cites James Barry RA, lamenting Barbauld's provincial existence: '[Barbauld], to the shame and loss of the public, is buried in a retirement at [Palgrave] actually making two-penny books for children; but the appearances may deceive us; some epic or other great work is, I trust, in hand, as the solace of retirement'.[30] Samuel Johnson was equally appalled by what he saw as Barbauld's descent into the nursery: she 'was an instance of early cultivation, but in what did it terminate? In marrying a little Presbyterian parson, who keeps an infant boarding school, so that all her employment now is "To suckle fools, and chronicle small beer".'[31] These most secular and dismissive comments suggest how little interest the London world had in her religious commitments beyond the social requirement of being a Christian. But it was in her years at Palgrave that Barbauld developed and extended her ideas of devotional piety, which informed her *Hymns in Prose for Children*, a set of prose poems imbued with both the feelings of sensibility and the cosmic connections to the sublimity of God.

It is also probably the case that when *Poems* (1773) was published by Johnson, Barbauld's immediate status in heterodox Dissenting circles was authorized by her role as a privileged daughter of the Warrington Divinity Tutor, John Aikin DD. The publication of *Poems* (1773) was mutually beneficial for the Warrington Academy and for Anna Barbauld herself. William Woodfall's review of the volume in the *Monthly Review* reminds its readers of Barbauld's place within the informal familial–pedagogic–religious network of Dissenting intellectuals, and her indebtedness to her social milieu: 'The Pupils of that very useful seminar [Warrington] . . . celebrated her genius, and diffused her praises far and wide; and some of her compositions have been read and admired by persons of the first taste and judgment in the republic of letters'.[32] Her niece, and to a certain extent her brother, borrowed her reflected light to develop themselves as literary people, but the most important intellectual interlocutors in her own education were her father and her friend and sometime mentor, Joseph Priestley.

The chief influence on Anna Aikin was her father. David Wykes' discussion in this volume of John Aikin DD (see Chapter 2) provides an excellent riposte to the tendency of literary and cultural critics to portray the Warrington Academy as exemplifying Dissenting academies more generally. Warrington was a Dissenting Academy reckoned to be the most heterodox and the most diverse in both its students and its curriculum. There, as Joseph Priestley was later to say, the Tutors 'were all . . . Arians' and many subsequently became Socinians.[33] The interest the Aikin family elicits from us might be a function of their being poised at the end of one set of religious institutions thrown up by the outcome of the Civil War and Restoration, and at the beginning of a new set in which religious tolerance, literary production and liberal politics would shape the cultural scene of the nineteenth century. This shifting from a religious movement that also fostered and engaged in secular activity to a liberal movement proposed a humanized, religious sensibility in the context of political reform.

Reading Wykes' chapter led me to understand much more clearly how different the values of the literary historian are to those of the historian of religion. While giving the reader a strong sense of what the elder Aikin was like as a thinker and a man, and the extent to which his own interests shaped his children's dedication to literary pursuits, Wykes shows how mistaken it is to locate the most intellectually interesting aspects of Dissent in the history and achievements of Warrington. There is no doubt that Warrington employed a good number of accomplished tutors. In addition to Aikin and Priestley there were other tutors whose contributions to literature and science, and whose support for progressive political positions made the Academy important for its secular achievements, including William Enfield, at whose school the young John Keats was educated, and the passionate Gilbert Wakefield.[34] Wykes insists on the *anomalous* character of Warrington's place in Dissenting culture, concluding that:

Although evidence of the best that Dissent could achieve, it did not fit the pattern of other eighteenth-century Dissenting academies. The Academy's reputation was founded on the excellence of its instruction in secular subjects: the teaching of science, languages and history. It did not compare with Daventry Academy, its main rival, in the teaching of theology, metaphysics or ethics.[35]

Wykes makes his argument even stronger when he looks at the low figures for students educated at Warrington who then went on to become Dissenting clerics, and he suggests that it may have been in part John Aikin's fault, given that he was not as distinguished in the theological studies that he was to teach for almost twenty years as he was in the 'grammar, oratory, and criticism' he was originally hired to teach as Tutor in *belles-lettres*.[36] Wykes' chapter argues that it was as a pedagogue at Kibworth, before he moved to Warrington, that Aikin made his foremost contribution to Dissent. On the other hand, the evidence Wykes provides suggests that Aikin's contribution to education more widely, and to the diffusion of his expertise in the classics, modern languages and literature, coupled with the large number of lay students at Warrington, was part of the assimilation of Dissenting education into the larger milieu of liberal culture. Although many of the courses of lectures given at Warrington had secular content, they were nonetheless taking place within the overall framework of the Dissenting academies. This makes sense in the light of the increasing importance to the nation of the industrial and financial power of Dissenting manufacturers and businessmen, many of whom sent their sons to Warrington where they encountered other young men who came from Established Church families that sought up-to-date education for their sons, creating a society of intellectual equals who would continue to know one another after leaving the Academy at Warrington.

Wykes tells us that John Aikin came to Warrington in 1758 as tutor in *belles-lettres*: the challenge was 'to form the Youth to a just Taste', and Aikin was the perfect candidate, being not only a knowledgeable classicist, but a lover of literature of all kinds. Even the classical scholar, Gilbert Wakefield, though often rather ungenerous and cranky when discussing Warrington in his *Memoirs*, wrote that Aikin *père*'s 'intellectual attainments were of a very superior quality indeed ... Every path of polite literature had been traversed by him, and traversed with success'.[37] When William Enfield delivered Aikin's funeral sermon, he did not neglect to speak of the minister's knowledge of the classics, depicting him as a person 'with all the discernment and feeling of a man of true taste'.[38] And one can understand why Wykes is quite right to be distressed that a 'modern author' has mistaken John Aikin DD for his son, John

Aikin MD – a confusion that turns out to be one made by a *literary* historian.

Though she stands at the centre of the Aikin circle, Anna Barbauld was, if not an indifferent, then a doctrinally amorphous Dissenter. McCarthy writes, 'on most creedal questions it is not at all clear what she believed; few of her admirers, complained a Unitarian journal in 1841, had any idea of her doctrinal beliefs. She was thought by contemporaries to be a Unitarian, and she is claimed by modern Unitarians; but some who knew her better were not so sure.'[39] Nonetheless the elements of Barbauld's religion can be seen fairly easily in her writing, even if they don't articulate Rational Dissent's doctrines. What they promote, instead, is a set of aesthetic values that are integrated into the language of piety and Christian worship. These values encourage the self-understanding that can elaborate and articulate morality on the basis of that understanding.

III

This brings me to my literary and speculative argument that in her inter-rogation of the inward life of persons in relation to the work of devotion to God (the engagement of what Charles Taylor discussed in his *Sources of the Self* as the 'internal' goods that displace the 'external' goods set out by an ever-watchful and, at times, punitive God), Anna Barbauld complicates by aestheticizing, and diminishes by reducing, the philosophical ground of Dissenting heterodoxy.[40] I suggest that without intending to, Barbauld participates in a dialectic of Dissent, a process in which secular concerns emerge from within institutions and doctrines of belief as they engage with the new knowledge of the seventeenth and eighteenth centuries and the broadening of those secular institutions within Britain that lived alongside religious ones.

In a more recent book, *A Secular Age*, Charles Taylor suggests that secularization should not be counterpoised to the religious grounding of knowledge and faith but is rather one of the outcomes of transformations immanent in religious activity. These outcomes are discernible in the transformations of Protestantism in the age of Newton and beyond, which in turn exacerbated a growing separation between the sublime God and the God of intimacy, domesticity and the human heart.[41] The sublime God's main task is to maintain the laws of the Universe, and so prevent such threats as a realignment of planets that could throw gravitational arrange-ments out of balance, and cause the universe itself to collapse. Taylor argues that providential arguments distance us from God and endow us with moral independence: 'First [God] made us, and endowed us with reason, and in some cases also, with benevolence, and it is these faculties which enable us to get things together, and carry out his plan.'[42] The distance between persons and the God who orchestrates the workings of the Universe opens a space for moral issues to be assessed and their principles articulated by attending to the voice of human interiority. Taylor presents the processes of secularization from the sixteenth through the eighteenth centuries as a slow and effective reorganization of the values and norms of a religious world into a set of norms concerned with 'freedom and mutual benefit'.[43]

Central to Taylor's discussion is what he calls 'providential Deism', which he argues is consistent with a number of foundational shifts, including (a) a constitutive shift from God as a human-like actor in the things and events of the world to the production of (b) an impersonal order of things which humanity can access through reason rather than through mystery, and which, as a result, places God and humanity at an increasing distance from one another, while at the same time (c) construing Christianity to be a historical religion, which has been 'obscured by accretions and corruptions'.[44] This is not to say that secularism is the only possible outcome of Dissent, but rather, that some of the fundamental categories of Nonconformist Christianity were the conditions of possibility for the development of institutions and discourses that could accommodate structures of feeling belonging to religion but also differentiate their intentions. So it may be wrong to consider secularization as an attack on religion but rather the result of a much larger process that begins deep within Protestant institutions so that by the mid-nineteenth century, literary liberalism is endorsed by the Unitarian movement as if it was an aspect of Dissenting religious culture. I want to add that Anna Barbauld is an instance of that process at work. Raised within the values of polite society in a milieu where Dissenting belief was provided with ways of knowing derived from the philosophical positions developed in the eighteenth century, Barbauld found in the discourses of sensibility and sympathy a way to defend belief against too much reason, while also being attached to its achievements.

Since the middle of the seventeenth century there have been many warnings of a dangerous drive towards freethinking and atheism by way of the Enlightenment, and in the twentieth century, with the growth of the soft sciences such as sociology, there were just as many celebrations of secularization and its triumph over the dogma, morality and institutions of the religious. It is not usually the British who are regarded as atheist-enlighteners, as natural philosophy emerged from and remained more securely tied to Christian doctrine and philosophy in the eighteenth century.[45] Nonetheless, ideas that appeared to undermine belief were an anxiety to those who saw an atheistic tendency in Rational Dissent.[46] To observers, Rational Dissenters such as Priestley seemed to be settling into a disenchanted state – the premonitory illness of the secular spirit. Even Jonathan Israel, the theorist of radical enlightenment as a tradition originating with Spinoza and continuing through the eighteenth century, who is most usually dismissive of the British contribution to the anti-clerical, anti-Rousseauvian 'preference for representative democracy', welcomes Priestley as a member of the radical enlightenment. Priestley was indeed an enlightenment man, and politically a radical, but he was a strong theist. As an adherent to the methodology of rational philosophy and natural philosophy, he was committed to the idea that Christian doctrine needs to be either factually or logically demonstrable. John Aikin and Priestley were both Arians in their first years at the Warrington Academy, believing that Christ, though divine, was not the equal of God. Priestley later became a Socinian, subscribing to the heresy that made the more radical claim that Christ was solely human. The combination of his politics and his religious position put Priestley in the line of fire by 'Church and King' rioters and Priestley's house was burned down in the Birmingham riots of 1791. For Priestley, the rigours of reason were not enticements to atheistic freethinking, but offered a method through which belief might be pursued.

By contrast, the Aikins were more conventional in their opinions and in their practices. What interests me here is that Barbauld's attractive status as a 'polite' Dissenter included her poetic humanizing of belief, which encouraged the focus on the self as moral arbiter. The power of her poetry to manage subjective religious experience within the conventions of the aesthetic was much greater than the power of Priestley's rationalism to undermine it. But there was a price to pay. By using the discourse of the aesthetic, questions of religious belief become questions of subjective aesthetic experience. Priestley, on the other hand, invoked the method of philosophy to build rational foundations for doctrine and belief. Was Rational Dissent as dangerous a pathway to atheism as was the aestheticization of belief? Fellow Dissenters may have feared that Rational Dissent would snare its adherents into unbelief; but devotional sensibility, as Anna Barbauld wrote it, may have reached more deeply and more kinds of Christians than anyone might have anticipated. In short, Anna Barbauld's poetic helped to spiritualize literature in the nineteenth century, something we see, for example, in Wordsworth's and Coleridge's meditative lyrics of the 1790s and, as I shall point out, even later in Shelley's poem of sublime and Godless Power in 'Mont Blanc'.

The families of Anna Barbauld's students and their children at the Palgrave school embraced her educational principles and programme fully, and it suggests that her practice of bringing divinity close to hand in her children's works was an attractive approach to offering a sympathetic God who might have joined the Restoration Society for the Reformation of Manners. Her response to the development of the impersonal order and the distanced God of providential Protestantism was to mediate God's separateness through the aesthetics of beauty. Her *Hymns in Prose for Children* (which was published in 1781 and stayed in print for years) urges its young readers to find their way from an immediate experience of beauty to an intuition of the ways in which God made Himself present through natural beauty.[47] In 'Hymn VI' of the series, she begins by addressing the 'Child of reason', who can think logically and know where she has been ('I have been wandering along the meadows, in the thick grass'), but the adult speaker tells the child to go back to the meadows and feel the presence of God everywhere. Barbauld had earlier approached the question of the distance between God and humanity by way of the category of the sublime. While Burke is often cited as a source for Barbauld's sense sublime, I think it is rather derived primarily from one of Addison's *Spectator* essays in 1712, where he, having become 'newtonian', writes about the power of the cosmos and our inability to synthesize it into a single concept or image as an analogy with our inability to know God. Having attributed to the natural philosophers the praise of gratifying and enlarging the work of the imagination, in *The Spectator* No. 420, we see how Addison produces both the theory and the sensation of the sublime:

when we survey the whole Earth at once, and the several Planets that lie within its Neighbourhood, we are filled with a pleasing Astonishment, to see so many Worlds hanging one above another, and sliding round their Axles in such an amazing Pomp and Solemnity. If, after this, we contemplate those wide Fields of *Ether*, that reach in height as far as from *Saturn* to the fixt Stars, and run abroad almost to an Infinitude, our Imagination finds its Capacity filled with so immense a Prospect, and puts itself upon the stretch to comprehend it. But if we rise yet higher, and consider the fixt Stars as so many vast Oceans of Flame, that are each of them attended with a different Sett of Planets, and still discover new Firmaments and new lights, that are sunk farther in those unfathomable Depths of *Ether*, so as not to be seen by the strongest of our Telescopes, we are lost in such a labyrinth of Suns and Worlds, and confounded with the Immensity and Magnificence of Nature.[48]

The transition from the visible to the only imaginable is here itself imperceptible – the verb is 'rising', which suggests the movement of the eyes ever upward and of the mind as well, and the *survey* becomes a *consideration* which adjusts into a *discovery* that is invisible to the eye, and even to 'the strongest of our Telescopes' – so it is that we are 'confounded with the Immensity and Magnificence of Nature'. It is the universe as we now understand it, or almost understand it, that creates the structure of sublime experience. Mr Spectator recognizes that he has provided a theory near the end of the essay:

> I think it may shew us the proper Limits, as well as the Defectiveness, of our Imagination; The Understanding, indeed, opens an infinite Space on every side of us, but the imagination, after a few faint efforts, is immediately at a standstill, and finds her self swallowed up in the immensity of the void that surrounds her.

In her greatest poem, the nocturne 'A Summer Evening's Meditation', Barbauld is quoting Addison, not Burke, and disclosing the doubleness of sublime experience.[49] It diminishes the subjectivity of the person by showing our limits and it offers the experience of God as incomprehensible in Himself, but available through the manageable aesthetic form of excess, the sublime:

> Seiz'd in thought
> On fancy's wild and roving wing I sail,
> From the green borders of the peopled earth,
> And the pale moon, her duteous fair attendant;
> From solitary Mars; from the vast orb
> Of Jupiter, whose huge gigantic bulk
> Dances in ether like the lightest leaf;
> To the dim verge, the suburbs of the system,
> Where chearless Saturn 'midst his wat'ry moons
> Girt with a lucid zone, in gloomy pomp,
> Sits like an exil'd monarch: fearless thence
> I launch into the trackless deeps of space,
> Where, burning round, ten thousand suns appear,
> Of elder beam;
>   . . .
>   Here must I stop,
> Or is there aught beyond? What hand unseen
> Impels me onward thro' the glowing orbs
> Of habitable nature; far remote,To the dread confines of eternal night,
> To solitudes of vast unpeopled space,
> The desarts of creation, wide and wild;
> Where embryo systems and unkindled suns

Sleep in the womb of chaos; fancy droops
And thought astonish'd stops her bold career.
But oh thou mighty mind! whose powerful word
Said, thus let all things be, and thus they were,
Where shall I seek thy presence? how unblam'd
Invoke thy dread perfection?

'A Summer Evening's Meditation' belongs to a tradition within English poetry of the 'nocturne', which begins with a mental journey from night to day-in-night as the vehicle for the assertion of the power of abstract thought when unburdened by the eye. The poem dramatizes the Addisonian sublime, and an article in the *Monthly Repository* of 1813 calls its lines 'true sublimity: our conceptions are elevated, our imagination is affected . . . and our expectations are still kept on the stretch'.[50] That phrase 'kept on the stretch' is lifted directly out of *Spectator* 420, 1712. The day's storm past, the speaker meditates in a darkening landscape, which opens her intellectual imagination: 'This dead of midnight is the noon of thought, / And wisdom mounts her zenith with the stars'. Once out into the void beyond the solar system, the speaker is accompanied by a reflection in which the mind is capable of asymptotically, as it were, approaching the limits of knowing. The poem begins as one which is set in the celebratory context of Newtonianism, in which the Universe is ordered, but only up to a point. The speaker is carried forward past the known to the unknown, which at first appears to be that which is *not yet* known by natural philosophy, and translates that question of knowledge into its aesthetic value enacted through her immediate experience of Addisonian sublimity. And surely in her vision of the 'solitudes of vast unpeopled space, / The desarts of creation, wide and wild; / Where embryo systems and unkindled suns / Sleep in the womb of chaos' we cannot help but hear the adumbration of Shelley's forbidding empty frozen mountains 'subject' to Mont Blanc's impersonal power: 'A desert peopled by the storms alone, / Save when the eagle brings some hunter's bone, / And the wolf tracks her there – how hideously / Its shapes are heaped around! rude, bare, and high, / Ghastly, and scarred, and riven'. But once the speaker has reached that place where her imagination gives out, she is able to reclaim her place as a supplicant to God, asking Him not to appear to her as the sublime, distanced God, but as the polite God, kind and gallant, who 'whispers comfort to the swelling heart abashed' residing with the blushing Miss Aikin. If this conclusion is cloying, it is nonetheless necessary to Barbauld's version of belief. In this poem Barbauld is drawn to both the Impersonal God of the Universe and to the perception of God at work in *this* world as a gentleman.

But she also makes a more significant claim – one that makes her a godmother to Romantic poetry. God, as Taylor intricately and persuasively argues in *A Secular Age*, is now to be found within one's self. So Barbauld seems to think as well, when in the presence of the vastness of the Universe and feeling the sublimity of the disengaged Newtonian God:

> At this still hour the self-collected soul
> Turns inward, and beholds a stranger there
> Of high descent, and more than mortal rank;
> An embryo GOD; a spark of fire divine
> Which must burn on for ages ...

It may be that our disappointment in the conventional conclusion comes from having heard the Prometheanism of the 'embryo God'. So even though she surrenders to providentialism, the poem again hints at the transformation of unknowable sublimity into romantic Prometheanism, in which the bringer of knowledge to mankind is martyred for that access, and self-knowledge struggles against both God's skyscape and from his providential presence. The theology of this poem is much more mixed up than is its earlier avatar, 'An Address to the Deity', a poem which brings us to the argument between Priestley and Barbauld over the best way to worship, both privately and in a congregation.

Barbauld's 'Address to the Deity' which was written in 1767 or 1768, is a much more quiescent version of how we are to be obedient to the God of the Universe through our perception of a link between a companionable God of small things and the self.[51] It was written, Priestley tells us, shortly after she heard him deliver a sermon on 'Habitual Devotion' in 1767, though he did not publish the sermon until 1781: 'it was the occasion of that excellent poem of Mrs. Barbauld, intitled *An Address to the Deity*'.[52] In that sermon, Priestley warns against losing one's perception of God through being too much of the world: 'The more imperfect of the middle classes will have their minds too much engrossed by this world, and the things of it, so as to exclude, in a very great degree, the apprehension of God, and of their relation to him.'[53] Priestley addressed this falling away from sensing the presence of God everywhere as a practical matter, and advocated the Lockean method of habituation, made precise through David Hartley's physiological version of the association of ideas.[54] Remind yourself of God as often as possible, and you will begin to automatically think of him and lead a good life:

An habitual regard to God promotes an uniform chearfulness of mind; it tends to dissipate anxiety, or melancholy, and may even, in some cases, prevent madness.

Without a regard to God, as the maker and governor of all things, this world affords but a gloomy and uncomfortable prospect.[55]

Nine years later, Barbauld wrote her own essay on how to worship, 'Thoughts on the Devotional Taste, on Sects, and on Establishments' as a preface to a volume of *Devotional Pieces, Compiled from the Psalms and the Book of Job*.[56]

In this essay, Barbauld argues that persons are becoming alienated from God because He appears increasingly to be abstract and not connected to the matters that engage the human heart and soul. She aims to rekindle a personal connection with God, and finding that subjective emotional attachment with a sense of aesthetic pleasure in the beauties provided by Him. Established now at Palgrave and dealing with children much younger than at Warrington, Barbauld must be thinking about the disputatious Warrington theological intellectuals when she rather harshly writes:

There is nothing more prejudicial to the feelings of a devout heart, than a habit of disputing on religious subjects. Free inquiry is undoubtedly necessary to establish a rational belief; but a disputatious spirit, and fondness for controversy, give the mind a sceptical turn, with an aptness to call in question the most established truths.[57]

She appears to be addressing natural philosophers when she distinguishes between the disengaged God and the God who can be invoked through a particular kind of devotional worship:

The philosopher offers up general praises on the altar of universal nature; the devout man, on the altar of his heart, presents his own sighs, his own thanksgivings, his own earnest desires: the former worship is more sublime, the latter more personal and affecting.[58]

Harkening back to her reading of Addison's essay on the cosmos, she finds that what is exciting for the imagination is a rebuke to our earthly worship of God: when we experience the sublimity of the Universe:

When we trace the footsteps of creative energy through regions of unmeasured space, and find still new wonders disclosed and pressing upon the view – we grow giddy with the prospect; the mind is astonished – confounded at its own insignificance ... the idea of communion with our Maker seems shocking, and the only feeling the soul is capable of in such a moment is a deep and painful sense of its own abasement.[59]

Here she partly repeats and partly confounds the sublime trip into outer space that she undertakes in 'A Summer Evening's Meditation', suggesting that the sensation of sublimity can have the unfortunate effect of making

God too overwhelming for human apprehension, and so act as a brake of sorts upon the devotional duties of Christians. The philosophers might be resistant to this, but what about the sublime in the quotidian lives of those middle classes that Priestley had referred to?

To find the way from the sublimity of God's universe to that 'spark divine' within each of us, Barbauld reinvents the Hartleian psycho-physiology that moves information along our nerves to the brain, by focusing on 'the passions' and, in turn, their aesthetic forms:

> [Devotion's] seat is in the imagination and in the passions, and it has its source in that relish we have for the sublime, the vast, and the beautiful, by which we taste the charms of poetry and other compositions that address our finer feelings.[60]

In short, the vast, the beautiful and the sublime will be the constituent elements of religious devotion, prompting 'our finer feelings' in the same way that aesthetically pleasing writing does. And by repeating these experiences, the practising Christian forms 'a taste' for worship. Anna Barbauld may have promoted devotional practices in order to safeguard the affective power of Christianity, but she was simultaneously constructing a hybrid aesthetico-religious discourse, deepening the sense of an independent emotional interiority within each of us, that cannot help but make us each more autonomous and less dependent on the God of the impersonal order. Here in Barbauld's œuvre the difference between the secular and the religious is unrecognizable – they appear to be the same thing. Barbauld struggles against the disengaged Christianity of the Rational Dissenters, arriving at a compromise with Rational Dissent that can be interpreted as either an aestheticized religion or a Christianized aestheticism.

Priestley was very disturbed by Barbauld's essay, in no small part, I think, because she had taken up the same subject and attacked Priestley and Rational Dissent with it. Readers of Barbauld's poetry will remember her light satire on Priestley's natural philosophical method in 'The Mouse's Petition', but also his pride in her poetry, reminding readers of his influence on her work. He wrote Barbauld a sharp letter when he read her essay, and he begins by saying that it is Barbauld herself who has asked for his thoughts on it, 'as my wife informs me that you wish to know what I think of your late publication'.[61] It is important to keep in mind, however, that the value of continuing practices of devotion was high for both Barbauld and Priestley. Priestley joins religious intensity to intellection; Barbauld joins the terrain of aesthetic judgement to the private worship of God. Jon Mee is quite right to say that Barbauld's problem with Priestley is not that he lacks 'feeling, but the regulatory manners of sensibility as she understood them in the 1770s'.[62] Yet this attention to manners, as Priestley thinks it has become for Barbauld, entails the reduction of morality to conduct. Nonetheless, it might be the case that Barbauld was alluding in her essay to the success of enthusiastic and evangelical sects in gathering together new recruits, in particular, in her subtler argument for devotion as a means of making everyday behaviour and love of God into a matter of habituation – the same end result as Priestley would endorse.

Priestley's consternation came from the insouciant manner in which Barbauld appeared to be reducing the content of Divinity to fashions of taste. And fashion is of great importance here. Priestley's Lockean philo-sophical position being that since taste is formed by habits of sensation, then surely different cultures will give rise to different ideas of what constitutes taste. Priestley objects to Barbauld identifying devotion as an aspect of aesthetic experience, like that of poetry, that 'relish for the sublime, the vast, and the beautiful, by which we taste the charms of poetry'. It is certain that Barbauld has given a hostage to Priestley's theology by assimilating belief to 'taste' as a relish, that indeed, he writes, 'we may do very well without'.[63] But while Priestley objects to what seems to be a trivialization of devotion, Barbauld is perhaps unwittingly building the foundations for the modification we find in the religious sectionalism of Rational Dissent, as its adherents came to campaign for secular as well as religious entitlements; and from theology to literature as an adequate vocation for polite persons of devotional taste. Priestley also addresses the point Barbauld makes when she says that 'a prayer strictly philosophical must ever be a cold and dry composition'.[64] It is hard to avoid noting the persistent and unattractive strain among English writers that became more pervasive from the 1790s onwards, in which the work of the intellect is considered to be inferior to a combination of received truths and intuitions inspired by the experience of English nature. And Priestley definitely has a point when he accuses her of having 'adopted the maxim ascribed to the Papists, viz. that "ignorance is the mother of devotion"'.[65]

The intellectually demanding approach of Joseph Priestley secured the philosophical advances of the eighteenth century to the doctrinal issues of Socianism, or at least demonstrated their companionability. The materials that Barbauld learned from her literary education inhabited the literary–philosophical ground of 'sympathy', 'sensibility' and the stretching of the inner life to accommodate the affections as a mode of moral being. She is becoming disaffected with Rational Dissent's theology, charging that a phil-osophical theology is too abstruse for the feelings that Christianity should evoke in the believer: 'upon the whole it is safer to trust to our genuine feelings, feelings implanted in us by the God of nature, than to any metaphysical subtleties'.[66] To this somewhat jejune assertion, Priestley replies, 'I see all the reason in the world to conclude, that those who are indifferent to religious truth [i.e., philosophy], have the least regard to religion under any description of it, and that they have the least of a devotional spirit.'[67]

Anna Barbauld returned to her family after the sorrows of defeated radicalism and the wrenching of her life by her husband's suicide, and she moved to Stoke Newington to be near to her brother John Aikin. When she returned to print, in her brilliant and bitter excoriation of contemporary politics, *Eighteen Hundred and Eleven*, she was no longer centrally concerned with matters of religion, but rather with traditions of political poetry and the exigencies of an exhausting war. I can only speculate that she was glad to be shot of the debates of her elders. As William Keach first pointed out to modern readers, the attacks on that poem were equally attacks on her person as an older woman, savaging Barbauld personally because she dared to write a political poem at the age of 69.[68] The distress she suffered at the hands of the critics suggests that she had failed to reckon on how cruel the world of letters could be when the God of polite society was no longer an Aikin.

NOTES

1. I am indebted to Dr Simon Mills, whose excellent Ph.D. dissertation on Joseph Priestley, *Joseph Priestley and the Intellectual Culture of Rational Dissent, 1752–1796* (Queen Mary, University of London, 2009) taught me an enormous amount about Priestley's philosophical development. Sadly, most of what I learned never made it into this chapter, which is about Anna Barbauld. But Mills' study did make me understand why Anna Barbauld found in Priestley a mentor and a worthy interlocutor. Thanks also to David Colclough, Felicity James and David Wykes for conversations and comments.
2. Conference held at Dr Williams's Centre for Dissenting Studies, 17 May 2008 (online at: www.english.qmul.ac.uk/drwilliams/events/c2008.html; accessed 23 May 2011).
3. See, for example, White, 'The "Joineriana"', 511–33; Deirdre Coleman, 'Firebrands, Letters and Flowers: Mrs Barbauld and the Priestleys', in Gillian Russell and Clara Tuite (eds.), *Romantic Sociability: Social Networks and Literary Culture in Britain, 1770–1840* (Cambridge University Press, 2002), 82–103, and in that same volume, Anne Janowitz, 'Amiable and Radical Sociability: Anna Barbauld's "Free Familiar Conversation"', 62–81.
4. These are the descriptions in apposition to each name in the *Dictionary of National Biography*, ed. Leslie Stephen, 1885 (London: Smith, Elder & Co., 1885), vol. 1.

5. *The Times*, Saturday, 16 April 1927, issue 44557, 12.
6. See Isobel Armstrong, 'The Gush of the Feminine: How Can We Read Women's Poetry of the Romantic Period?', in Paula Feldman and Theresa M. Kelley (eds.), *Romantic Women Writers: Voices and Countervoices* (Hanover, NH: University of New England Press, 1995), 13–32; and in the same volume, William McCarthy, '"We Hoped the Woman was Going to Appear": Repression, Desire, and Gender in Anna Letitia Barbauld's Early Poems', 113–37; Mellor, 'The Female Poet and the Poetess', 261–76.
7. McCarthy, *Anna Letitia Barbauld*. I discuss the biography at some length in a review of it in *Studies in Romanticism*, 48 (2009), 713–29.
8. I have elsewhere given an account of the family's reputation machine, 'Memoirs of a Dutiful Niece: Lucy Aikin and Literary Reputation', in Glen and Hamilton, *Repossessing the Romantic Past*, 80–98.
9. William Enfield, *A Funeral Sermon, Occasioned by the Death of the Late Rev. John Aikin, D. D.* (Warrington: W. Eyres, for J. Johnson, London, 1781), 18.
10. Anna Barbauld, 'A Character', in McCarthy and Kraft, *Poems of Anna Letitia Barbauld*, 69.
11. Barbauld, 'William Enfield', *The Poems*, 68.
12. Le Breton, *Memoirs*, 196.
13. Francis E. Mineka, *The Dissidence of Dissent: The Monthly Repository, 1806–1825* (Chapel Hill, NC: University of North Carolina Press, 1944), 39, 44.
14. For the importance of the *Monthly Repository* to Victorian poetry, see Isobel Armstrong, *Victorian Poetry: Poetry, Poetics, and Politics* (London: Routledge, 1993), 25.
15. Mineka, *Dissidence of Dissent*, 84.
16. John Guillory, 'The English Common Place: Lineages of the Topographical Genre', *Critical Quarterly*, 33(4) (1991), 3–27. This excellent article is among the first to consider Barbauld in relation to the politics of Dissenting assimilation.
17. Aikin, *Memoir of John Aikin*, I, 4.
18. McCarthy, *Anna Letitia Barbauld*, 105–7.
19. Le Breton, *Memoirs*, x–xi.
20. *Critical Review*, 3(23) (1811), 426.
21. Aikin, *Memoirs of the Court of Queen Elizabeth*, I, V, VII.
22. *Monthly Repository*, 17 (1822), 771.
23. McCarthy and Kraft, *Poems of Anna Letitia Barbauld*, 277.
24. Tyson, *Joseph Johnson*, 163.
25. John Aikin, 'To Gilbert Wakefield, A. B. on his Liberation from Prison', *Monthly Magazine* (June 1801), 422; Gilbert Wakefield, 'To John Aikin, MD', *Monthly Magazine* (July 1801), 513–14; see also Lucy Aikin, 'To the Memory of Gilbert Wakefield', *Monthly Magazine* (October 1801), 220–1.
26. Anna Barbauld, 'Essay on Akenside's Poem', in Mark Akenside, *The Pleasures of the Imagination* (London: T. Cadell, 1795); *The British Novelists*, ed., Anna Barbauld, 50 vols. (London: J. Rivington, 1810).

27. Barbauld, 'On Mrs. Priestley's Leaving Warrington', McCarthy and Kraft, *The Poems*, 2.
28. Barbauld, 'To Dr. Aikin on his Complaining that She Neglected Him, October 20th 1768', McCarthy and Kraft, *The Poems*, 18.
29. *The Ladies New and Polite Pocket Memorandum-Book for 1778* (London: J. Johnson, 1777), iv–v.
30. Elizabeth Eger, 'Representing Culture: "The Nine Living Muses of Great Britain" (1779)', in Eger, Grant *et al.* (eds.), *Women, Writing and the Public Sphere 1700–1830* (Cambridge University Press, 2001), 104–26 (117).
31. Cited in Betsy Rodgers, *A Georgian Chronicle: Mrs. Barbauld and Her Family* (London: Methuen, 1958), 71.
32. William Woodfall, *Monthly Review*, 48 (1773), 54.
33. Bright, *Historical Sketch*, 12.
34. See Nicholas Roe's study of Keats for a discussion of Enfield's impact as a pedagogue, *John Keats and the Culture of Dissent* (Oxford: Clarendon Press, rev. edn 1998).
35. See Chapter 2 in this volume.
36. *Ibid.*
37. Gilbert Wakefield, *Memoirs* (London: J. Johnson, 1804), 219–20.
38. Enfield, *A Funeral Sermon*, 6–7.
39. McCarthy, *Anna Letitia Barbauld*, 153.
40. Charles Taylor, *Sources of the Self: The Making of the Modern Identity* (Cambridge University Press, 1989).
41. Charles Taylor, *A Secular Age* (London: Belknap Press, 2007), 221–69.
42. Taylor, *A Secular Age*, 221.
43. *Ibid.*
44. *Ibid.*
45. See Steven Gaukroger, *The Emergence of a Scientific Culture: Science and the Shaping of Modernity 1210–1685* (Oxford University Press, 2006), for a detailed discussion of the links between theology and the development of natural philosophy.
46. Margaret C. Jacobs, *The Radical Enlightenment: Pantheists, Freemasons and Republicans* (London: George Allen & Unwin, 1981), 87.
47. McCarthy and Kraft, *Selected Poetry*, 234.
48. *The Spectator*, no. 420, Wednesday 2 July 1712.
49. Barbauld, 'A Summer Evening's Meditation', *The Poems*, 81–4.
50. 'Essay on the Infinity of Creation', *Monthly Repository*, 8 (1813), 13–14.
51. Barbauld, 'An Address to the Deity', *The Poems*, 4–6.
52. Joseph Priestley, *Two Discourses; 1. On Habitual Devotion, 2. On the Duty of not Living to Ourselves* (Birmingham: J. Johnson, 1782), v.
53. *Ibid.*, 5.
54. *Ibid.*, iv. Priestley credits Hartley in the preface to the 1781 publication of 'On Habitual Devotion': 'I have availed myself of Dr. Hartley's theory of the human affections, the excellence of which is, that it not only explains, with wonderful simplicity, many phenomena of the mind, but

also leads to a variety of practical applications, and those of the most valuable kind'.

55. Priestley, *Two Discourses*, 9–10.
56. Anna Barbauld, *Devotional Pieces, Compiled from the Psalms and the Book of Job, to which are Prefixed, Thoughts on the Devotional Taste, on Sects, and on Establishments* (London: J. Johnson, 1775).
57. *Ibid.*, 6.
58. *Ibid.*, 13–14.
59. *Ibid.*, 11.
60. *Ibid.*, 3.
61. John Towill Rutt, *Life and Correspondence of Joseph Priestley, LLD, FRS*, 2 vols. (London: R. Hunter, 1831), 1, 278.
62. Jon Mee, *Romanticism, Enthusiasm, and Regulation* (Oxford University Press, 2002), 175. Mee characterizes Priestley's irritation with Barbauld as a function of his seeing her notion of feelings as an instance of empty manners rather than 'the sublime of free enquiry' (*ibid.*). But Priestley is not interested in aesthetic categories when it comes to devotion – he is concerned with the religious question of how to remind the busy world that God is present in everything and at all times. I also think that Mee neglects Priestley's commitment to religious doctrine – for Priestley, taste is a trivial category. Barbauld's framework is heavily dependent on literary categories, which in the case of 'sensibility' distances questions of doctrine from the forms of devotion that she explicitly grounds in the language of aesthetics.
63. Rutt, *Life and Correspondence of Joseph Priestley*, 11, 280.
64. Barbauld, *Devotional Pieces*, 14.
65. Rutt, *Life and Correspondence of Joseph Priestley*, 11, 282.
66. Barbauld, *Devotional Pieces*, 15.
67. Rutt, *Life and Correspondence of Joseph Priestley*, 11, 284.
68. William Keach, 'A Regency Prophecy and the End of Barbauld's Career', *Studies in Romanticism*, 33 (1994), 569–77.

Bibliography

MANUSCRIPT SOURCES

BODLEIAN LIBRARY, OXFORD

MS Montagu Collection d21, fos. 258–9 [William Shepherd to Walter Wilson, 3 Dec. 1841].

CONGREGATIONAL LIBRARY, LONDON

MS 11. e. 43 [Doddridge's cash book, 1730–4].

HARRIS MANCHESTER COLLEGE, OXFORD

MS Warrington 2 [Minute book of Warrington Academy, 1757–75].
William Shepherd MS Collection in 26 vols. [vols. 11, 111, x].

JOHN RYLANDS UNIVERSITY LIBRARY, UNIVERSITY OF MANCHESTER

Turner, MS Letterbook, Unitarian College Archive.
Benson MS 166 [John Hodgson, Lincoln, to George Benson, 11 Dec. 1751].
Eng. MS 1209 (10, 14–16) [Philip Doddridge to his wife Mercy, 17 Jul. 1733, 15, 19, 25 Jun. 1734].

LINNEAN SOCIETY LIBRARY, LONDON

Pulteney MSS, Coltman letter 19 [John Coltman to Richard Pulteney, 2 Jun. 1790].

LIVERPOOL RECORD OFFICE

Currie Papers, 920 CUR 55–7; fl58 [John Aikin to James Currie, 16 Nov. 1790; Dr Currie to Dr Priestley, undated].
Nicholson Papers, 920 NIC. 5/8/7–9; 9/12/4; 9/12/5. [Matthew Nicholson to his father, [7], 8 Feb. 29 Apr. 1764; Enfield to Clayton, 23 Dec. 1789; Enfield to Clayton, 22 Mar. 1790].

MELBOURNE UNIVERSITY ARCHIVES

Bright Family Papers; Papers of Henry Bright, Section I, vol. II, 25ff. [A. and B. Heywood of Liverpool, correspondence with Henry Bright 1770–1].

PENNSYLVANIA HISTORICAL SOCIETY

MS, Gratz Collection [Joseph Buckminster to John Aikin, 2 Jun. 1809].

RECORD OFFICE FOR LEICESTERSHIRE, LEICESTER, AND RUTLAND

15 D 57/45 [John Coltman's memorandum or commonplace book].
15 D 57/448 [Samuel Coltman, 'Time's Stepping Stones – or some Memorial of four generations of a family – by an Octogenarian member of the same'].

SHROPSHIRE ARCHIVES

6000/15932 [William Turner to Richard Astley, 16 Jun. 1812].

VASSAR COLLEGE LIBRARY

Special Collections [Barbauld to Miss Harris, Apr. 1812?].

WARRINGTON PUBLIC LIBRARY, WARRINGTON

MS Bound Volume, James Kendrick, 'Profile of Warrington Worthies, Autographs and Letters', n.d., Local History Collection.

WARWICKSHIRE RECORD OFFICE

Pennant Papers, CR 2017 TP 3/18; TP 33/2–3; 14; TP 154/1–7; TP 155/1–4. [John Aikin sen. and John Aikin jun. to Thomas Pennant].
Pennant Papers CR 1017/TP 155/4. [John Aikin jun. to Thomas Pennant, 30 Mar. 1796].

DR WILLIAMS'S LIBRARY, LONDON

MS 38.106 [Minutes of the Protestant Dissenting Ministers of the Three Denominations, 12 May 1772, 10 Jun. 1772 and 28 May 1773].
MS NCL LI/10/35 [Doddridge to Clark, 20 Jul. 1737].
Walter Wilson MSS, A.8.63.

PRIMARY SOURCES

A Report on the State of the Warrington Academy, by the Trustees at Their Annual Meeting, 1 July 1762.

Accum, Frederick, *A Practical Essay on the Analysis of Minerals* (London: printed for the author, 1804).

Aikin, Anna Letitia, *Poems* (London: J. Johnson, 1773).

Aikin, Arthur, *Journal of a Tour of North Wales and Part of Shropshire* (London: J. Johnson, 1797).

(ed.), *The Annual Review and History of Literature*, from 1802, vol. 1 (London: T. Gillet, 1803), with preliminary prospectus.

A Manual of Mineralogy (London: Longman, 1814).

An Address delivered on 27 May 1817 at the Annual distribution of Rewards of the Society for the Encouragement of Arts, Manufactures and Commerce (London: T. Woodfall, 1817).

Illustrations of the Arts and Manufactures (London: J. van Voorst, 1841).

Aikin, Arthur and Charles Rochemont Aikin, *A Dictionary of Chemistry and Mineralogy*, 2 vols. (London: W. Phillips, 1807).

An Account of the Most Important Recent Discoveries and Improvements in Chemistry and Mineralogy, An Appendix to the Dictionary of Chemistry and Mineralogy (London: W. Phillips, 1814).

Aikin, John, *A Treatise on the Situation, Manners and Inhabitants of Germany and the Life of Agricola by C. Cornelius Tacitus* (Warrington: W. Eyres for J. Johnson, 1772).

Essay on the Application of Natural History to Poetry (Warrington: W. Eyres for J. Johnson, 1777).

Biographical Memoirs of Medicine in Great Britain from the Revival of Literature to the Time of Harvey (London: J. Johnson, 1780).

The Calendar of Nature (Warrington: W. Eyres for J. Johnson, London, 1784).

England Delineated, or a Geographical Description of Every County in England and Wales with a Concise Account of Its Most Important Products, Natural and Artificial (London: J. Johnson, 1788).

An Address to the Dissidents of England on their Late Defeat (London: J. Johnson, 1790).

The Spirit of the Constitution and that of the Church of England, compared (London: J. Johnson, 1790).

Food for National Penitence (London: J. Johnson, 1793).

Letters from a Father to his Son, vol. I (London: J. Johnson, 1793); vol. II (London: J. Johnson, 1800).

A Description of the Country from Thirty to Forty Miles Around Manchester (London: John Stockdale, 1795).

England Delineated; or, a Geographical Description of Every County in England and Wales: with a Concise Account of its Most Important Products, Artificial and Natural (London: J. Johnson, 1795).

(ed.), *The Spleen, and other Poems*, by Matthew Green (London: Thomas Cadell and William Davies, 1796).

General biography; or lives, critical and historical, of the most eminent persons of all ages, countries, conditions, and professions, 10 vols. (London: J. Johnson, 1799–1815).

(ed.), *The Poetical Works of John Milton, from the text of Dr. Newton: with a critical essay by J. Aikin*, 4 vols. (London: J. Johnson, 1801).

'To Gilbert Wakefield, A. B. on His Liberation from Prison', *Monthly Magazine* (June 1801).

Geographical Delineations, or a Compendious View of the Natural and Political State of all Parts of the Globe, 2 vols. (London: J. Johnson, 1806; Philadelphia: F. Nichols, 1807).

Geographical Delineations, or a Compendious View of the Natural and Political State of all parts of the Globe, 2nd edn in one volume (Philadelphia, PA: F. Nichols, 1807).

(ed.), *The Art of Preserving Health*, by John Armstrong (Walpole, NH: Thomas & Thomas, 1808).

Annals of the Reign of King George the Third; From Its Commencement in the Year 1760, to the General Peace in the Year 1815, 2 vols. (London: Longman, 1816).

England Described, being a Concise Delineation of Every County in England and Wales (London: Baldwin, Cradock and Joy, 1818).

Aikin, John and Anna Letitia, *Miscellaneous Pieces in Prose* (London: J. Johnson, 1773).

Aikin, John, and Anna Letitia Barbauld, *Evenings at Home, or the Juvenile Budget Opened*, 6 vols. (London: J. Johnson, 1792–6).

Aikin, Lucy, 'To the Memory of Gilbert Wakefield', *Monthly Magazine* (October 1801), 220–1.

The Travels of Rolando, 4 vols. (London: Richard Phillips, 1804).

Epistles on Women, Exemplifying Their Character and Condition in Various Ages, and Nations. With Miscellaneous Poems. By Lucy Aikin (London: Johnson, 1810).

Memoirs of the Court of Queen Elizabeth, 2 vols. (London: Longman, 1818).

Memoirs of the Court of King James I, 2 vols. (London: Longman, 1822).

Memoir of John Aikin, MD with a Selection of Miscellaneous Pieces, Biographical, Moral and Critical, 2 vols. (London: Baldwin, Cradock and Joy, 1823).

(ed.), *The Works of Anna Lætitia Barbauld. With a Memoir by Lucy Aikin*, 2 vols. (London: Longman, 1825).

Memoirs of the Court of King Charles I, 2 vols. (London: Longman, 1833).

'Review of *The Life of William Roscoe*', *Edinburgh Review* 58(117) (July 1833), 65–86.

Memoirs, Miscellanies and Letters of the Late Lucy Aikin, ed. Philip Hemery Le Breton (London: Longman, 1864).

Epistles on Women and Other Works by Lucy Aikin, eds. Anne K. Mellor, and Michelle Levy (Peterborough, ON: Broadview Press, 2011).

Alcott, A. Bronson, *Concord Days* (1872; rpt. Philadelphia, PA: Albert Saifer, 1962).

Anderson, Peter John (ed.), *Roll of Alumni in Arts of the University and King's College of Aberdeen, 1596–1860* (Aberdeen, 1900).

234 *Bibliography*

25 Bibliography

The Annals of Philosophy or Magazine of Chemistry, Mineralogy, Mechanics, Natural History, Agriculture and the Arts, from 1813: London.

The Annual Biography and Obituary, for the Year 1819 (London: Longman, 1819).

The Annual Review and History of Literature, from 1807: London.

Arnold, Matthew, *Culture and Anarchy and Other Writings*, ed. Stefan Collini (Cambridge University Press, 1993).

Arnould, Sir Joseph *Life of Thomas, First Lord Denman, formerly Lord Chief Justice of England*, 2 vols. (Boston, MA: Estes & Lauriat, 1874).

Aspland, Robert, 'Memoir of the Late Rev. Jeremiah Joyce', *Monthly Repository*, 12 (1817), 697–704.

Austen, Jane, *Persuasion* (Peterborough, ON: Broadview Press, 1998).

Barbauld, Anna Letitia, *Devotional Pieces, Compiled from the Psalms and the Book of Job, to which are Prefixed, Thoughts on the Devotional Taste, on Sects, and on Establishments* (London: J. Johnson, 1775).

Hymns in Prose for Children (London: J. Johnson, 1781).

An Address to the Opposers of the Repeal of the Corporation and Test Acts, 3 March 1790 (London: J. Johnson, 1790).

Remarks on Mr. Gilbert Wakefield's Enquiry into the Expediency and Propriety of Public or Social Worship (London: J. Johnson, 1792).

Civic Sermons to the People. Number II. From Mutual Wants Springs Mutual Happiness (London: J. Johnson, 1792).

'Essay on Akenside's Poem', in Mark Akenside, *The Pleasures of the Imagination* (London: T. Cadell, 1795).

(ed.), *The British Novelists*, 50 vols. (London: J. Rivington, 1810).

Eighteen Hundred and Eleven: A Poem (London: J. Johnson, 1812).

A Legacy for Young Ladies. Consisting of Miscellaneous Pieces in Prose and Verse. By the late Mrs. Barbauld, ed. Lucy Aikin (London: Longman, 1826).

The Poems of Anna Letitia Barbauld, ed. William McCarthy and Elizabeth Kraft (Athens, GA: University of Georgia Press, 1994).

Anna Letitia Barbauld: Selected Poetry and Prose, ed. William McCarthy and Elizabeth Kraft (Peterborough, ON: Broadview Press, 2002).

Barbauld, Rochemont, *The Duty of Promoting the Welfare of the Rising Generation: Represented in a Sermon Preached at St. Thomas's, Jan. 2, 1792. For the Benefit of the Charity-School, in Gravel-Lane, Southwark* (London: H. Goldney, 1792).

Belsham, Thomas, *Memoirs of the late Reverend Thomas Belsham: including a brief notice of his published works, and copious extracts from his diary, together with letters to and from his friends and correspondents*, ed. John Williams (London: privately printed, 1833).

Bloomfield, Robert, *The Letters of Robert Bloomfield and his Circle*, ed. Tim Fulford and Lynda Pratt, *Romantic Circles* (available online at: www.rc.umd.edu/editions/bloomfield_letters; accessed 25/01/11).

Brayley, E. W. (ed.), *The Beauties of England and Wales; or Delineations Topographical, Historical, and Descriptive, of Each County* (London: J. Harris, 1808).

Bright, H. A., *A Historical Sketch of Warrington Academy* (Liverpool: pr. T. Brakell 1859).

Burke, Edmund, *Reflections on the Revolution in France*, ed. L. G. Mitchell (Oxford University Press, 1993).

Cappe, Catharine, *Discourses chiefly on Devotional Subjects, by the late Reverend Newcome Cappe. To which are prefixed Memoirs of his Life by Catharine Cappe* (York: privately printed, 1805; 2nd edn, 1816).

Cappe, Newcome, *A Sermon Preached on Thursday, the twenty-ninth of July, MDCCLXXXIV, the late Day of National Thanksgiving* (York: A. Ward for J. Johnson, London, 1784).

Carlyle, Thomas, *Heroes, Hero-Worship, and the Heroic in History* (New York, NY: Alden, 1888).

The Works of Thomas Carlyle, ed. H. D. Traill, centenary edn, 30 vols. (New York, NY: Scribner's, 1896–1901).

Carter, Elizabeth, *A Series of Letters between Mrs. Elizabeth Carter and Miss Catherine Talbot, from the Year 1741 to 1770. To which are added, Letters from Mrs. Elizabeth Carter to Mrs. Vesey, between the Years 1763 and 1787*, ed. Montagu Pennington, 2 vols. (London: Rivington, 1808).

Chapone, Hester Mulso, *The Works of Mrs. Chapone*, new edn (Edinburgh, 1807).

The Child's New Play-Thing: Being a Spelling-Book Intended to Make the Learning to Read a Diversion Instead of a Task, 8th edn (London, 1763).

Christian Reformer or New Evangelical Miscellany, from 1815: London.

Coleridge, Samuel Taylor, *The Poems of Samuel Taylor Coleridge*, ed. Ernest Hartley Coleridge (Oxford University Press, 1912).

Crabb Robinson, Henry, *Henry Crabb Robinson on Books and Their Writers*, ed. Edith Julia Morley, 3 vols. (London: J. M. Dent, 1938).

Critical Review or Annals of Literature, from 1756: Edinburgh.

Cronstadt, A. F., *An Essay towards a System of Mineralogy, translated from the Swedish by Gustav von Engerstrom to which is added a Treatise on the Pocket Laboratory, by the translator, including revisions and comments by E. M. Da Costa* (London: E. and C. Dilly, 1770).

Davidson, Robert, *Elements of Geography Short and Plain* (London: T. Wilkins, 1787).

Doddridge, Philip, *Family Expositor, or, A Paraphrase and Version of the New Testament. With critical notes; and a Practical Improvement of each Section*, 6 vols. (1739–56).

Correspondence and Diary of Philip Doddridge, ed. J. D. Humphreys (London: Colburn and Bentley, 1829–31).

[Dufresnoy, Nicholas Lenglet], *Geography for Children*, 14th edn (London: J. Johnson, 1783).

Eaton, D. I. (ed.), *Politics for the People* (London: Hogs Wash, 1794).

The Eclectic Review, from 1805: London.

The Edinburgh Review or the Critical Journal, from 1802: Edinburgh.

Eliot, George, *Middlemarch* (London: Penguin, 1985).

Emerson, Ralph Waldo, *The Journals and Miscellaneous Notebooks*, vol. XI, ed. A. W. Plumstead *et al.* (Cambridge, MA: Harvard University Press, 1975).

Enfield, William, *A Funeral Sermon, Occasioned by the Death of the Late Rev. John Aikin, DD* (Warrington: W. Eyres, for J. Johnson, London, 1781).

Evans, John, *A Sermon on the Decease of the Rev. Hugh Worthington of Salters Hall, Islington* (London: privately printed, 1813).

The Geography of England: Done in the Manner of Gordon's 'Geographical Grammar' (London: T. Dodsley, 1744).

Gibbon, Edward, *The Rise and Decline of the Roman Empire* 8 vols. (London: Murray, 1887).

Gilpin, William, *Observations on the Western Parts of England relative Chiefly to Picturesque Beauty* (London: T. Cadell, 1798).

Goldsmith, Oliver, *Collected Works of Oliver Goldsmith*, ed. Arthur Friedman, 5 vols. (Oxford: Clarendon Press, 1966).

Gore's General Liverpool Advertiser.

Gough, Richard, *British Topography. Or, an Historical Account of What has been Done for Illustrating the Topographical Antiquities of Great Britain and Ireland*, 2 vols. (London: T. Payne and Son, 1780).

Hartley, David, *Observations on Man, His Frame, Duty and Expectations* (London: S. Richardson, 2 vols. 1749, repr. 1791, 1799).

Hays, Mary, *Female Biography, or Memoirs of Illustrious and Celebrated Women, of all Ages and Countries Alphabetically Arranged*, 6 vols. (London: Richard Phillips, 1803).

Hazlitt, William, *The Complete Works of William Hazlitt*, ed. P. P. Howe, 20 vols. (London and Toronto: J. M. Dent).

Heron, Robert, *Scotland Delineated, or a Geographical Description of every Shire in Scotland, Including the Northern and Western Isles* (Edinburgh: James Neill, 1791).

Horace, *Horace: The Odes and Epodes*, ed. and trans. C. E. Bennet (Cambridge, MA: Harvard University Press, 1952).

Hunter, Joseph, *Familiae minorum gentium*, ed. John W. Clay, 4 vols., Harleian Society, 37 (London, 1894–6).

Hutcheson, Francis, *An Essay on the Nature and Conduct of the Passions and Affections, with Illustrations on the Moral Sense* (1728; ed. Aaron Garrett (Indianapolis, IN: Liberty Fund, 2002)).

Philosophiae Moralis Institutio Compendiaria, with a Short Introduction to Moral Philosophy (1747; ed. Luigi Turco (Indianapolis, IN: Liberty Fund, 2007).

Joyce, Jeremiah, *A Sermon Preached 23 February 1794, to Which is Added an Appendix, An Account of the Author's Arrest for Treasonable Practices* (London: privately printed, 1794).

An Account of Mr Joyce's Arrest for Treasonable Practices (London: Chevening House, 1795).

Kippis, Andrew, *A Vindication of the Protestant Dissenting Ministers, with Regard to their Late Application to Parliament* (London: 1772). Reviewed in *Monthly Review* 47 (1772), 101–7.

The Ladies New and Polite Pocket Memorandum-Book for 1778 (London: J. Johnson, 1777).

Le Breton, Anna Letitia (ed.), *Correspondence of William Ellery Channing, DD, and Lucy Aikin, from 1826 to 1842* (London: Williams and Norgate; Boston, MA: Roberts Brothers, 1874).

　Memoir of Mrs. Barbauld, Including Letters and Notices of Her Family and Friends (London: George Bell, 1874).

　Memories of Seventy Years by one of a literary family, ed. Mrs Herbert Martin (London: Griffith & Farran, 1883).

Le Breton, Philip Hemery (ed.), *Memoirs, Miscellanies and Letters of the Late Lucy Aikin* (London: Longman, 1864).

Lindsey, Theophilus, *A Sermon Preached at the Opening of the Chapel in Essex-House, Essex-Street* (1774).

[Lister, T. H.], 'The Waverley Novels', *Edinburgh Review* 55 (April 1832), 61–79.

Literary Gazette, and Journal of Belles Lettres, Arts and Sciences, from 1817: London.

Livy, *Livy*, ed. and trans. B. O. Foster, vol. 1 (New York, NY: G. P. Putnam's Sons, 1925).

Martineau, Harriet, *Autobiography*, ed. Linda H. Peterson (Peterborough, ON: Broadview, 2007).

Monthly Magazine of Politics, Literature, Art, Science and Belles Lettres, from 1796: London.

Monthly Repository of Theology and General Literature, from 1806: London.

Murch, Jerom, *A History of the Presbyterian and General Baptist Churches in the West of England* (London: Hunter, 1835).

New College 24th June, 1789 [printed handbill BL 4406.g.2 [134]].

Nuttall, G. F. (ed.), *Calendar of the correspondence of Philip Doddridge*, Historical Manuscripts Commission, JP 26 (1979).

Paterson, Samuel, *Joineriana: Or the Book of Scraps* (London: J. Johnson, 1772).

[Peabody, W. B. O.], Review of *The Works of Anna Lætitia Barbauld*, *Christian Examiner*, 3(4) (1826), 299–315.

Peile, John (ed.), *Biographical register of Christ's College 1505–1905 and of the earlier foundation, God's House 1448–1505*, 2 vols. (Cambridge University Press, 1913).

Percival, Thomas, *A Short View of the Grounds and Limits of Taxes, addressed to the Manchester Literary and Philosophical Society* (Warrington: privately printed, 24 March 1785).

Philosophical Magazine, from 1798: London.

Pinkerton, John, *Modern Geography* (London: T. Cadell and Davies, 1802; 1803).

Price, Richard, *The Correspondence of Richard Price, vol. III*, ed. W. Bernard Peach (Durham, NC: Duke University Press, 1994).

Priestley, Joseph, *An Essay on a Course of Liberal Education for Civil and Active Life* (London: C. Henderson, 1768).

　Two Discourses; 1. On Habitual Devotion, 2. On the Duty of not Living to Ourselves (Birmingham: J. Johnson, 1782).

　Miscellaneous Observations relating to Education, More especially as it Respects the Conduct of the Mind (Bath: R. Cruttwell, 1788).

　The proper objects of education in the present state of the world: represented in a discourse, delivered on Wednesday, April 27, 1791, at the meeting-house in the

Old-Jewry, London; to the supporters of the New College at Hackney (London: Johnson, 1791).

Heads of Lectures on a Course of Experimental Philosophy, particularly including Chemistry (London, New College, Hackney: G. Smallfield, 1794).

The Theological and Miscellaneous Works of Joseph Priestley, LLD FRS &c., ed. John Towill Rutt, 25 vols. (1817–31, rpt. New York, NY: Kraus Reprint, 1972).

Rickards, E. C., 'Mrs Barbauld and her Pupil', *Murray's Magazine*, 10 (1891), 706–26.

Rowe, Elizabeth, *The Poetry of Elizabeth Singer Rowe*, ed. Madeleine Forell Marshall (Lewiston, NY: Edwin Mellon, 1987).

Rutt, John Towill, 'An Account of Jeremiah Joyce', *Monthly Repository*, 12 (1817), 357–61.

Life and Correspondence of Joseph Priestley, LLD, FRS, 2 vols. (London: R. Hunter, 1831).

Seddon, John, 'Brief Memoir of Rev. John Seddon, of Warrington, with Selections from His Letters and Papers. No. 1; No. 3', *Christian Reformer*, N S 10 (1854), 225, 230–31, 626.

Shepherd, William, *Every Man his Own Parson* (Liverpool: privately printed, 1791).

A Selection from the Early Letters of Revd William Shepherd LLD (Liverpool: H. Bradley, 1855).

Southey, Robert, *Life and Correspondence*, ed. Cuthbert Southey, 6 vols. (1849–50).

New Letters of Robert Southey, ed. Kenneth Curry, 2 vols. (New York, NY: Columbia University Press, 1965).

The Spectator, 1711–12, 1714, London.

Taylor, William, *A Memoir of the Life and Writings of the Late William Taylor*, 2 vols. (London: John Murray, 1843).

Toulmin, Joshua, *The Character and Reward of the Faithful Servant, considered and improved in a sermon, preached at Bridgwater, in the county of Somerset, on Lord's Day, March 10, 1793; on occasion of the much-lamented Death of the Rev. Thomas Watson* (Taunton, [1793]).

Trimmer, Sarah, *Guardian of Education*, 2 (1803).

Turner, W., 'Historical Account of the Warrington Academy', *Monthly Repository of Theology and General Literature*, 8.01–05 (1813), 85–94, 161–72.

'Historical Account of Students educated in the Warrington Academy', *Monthly Repository of Theology and General Literature*, 9(100–5) (1814), 201–5, 263–8, 385–90, 525–30, 594–9.

Virgil, *The Eclogues*, ed. and trans. Guy Lee (London: Penguin Classics, 1984).

von Humboldt, Alexander, *Researches Concerning the Institutions and Monuments of the Ancient Inhabitants of America*, trans. H. M. Williams, 2 vols. (London: Longman, 1814).

Wakefield, Gilbert, 'To John Aikin, MD', *Monthly Magazine* (July 1801).

Memoirs of the Life of Gilbert Wakefield, BA, new edn, 2 vols. (London: J. Johnson, 1804).

Watts, Isaac, *Divine Songs Attempted in Easy Language for the Use of Children* (1715; ed. J. H. P. Pafford (Oxford University Press, 1971)).

A Treatise on the Education of Children and Youth, 2nd edn (London, 1769).
Young, Arthur, *Extracts from Mr. Young's Six months tour through the north of England, and from the letter of an unknown author, published in the London Magazine, for October, 1772, on the subject of canal navigations. Addressed to the Right Honourable the Lord Mayor, aldermen, and common-council of the City of London by James Sharpe* (London: London Magazine, 1772).

SECONDARY SOURCES

Acosta, Ana M., 'Spaces of Dissent and the Public Sphere in Hackney, Stoke Newington, and Newington Green', *Eighteenth-century Life*, 27 (2003), 1–27.
Allen, D. E., *The Naturalist in Britain. A Social History* (London: Penguin 1978).
Anderson, John M., '"The First Fire": Barbauld Rewrites the Greater Romantic Lyric', *SEL*, 34 (1994), 719–38.
Annan, Noel, 'The Intellectual Aristocracy', in J. H. Plumb (ed.), *Studies in Social History: A Tribute to G. M. Trevelyan* (London, New York, NY and Toronto: Longman, 1955), 241–87.
Armstrong, Isobel, *Victorian Poetry: Poetry, Poetics, and Politics* (London: Routledge, 1993).
'The Gush of the Feminine: How Can We Read Women's Poetry of the Romantic Period?', in Paula Feldman and Theresa M. Kelley (eds.), *Romantic Women Writers: Voices and Countervoices* (Hanover, NH: University of New England Press, 1995), 13–32.
Axon, E. (ed.), *Memorials of the Nicholson Family* (Kendal: privately printed, 1928).
Barker-Benfield, G. J., *The Culture of Sensibility: Sex and Society in Eighteenth-century Great Britain* (Chicago, IL and London: University of Chicago Press, 1992).
Baylen, Joseph O. and Norbert J. Gossman, *A Biographical Dictionary of Modern British Radicals*, 3 vols. (Hassocks: Harvester Press, 1979–88).
Beale, C. H., *Catherine Hutton and Her Friends* (Birmingham: Cornish Brothers, 1895).
Billson, C. J., *Leicester Memoirs* (Leicester: Edgar Backus, 1924).
Bott, Elizabeth, *Family and Social Networks* (London: Tavistock Publications, 1971).
Braithwaite, Helen, *Romanticism. Publishing and Dissent: Joseph Johnson and the Cause of Liberty* (Basingstoke: Palgrave Macmillan, 2003).
Brantley, Richard E., *Wordsworth's 'Natural Methodism'* (New Haven, CT: Yale University Press, 1975).
Coordinates of Anglo-American Romanticism: Wesley, Edwards, Carlyle and Emerson (Gainesville, FL: University Press of Florida, 1993).
Brock, W. H. and A. J. Meadows, *The Lamp of Learning: Two Centuries of Publishing at Taylor & Francis* (London and Bristol, PA: Taylor & Francis, 1998).
Brooks, Marilyn L., 'John Aikin (1747–1822)', *Oxford DNB* (Oxford University Press, 2004) (available online at: www.oxforddnb.com/view/article/230).

Brown, Philip Anthony, *The French Revolution in English History* (1918; London: Frank Cass, 1965).

Brown, Richard, *Church and State in Modern Britain, 1700–1850* (London: Routledge, 1991).

Bruckner, Martin, 'Lessons in Geography: Maps, Spellers and other Grammars of Nationalism in the Early Republic', *American Quarterly*, 51 (1999), 310–43.

Brunton, Deborah, *The politics of vaccination: practice and policy in England, Wales, Ireland, and Scotland, 1800–1874* (Rochester, NY: University of Rochester Press, 1988).

Burstein, Miriam, *Narrating Women's History in Britain, 1770–1902* (Aldershot: Ashgate, 2004).

Clark, J. C. D., *English Society 1688–1832* (Cambridge University Press, 1985).

Coleman, Deirdre, 'Firebrands, Letters and Flowers: Mrs Barbauld and the Priestleys', in Russell and Tuite, *Romantic Sociability*, 82–103.

Coveney, Peter, *Poor Monkey: The Child in Literature* (London: Rockliff, 1957).

Cragwall, Jasper, 'Wordsworth and the Ragged Legion; Or, the Lows of High Argument', in Eugene Stelzig (ed.), *Romantic Autobiography in England* (Farnham, Surrey: Ashgate, 2009), 179–94.

Cripps, E. C., *Plough Court. The Story of a Notable Pharmacy 1715–1927* (London: Allen & Hanbury, 1927).

Cunningham, Andrew, 'Medicine to Calm the Mind: Boerhaave's Medical System, and Why it Was Adopted in Edinburgh', in Andrew Cunningham and Roger French (eds.), *The Medical Enlightenment of the Eighteenth Century* (Cambridge University Press, 1990), 40–66.

Daniels, Stephen and John Bonehill (eds.), *Paul Sandby. Picturing Britain* (London: Royal Academy, 2009).

Davidoff, Leonore and Catherine Hall, *Family Fortunes: Men and Women of the English Middle Class, 1780–1850*, 2nd edn (London: Routledge, 2002).

Dick, Malcolm (ed.), *Joseph Priestley and Birmingham* (Studley: Brewin Books, 2005).

Dinwiddy, J. R., *From Luddism to the First Reform Bill* (Oxford: Blackwell, 1986).

Ditchfield, G. M., 'The Parliamentary Struggle over the Repeal of the Test and Corporation Acts, 1787–90', *English Historical Review*, 89 (1974), 551–77.

'Debates on the Test and Corporation Acts, 1787–90', *Bulletin of the Institute of Historical Research*, 50(121) (1977), 69–81.

Dzelzainis, Ella, 'Reason vs Revelation: Feminism, Malthus, and the New Poor Law in Narratives by Harriet Martineau and Charlotte Elizabeth Tonna', *19: Interdisciplinary Studies in the Long Nineteenth Century*, 2 (2006).

Eger, Elizabeth, 'Representing Culture: "The Nine Living Muses of Great Britain" (1779)', in Eger, Grant *et al.* (eds.), *Women, Writing and the Public Sphere 1700–1830* (Cambridge University Press, 2001), 104–26.

Elliott, Paul and Stephen Daniels, '"No Study so Agreeable to the Youthful Mind": Geographical Education in the Georgian Grammar School', *History of Education*, 39 (2010), 15–33.

Ellis, Grace A., *A Memoir of Mrs. Anna Lætitia Barbauld, with Many of Her Letters* (Boston, MA: Osgood, 1874).

Evans, George E., *A History of Renshaw Street Chapel and its Institutions, with some Account of the former chapels Castle Hey and Benn's Garden* (London: C. Green, 1887).

Felber, Lynette (ed.), *Clio's Daughters: British Women Making History, 1790–1899* (Newark, DE: University of Delaware Press, 2007).

Fitzpatrick, Martin, 'Priestley Caricatured', in A. Truman Schwartz and John G. McEvoy (eds.), *Motion Toward Perfection: the Achievement of Joseph Priestley* (Boston, MA: Skinner House Books, 1990), 161–218.

Frye, Northrop, *Anatomy of Criticism* (Princeton University Press, 1957).

Fulton, John F., 'The Warrington Academy (1757–1786) and Its Influence upon Medicine and Science', *Bulletin of the Institute of History of Medicine*, 1(2) (1933), 50–80.

Fyfe, Aileen, 'Reading Children's Books in Late Eighteenth-century Dissenting Families', *Historical Journal*, 43 (2000), 453–73.

Gardiner, William, *Music and Friends: Or, Pleasant Recollections of a Dilettante* (London: Longman; Leicester: Combe and Crossley, 1838).

Garfinkle, Norman, 'Science and Religion in England 1790–1800', *Journal of the History of Ideas*, 26 (1955), 376–88.

Gaukroger, Steven, *The Emergence of a Scientific Culture: Science and the Shaping Of Modernity 1210–1685* (Oxford University Press, 2006).

Gay, John G., *The Geography of Religion in England* (Basingstoke: Macmillan, 1971).

Gleadle, Kathryn, *The Early Feminists: Radical Unitarians and the Emergence of the Women's Rights Movement, 1831–5* (New York, NY: St Martin's Press, 1995).

Goodwin, Albert, *The Friends of Liberty: The English Democratic Movement in the Age of the French Revolution* (London: Hutchinson, 1979).

Gordon, Alexander, 'Simpson, John (1746–1812)', rev. M. J. Mercer, *Oxford DNB* (Oxford University Press, 2004) (available online at: www.oxforddnb.com/view/article/25586).

Graff, Gerald, *Professing Literature: An Institutional History* (University of Chicago Press, 1987).

Gray, Mike, 'Joseph Priestley in Hackney', *Enlightenment and Dissent*, 2 (1983), 107–10.

Grayling, A. C., *The Quarrel of the Age. The Life and Times of William Hazlitt* (London: Phoenix, 2000).

Greer, S., *The Emerging City: Myth and Reality* (New York, NY: Free Press, 1962).

Guest, Harriet, *Small Change: Women, Learning, Patriotism, 1750–1810* (University of Chicago Press, 2000).

Guillory, John, 'The English Common Place: Lineages of the Topographical Genre', *Critical Quarterly*, 33(4) (1991), 3–27.

Haakonssen, Knud (ed.), *Enlightenment and Religion: Rational Dissent in Eighteenth-century Britain* (Cambridge University Press, 1996).

Haakonssen, Lisbeth, *Medicine and Morals in the Enlightenment: John Gregory, Thomas Percival, and Benjamin Rush* (Amsterdam and Atlanta, GA: Rodopi, 1997).

Hanson, Craig Ashley, *The English Virtuoso: Art, Medicine, and Antiquarianism in the Age of Empiricism* (Chicago, IL and London: University of Chicago Press, 2009).

Harris, James A., *Of Liberty and Necessity: The Free Will Debate in Eighteenth-century British Philosophy* (Oxford: Clarendon Press, 2005).

Harris, José (ed.), *Civil Society in British History: Ideas, Identities and Institutions* (Oxford University Press, 2003).

Henriques, Ursula, *Religious Toleration in England 1787–1833* (University of Toronto Press, 1961).

Holt, R. V., *The Unitarian Contribution to Social Progress in England* (London: Allen & Unwin, 1938).

Hoselitz, Bert F., 'Economic Growth – Non-Economic Aspects', *International Encyclopaedia of the Social Sciences* (London and New York, NY: Macmillan/ Free Press, 1968).

Hudson, Derek and Kenneth W. Luckhurst, *The Royal Society of Arts 1754–1954* (London: John Murray, 1954).

Hunt, L. B. and P. D. Buchanan, 'Richard Knight 1768–1844: A Forgotten Chemist and Apparatus Designer', *Ambix*, 31, pt 2 (1984), 57–67.

Hutt, Marten, 'Maintaining "the Dignity of a Liberal and Learned Profession": John Aikin's *Biographical Memoirs of Medicine in Great Britain* (1780)', *Transactions of the Unitarian Historical Society*, 31 (1998), 302–10.

Hyde, Ralph, *Panoramania! The Art and Entertainment of the 'All-Embracing' View* (London: Trefoil, 1988).

Inkster, Ian, 'Science and Society in the Metropolis. A Preliminary Examination of the Social and Institutional Context of the Askesian Society of London', *Annals of Science*, 34 (1977), 1–32.

'London Science and the Seditious Meetings Act of 1817', *British Journal for the History of Science*, 12 (1979), 192–6.

'Potentially Global: "Useful and Reliable Knowledge" and Material Progress in Europe, 1474–1914', *International History Review*, 28 (2006), 237–86.

'Seditious Science: A Reply to Paul Weindling', *British Journal for History of Science*, 14 (1981), 181–7.

Issitt, John, *Jeremiah Joyce. Radical, Dissenter and Writer* (Aldershot: Ashgate, 2006).

Jacobs, Margaret C., *The Radical Enlightenment: Pantheists, Freemasons and Republicans* (London: George Allen & Unwin, 1981).

Janowitz, Anne, 'Amiable and Radical Sociability: Anna Barbauld's "free familiar conversation"', in Russell and Tuite, *Romantic Sociability*, 62–81.

'Memoirs of a Dutiful Niece: Lucy Aikin and Literary Reputation', in Heather Glen and Paul Hamilton (eds.), *Repossessing the Romantic Past* (Cambridge University Press, 2006), 80–97.

'William McCarthy, Anna Letitia Barbauld: Voice of the Enlightenment: Book Review', *Studies in Romanticism*, 48 (2009), 723–9.

Jones, Diana K., 'Aikin, John (1713–1780)', *New Oxford DNB* (Oxford University Press, 2004) (available online at: www.oxforddnb.com/view/article/229).

Keach, William, 'A Regency Prophecy and the End of Barbauld's Career', *Studies in Romanticism*, 33 (1994), 569–77.

Kelly, Gary, 'Romanticism and the Feminist Uses of History', in Damian Walford Davies (ed.), *Romanticism, History, Historicism: Essays on an Orthodoxy* (New York, NY: Routledge, 2009), 163–80.

Kennedy, Thomas C., 'From Anna Barbauld's *Hymns in Prose* to William Blake's *Songs of Innocence and of Experience*', *Philological Quarterly*, 77(4) (1998), 359–76.

King, Lester S. *The Medical World of the Eighteenth Century* (University of Chicago Press, 1958).

Kinnell, Margaret, 'Publishing for Children, 1700–1780', in Peter Hunt (ed.), *Children's Literature: An Illustrated History* (Oxford University Press, 1995), 26–45.

Knight, Frida, *University Rebel, the Life of William Frend 1757–1841* (London: Victor Gollancz, 1971).

Kraft, Elizabeth, 'Anna Letitia Barbauld's "Washing-Day" and the Montgolfier Balloon', *Literature and History*, 4(2) (1995), 25–41.

Krawczyk, Scott, *Romantic Literary Families* (New York, NY and Basingstoke: Palgrave Macmillan, 2009).

Kucich, Greg, 'Romanticism and Feminist Historiography', *The Wordsworth Circle*, 24(3) (summer 1993), 133–40.

'"This Horrid Theatre of Human Sufferings": Gendering the Stages of History in Catharine Macaulay and Percy Bysshe Shelley', in Thomas Pfau (ed. and introd.) and Robert F. Gleckner (ed.), *Lessons of Romanticism: A Critical Companion* (Durham, NC: Duke University Press, 1998), 448–65.

'Women's Historiography and the (Dis)Embodiment of Law: Ann Yearsley, Mary Hays, Elizabeth Benger', *Wordsworth Circle*, 3(1) (winter 2002), 3–7.

Kuper, Adam, *Incest and Influence: The Private Life of Bourgeois England* (Cambridge, MA: Harvard University Press, 2009).

Laslett, Peter, *The World We Have Lost* (New York, NY: Scribner, 1966).

The World We Have Lost: Further Explored, 3rd edn, rev. (London: Routledge, 2002).

Laudan, Rachel, 'Ideas and Organizations in British Geology: A Case Study in Institutional History', *Isis*, 68 (1977), 527–38.

Laurence, Anne, 'Women Historians and Documentary Research: Lucy Aikin, Agnes Strickland, Mary Anne Everett Green, and Lucy Toulmin Smith', in Joan Bellamy, Anne Laurence and Gillian Perry (eds.), *Women, Scholarship and Criticism c.1790–1900* (Manchester University Press, 2000), 125–41.

Levy, Michelle, *Family Authorship and Romantic Print Culture* (New York, NY and Basingstoke: Palgrave Macmillan, 2008).

Lincoln, Anthony, *Some Political and Social Ideas of English Dissent, 1763–1800* (Cambridge University Press, 1938).

Looser, Devoney, *British Women Writers and the Writing of History, 1670–1820* (Baltimore, MD: Johns Hopkins University Press, 2000).

Maitzen, Rohan, *Gender, Genre, and Victorian Historical Writing* (New York, NY and London: Garland, 1998).

Major, Emma, 'The Politics of Sociability: Public Dimensions of the Bluestocking Millennium', *Huntington Library Quarterly*, 65(1–2) (2002), 175–92.
'"Nature, Nation and Imagination"; Robert Mayhew, William Gilpin and the Latitudinarian Picturesque', *Eighteenth-century Studies*, 33 (2000), 349–66.
'Nature, Nation and Imagination: Barbauld's Taste for the Public', *ELH*, 74 (2007), 909–30.
Mayhew, Robert J., 'Geography in Eighteenth-century British Education', *Paedogogica Historica*, 34 (1998), 731–69.
Enlightenment Geography: The Political Languages of British Geography 1650–1850 (Basingstoke: Macmillan, 2000).
McCann, Andrew, *Cultural Politics in the 1790s: Literature, Radicalism and the Public Sphere* (Basingstoke: Macmillan, 1999).
'"We Hoped the Woman Was Going to Appear": Repression, Desire, and Gender in Anna Letitia Barbauld's Early Poems', in Paula Feldman and Theresa M. Kelley (eds.), *Romantic Women Writers: Voices and Countervoices* (Hanover, NH: University of New England Press, 1995), 125–30.
McCarthy, William, 'The Celebrated Academy at Palgrave: A Documentary History of Anna Letitia Barbauld's School', *Age of Johnson*, 8 (1997), 279–392.
'Mother of All Discourses: Anna Barbauld's *Lessons for Children*', *Princeton University Library Chronicle*, 60 (1999), 196–219.
'A "High-Minded Christian Lady": The Posthumous Reception of Anna Letitia Barbauld', in Harriet Kramer Linkin and Stephen C. Behrendt (eds.), *Romanticism and Women Poets: Opening the Doors of Reception* (Lexington, KY: University Press of Kentucky, 1999), 165–91.
'Why Anna Letitia Barbauld Refused to Head a Women's College: New Facts, New Story', *Nineteenth-century Contexts*, 23(3) (2001), 349–79.
Anna Letitia Barbauld: Voice of the Enlightenment (Baltimore, MD: Johns Hopkins University Press, 2008).
McCarthy, William and Elizabeth Kraft, *The Poems of Anna Letitia Barbauld* (London: University of Georgia Press, 1994).
McNeil, Maureen, *Under the Banner of Science: Erasmus Darwin and his Age* (Manchester University Press, 1987).
Mead, G. H., *Mind, Self and Society* (University of Chicago Press, 1967).
Mee, Jon, *Romanticism, Enthusiasm, and Regulation* (Oxford University Press, 2002).
Mellor, Anne K., 'The Female Poet and the Poetess: Two Traditions of British Women's Poetry, 1780–1830', *Studies in Romanticism*, 36 (1997), 261–76.
Mothers of the Nation: Women's Political Writing in England, 1780–1830 (Bloomington, IN: Indiana University Press, 2000).
Mellor, Anne K. and Michelle Levy, 'Introduction', in Anne K. Mellor and Michelle Levy (eds.), *Epistles on Women and Other Works* by Lucy Aikin (Peterborough, ON: Broadview, 2011).
Mercer, M. J., 'Addington, Stephen (1729–1796)', *New Oxford DNB* (Oxford University Press, 2004) (available online at: www.oxforddnb.com/view/article/152).

Merton, Robert, 'Patterns of Influence: A Study of Interpersonal Influence and of Communications Behaviour in a Local Community' (1948), reprinted in Merton, *Social Theory and Social Structure* (New York, NY: Free Press, 1968), 91–110.

'Social Conformity, Deviation, and Opportunity Structures', *American Sociological Review*, 24 (1959), 177–89.

Sociological Ambivalence and Other Essays (New York, NY: Free Press/ Macmillan, 1976).

Miller, D. P., 'Method and the "Micropolitics" of Science: The Early Years of the Geological and Astronomical Societies of London', in J. A. Schuster and R. R. Yeo (eds.), *The Politics and Rhetoric of Scientific Method* (London: Reidel, 1986), 227–57.

Mills, Simon, 'Joseph Priestley and the intellectual culture of Rational Dissent, 1752–1796', unpublished Ph.D. (University of London, 2009).

Mineka, Francis E., *The Dissidence of Dissent: The Monthly Repository, 1806–1825* (Chapel Hill, NC: University of North Carolina Press, 1944).

Mitchell, Rosemary Ann, '"The Busy Daughters of Clio": Women Writers of History from 1820 to 1880', *Women's History Review*, 7 (1998), 107–34.

Myers, Mitzi, 'Of Mice and Mothers: Mrs. Barbauld's "New Walk" and Gendered Codes in Children's Literature', in Louise Wetherbee Phelps and Janet Emig (eds.), *Feminine Principles in Women's Experience in American Composition and Rhetoric* (University of Pittsburgh Press, 1995).

Nicholson, Francis, 'The MS of William Shepherd at Manchester College, Oxford', *Transactions of the Unitarian Historical Society*, 2(4) (1922), 119–30.

O'Brien, P. K., 'The Reconstruction, Rehabilitation and Reconfiguration of the British Industrial Revolution as a Conjuncture in Global History', *Itinerario*, 26 (2000), 118–36.

Paget, Alfred Henry (ed.), *Epitaphs in the Graveyard and Chapel of the Great Meeting Leicester* (Leicester: privately printed, 1912).

Parry, Noel and José Parry, *The Rise of the Medical Profession: A Study of Collective Social Mobility* (London: Croom Helm, 1976).

Porter, Roy, *The Greatest Benefit to Mankind: A Medical History of Humanity* (London and New York, NY: W. W. Norton, 1997).

Enlightenment. Britain and the Creation of the Modern World (London: Penguin, 2000).

Ready, Kathryn, 'The Enlightenment Feminist Project of Lucy Aikin's *Epistles on Women* (1810)', *History of European Ideas*, 31 (2005), 435–50.

Rivers, Isabel, *Reason, Grace, and Sentiment: A Study of the Language of Religion and Ethics in England, 1660–1780*, 2 vols. (Cambridge University Press, 2000).

The Defence of Truth Through the Knowledge of Error: Philip Doddridge's Academy Lectures (London: Friends of Dr Williams's Library, 2003).

'Doddridge, Philip (1702–1751)', *New Oxford DNB* (Oxford University Press, 2004) (available online at: www.oxforddnb.com/view/article/7746).

Rivers, Isabel and David L. Wykes, *Joseph Priestley, Scientist, Philosopher, and Theologian* (Oxford University Press, 2008).

Roberts, Marie Mulvey and Roy Porter (eds.), *Literature and Medicine during the Eighteenth Century* (London and New York, NY: Routledge, 1993).

Robinson, Eric, 'The English "Philosophes" and the French Revolution', *History Today*, 6 (1956), 116–21.

Robinson, Harry, 'Geography in Dissenting Academies', *Geography*, 36 (1951), 179–86.

Rodgers, Betsy, *A Georgian Chronicle: Mrs. Barbauld and Her Family* (London: Methuen, 1958).

Roe, Nicholas, *John Keats and the Culture of Dissent* (Oxford: Clarendon Press, rev. edn 1998).

Ross, Marlon, 'Configurations of Feminine Reform: The Woman Writer and the Tradition of Dissent', in Carol Shiner Wilson and Joel Hafner (eds.), *Revisioning Romanticism: British Women Writers, 1776–1837* (Philadelphia, PA: University of Pennsylvania Press, 1994), 91–110.

Rothstein, D., 'Culture Creation and Social Reconstruction: the Socio-Cultural Dynamics of Intergroup Contact', *American Sociological Review*, 37 (1972), 671–8.

Rousseau, G. S., *Enlightenment Borders: Pre- and Post-Modern Discourses Medical, Scientific* (Manchester University Press, 1991).

Routley, Erik, *English Religious Dissent* (Cambridge University Press, 1960).

Russell, Gillian and Clara Tuite (eds.), *Romantic Sociability: Social Networks and Literary Culture in Britain, 1770–1840* (Cambridge University Press, 2006).

Ruston, Alan R., *Unitarianism and Early Presbyterians in Hackney* (Oxley: privately printed, 1980 [British Library: X.200/40127]).

Seed, John, 'Unitarian Ministers as Schoolmasters, 1780–1850: Some Notes', *Transactions of the Unitarian Historical Society*, 17 (1979–82), 170–6.

'Jeremiah Joyce, Unitarianism and the Vicissitudes of the Radical Intelligentsia in the 1790s', *Transactions of the Unitarian Historical Society*, 17(3) (April 1981), 97–108.

'"A Set of Men Powerful Enough in Many Things": Rational Dissent and Political Opposition in England, 1770–1790', in Knud Haakonssen, *Enlightenment and Religion*, 140–68.

Sekora, John, *Luxury: The Concept in Western Thought, Eden to Smollett* (Baltimore, MD: Johns Hopkins University Press, 1977).

Sellers, Ian, 'William Roscoe, the Roscoe Circle and Radical Politics in Liverpool 1787–1807', *Transactions of Historical Society of Lancashire and Cheshire*, 12 (1968), 45–62.

Shefrin, Jill, '"Make It a Pleasure and not a Task": Educational Games for Children in Georgian England', *Princeton University Library Chronicle*, 60 (1999), 251–75.

Shryock, Richard H., 'The Rise of Modern Scientific Medicine', *Studies in the History of Science* (Port Washington, NY: Kennikat Press, 1941).

Smiles, Sam, *Eyewitness: Artists and Visual Documentation in Britain, 1770–1830* (Aldershot: Ashgate, 2000).

Smith, Bonnie, *The Gender of History: Men, Women, and Historical Practice* (Cambridge, MA: Harvard University Press, 1998).

Smith, Orianne, "'Unlearned and Ill-Qualified Pokers into Prophecy": Hester Lynch Piozzi and the Female Prophetic Tradition', *Eighteenth-century Life*, 28(2) (2004), 87–112.

Spadafora, David, *The Idea of Progress in Eighteenth-century Britain* (New Haven, CT: Yale University Press, 1990).

Spongberg, Mary, *Writing Women's History since the Renaissance* (New York, NY and Basingstoke: Palgrave Macmillan, 2002).

Stephen, Leslie (ed.), *Dictionary of National Biography*, 1885 (London: Smith, Elder, & Co., 1885).

Stevenson, John, *Popular Disturbances in England 1700–1870* (London: Longman, 1979).

Stone, Lawrence, *The Family, Sex and Marriage in England 1500–1800* (Harmondsworth: Penguin, 1979).

Tadmor, Naomi, *Family and Friends in Eighteenth-century England: Household, Kinship, and Patronage* (Cambridge University Press, 2000).

Taylor, Charles, *Sources of the Self: The Making of the Modern Identity* (Cambridge University Press, 1989).

A Secular Age (London: Belknap Press, 2007).

Terry, Richard G., *Poetry and the Making of the English Literary Past* (Oxford University Press, 2001).

Thomas, Helen, *Romanticism and Slave Narratives: Transatlantic Testimonies* (Cambridge University Press, 2000).

Thompson, E. P., *The Making of the English Working Class* (1963; London: Penguin, 2002).

Topham, Jonathan R., 'Technicians of Print and the Making of Natural Knowledge', *Studies in History and Philosophy of Science*, 35(2) (2004), 391–400.

Torrens, H. S., 'Arthur Aikin's Mineralogical Survey of Shropshire 1796–1816 and the Contemporary Audience for Geological Publications', *British Journal for the History of Science*, 16 (1983), 111–53.

Tyson, Gerald P., *Joseph Johnson: A Liberal Publisher* (Iowa City, IA: University of Iowa Press, 1979).

Vickers, Neil, *Coleridge and the Doctors 1795–1806* (Oxford University Press, 2004).

Waddington, Ivan, *The Medical Profession in the Industrial Revolution* (Dublin: Gill & Macmillan, 1984).

Walker, Gina Luria, *Mary Hays (1759–1843). The Growth of a Woman's Mind* (Aldershot: Ashgate, 2006).

Watts, Michael, *The Dissenters: From the Reformation to the French Revolution* (Oxford University Press, 1978).

Watts, Ruth, *Gender, Power and the Unitarians in England 1760–1860* (London and New York, NY: Longman, 1998).

Webb, R. K., 'Belsham, Thomas (1750–1829)', *New Oxford DNB* (Oxford University Press, 2004) (available online at: www.oxforddnb.com/view/article/2066).

Webster, Charles and Jonathan Barry, 'The Manchester Medical Revolution', in Barbara Smith (ed.), *Truth, Liberty, Religion: Essays Celebrating Two Hundred Years of Manchester College* (Oxford: Manchester College, 1986), 165–84.

Welch, d'Alté A., *A Bibliography of American Children's Books Printed prior to 1821* ([Worcester, MA:] American Antiquarian Society, 1972).

Wells, Roger, *Insurrection. The British Experience 1795–1803* (London: Alan Sutton, 1983).

White, Daniel, 'The "Joineriana": Anna Barbauld, the Aikin Family Circle, and the Dissenting Public Sphere', *Eighteenth-century Studies*, 32(4) (1999), 511–33.

Early Romanticism and Religious Dissent (Cambridge University Press, 2006).

Willey, Basil, *The Eighteenth Century Background* (London: Chatto & Windus, 1946).

Williams, Carolyn D., 'Cogan, Thomas (1736–1818)', *Oxford DNB* (Oxford University Press, 2004) (available online at: www.oxforddnb.com/view/article/5813).

Wiltshire, John, *Samuel Johnson in the Medical World: The Doctor and the Patient* (Cambridge University Press, 1991).

Withers, Charles W. J., 'Eighteenth-Century Geography: Texts, Practices, Sites', *Progress in Human Geography*, 30 (2006), 711–29.

Woodward, H. B., *The History of the Geological Society of London* (London: Geological Society, 1907).

Wykes, David L., 'The Reluctant Businessman: John Coltman of St Nicholas Street, Leicester (1727–1808)', *Transactions of the Leicestershire Archaeological and Historical Society*, 69 (1995), 71–85.

'The Contribution of the Dissenting Academy to the Emergence of Rational Dissent', in Knud Haakonssen, *Enlightenment and Religion*, 99–139.

'Joseph Priestley, Minister and Teacher', in Rivers and Wykes, *Joseph Priestley, Scientist, Philosopher, and Theologian*.

Zemon Davis, Natalie, '"Women's History" in Transition: The European Case', *Feminist Studies*, 3 (spring–summer, 1976), 83–103.

'Gender and Genre: Women as Historical Writers, 1400–1820', in Patricia H. Labalme, *Beyond Their Sex: Learned Women of the European Past* (New York University Press, 1980), 153–82.

Index